The African Conundrum:
Rethinking the Trajectories of Historical, Cultural, Philosophical and Developmental Experiences of Africa

I0086105

Edited by

Munyaradzi Mawere, Tapuwa R. Mubaya & Jowere Mukusha

Langaa Research & Publishing CIG
Mankon, Bamenda

Publisher:
Langaa RPCIG
Langaa Research & Publishing Common Initiative Group
P.O. Box 902 Mankon
Bamenda
North West Region
Cameroon
Langaagrp@gmail.com
www.langaa-rpcig.net

Distributed in and outside N. America by African Books Collective
orders@africanbookscollective.com
www.africanbookscollective.com

ISBN-10: 9956-764-44-2

ISBN-13: 978-9956-764-44-0

List of Contributors

Munyaradzi Mawere holds a PhD in Social Anthropology from the University of Cape Town (UCT) in South Africa. Professor Mawere also holds a Master's Degree in Social Anthropology from UCT, a Master's Degree in Development Studies, and Master's Degree in Philosophy and B. A. (Hons) Degree in Philosophy from the University of Zimbabwe. He is currently Professor in the Department of Culture and Heritage Studies at Great Zimbabwe University. Before joining this university, Professor Mawere was a lecturer at the University of Zimbabwe and at Universidade Pedagogica, Mozambique, where he has worked in different capacities as a Senior lecturer, Assistant Research Director, Postgraduate Co-ordinator and Associate Professor. He has an outstanding publishing record of more than one hundred and twenty pieces of work which include more than twenty-five books and over a hundred book chapters and papers in scholarly journals. Professor Mawere has published extensively on poverty and community development, knowledge studies, political anthropology, science and technology studies (STS), environment and agrarian issues, democracy and African states, coloniality, decoloniality and transformation, African philosophy and political systems, culture and heritage studies. Some of his bestselling books are: *Humans, Other Beings and the Environment: Harurwa (Edible stinkbugs) and Environmental Conservation in South-eastern Zimbabwe* (2015); *Democracy, Good Governance and Development in Africa: A Search for Sustainable Democracy and Development,* (2015); *Culture, Indigenous Knowledge and Development in Africa: Reviving Interconnections for Sustainable Development* (2014); *Harnessing Cultural Capital for Sustainability: A Pan Africanist Perspective* (2015); *Divining the Future of Africa: Healing the Wounds, Restoring Dignity and Fostering Development,* (2014); *African Cultures, Memory and Space: Living the Past Presence in Zimbabwean Heritage* (2014); *African Philosophy and Thought Systems: A Search for a Culture and Philosophy of Belonging* (2016); *Colonial Heritage, Memory and Sustainability in Africa: Challenges, Opportunities and Prospects* (2016); *Underdevelopment, Development and the*

Future of Africa (2017), and *Theorising Development in Africa: Towards Building an African Framework of Development* (2017).

Raymond Ogunade is a PhD holder and was a Fulbright Fellow (2011) and the Association of Commonwealth Universities Fellow (2010/2011) at UCSB, USA and Swansea University, Wales, UK respectively. He is also a Prize Award Winner of the prestigious Science and Religion Course Programme (2001), Centre for Theology and the Natural Sciences, Berkeley, California. His research interests include: Sociology of Religion, African Religion, Inter-faith Dialogue, and the Interface between Religion and Science. Besides having authored/edited two books, Dr Ogunade has published widely in internationally acclaimed peer review academic Journals. He teaches Comparative Religion in the Department of Religions, University of Ilorin, Nigeria.

Takavafira Masarira Zhou is an environmental historian, a Lemba, and Human Rights defender. He is a holder of B.A. General Degree, B.A. Special Honours Degree in History, Master's Degree in African History, Graduate Certificate in Education, and D.Phil. in Environmental History from the University of Zimbabwe. Dr Zhou was a Teaching Assistant in the History Department at the University of Zimbabwe (1991-1995), and a History Lecturer at Mutare Teachers' College (2002-2004). As a History Lecturer at Great Zimbabwe (2004-2008), he helped to transform the history subject area into the Department of History and Development Studies. He was a technical advisor (researcher) in Zimbabwe Constitution Select Committee (2010-2011) that produced Zimbabwe's new Constitution in 2013. As a member of the National Education Advisory Board (2009-2013), he helped the then Ministry of Education, Sports, Arts and Culture in strategic planning, resource mobilisation and policy formulation during the period of Inclusive Government in Zimbabwe. Currently, Dr Zhou is the president of the Progressive Teachers' Union of Zimbabwe, and treasurer of the Non-Aligned Teachers' Unions of Southern Africa (ANTUSA). He has published on African agriculture; white settler farming; environmental impact of mining in Zimbabwe; peace and security in Africa; History curricula changes in Zimbabwe; poverty, natural resources 'curse' and underdevelopment in Africa; post-2016 Africa's development; and general history and politics of Zimbabwe.

Ogunbiyi, Olatunde Oyewole is a PhD holder and a lecturer of Comparative Religious Studies and African Religion in the Department of Religions, University of Ilorin, Ilorin, Nigeria. He specialises in the appraisal of the representations of Religions in Movies with special emphasis on African Religion and Nigerian movies for a global audience. He has attended conferences abroad and in Nigeria to present papers on African Religion and movies, digging into the nuances of African Religion for global attention.

Fortune Sibanda received his D.Phil. in Religious Studies from the University of Zimbabwe in 2015. He lectures in the Department of Philosophy and Religious Studies, Simon Muzenda School of Arts, Culture and Heritage Studies, Great Zimbabwe University, Masvingo. Dr Sibanda has widely published articles in refereed journals and book chapters on various themes from a religious perspective such as New Religious Movements, Avenging Spirits, Land, Indigenous Ways of Knowing, Human rights issues and the Environment in the African context. In addition to afore mentioned areas of publication, his research interests include religion and law, religion and media, religion and disability, religion and diet as well as religion and gender issues.

Tapuwa Raymond Mubaya is a Lecturer at Great Zimbabwe University and a PhD candidate at Tilburg University, Netherlands. Before joining Great Zimbabwe University, Mr. Mubaya worked for National Museums and Monuments of Zimbabwe (NMMZ) for eight years as the Curator of Archaeology and Head of the Great Zimbabwe Monument Conservation Centre. Currently he is heading the Department of Heritage Studies at Great Zimbabwe University. Mr Mubaya holds a Master of Arts Degree in Heritage Studies from the University of Zimbabwe. He is also a member of the Association of Southern African Professional Archaeologists (ASAPA) and the Zimbabwe Association of Professional Archaeologists and related Disciplines (ZAPAD. His current research interests are focussed on heritage management and conservation, cultural tourism and museums. Mubaya has written and published fourteen articles in internationally esteemed scholarly journals and is the co-editor/author of the books: *African Cultures, Memory and Space: Living the Past Presence in Zimbabwean Heritage* (2014) and *Colonial Heritage, Memory and Sustainability in Africa: Challenges, Opportunities and Prospects* (2016); and co-author of *African Philosophy and Thought Systems: A Search for a Culture and Philosophy of Belonging* (2016).

Ibrahim, Bashir Olaitan is a lecturer in the Department of History and International Studies of the University of Ilorin, Nigeria. He holds a PhD in Economic History but with special interest in industrialisation. He has handled many research projects and taught many courses on economic history. Dr Ibrahim has published extensively in internationally acclaimed peer review journals. Besides, Dr Ibrahim is a Board Member of many professional bodies among which includes Historical Society of Nigeria, International Research and Development Institute, and Research and Development Network, among others. He is also a sportsman of note.

Fidelis Peter Thomas Duri is a lecturer in the Department of History and Development Studies at Great Zimbabwe University. He is a holder of a PhD in History from the University of the Witwatersrand in Johannesburg, South Africa. He has published a number of books and articles which focus on environmental history, socio-cultural dynamics, subaltern struggles, African border studies and politics in Zimbabwe during the colonial and post-colonial periods. He has also reviewed and edited a number of scholarly books and articles and is also a member of the editorial boards of international journals such as the *Zimbabwe Journal of Historical Studies* and the *International Journal of Developing Societies*.

Jowere Mukusha is a Philosophy Lecturer at Great Zimbabwe University. He is a holder of a Master of Arts Degree in Philosophy, B.A. (Hons) Philosophy, and Diploma in Education. Mukusha teaches the following courses: African Philosophy, Theory of Knowledge, Philosophy of Education, Introduction to Problems of Philosophy & A Survey of Major Philosophical Trends. He is also a specialist in International Human Rights Exchange (IHRE) and a Peer Educator.

Ephraim Taurai Gwaravanda holds a Doctor of Literature and Philosophy in Philosophy from the University of South Africa (UNISA). He also holds a Master of Arts Degree in Philosophy (University of Zimbabwe) and a Bachelor of Arts Honours Degree in Philosophy (University of Zimbabwe). He is a Senior Lecturer in Philosophy in the Department of Philosophy and Religious Studies at Great Zimbabwe University where he teaches Advanced Logic, Metaphysics and Philosophy of Law. His research interests are in the areas of Philosophy of Development, Indigenous Knowledge Systems, Globalisation, Epistemic Justice, Governance and Philosophy of Law. He has published several articles with international peer reviewed journals.

Erasmus Masitera is a lecturer in the Department of Philosophy and Religious Studies at the Great Zimbabwe University, Masvingo. Erasmus holds an Honours Degrees in Philosophy from Arrupe College, Harare; M.A Philosophy, University of Zimbabwe, Harare; and recently completed D.Phil. studies at the University of Pretoria, South Africa. Dr Masitera is interested in researches that straddle traditional, social and political issues and connected philosophies. He has also published widely in the aforementioned areas, in in internationally acclaimed peer review journals. Some of his publications are book chapters.

Silibaziso Mulea is a Temporary Full-Time lecturer of Tshivenda in the Department of African Languages and Literature at Great Zimbabwe University. She holds a Master's Degree in Tshivenda from the University of Venda as well as a Diploma in Education from United College of Education. She is currently a registered PhD candidate with the University of South Africa. Her research interests include but not limited to culture, Indigenous Knowledge Systems and onomastics.

Costain Tandi is a Graduate teacher for Advanced level History and Sociology as well as Head of Department (Humanities) at Rufaro

High School in Chatsworth, Zimbabwe. He holds a Master of Arts Degree in Development Studies from Midlands State University; Bachelor of Arts 4th year Honours Degree in History from Great Zimbabwe University; Bachelor of Arts General Degree from the University of Zimbabwe; Graduate Certificate in Education from Great Zimbabwe University; An Executive Certificate in Project and Program Monitoring and Evaluation from the University of Zimbabwe; and An Executive Certificate in Project Management from the University of Zimbabwe. Tandi has six publications and his research interests include but not limited to Indigenous Knowledge Systems, Climate Change and Variability, Rural Poverty, Agriculture and Community Development.

ODEIGAH, Theresa Nfam is a holder of a B.A Degree in History; M.A. (History), PGDE, and PhD (History). She is a lecturer in the Department of History and International Studies at the University of Ilorin, Kwara State, Nigeria. She is an Economic Historian specialising in the Niger Delta Region of Nigeria. She has published widely in scholarly journals in the area of economic history.

Tendai Chibaya is a lecturer in the School of Hospitality, Tourism and Culture at Great Zimbabwe University. She holds a Bcom (Hons) in Tourism and Hospitality Management and MCom in Tourism and Hospitality Management (MSU). Currently, she is a PhD candidate at North West University, Potchefstroom Campus, South Africa. Her research interests are in human resources management, events management, tourism marketing and religious tourism.

Kilibone Choeni is a lecturer in the Department of African Languages and Literature at Great Zimbabwe University. She is a holder of a Master's Degree in Tshivenda from the University of Venda and a Post-Graduate Diploma in Education from the Great Zimbabwe University. Her research interests are but not limited to culture, literature and onomastics.

Peter Machenjera is a History school teacher and a trade unionist. He is a holder of a B.A. General Degree and B.A. Special Honours

Degree in History from Great Zimbabwe University. He also holds a Master of Arts Degree in African History with Midlands State University (MSU) where he was awarded an MSU book prize for excelling. He is currently employed as a History teacher at Mazungunye Government High School, in Bikita. He is also the current national Progressive Teachers' Union of Zimbabwe (Ptuz) secretary for information and publicity. Machenjera has presented various conference papers in Zimbabwe and SADC region on cutting-edge issues in teacher-education and history. Though he has just made a breakthrough in publication he has immerse enthusiasm in historical related research, especially environmental and contemporary issues.

Table of Contents

Chapter One
Reawakening the Giant Lion:
A Rethinking of the African Conundrum……..…..…….……1
Munyaradzi Mawere

Chapter Two
'Cultural Heritage is Our Right, Our Dignity':
Rethinking the Concept and Use of
Heritage in Zimbabwe……………………………………13
Tapuwa Raymond Mubaya & Munyaradzi Mawere

Chapter Three
Colonialism, Poverty and [Under-]
development in Africa……..……………...………………33
Takavafira Masarira Zhou & Peter Machenjera

Chapter Four
The Resilience and Challenges of Yoruba
Religious Worship in Modern Context…………………...97
Raymond Ogunade

Chapter Five
On the Philosophy and Historicity
of the Development Agenda:
Problematising African Nationalism
in the Context of Zimbabwe's Land
Question since the Colonial Period…………………… 121
Fidelis P.T. Duri

Chapter Six
Indigenous Religion and Security
Regimens in Africa: A Study of the Yoruba
Vigilante Groups in Southwest Nigeria………….....……… 167
Ogunbiyi Olatunde Oyewole

Chapter Seven

Epistemic (In-)justice and African
(Under-)development..185
Ephraim Taurai Gwaravanda

Chapter Eight

Markets and Indigenous Technology in
Ilorin Emirate Before 1900: A Hermeneutical
and Historical Analysis... 205
Ibrahim Bashir Olaitan

Chapter Nine

Interrogating the Role of Non-state Actors in
the Development Agenda of the Global South................. 223
Munyaradzi Mawere & Costain Tandi

Chapter Ten

Servant Leadership and the Paradox
of Africa's [Under-]development
Predicament..243
Fortune Sibanda

Chapter Eleven

Dilemmas and Controversies Surrounding the
Land Debacle in Zimbabwe: Appropriating Some
Ideas from the Shona *Unhu (Ubuntu)* Justice.................... 267
Erasmus Masitera

Chapter Twelve

The Trans-Atlantic Slave Trade from the
15th -19th Centuries: A Major Setback to the
Development of the Indigenous Economy of
the Niger Delta Region of Nigeria...............................287
Odeigah, Theresa Nfam

Chapter Thirteen
'Eating a Pig in a Pie?' - A Philosophical
Paradox of Women Rights in Human
Rights Discourse in Zimbabwe...303
Jowere Mukusha

Chapter Fourteen
Female Initiation as a Preventative
Measure to Teenage Pregnancy:
A Reflection on Zimbabwe's
Vhavenda Cultural Practices...323
Silibaziso Mulea & Kelibone Choeni

Chapter Fifteen
Pentecostalism as a Drive for Religious
Tourism Development in New Millennium
Zimbabwe...343
Tendai Chibaya

Chapter One

Reawakening the Giant Lion:
A Rethinking of the African Conundrum

Munyaradzi Mawere

Introduction

Africa is a puzzle – a conundrum of no match! The conundrum of Africa is located within its paradoxes. As Mazrui (1982) rightly points out, there are six paradoxes central to understanding Africa: First, that Africa was the birthplace of man – the cradle of mankind, but the last to be made habitable in a modern sense. Second, that although Africans have not been the most abused group of people in modern history, they have been the most humiliated. Third, that Africa is the most different from the West culturally, but is westernising very quickly. Fourth, that Africa possesses extreme natural wealth, but its people are very poor. Fifth, that Africa is huge, yet very fragmented. Sixth, that Africa is geographically central, but politically marginal.

Taking it from Mazrui's analysis of the African continent's condition, one notes that Africa is an enigma with an astounding conundrum. Indeed, Africa is not merely a brainchild of a modern, imperial or colonial experience. Nor is Africa merely a poor continent always in need of foreign aid from the former colonial "masters" and the so-called developed countries. Africa might be economically needy, politically unstable, and in part socially chaotic, and/or suffering from civil wars and social unrest. But Africa is more than this! It is certainly different from the pejorative sniping labellings and unabashed caricaturing portrayed in the Western controlled mass media. It is certainly a continent full of political and socio-economic potentials; some being thwarted and overgrown before seeing the sun like the grass of the equatorial. As noted by Mazrui, the continent has been the cradle of civilisation in the pre-colonial era, with diverse rich cultures, spiritual, philosophical and economic development.

1

Historically, Africa, particularly Egypt is renowned for its ancient shaduf [irrigation] system that was developed many years before Europe and the Americas realised their civilisations. Africa is also renowned for the magnificent and majestic architectural structures such as Great Zimbabwe Monuments, Mapungumbwe Monuments, the Egyptian Pyramids, and many other World Heritage Sites scattered across the continent. It is also renowned for its appealing life-giving moral philosophies such as Ubuntu/Unhu/Vumunhu and MA'AT, among others. Besides, with the help of the unstinting efforts by extraordinarily decorated heroes such as Kwame Nkrumah, Julius Nyerere, Amical Cabral, Frantz Fanon, Nawal El Saadawi, Stephen Biko, Nelson Mandela, Samora Machel, Robert Mugabe, and many others, Africa has had a long history of successful struggle against slavery, colonial exploitation and other inhumane and bastard pogroms instituted against her. This is not to count the rich reserves of natural resources such as minerals, wildlife, forests, and plenty sunlight that Africa enjoys more than many other continents of the world. Why then Africa is considered poor?

Indeed, Africa today remains trapped and deeply entangled in a cobweb of mangled situations and histories that make the continent difficult to remain neutral or at least to treat its problems with folded hands. It is worth noting that like a young girl deflowered before the age, all the successes and potentials of Africa have been shattered before their blooming stage and full realisation, mainly by malicious external forces. In fact, due to external forces exerted on the continent ranging from slavery, colonialism, capitalism, westernisation and globalisation, Africa's political and socio-economic development agenda was hijacked before "landing" like an aeroplane caught in the Bermuda mist. Consequently, the development compass of the African continent has been lost, forcing Africa to gullibly and desperately accept any development model and theory from outside, even those from the former colonisers which under normal circumstances should be treated with the highest degree of suspicion. Five grand questions arise: 'What "stage" or "state" of development Africa could have been in had it not been colonised? How can Africa go about its enduring quandary and nerve-chilling problems that have haunted her since the dawn of colonialism? What were the impacts of colonialism on the development direction of Africa? What are the impacts of foreign imposed development theories and models on African cultures, politics and progression? What should be done for Africa to realise its sustainable development goals?'

More so, given Africa's opulent cultural diversity, multifaceted philosophy of life, and multifarious "traditional" political systems with bottomless roots in the beliefs, worldviews, customs, spiritual rituals, and the legacy of the sages, one could ask: How can Africa's rich philosophy of life contribute to the global peace and development? How would this contribution improve the condition of life, and the wellbeing of the African continent? How could African worldviews play a role in today's debates on global peace and development? How could this contribution resolve the existing political and socio-economic trauma, eliminate the overloaded elements of the civil wars, and more importantly, improve the socio-economic and human development of Africa?

While the effects of Africa's hijacking by the Global North imperialists seem to be insignificant in light of the call for globalisation and internationalisation, a reconsideration of its deepening effects in the 21st century where global problems such as global warming, famine, drought, poverty and underdevelopment are a menace, is more urgent than ever. So, is the meticulous rethinking of Africa's colonialistic and Eurocentric stereotype panoramas. There is ample evidence that by imbibing from its past in a forward looking reflective approach, Africa will wean itself from underdevelopment and promote sustainable development, perhaps more miraculously than the Chinese magic.

In the light of the above, I argue for the need to rethink the African conundrum and to reawaken the giant lion, Africa, from its deep slumber. It is out of the realisation and consciousness of the highlighted obtaining reality, that the esteemed editors and contributors to this impeccable volume have decided to call for a *volte face* and a reconsideration of the African historical bastardisation, cultural manglement, and development predicament by undertaking a book project that focuses on the trajectories of historical, cultural, philosophical and underdevelopment experiences of Africa. Basing

3

on the fervent hope that crumpling the clichés, stereotypes and sad realities of Africa is long overdue but never too late a process to begin, all those who contributed to this volume staunchly believe that the text will go a long way to re-invigorate, re-invent and re-theorise Africa and reverse its fortunes in a manner that would extinguish the fire of poverty and propel the continent's sustainable development agenda.

In between the pages: The ongoing search for Africa's progress

All concerned Africans long for peace, stability and progress on the continent. Why, then, there seem to be more regression than progression in the cultural, economic and political sense? Is this because in Africa, we have more people longing for regression than we have those longing for peace and development? This book seeks to answer these questions with some profound dexterity.

Tapuwa R. Mubaya and Munyaradzi Mawere's must read chapter two circumspectly documents the controversies surrounding the conceptualisation and deployment of the concept of 'cultural heritage'. For Mubaya and Mawere, the varied interpretation and abuse of heritage is pervasive in formerly colonised states such as those of African societies, where the debates and hullabaloos surrounding the concept have been invoked by the colonial legacy. Whatever the case might be, the duo underlines the need to clear away the controversies. This need is more urgent now than ever given that, as Wiredu (1996) tells us, we live in times "marked by a certain intellectual anomaly [...] in a cultural flux characterised by a confused interplay between an indigenous cultural heritage and foreign cultural legacy of a colonial origin" (p. 1). As Wiredu further notes, "implicated at the deepest reaches of this cultural amalgam is the superimposition of Western conceptions of the good upon African thought and conduct" (Ibid). On the basis of their findings and the underscored observations, Mubaya and Mawere conclude their chapter by urging African governments, researchers and scholars alike to use their imaginative powers and creative insights to productively analyse African problems and solve them using African bred solutions.

In their chapter three, Takavafira Zhou and Peter Machenjera trouble the question of development of underdevelopment and poverty in Africa. The duo gives a critical analysis of the past historical process of the development of underdevelopment and poverty in Africa, where they identify colonialism as the major actor responsible for the economic ills in the continent. In Zhou and Machenjera's words "colonialism was responsible for the creation of arbitrary border designs, political subjugation, economic disarticulation and impoverishment of Africa's societies". Thus, for Zhou and Machenjera, the economic underdevelopment and poverty being experienced in Africa should be understood as part of the legacy of colonialism, which in fact, was responsible for the plundering, wrecking, siphoning and expatriation of African riches.

Raymond Ogunade's chapter four tussles head on with the question of religion in Nigeria, particularly the religion of the Yoruba people. While focusing on the Yoruba people of Nigeria, the chapter also includes the Yorubas in the diaspora, for example, those living in countries such as Brazil, Cuba, Republic of Benin, Togo, United Kingdom, France, India, Japan, and the United States of America. Basing on his findings, Ogunade argues that the Yoruba people, both inside and outside Nigeria, continue to practice their indigenous religious faith. This is in spite of the challenges of modernity and foreign religions such as Christianity and Islam, which for the greater part have destabilised African Tradition Religions and cultures. Yet, though destabilising, Ogunade is quick to observe that the challenges encountered by the Yoruba Religion have helped it to deploy some of the modern media of propagation in a way that instead of weakening the Yoruba Religion, has made it even much stronger to attract more and more followers.

In his chapter five, Fidelis Duri wittingly problematises African "nationalism as a philosophy in the context of development discourses in general and the land question in particular in Zimbabwean history since the colonial period". On this note, Duri cross-examines a gamut of ambiguities "such as continuities and discontinuities, consistencies and inconsistencies," particularly in the manner that the philosophy of African nationalism is often applied in Zimbabwe since the beginning of the anti-colonial struggle when it comes to the land question. Duri, thus, concludes that as far as the land question in Zimbabwe is concerned, the application of African nationalism as a philosophy of unity, peace and harmony, has remained loaded with contestations and ambiguities. Yet, Duri is quick to note that the manipulation of the African philosophy of nationalism should not be understood as lack of well-laid principles, but only as a testimony of the elite who inconsistently implements the philosophy in a manner that suits their political and economic agenda.

Chapter six by Ogunbiyi Olatunde Oyewole interrogates indigenous religions and security regimes in Nigeria. The chapter boldly and audaciously points on the apparent reluctance of the Police Force in Nigeria to arrest the steady rise of crime across the country as responsible for the birth of alternative crime control agencies such as the indigenous vigilante groups of Yoruba in South-west Nigeria. Basing on this observation, Oyewole hails indigenous security regimes as much better in terms of security provision as compared to the modern Police Force which is more corrupt, unorganised and squanterous. Taking it from his field trips and interviews carried out during research for the chapter, Oyewole concludes that the indigenous security groups of the Yorubaland are more efficient and remarkably supportive of the people than the modern Police Force. This revelation, for Oyewole, calls for the need for a serious overhauling of Nigeria's State Police Force to effectively address the security challenges plaguing the country and the continent at large.

In an ingeniously research fashion, Ephraim Gwaravanda's chapter seven examines "the influence of epistemic injustice on both African indigenous knowledge systems and African development". Gwaravanda, as with Zhou and Machenjera, argues that colonialism was responsible for the cultivation of ignorance and underdevelopment in Africa, especially if we are to consider its hegemonic tendency of marginalising other people's knowledge systems. Gwaravanda, thus, advances the critical argument that "Africans were deprived of their epistemological heritage such that it was difficult for them to appreciate and advance their own worldviews after the creation of knowledge vacuum by colonialism".

Yet, as Gwaravanda further argues, any meaningful development should respond to the needs, problems and challenges of a given culture. Thus, Gwaravanda concludes that in order to close the historical epistemological vacuum that was created by Westerners in Africa, there is need to first of all liberate the African people's minds after which the significance and centrality of the African epistemological paradigm is defended as the bedrock for African development.

In his chapter eight, Ibrahim Bashir Olaitan dissects and critically provides a nuanced and complicated analysis of the markets and indigenous technology in Ilorin Emirate before 1900. On this note, Olaitan exhibits the technological dynamics and commercial capabilities of the people of Ilorin Emirate before 1900, noting that before destabilisation by colonialism these people's economy was vibrant and promising. This is in contrast to the argument put forward by people like Trevor-Ropers, who argue that Africans have no past and therefore no history. The gist of this chapter, therefore, is to prove that even before the contact of Africa with Europe, the former had an organised political and economic system as both males and females in African towns like Ilorin were highly enterprising. As Ibrahim gives as examples of enterprising adventures of the people of Ilorin, "apart from farming in which both sexes jointly practice, especially at the harvest stage, there were some specific crafts which were regarded as exclusively preserved for women or men". All these practices thrived years before the contact of Africa with Europe.

In chapter nine, Munyaradzi Mawere and Costain Tandi critically dissects and wades into the debates on the role of non-state actors (NSAs) such as Non-Governmental Organisations (NGOs), Transnational Corporations (TNCs) and Civil Society Organisations (CSOs) in the development agenda of the Global South, particularly that of Africa. In their attempt to provide a nuanced and better understanding of the current role of non-state actors in Africa, the duo tries to clear, with the aid of examples, the controversies surrounding NSAs' role on Africa's development efforts and agenda. From their findings, Tandi and Mawere argue that it is untrue to say that Africa is underdeveloped. Instead, Africa is overexploited both intellectually and materially by NSAs which in most cases act as agents of imperialists. Thus, for Mawere and Tandi, more harm than good have been inflicted by the activities of NSAs in Africa such that all activities of NSAs from the North are worth blanketing and identifying with suspicions as controversial and unethical. Yet, Mawere and Tandi are quick to note that due to the uncertainty resulting from the contradicting activities of NSAs, where in some instances the activities are detrimental and in others genuine assistance is rendered, further research and analysis on the subject is peremptory and indeed more than necessary.

Fortune Sibanda's chapter ten creatively looks at servant leadership, but with a special focus on Zimbabwe and Africa in general. Sibanda uses his concept of servant leadership to make a case for Zimbabwe and Africa at large, where he argues that such leadership can go a long way to serve as a remedy for underdevelopment. Drawing his allegory from the discipline of Religious Studies, Sibanda equates servant leadership with the biblical teaching of Jesus Christ and also with the leadership captured in the African leadership philosophy of *Ubuntu/Unhu/Vumunhu* (humanness). Basing on such analysis, Sibanda believes that the reinvention of such teachings and leadership has the potential to resuscitate sustainable development for the 21st century Africa given that servant leadership has the capacity to resolve problems in the socio-economic and political spheres. It also has the potential to build good relational networks based on responsibility, accountability, relevance, and ethics, which in no doubt will help to deal with leadership failures and corruption in Zimbabwe's 21st century political arena.

Erasmus Masitera's chapter eleven meticulously and wonderfully cross-examines the land reform programmes in post-independent Zimbabwe. In particular, Masitera meticulously examines the dilemmas and controversies surrounding the land issue in Zimbabwe. He cleverly scrutinises and reveals the different dominant problems in the Zimbabwean land question. For him, these dominant problems are numbered four, with the first one resting on protracted disagreement over land ownership between the African indigenous peoples and the European settlers. The second problem, he notes, rests on all the land redistribution programmes that Zimbabwe has experienced since the dawn of colonialism which all seem to have been informed by injustices of some sorts. His problem number three is what he calls "the problem of rectification", which tries to take into consideration the injustices that have occurred in the past. His fourth and last problem probes the critical question on how real justice could be attained after many instances of unjust land redistribution programmes throughout the history of Zimbabwe. In his attempt to throw light on all these identified problems and controversies, Masitera acutely employs the philosophy of justice of Unhu/Ubuntu/Vumunhu, with which he argues, has the potential to address the political injustices and social ills that have occurred throughout the history of land reform in Zimbabwe.

Chapter twelve by Odeigah Theresa Nfam re-thinks the effects on Nigeria of the trans-Atlantic Slave Trade from the 15th to the 19th century. Odeigah argues that the effects were largely negative as they resulted in the staggering of development and indigenous economy of the Niger Delta Region. In Odeigah's words "the negative effects of the trans-Atlantic Slave Trade in Nigeria included among others, the collapse of the thriving Niger Delta indigenous economy". It also included a great reduction in agricultural productivity in the Niger Delta Region as well as that of palm oil production, salt production, fishing, trading, and hunting, which all flourished before the advent of trans-Atlantic Slave Trade and subsequently, colonialism. Thus, basing on her findings, Odeigah argues that the trans-Atlantic slave trade has remained a major setback to the economy and development of the Niger Delta Region and Nigeria in general.

Drawing on his wealth experiences and researches, Jowere Mukusha in his thought provoking chapter thirteen, tackles heads on the controversial question of human rights in patriarchal societies with respect to a gamut of areas such as culture, land, democracy and education. He conscientiously argues that the struggle for the need to respect human rights in Africa and Zimbabwe in particular, have ushered in the paradox of women rights in Africa. Mukusha is apt to equate the nature and scope of the women rights paradox to the saying: 'Eating a pig in a pie.' This, Mukusha does on the pretext of the susceptibility of women to women's human rights abuse which in fact continues despite the women's existential presence in the realm of humanity. To avoid the 'eating a pig in a pie' paradoxical scenario that obtains in many realms in Zimbabwe and elsewhere on the continent, Mukusha encourages a reverse on the socialisation of both men and women, where the former are socialised to become both protectors and sexual predators while the latter are socialised to become weak and sexual preys.

Chapter fourteen by Silibaziso Mulea and Kelibone Choeni audaciously interrogates the female initiation practice as a preventative measure to teenage pregnancy mong the Vhavenda people of Zimbabwe. With the fast changing cultural practices in Zimbabwe as a result of globalisation and westernisation, the duo reveals that "in Zimbabwe, indigenous methods of preventing teenage pregnancy have since been abandoned" in favour of the so-called "modern methods", which however, cause more harm than good to both the country's development efforts and cultural heritage. Why this is the case is that most of the so-called "modern programmes and methods boost the youths' sexual appetite" other than controlling their sexual desires. This results in recklessness on the youths' reproductive health which in turn disrupts culture and the wheels of development in the country. Basing on their findings, Mulea and Choeni, thus, argue for the revitalisation of traditional cultural rites of passages of initiation as a way of curbing teenage pregnancy, nurturing culture, and fostering development.

In the last and 15th chapter, Tendayi Chibaya catechises the impact of Pentecostalism on religious tourism development in present-day Zimbabwe. She observes that the new millennium Pentecostal Churches such as the Emanuel Makandiwa's United Family International Church (UFIC) and the Walter Magaya's Prophetic Healing and Deliverances (PHD) Ministries, which were born in 2010 and 2012 respectively by charismatic prophets, are fast attracting a lot of religious tourists from near and far. From this observation, Chibaya is curious to investigate the contribution of Pentecostalism to the tourism sector in Zimbabwe. To that effect, she uses the Zimbabwe's PhD Ministries and UFI Church as case studies to discuss "the link between the Pentecostal-led Christian revivalism and the resuscitation of Zimbabwe's tourism sector". She concludes that the presence of the two Pentecostal ministries – UFIC and PHD – among others, is fast boosting Zimbabwe's tourism sector.

This is a must read volume for all those who are interested in understanding the African condition and conundrum in the new millennium.

References

Mazrui, A. 1982. 'A confluence of three cultures,' *April/May 1982 Research News: Ali Mazrui Papers,* Bentley Library.
Wiredu, K. 1996. *Cultural Universals and Particulars: An African Perspective*, Bloomington: Indiana UP.

Chapter Two

'Cultural Heritage is Our Right, Our Dignity': Rethinking the Concept and Use of Heritage in Zimbabwe

Tapuwa Raymond Mubaya & Munyaradzi Mawere

'Cultural heritage is our right, our dignity' (Mawere 2015: Interview Notes from Binga).

Introduction

In the milieu of formerly colonised states such as those of African societies, the idea of heritage is not only controversial but invokes acrimonious debates. The controversies surrounding the concept of heritage have resulted from the colonial legacy which in turn has evoked differing interpretations and sometimes abuse or complete misuse of the concept by the government, ethnic, religious, political, and cultural groups, as well as academics across disciplines. In African societies such as Zimbabwe, the controversies and acrimonious debates surrounding the concept and conceptualisation of heritage are worth examining today than ever before because we live in times of cultural crisis; a time that westernisation and globalisation are taking the toll. We live in times "marked by a certain intellectual anomaly [...] in a cultural flux characterised by a confused interplay between an indigenous cultural heritage and foreign cultural legacy of a colonial origin. Implicated at the deepest reaches of this cultural amalgam is the superimposition of Western conceptions of the good upon African thought and conduct" (Wiredu 1996: 1). It is at this time that critical scholars are challenged to re-imagine, rethink, and proffer solutions to Africa's diverse problems, especially where Western-biased solutions have proven deficient and working against context-based problems. This re-imagination and rethinking of heritage in Africa is necessary today not only for the reason highlighted above, but for the other major reason to do with Western logocentrism as seen in the racist philosophies of Hume, Kant, Hegel, and Levy-Bruhl, among others, which denied Africans their right to rationality as humans and their dignity as a people. This is concordant with Mudimbe's (1988) view that it should be noted that colonialism involved the complete "domination of physical space, the reformation of *natives'* minds, and the integration of local economic histories into the Western perspective" (p. 2). It is from the perspective of this Western-imposed cultural, religious and intellectual outlook that scholars like Masoga and Kaya (2007: 154) argue:

> The silence imposed on Africa's history needs to be shattered. Africans and their heroic struggles, victories, and creative energies need to be rediscovered, promoted and celebrated. Since knowledge is not produced in a vacuum, knowledge production, documentation and dissemination must reflect African realities not constructed through Eurocentric prisms.

Indeed, "African epistemologies and realities were caricatured, denigrated, dismissed and relegated to the dustbin of oblivion to be forgotten once and for all" (Mawere 2014: 3). All these have resulted in the loss of identity – cultural and religious – and the alienation of African personality in global legal and political spheres.

Given the reality that colonialism together with the previous trans-Atlantic slave episode involved the protracted physical and intellectual enslavement of the African peoples, there may never be any genuine socio-economic, cultural, legal and political development in Africa, without the physical and intellectual emancipation of the Africans. In this process of emancipation, the rethinking of heritage in terms of both conceptualisation and usage in contemporary Africa is not only preponderant, but more urgent than ever before. Yet, the challenge for African scholars and theorists of Africa alike remains how, on the basis of justice and rationality, to deconstruct, reconstruct, and critically sift African thought from Eurocentric thought that is largely biased and mired with deliberate anthropological misrepresentations of Africa.

Drawing examples largely from Zimbabwe and the claim above by the BaTonga people during fieldwork by one of the authors of this chapter that "cultural heritage is our right, our dignity", the present chapter examines how the government is emphasising a mono-conservation methodology (adopted from Western modernist science) in conserving and managing cultural heritage sites (Mawere 2016). Hitherto, the government is doing this in a manner that is both suppressive and exclusive to the bearers and custodians of the heritage sites concerned. Backed by the outdated and out-of-context heritage legislation which is deeply rooted in colonial philosophy, the government through its inherited institutional arms legally owns heritage which practically belongs to the people. Thus, the move by the government to legally separate the people from their heritage is perceived as tantamounting to denying them the right to own and manage their heritage. Yet, at another level, to separate the government from the people seems to be impossible a thing given that in countries that purport to be guided by the principles of [representative] democracy such as Zimbabwe, government is the people and the people is the government.

It is in view of these complexities and the apparent conflict between the people and government when it comes to heritage ownership and management that the present chapter draws from recent fieldwork findings in Zimbabwe with the intention to rethink heritage. This is done in the pretext that both the government's heritage framework and the experiences of the deep-seated ways in which communities relate to their sites and the insights gained from interacting with them need serious rethinking in order to harmonise both parties in ways that foster eternal peace and mutuality.

What heritage is and is not

The discourse on heritage is mired with controversies of epic proportions which are normally compounded by the conceptualisation of the term "heritage". This being the case, the concept of heritage has, over the years, received different interpretations from special interest groups, which makes it difficult to achieve a unitary or universally agreed definition (Mubaya and

Mawere 2014). The complexity in the conceptualisation of heritage is further worsened by the fact that heritage is a dynamic, fluid and evolving term which keeps on changing its meaning over time. Yet, despite misconceptions, contradictions and disagreements on the conceptualisation and usage of heritage, what different interest groups seem to agree is that heritage resources (whether natural or cultural) are invaluable assets that require special protection, conservation (or preservation) and attention from all concerned groups (ibid). Confirming this, UNESCO-ICCROM (2006) observes that although heritage is by no means uniformly desirable, it is widely viewed as a precious and irreplaceable resource, crucial to personal and collective identity and dignity as well as self-respect. And, for this reason, people sometimes go to great lengths, often at huge expenses, to protect and celebrate the heritage they already possess, to find and enhance what they feel they need, and to restore and recoup what they have lost (Mubaya and Mawere 2014). We should be quick, however, to underline that what appears to be at the centre of the conceptual confusion of the term "heritage" is the fact that the criterion employed in defining heritage resources vary from one country to another and even from one community to another (see also Ndoro 2008). This means that what may be considered as heritage in one country (or one society) may not be necessarily regarded as such in another. This brings to the fore the point that heritage is created and defined by the communities who uphold it. It is against this background that the concept of heritage has enjoyed a plethora of definitions, some of which are scholarly and others religiously and legally informed (Mubaya and Mawere 2014).

As alluded to above, the term "heritage" in its everyday commonplace sense has attracted many criticisms. Some of the criticisms levelled against it are that it commodifies the past, it oversimplifies, it fossilises or constrains or it appropriates history to the nation state. But at the same time it is of paramount importance to note that heritage has grown into a deeply, socially embedded attitude that sits at the heart of the culture of most people across the globe. We must therefore hasten to confess that while issues related to heritage are inevitably complex to address in their entirety in this chapter, they are worthy of concentrated interrogation particularly in culturally diverse and historically fragile situations like those of Zimbabwe. In fact, although this is not the place for a lengthy analysis of the word "heritage" or of its uses and abuses, it is sufficient to say that the word is neither neutral nor unproblematic, and that the word itself, let alone the things it denotes, can be highly contested.

Taking it from its French origin, the term 'heritage' is derived from *heriter* which means something passed on from an earlier generation to the next. This understanding of heritage relates it to history, which owes its origins from a Latin term *historia* meaning inquiry (Fisher 2010). However, Lowenthal (1998) insists that history and heritage are two different worlds apart. He, in fact, argues:

> History and heritage transmit different things to different audiences. History tells all who will listen what has happened and how things came to be as they are. Heritage passes on exclusive myths of origin and continuance, endowing a select group with prestige and common purpose […]. History is for all, heritage for (us) alone (p. 128-129).

Besides, heritage has been accused of being unscientific and an area that invests in emotions of, and allegiance to, imagined collective identities (Grever, De Bruijn and Van Boxtel 2012). Lowenthal (1996) captures this critique aptly arguing that unlike history which is universally accessible and testable, heritage is "tribal, exclusive, patriotic, redemptive or self-aggrandising' and is not primarily concerned with 'checkable fact but credulous allegiance" (p. 120-121). Lowenthal goes on to argue that heritage embodies feelings of the past that shape identities and the historical materials that are harnessed to sustain them. For him, heritage's approach to the past is largely presentist and not particularly concerned with historical accuracy (Mawere 2016). Contrary to this approach is that of history, he argues further, which adheres to stipulated methods and ethics involving rigorous research, evidence, and rational arguments. In his comparison of heritage and history, Lowenthal (1998), thus argues:

> Heritage diverges from history not in being biased but in its attitude towards bias. Neither enterprise is value-free. But while

historians aim to reduce bias, heritage sanctions and strengthens it. Bias is a value that history struggles to exercise; for heritage, bias is a nurturing virtue (p. 122).

As Seixas (2014) has emphasised, the primacy of history is evidence not authority given that heritage tends to be celebratory while history critiques the past. In other words, heritage emphasises on the continuity from the past while history scrutinises and sometimes critiques or challenges the perceived links between the past and the present (Gadamer 1987). As that may be, heritage is the result of a selection process. It is not everything from our history. The aim of heritage protection is to pass on this selection of things with their values intact and in authentic condition.

Heritage can also be defined as our legacy from the past, what we live with in the present, and what we pass on to future generations, to learn from, to marvel at and to enjoy (SAHRA 2005). Following this interpretation, heritage reflects the dynamic character of something that has been developed, built or created, interpreted and re-interpreted throughout history, and transmitted from generation to generation. In other words, heritage assumes the becomings and unbecomings that come along with change and time, yet it inherently comprises those things in the natural and cultural environment around us that we have inherited from previous generations – or were sometimes created by the current generation – and that we, as communities and societies, think are so important that we want to pass them on to future generations. Generally, these things can be tangible (sites, buildings and artefacts) and intangible (practices and skills embodied in people). Contrarily, it is fundamental to note that heritage is not simply about the past, but is also about the present and the future hence a heritage that is disjoined from the past and the present has limited value. Instead, heritage involves continual creation, re-creation – becoming and unbecoming – and transformation. For instance, one can make heritage by adding new ideas to old ones or simply by modifying them.

We should point out, however, that even with all the seemingly incompatible divergences between heritage and history discussed above, it remains a fact that history and heritage converge, complement and overlap each other (Mawere 2016). Both are, for example, approaches to the study of the past and their relationship as approaches is dialectical (Seixas 2014). More so, both heritage and history tend to be selective but strive to represent the totality and accuracy of the past (Lowenthal 1985). We however underline that heritage largely involves 'framing the past" and can become "as little more than bogus history' (Johnson 1999: 187) such that 'all that constitutes heritage enjoys the backing of history' (Tejaswi 2011: 1).

Though viewing history and heritage as separate practices, these overlaps prompted Lowenthal (1998) to identify some symbiotic relationships between them, particularly the manner in which heritage can be derived from historical narratives and the way in which heritage delivers history to the ordinary people. Lowenthal (1996: 250) argues:

> *Heritage experts* feel compelled to cloak (their) wares in historical authenticity. Material relics are scrutinised, memories retrieved, archives examined, monuments restored, re-enactments performed, and historic sites interpreted with painstaking precision. Heritage apes scholarship with factoids and footnotes (p. 250).

What becomes evident from this discussion is that both heritage and history are approaches for the study of the past. They overlap and depend on each other in the sense that they derive their content about the past from each other (Mawere 2016). More importantly, both approaches are vulnerable to manipulation by various constituencies such as politics to address agendas of the time, which explains why there are divergent interpretations and deployment of heritage by the government and the local communities in Zimbabwe. It is also for the same reason that scholars like Munjeri (2003) argue that cultural heritage is a medium through which identity; power and society are produced and reproduced.

Drawing on the different interpretations of heritage elaborated herein, we, underscore that the term heritage can be used in three separate but closely linked ways:

i). Heritage can be used descriptively to refer to those objects that people as a community worry about conserving;

ii). Heritage can be used in an active sense to refer to the philosophy of looking after and exploiting "precious" resources;

iii). Heritage can be used as an object, action, product or process wholesomely or separately.

The heritage landscape and framework in Zimbabwe

The heritage landscape and the framework of operations in Zimbabwe can best be understood through historical and hermeneutical lenses. As such, we critically unravel these by dissecting the historical matrix of the modern day Zimbabwe right through its three major historical epochs namely, pre-colonial, colonial and contemporary.

The pre-colonial era

In Zimbabwe, as elsewhere in Africa, formal heritage management as it is recognised today came as an appendage of the colonial package (see Mubaya 2015; Maradze 2003). Before the advent of colonialism, indigenous interpretations along with their context-based management systems were used to protect and conserve cultural heritage sites. These included taboos, restrictions, myths, legends and folktales, and traditional ceremonies (cf. Mawere 2015: 3). It is important to note that these indigenous mechanisms of conserving heritage were effective in ensuring the continual survival of heritage sites. This is evidenced by the fact that the majestic cultural structures we see today such as the renowned Great Zimbabwe Monuments and many such similar and unparalleled structures across the country have survived for hundreds of years, implying they owe their existence to some form of management, which are certainly based on indigenous practices (Mubaya *et al* 2015). Add to that, pre-colonial communities had a strong, unlimited and untainted relationship with cultural heritage sites especially those which were imbued with sacred or spiritual values. By and large, the indigenous people related with cultural heritage sites for various reasons. For instance, groves, caves, pools and trees were considered as the abodes of the ancestors hence, they were highly respected. To ensure that heritage resources were utilised in a sustainable manner, local chiefs were appointed by spirit mediums to be the custodians of such sacred sites. This safeguarded the religious value and physical integrity of places like groves and pools, hence their conservation.

Heritage during the colonial period

The advent of colonialism brought with it several factors that led to the denigration of indigenous methods of heritage conservation Legal instruments enacted by the colonial government such as the Land Apportionment Act of 1930 and the Land Tenure Act of 1959 saw people being forcibly removed from their ancestral land and relocated to unproductive areas known as reserves (Mataga 2014; Maradze 2003). This was meant to pave way for *white* commercial farms. Resultantly, the indigenous people were alienated from their heritage and regrettably, some cultural heritage sites became part of these commercial farms, thereby limiting access to the local people. Examples of cultural heritage sites that were affected as such include Nharira Hills in Mazowe Valley and Tsindi National Monument in Marondera. Having been moved hundreds of kilometres away from their places of origin, the locals were divorced from their heritage both physically and spiritually (Maradze 2003). The effect of this was that indigenous communities who for generations lived with heritage sites and formed their relationships with these sites were sidelined, as scientific values and conservation ideals took the centre stage (Smith, 1994, 2001; Smith & Waterton, 2009; Meskell, 2011). This was a recipe for clashes, conflicts and misunderstandings between the government of the time and the concerned communities.

As a way of ensuring that the indigenous people were completely alienated from their heritage the colonial government also tampered with the traditional leadership system. Chiefs who used to be appointed by spirit mediums were now being appointed by the colonial government. Thus, both the spirit mediums and the chiefs were relegated from the centre of the management equation to the periphery. To make matters worse, Euro-centric legislation that was unsympathetic to customary ways of conserving heritage were crafted and enforced irrespective of the context. Cases in point include the

Historical Monuments Act of 1937 and the National Museums and Monuments Act of 1972, among others. These two heritage legal instruments, despite excluding the communities from managing and conserving heritage, recognised heritage sites as state properties (Maradze 2003). This meant that once a place was proclaimed a National Monument, it was an offense for local people to freely access and let alone perform cultural and other such activities at these sites. Unfortunately, this legalistic approach to the conservation of heritage did not recognise and accommodate the interests and aspirations of the local people who happen to be the owners and custodians of cultural heritage (see also Mataga 2014).

Heritage in post-colonial Zimbabwe

In 1980, the postcolonial state inherited an official heritage canon that was at odds with the realities of local communities. This is demonstrated by the fact that there was no major policy shift in heritage policies. Heritage institutions have continued to be governed by the legislation inherited from the colonial era, with only cosmetic changes such as titles to be in congruence with the new nomenclature (Mataga 2014). Precisely, the government is at the centre while the different communities which authored the heritage are pushed to the periphery. For Smith, this state of affairs which she coined the Authorised Heritage Discourse (AHD) privileges the position of experts (and/or the government), who are seen as:

> stewards or caretakers of the past [...] and the idea that the proper care of heritage, and its associated values, lies with the experts, as it is only them who have the abilities, knowledge and understanding to identify the innate value and knowledge contained at and within historically important sites and places (Smith 2006: 29-30).

This has created an antagonistic and suspicious relationship of accusations and counter-accusations whereby the government views the communities as potential threat to the heritage while the communities are also blaming the government of excluding and denying them the right to manage and conserve their own heritage. Conflicts between locals and the government have therefore become inevitable, with heritage sites acting as conflicting grounds. The National Museums and Monuments of Zimbabwe (NMMZ), the organisation in charge of heritage sites in the country, has for instance, learned through experience that adopting a 'solo approach' which excludes locals in matters of heritage is counter-productive and potentially destructive as the locals always feel excluded and denied the right to exploit what is rightfully theirs (Mawere *et al.* 2013).

Heritage is our right, our dignity: Notes from the field

From the foregoing it is apparent that the utilisation of cultural heritage in Zimbabwe is a contested terrain especially between the government and the different concerned source communities. For instance, as a way of reclaiming their cultural heritage rights, the BaTonga people of north-western Zimbabwe have developed systems and mechanisms of challenging the relentless ideological residuals of colonialism still operational and embedded in current heritage practices of Zimbabwe by constructing their own local community museum- the BaTonga Community Museum (BCM). As a people, the BaTonga ethnic group as well as their culture have, since the colonial era, been marginalised by the Zimbabwean government (Mawere 2016). This resonates with Chikozho's earlier observations that the BaTonga people were not only politically affected by the colonial and post-colonial governments of Zimbabwe, but were also socially excluded. By marginalisation (which is also known as social exclusion), we mean "social disadvantage and relegation of individuals or the entire community to the periphery of the society socially, politically, economically and culturally" (Mawere 2016: 19; cf. Silver 1994). As Lewis & Lockheed (2006: 49) argue, 'marginalisation sidelines certain population groups. It *restricts* excluded groups' economic mobility and *prevents* them from receiving the social rights and protections meant to be extended to all citizens.' This means that:

> marginalisation has, as its effects, some individuals or the entire community of some people (in this case the BaTonga) being

systematically blocked, partially or totally, from accessing various resources, opportunities, and rights that are normally accessible to other members of a different group of the same society (Mawere 2016: 20).

It is in this view that the BaTonga people felt excluded by the government to the extent that they thought it necessary to reclaim their heritage right by conceiving the idea of establishing the BaTonga Community Museum in 2000. The idea, which as highlighted above, was initiated by the BaTonga people with the assistance of the Binga Crafts Centre Management Board, and MS Zimbabwe (Danish Association for International Cooperation) and the Binga Rural District Council, was meant to present the life, history and culture of the Tonga people in Zimbabwe in a way that preserves their dignity and right as a people. This was echoed by an interlocutor during fieldwork by one of the authors of this chapter, who had this to say.

The BCM belongs to the community as a whole. It belongs to us! Unfortunately, this is not what is obtaining in reality. It is even confusing not only for me but for many other headmen and community members here in Binga. At one time you hear that the site is a national asset and at another time you hear it belongs to the local community. Truly speaking even the name of the site bears testimony to the fact that the BCM belongs to the local community. But sometimes we are divorced from the site which leaves us with no power and control over the site. Although National Museums and Monuments of Zimbabwe (NMMZ) is trying to infuse the local leadership and community members in general in the management and daily activities at the museum, in reality we feel like we are more of stakeholders than owners of the site (Mawere 2016: 48-49).

The above understanding of heritage as a right and wellspring of human dignity was also expressed in another community in south-eastern Zimbabwe. In fact, what we harvested from the BaTonga Community reverberates with Chief Charumbira's (President of the Zimbabwe Council of Chiefs) famous statement during a workshop convened to discuss and revise the Zimbabwe's culture heritage legislation in 2005. He is quoted to have said on behalf of other

Chiefs: "We are not stakeholders; we are the owners of this heritage" (Chirikure and Pwiti 2008: 468). This reality even makes one to ascertain that the ownership and management of cultural property is mired with complexities and controversies which often results in conflicts between the government and the local communities.

Also, to demonstrate that heritage encompasses and enmeshes human dignity, the local people around Domboshava Monument in Mashonaland East Province of Zimbabwe retaliated when denied access to carry out their rituals in the monument. With their claim that the government should recognise them as owners and not merely stakeholders, they obliterated the rock paintings with paint. Besides, they also burned down the curio shop that was erected at the monument by the government. When one of the authors of this chapter interviewed some of the locals on why they revolted against the government, the common answer that he received was "heritage is our right: it is our dignity and the government had no right whatsoever to deny us access to our shrine" (Mawere 2015: Field notes from Binga).

Examples of claims of the locals that heritage is the seedbed of human dignity and a fundamental right to the people, are numerous across many other communities in Zimbabwe. In Chibvumani community, the discontentment among members of the public and communities around the monument who felt being denied their right to Chibvumani Monument was revealed by Mr. Tamirepi (Village head to which Chibvumani falls under his jurisdiction) who complained of NMMZ officers who just go to the monument without their knowledge and approval (Interview with Mr. Tamirepi, 20/07/2011). Another strong sign of discontentment was brought to surface in 1998 when the then NMMZ Regional Director was chased away from the site when he decided to pass by on his way to Mutare (third largest city in Zimbabwe located near the border with Mozambique) (Interview with Mr. Chigiya 23/06/12 at Mamutse Primary School).

It is worth noting that the tactics that are employed by the disgruntled communities who seek to reclaim their right and perceivably lost dignity normally have serious negative effects to the sustainable use and management of heritage. Thus, in the ensuing section, we proffer different ways in which the conservation and utilisation of cultural heritage could be sustainably done and in a way that fosters eternal peace and justice.

The way forward

The participation of local communities is essential for the protection and preservation of heritage because the sites and monuments constitute part of the living traditions of indigenous people. The protection of heritage must therefore be based on the effective collaboration of professionals from a variety of fields and disciplines (Gaetan Juillard 2007). In addition, it also requires that government authorities and departments cooperate with each other as well as with researchers, academics, private enterprises and most especially with the local community members who are key stakeholders and custodians of heritage sites. It is these stakeholders who live with the heritage being conserved. Public participation is essential especially when the heritage of the indigenous people is involved (ICOMOS Charter 1990). Article 6 of the ICOMOS Charter acknowledges that local commitment and participation is essential, particularly where questions being dealt with concern the heritage of local cultural groups or indigenous people.

In the context of denial of their humanity, suppression of their ideas, and the domination and exploitation by the West that followed, African scholars must use their imaginative powers and creative insights "to project into the future, dream up ideal situations and work incessantly and tenaciously toward the accomplishment of these ideals no matter the difficulties confronting us" (Okoro: np). This is to say that African scholars should come up with a hermeneutic that critically and analytically interpret the African condition and propose African initiated solutions. We are advocating and arguing for a situation whereby people who are well grounded in the cosmology and ontology of the African cultures solve these seemingly irresolvable heritage issues using African philosophical lenses and approaches that most suit their context (Mubaya *et al* 2015). There is need for Africans to dig deeper into our cultural labyrinths and identify the deferent indigenous heritage conservation practices that our forebears used as their fronts and springboards of civilisation (ibid).

Yet in doing so, as in trying to pursue Socrates' (469-399BC) great assertion as far back as the mid-fifth century BC: "*Man*[1] *know thyself*" bump into another big challenge. The question remains: 'In his evaluation of ideological and even philosophical trends that have since these two millennia animated man's self-understanding and cultural values, is man progressing in his task of answering that basic Socratic question: *Man Know thyself* or is he alienating himself more and more from his identity and his mission? Has culture been a progressive expression of the perfection of man, are more 'advanced' (time-wise) cultures a proof of growth or are we to rediscover the germ of man's highest point of cultural expressions consistent with his origin, nature, goal and destiny in the distant past?

Also, in multiculturalist societies across Zimbabwe and Africa today, there is need to promote citizen education. We argue here that multiculturalism offers a better educational alternative to multi-ethnic societies as those of Zimbabwe. This suggestion is proffered on the assumption that *Ceteris Peribus* (all things being equal) multicultural education nurtures citizenship education, and explicitly connects the concepts of *Pluribus ad Unum* (unity in diversity) to create an inclusive, just, and harmonious society where peace and justice are expected to prevail.

Conclusion

This chapter has drawn from scholarship on cultural heritage studies and our recent field researches in contemporary Zimbabwe the extent to which heritage is being used in negotiating and validating social and cultural claims for both government and communities, especially those in the countryside where the bulk of the heritage is housed. Specifically, the chapter has focused on ways in which cultural heritage plays a part in broader contestations around

---

[1] In this chapter, we use the expression, 'Man' in a generic sense to mean, human beings (whether male and female) except where the context explicitly connotes otherwise. On the same note, the personal pronoun 'his' and its other derivatives, is used generically to mean human beings, whether male or female.

identity, cultural rights and claims of power and ownership. We advanced this from the understanding that heritage is a social construction and a mode of cultural production (see also Kirshenblatt- Gimblett, 1995; Graham, *et al*, 2000; Peckham 2003; Harvey, 2007; Smith 2006). As a result of this realisation, it is evident that the African people's heritage gives them self-identity, self-confidence and self-respect. More specifically, it allows them to be in harmony with their physical and spiritual environment given that for the traditional Africans, cultural heritage is their antennae into the unknown future and their reference point into their past. We have, however, underscored how meanings of heritage have been constructed and institutionalised in Zimbabwe, and how this elicits responses from local communities warrants careful examination and rethinking to ensure that justice and the mutuality between government and local communities prevail.

References

Chirikure, S., & Pwiti, G. 2008. Community Involvement in Archaeology and Cultural Heritage Management: An Assessment from Case Studies in Southern Africa and Elsewhere, *Current Anthropology* 49 (3): 467-485.

Chirikure, S. C. Manyanga, M., Ndoro, W., & Pwiti, G. 2010. Unfulfilled promises? Heritage Management and Community Participation at some of Africa's Cultural Heritage Sites. *International Journal of Heritage Studies,* 16 (1–2): 30–44.

Fairclough, G. *et al.* (Eds), 2008. *The Heritage Reader,* London: Routledge.

Fisher, J. L. 2010. *Pioneers, settlers, and aliens, exiles: The decolonisation of white identity in Zimbabwe,* Australian National University Press: Canberra.

Fontein, J. 2006. *The silence of Great Zimbabwe: Contested landscapes and the power of heritage,* Weaver Press: Harare.

Gadamer, H. G. 1987. 'The problem of historical consciousness,' In: P. Rabinow and W.M. Sullivan, (Eds), *Interpretive social science: A second look*, Berkeley: University of California Press, pp.82-140.

Graham, B., Ashworth, G. J., and Tunbridge, J. E. 2000. *A Geography of Heritage*, London: Arnold.

Grever, M. De Bruijin, P. and Van Boxtel, C. 2012. Negotiating historical distance: Or how to deal with the past as a foreign country in heritage education, In: *Paedagogica Historica*, Volume 46, Number 6, p.878.

Harvey, D. C. 2007. Heritage Pasts and Heritage Presence: Temporality, Meaning and the Scope of Heritage Studies, in Smith, L. J. (Ed), *Cultural Heritage Critical Concepts in Media and Cultural Studies*, London & New York: Routledge, pp 319-338.

Herwitz, D. 2011b. Monument, Ruin and Redress in South African, *Paper presented at the NRF Archive and Public Culture workshop,* 30 August-01 September, University of Cape Town.

ICOMOS, 1990. *Charter for the Protection and Management of the Archaeological Heritage*, International Council of Monuments and Sites.

Johnson, N. C. 1999. Framing the past: Time, space and the politics of heritage tourism in Ireland, In: *Political Geography*, Volume 18, pp.187–207.

Kirshenblatt-Gimblett, B. 1995. Theorizing Heritage, *Ethnomusicology,* 39 (3): 367–380.

Lang, G. 1936. "Culture," In: Linton, R. *The Study of Man*, New York: New York.

Linton, R. 1936. *The Study of Man*, New York: New York.

Logan, W.S. 2007a. 'Closing Pandora's Box: Human Rights Condrums in Cultural Heritage Protection,' In: Silverman and D. F. Ruggles, (Eds). *Cultural Heritage and Human Rights*, New York: Springer, pp. 33-52.

Lowenthal, D. 1996. *Possessed by the past: The heritage crusade and the spoils of history*, The Free Press: New York.

Lowenthal, D. 1998. *The heritage crusade and the spoils of history*, Cambridge University Press: Cambridge.

Manyanga, M. 2003. Intangible Cultural Heritage and the Empowerment of Local Communities:

Manyanga (Ntaba zi ka mambo) Revisited. *Proceedings of the 14th ICOMOS General Assembly,* 27–31

October, Victoria Falls. http://www.international. icomos.org/victoriafalls2003/papers/C3-5- Munyaradzi.pdf. (Accessed 11 June 2011).

Manyanga, M. 1999. The Antagonism of Living Realities: Archaeology and Religion, *Zimbabwe,* 6, pp 9–15.

Matenga, E. 2011. *The Soapstone birds of Great Zimbabwe: Archaeological Heritage, Religion and Politics in Postcolonial Zimbabwe and the Return of Cultural Property,* Department of Archaeology and Ancient History, Uppsala University.

Mawere, M. 2014. *Culture, indigenous knowledge and development in Africa: Reviving interconnections for sustainable development,* Langaa RPCIG: Bamenda.

Mawere, M. 2015. *Humans, Other Beings and the Environment: Harurwa (Edible Stinkbugs) and Environmental Conservation in Southeastern Zimbabwe,* Cambridge Scholars Publishing: Cambridge.

Mawere, M. 2016. *Heritage Practices for Sustainability: Ethnographic Insights from the BaTonga Community Museum in Zimbabwe,* Langaa Publishers: Bamenda.

Mawere, M., Mubaya, T. R., & Sagiya, M. E. 2013. Challenges, Dilemmas and Potentialities for Poverty Relief by Heritage Sites in Zimbabwe: Voices from Chibvumani Heritage Site Stakeholders**,** *Journal of Sustainable Development in Africa,* 15 (1): 186-198.

Meskell, L. 2011. *The Nature of Heritage: The New South Africa,* Wiley-Blackwell: London.

Masoga, A. M., & Kaya, H. 2007. Building on the Indigenous: An Appropriate Paradigm for Sustainable Development in Africa" in Gerard Walmsley (ed.), *African Philosophy and the Future of Africa,* Cultural Heritage and Contemporary Change Series II, Africa, Volume 14, Washington, D.C, pp. 153-169.

Mubaya, T. R., Mawere, M and Chikozho, J. 2015. 'The Unsung Dimension of Great Zimbabwe National Monument: A critique,' In: Mawere, M., & Mwanaka, T. R. 2015. *Democracy, Good Governance and Development in Africa,* Langaa Research and Publishing CIG: Bamenda.

Mubaya, T. R. & Mawere, M. 2014. 'Heritage Typologies and Organisations in Zimbabwe: Questions, Insights and Policy

Implications,' In: Mawere, M. & Mubaya, T. R. (Eds,). 2014. *African Cultures, Memory and Space: Living the Past Presence in Zimbabwean Heritage,* Langaa Research and Publishing Common Initiative Group, Mankon, Bamenda, Cameroon, p. 179-208.

Mudimbe, V. Y. 1988. *The invention of Africa: Gnosis, philosophy and the order of knowledge,* Indiana University Press: Bloomington and Indianapolis.

Mukamuri, B. 1995. "Local Environmental Conservation Strategies: Karanga Religion. Politics and Environmental Control," *Environment and History* 1 (3): 297-3.

Munjeri, D. 2009. Following the Length and Breadth of the Roots: Some dimensions of Intangible Heritage, in, Smith, L., and Akagawa. N. (Eds), *Intangible Heritage.* London: Routledge, pp 131-150.

Munjeri, D. 2003. Anchoring African Cultural and Natural Heritage: The Significance of Local Community Awareness in the Context of Capacity-Building, *World Heritage Papers, 13*: 76-81.

Muringaniza, J. 1998. *Community participation in archaeological heritage management in Zimbabwe: The case of Old Bulawayo,* MPhil thesis, University of Cambridge.

Ndoro, W. Mumma, A. and Abungu, G. (eds.) 2008. *Cultural Heritage and the Law: Protecting Immovable Heritage in English Speaking Countries of Southern Africa.* ICCROM Conservation Studies 8. Rome: ICCROM.

Ndoro, W. 2005. Your Monument, Our Shrine: The Preservation of Great Zimbabwe. Rome; ICCROM.

Okoro, C. nd. *"www.unilag.edu.ng/opendoc.php?sno=3609&doctype=doc...$, (Accessed 12/02/2016).'*

Peckham, R. S. 2003. *Rethinking Heritage: Cultures and Politics in Europe.* London: I. B. Tauris.

Pwiti, G. and Mvenge, G. 1996. Archaeologists, tourists and rainmakers: problems in the management of rock art sites in Zimbabwe: a case study of Domboshava Monument, In: *Aspects of African Archaeology,* Pwiti, G & Soper R. (Eds), 817- 824. Harare: University of Zimbabwe.

Pwiti, G. 1996. *Continuity and Change: An archaeological study of farming communities in Northern Zimbabwe 500- 1700,* Uppsala: Uppsala University.

Pwiti, G., and G. Mvenge. 1996. 'Archaeologists, Tourists, and Rainmakers: Problems in the

Management of Rock Art Sites in Zimbabwe, a Case Study of Domboshava National Monument,' In: Pwiti, G., and Soper, R. (Eds). *Aspects of African archaeology: Papers from the 10th Congress of the Pan-African Association for Prehistory and Related Studies.* Harare: University of Zimbabwe Publications, pp 817–24.

Pwiti, G., and Ndoro, W. 1999. The legacy of Colonialism: Perceptions of the Cultural Heritage in Southern Africa with Special reference to Zimbabwe. *African Archaeological Review 3, 16,* 143 153.

SAHRA, 2005. *South African Heritage Resources Newsletter,* 1, (1).

Seixas, P. F. 2014. History and heritage: What is the difference? In: *Canadian Issues,* pp.12-17.

Smith, L., and Waterton, E. 2009. *Heritage, Communities and Archaeology,* London: Duckworth.

Smith, L.J. 2006. *The Uses of Heritage,* London: Routledge.

Smith, L. 1994. Heritage Management as Postprocessual Archaeology? *Antiquity,* 68, pp 300-309.

Tejaswi, S. 26 May 2011. 'What is the relationship between history and heritage?' downloaded from www.preservearticles.com, (Accessed 10 October 2015).

UNESCO World Heritage Centre. 2004. Linking universal and local values, World Heritage Papers 13. Paris: UNESCO.

UNESCO-ICCROM 2006. Introducing Young People to the Protection of Heritage Sites and Historic Cities: A Practical Guide for School Teachers in the Arab Region.

Wiredu, K. 1996. *Cultural Universals and Particulars: An African Perspective,* Indiana University Press, Bloomington.

Chapter Three

Colonialism, Poverty and [Under-] development in Africa

Takavafira Masarira Zhou & Peter Machenjera

Introduction

When compared to the Western World and other parts of the world, Africa is too far behind in terms of development. For years, historians were not in agreement as to what really contributed to the underdevelopment of Africa. Most African leaders and other Afro-centric historians have tended to blame past phenomena such as colonialism as the major culprits for underdevelopment of Africa while Euro-centric historians pinned the blame on failure by Africans to embrace the gains of colonialism. Considering these debates around the underdevelopment of Africa, this chapter, therefore, explores the political, economic and socio-cultural effects of colonialism on the development of Africa. The first part of this chapter argues that colonialism was responsible for the creation of arbitrary border designs, political subjugation, economic disarticulation and impoverishment of Africa's societies. It is our argument that the poverty being experienced in Africa should be understood as part of the legacy of colonialism since it was characterised by plundering, wrecking, siphoning and expatriation of African resources, relegating Africa to a dependent status. In most parts of Africa, colonial rule left a legacy of intense commitment to independence but few ideas regarding appropriate economic and social policies. The colonial era was a miserable epoch for the Africans, which entrenched their marginalisation and bastardisation, let alone underdevelopment of Africa in even far worse conditions than those experienced before. Colonialism was not merely a system of exploitation, but one whose essential purpose was to repatriate the profits to the so-called 'mother countries' or empires. This amounted to consistent expatriation of surplus produced by African labour from African resources. Resonating with dependency theorists, such as Baran (1973), Frank (1972), Furtado (1973) and Rodney (1972), we argue that colonialism even meant the development of Europe and other parts of the world as part of the same dialectical process that underdeveloped Africa. Like any other process instigated by the external forces, colonialism was responsible for the entrenchment of a new political system and 'robbery' economy whose permanent cancer in Africa has been ethnic fragmentation and struggles, patronage politics, civil conflict, inequality, underdevelopment and poverty. In this light, the present chapter argues that Africa's poverty today can be understood more through the lenses of colonialism, among other points of references, because it frustrated capabilities due to asset deprivation (land, markets, information, credit, and others), inability to afford decent health and education, and lack of power.

Yet, sound as this appears; to continue to blame colonialism *per se* for the underdevelopment and poverty of Africa many decades after most countries have gained independence as the dependency theorists do, is too simplistic and untenable. This is not to discount the continued negative effects of imperialism and neo-colonialism, but a sheer understanding that for Africa to turn things around, it must take responsibility for its own actions. While it is a historical fact that colonialism and Western imperialism did not leave Africa in good shape, we argue in the second part of this chapter that, Africa's condition has been made immeasurably worse by internal factors: poverty of leadership, systematic corruption, capital flight, resource/economic mismanagement, senseless civil wars, political tyranny, flagrant violations of human rights, and military vandalism. It is our argument that the attribution of Africa's underdevelopment and poverty to external factors alone is intellectually deficient as pragmatism and scientific scholarship demand, at the very least, an unerring scrutiny of all causative factors, both internal and external. Conversely, Africa is in bandages because most of its leaders looked only one way – at the external.

The present chapter, therefore, gives a cogent analysis of the past historical process of the development of underdevelopment and poverty in Africa, with a view to foster the present and future development of Africa.

Conceptions of Colonialism, poverty [under-] development in Africa

Colonialism refers to extension of direct foreign control of African territories from the second half of the 19th century by European powers. This control was not only accompanied by political subjugation but also economic and social exploitation. Although, foreign political domination ended when African states attained independence from the 1960s, indirect control (neo-colonialism) has continued to the present day through unequal trade and capitalist investment/aid. Poverty is simply a condition of lack, whereby people do not have access to basic necessities of life. It is characterised by inadequate shelter, that is, improperly constructed, overcrowded, and lacking in basic services such as water and sanitation, as well as homelessness. Ramlogan (2004: 140) asserts that "poverty, in its most extreme form, is the condition that exists when people lack the means to fulfil basic human needs, adequate and nutritious food, clothing, housing, clean water, and health services." Similarly, Narayan *et.al* (2000: 4-5) define poverty as multidimensional deprivation that "includes hunger, illiteracy, illness and poor health, powerlessness, voicelessness, insecurity, humiliation, and lack of access to basic infrastructure." In this context, the identification of poor people in Africa first requires a determination of what constitutes basic needs.

Development has been conceptualised in many different ways by scholars. Ayittey (1999: 30) defines development as an improvement in living conditions for the average person. This entails not only increased income but also better access to education, health, and nutrition. The British economist, Dudley Seers (1969: 2-6) argues that development is a creation of opportunities for the realisation of human potential. It is his conviction that if poverty, unemployment and inequality have declined from high to low, then the country can be said to enjoy a period of development. Todaro (1992: 100-102) views development as embracing three core values: firstly, the satisfaction of basic physiological needs; secondly, self-esteem;

thirdly, freedom from man's servitude to nature, ignorance, other men, misery, institutions and dogmatic beliefs. At the level of the individual, it implies increased skill and capacity, greater freedom, creativity, self-discipline, responsibility and material well-being. Arguably, development does not only encompass Seers' satisfaction of basic needs and Ayittey's pro-poor policy, but also emotional, spiritual and political needs. Underdevelopment is an anti-thesis of development and is punctuated by insecurity, economic backwardness, poverty, adverse living conditions, limited access to education, deplorable health and nutrition. At all times, one of the ideas behind underdevelopment is a comparative one as the economic conditions of a country at two different periods can be compared, let alone the economies of any two or sets of countries at any given period in time. A more indispensable component of modern underdevelopment is that it expresses a particular relationship of exploitation of a country by either another country or ruling elite. This chapter examines the intricate relationship of both colonialism and independent African ruling elites, to poverty and underdevelopment in Africa. It is a paradox of history that the underdeveloped countries of Africa are the ones with the greatest wealth of natural resources and human capital and yet the poorest in terms of goods and services presently provided by and for their citizens. In order to do justice to the link between colonialism and underdevelopment of Africa, it is imperative to briefly outline the pre-colonial political, economic and social dimensions of African states and communities.

Africa before the advent of colonialism

Contrary to Eurocentric perceptions of pre-colonial Africa as the land of the "unhistorical, undeveloped spirit exhibiting the natural man in his completely wild and untamed state", much political, economic and social development was achieved in this period (Zhou, 2013: 23; Bohannan, 1964). The rise of states was itself a form of political development, which increased the scale of African politics and merged small ethnic groups into wider identities suggestive of nations. Egypt, Ethiopia (Axum), Ghana, Mali, Songhai and Nubia are typical examples of great developed states in pre-colonial Africa (James, 1986; Ki-Zerbo and Niane, 1997: 77-89; Boahen *et al.* 1986: 3-37; Oliver and Fage, 1962: 46-49, 85-90). The regions of Yorubaland, Dahomey, the inter-lacustrine kingdoms and Zululand are also examples of leading forces in the political development which was taking place in Africa right up to the eve of colonisation. They were not the only leading forces, and even where the states were territorially much smaller, there were observable advances in political organisation.

In the Western Sudan, the Hausa states were heirs to the political and commercial traditions of the great states after the fall of Songhai in the 17th century; and early in the 19th century, the Sokoto Caliphate with its centre in Hausaland emerged as one of the largest political units ever established on the African continent (Webster *et.al*, 1990: 13-14). Conversely, much political and economic development had ensued in Africa long before the advent of colonialism. In the 1880s, a military genius and political innovator, Samori Toure, established the Mandinka state with a political administration where a sense of loyalty prevailed over and above clans, localities and ethnic groups (Webster *et al.* 1990: 181-86). Zimbabwe also showed great ingenuity, dexterity and technology (including masonry) with only slight interference from Europeans (Hull, 1981: 17-21). The process of political centralisation saw the emergence of the Luba-Lunda Kingdoms in Central Africa from the 15th century. The several small states on the island of Madagascar had by the 18th century, given way to the powerful Merina kingdom (Boahen *et al.* 1990: 108). Arguably, as long as any African society could at least maintain its inherited advantages springing from many centuries of evolutionary change, then for so long could the superstructure continue to expand and give further opportunities to whole groups of people, to classes and to individuals. Certainly, no one starved while others stuffed themselves and threw away the excess.

As much as African leaders were also judiciary judges, they were not above the law. They had to obey the law and their power and position rested on the will of the people. Among the Igbo, Tiv, Mende, Fante, Temme and Kru of West Africa, leaders were spokespersons, powerless to act without popular consent (Webster *et al.* 1990: 199-200). Even in centralised states, checks and balances existed in which a council of advisers, council of elders and traditional leaders ensured some semblance of democracy from leaders. Writing about Ashanti courts Casely (1911: 251) states:

> ... the King sits with his Councillors; and the Court is an open one, which any member of the community may attend. There is no secrecy about the proceeding. The complainant states his case as fully as he can, and he is given a patient hearing. In the course of this statement questions are freely asked him by the Councillors, and doubtful points elucidated. The process is gone through with the defendant, and with the witness called by either party. The council then retires to deliberate upon the facts, and its verdict is given by the King's Linguist.

Economically, pre-colonial states had diversified economies. The best organised state on the West African coast in the 19th century was Dahomey (now Benin) with a planned diversified economy punctuated by palm oil production, livestock and food crop production, specialisation on certain crops by provinces and districts, balance between production and consumption of livestock, local and long distance trade, census and a host of taxes (Webster et al. 1990: 83-84). Such diversified economy and advanced administration was destroyed by the French after their conquest of Dahomey as they pushed the peasants back into poverty and misery from which their ancestors had raised themselves during the period of Dahomey's pre-colonial greatness. Cobbing (1976) has shown that despite a harsh environmental climate in Matabeleland in pre-colonial period, the Ndebele state developed a diversified economy based on crop cultivation, livestock rearing, local industry, and internal and external trade. Arguably, innovations and ingenuity by Africans in spite of arid conditions, demonstrated the triumph of humanity over geography.

One way of judging the level of economic development in Africa prior to the advent of colonialism is through the quality of the products. According to Rodney (1972: 50), through North Africa, Europeans became familiar with a superior brand of red leather from Africa which was termed 'Morocco leather.' In fact, it was tanned and dyed by Hausa and Mandinka specialists in Northern Nigeria and

Mali. Many more impressive items were displayed when direct contact was established between Europeans and Africans on the East and West Coasts. Rodney (1972: 50) posits that, "as soon as the Portuguese reached the old kingdom of Kongo, they sent back word on the superb local cloths made from bark and palm fibre – and having a finish comparable to velvet. The Baganda were also expert bark-cloth makers." Yet, Africa had even better to offer in the form of cotton cloth, which was widely manufactured before the coming of the Europeans. The city of Kano in present day Nigeria became the 'Manchester of West Africa' in pre-colonial Africa. Its cloth sales amounted to at least 300,000,000 a year in the 1850s, a figure equivalent to about £40,000 (Tidy and Leeming, 1987: 67-68). The Kano cloth industry was aided by the existence of three favourable conditions: two locally grown raw materials, cotton and indigo; a large consumer market; and the highly efficient distributive network organised by Hausa traders over a large region. Well into the 20th century, local cottons from the Guinea coast were stronger than Manchester cottons. Once European products reached Africa, Africans too were in a position to make comparisons between their commodities and those from outside. The local copper continued to be preferred to the imported item in Katanga and Zambia, while the same held true for iron in places like Sierra Leone and Zimbabwe. It, therefore, remains to be seen how such progress was reversed by colonialism with the consequent entrenchment of underdevelopment.

Indeed, it was at the level of scale that African manufacturers had not made a breakthrough in the pre-colonial period. The cotton looms were small, the iron smelters were small, and the pottery was turned slowly by hand and not on a wheel. Yet some changes were taking place in this context. As much as under communalism, each household met its own needs by making its own clothes, pots and mats, care must be taken to note that economic expansion from there on was associated with specialisation and localisation of industry – people's needs being met by exchange. This trend was displayed in the principal African manufacturers, and notably in the cloth industry. Cotton fibre had to be ginned (separated from the seed), then carded and spun into yarn, before being woven. The yarn or the woven cloth had to be dyed, and the making of the dye itself was a complex process. As propounded by Rodney (1972: 51), there was a time when all these stages were performed by a single family or rather by the women in a single family, as in Yorubaland. All the same, economic development was mirrored in the separation of dyeing from cloth-making, and the separation of spinning from weaving. Arguably, each separation marked greater specialisation and quantitative and qualitative changes in output.

Like Europe, Africa had elements of guild system – an association of specialists passing on their skills by training apprentices. At Timbuktu, there were tailoring guilds, while in Benin guilds of a very restricted caste type controlled the famous brass and bronze industry. In Nupe (now Northern Nigeria) the glass and beads industry operated on a guild basis (Boahen *et al.* 1986: 19-20). Each Nupe guild had a common workshop and a master. The master obtained contracts, financed the guild, and disposed of the product. Both his relatives as well as strangers were free to enter the guild and learn the various specialised tasks within the glass industry. What this amounted to was simply that there was increasing specialisation and division of labour.

It is noteworthy that prior to the establishment of colonial rule, Africa was developing at its own pace with engagements between Africans and foreigners being on mutual understanding and benefits for the two groups. Hrituleac (2011: 14) argues that in pre-colonial Africa, farmers and peasants were producing for either their own use or to trade for other goods though the concept of production for the global market did not exist for them. As much as Africans looked after themselves with little reference to the global world, the vast majority of African communities fulfilled at least a few of their needs by trade. Africa was a continent of innumerable trade routes. Some extended for huge distances like the routes across the Sahara or the routes connected with Katanga copper. Settles (1996: 3) argues that prior to the advent of colonialism; Africa was not economically isolated from the rest of the world. Indeed African states had engaged in international trade from the time of the pharaohs of ancient Egypt and West Africa had specifically developed extensive international trading system during the era of Ghana, Mali and Songhai. These huge empires relied on the taxing of foreign trade to finance government expenditure. Conversely, Africans were in charge of their destiny and the foreigners' operations in Africa were not all that hegemonic. As such, African countries in pre-colonial period enjoyed their independence and sovereignty, and could effectively tap and harness their resources for economic development, a situation that increasingly became difficult under colonial rule.

It was, however, trade between neighbouring societies that was more important in the pre-colonial period. Various communities were producing surplus of given commodities which could be exchanged for items they lacked. In this way, the salt industry of one locality would be stimulated while the iron industry would be encouraged in another. As put forward by Rodney (1972: 52) "the trade so readily distinguishable in every part of the continent between the 10th and 15th centuries was an excellent indicator of economic expansion and other forms of development which accompanied increasing mastery over the environment." Noteworthy is the fact that, in independent indigenous economies, families operated as autonomous, self-sufficient units. Muzaale (1987: 80) argues that prior to the advent of colonialism, rural economies operated independently of pressures of international economy and a modern state economy. Questions concerning access to productive assets, of production and distribution of output and of disposal of surplus production were virtually entirely matters for family decision. As much as it is true that those pre-colonial economies often suffered from disasters such as drought and floods, it is noteworthy that there were institutionalised intercommunity voluntary exchange relationships that provided cover against such contingencies.

It was noticeable before the advent of colonialism that barter trade was giving way to some forms of money exchange as some items began to be used as the standard for measuring other goods and could, therefore, be kept as forms of wealth easily transformed into other commodities when the need arose. Salt, cloth, iron hoes and cowry shells were popular forms of money in Africa – apart from gold and copper, which were much rarer and therefore restricted to measuring things of great value (Rodney, 1972: 52). Rodney further argues that in a few places, such as North Africa, Ethiopia and

Congo, the monetary systems were quite sophisticated, indicating that the economy was far removed from simple barter and subsistence. Arguably, the expansion of the productive forces was accompanied by many other changes of socio-political nature in pre-colonial Africa. As such, agricultural practices, industry, trade, money and political structures were inseparable – each interacting with the other.

Colonialism and the legacy of poverty and underdevelopment in Africa

Of all the external factors used to explain poverty and underdevelopment in Africa, the most frequently used has been that of the legacy of European colonialism. As reflected above, African societies were developing independently until they were taken over directly and indirectly by the capitalist powers from the second half of the 19th century. According to Blanton, Mason and Athow (2001: 476), the industrial revolution in Europe created a high demand for agricultural goods and raw materials. In order to guarantee supplies of these commodities, the Europeans used colonialism to assume direct administrative control over the territories that produced them. Zhou (2017) posits that between 1885 and 1912 all the countries in the African continent, except Ethiopia and Liberia, were overrun by European led military forces and brought under European colonial rule. Admittedly, when Africans were forced to relinquish power entirely to colonialists, this itself was a form of underdevelopment. Subsequently, exploitation increased and the export of surplus ensued, depriving the societies of the benefit of their natural resources and labour, thereby further entrenching the development of underdevelopment and underdevelopment of development.

The negative impact of colonialism in political terms was quite dramatic. Overnight, African political states lost their power, sovereignty, independence, and meaning, and with them the right of Africans to shape their own destiny, plan their own development, determine their own strategies and priorities and borrow freely from the outside world at large the latest and most appropriate technology. As Boahen (1990: 330) puts it, "colonialism deprived Africans of one of the most fundamental and inalienable rights of a people, the right to liberty." Indeed, the advent of colonialism did not only entail loss of independence by African communities but also imposition of brutal foreign system of administration. As much as certain traditional rulers were kept in office, and the formal structure of some kingdoms was partially retained, it is noteworthy that the substance of political life was quite different. Political power had passed into the hands of foreign overlords. In as much as numerous African states in pre-colonial Africa had passed through the cycle of growth and decline, colonial rule was different. So long as it lasted, not a single African state could flourish. Arguably, colonialism was largely a one-armed bandit with the consequent entrenchment of poverty and underdevelopment in Africa.

Boahen *et al.* (1990), and Oliver and Fage (1962: 119-214), note that colonialism crushed by force the surviving states of North Africa; that the French wiped out the large Muslim states of the Western Sudan, as well as Dahomey and the kingdoms in Madagascar; that the British eliminated Egypt, the Madhist Sudan, Asante, Benin, the Yoruba kingdoms, Swaziland, the Ndebele, Zulu, Lozi and the East African Lake kingdoms as great states. A multiplicity of smaller and growing states were also removed from the face of Africa by Belgians, Portuguese, British, French, Germans, Spaniards and Italians. The majority of African leaders were killed in the initial primary resistance or captured and deported. In West Africa Jaja of Opobo was deported to West Indies, Nana of Itsekiri to Gold Coast, Prempe of Asante to Sierra Leone, and Samori Toure of Mandinka to Gabon (Webster *et al.* 1990: 185,191,199). It is noteworthy that the wars of conquest were also a source of retardation in Africa as they immiserated African communities. A case in point was the 1881-1898 Franco-Mandinka war that had devastating effects as the French mercilessly destroyed villages and people sympathetic to Samori Toure. By 1898, thousands had died (the population was reduced to one-third of the original size); the land was ruined and depopulated, while the remaining population was in a state of misery and starvation (Webster et al. 1990: 185-186). Colonialism, therefore, entrenched poverty and underdevelopment in Africa.

States that appeared to survive colonialism were nothing but puppet creations. For instance, the Sultan of Morocco retained nominal existence under colonial rule which started in 1912; and the same applied to the Bey of Tunis (Boahen *et al.* 1990: 146-148; Rodney, 1972: 246-247). However, Morocco and Tunis were just as much under the trajectory of French colonial administrators as neighbouring Algeria, where the rulers were removed altogether. All forms of administration by the Germans, British, Portuguese, Belgians and French were fundamentally brutal and exploitative, with minor differences in degree rather than in kind. The so called indirect rule by the British, assimilation and association by the French and Portuguese, were tissues of misrepresentation and patent *obiter-dicta* for oppression, racism and exploitation. African chiefs lost their traditional character and freedom. They became independent of their people and instead were transformed into agents of colonialism, maintaining colonial law and order. In practice this entailed the maintenance of conditions most favourable to the expansion of capitalism and the plunder of Africa. As such, African rulers who were chosen to serve as agents of foreign colonial rule were quite obviously nothing but puppets.

The Portuguese and French were in the habit of choosing their own African 'chiefs.' The British were obsessed with chiefs so much that they created 'warrant chiefs' in Eastern Nigeria where there were no chiefs in pre-colonial period, just as the French created 'chiefs' in Futa Jalon (Afigbo *et al.* 1992: 3-14). All other colonial powers found it convenient to create 'superior' or 'paramount' rulers. Very often, the local population hated and despised such colonial stooges. The 'warrant chiefs', with their unrestrained authority and control of the courts, were seen by the people as miniature tyrants. Not surprisingly, when in 1929 the British tried to impose direct taxation in Igboland, and the famous Women Riots followed, the main targets of attack were the warrant chiefs (Webster *et al.*, 1990: 206). There were traditional rulers such as the Sultan of Sokoto, the Kabaka of Buganda and the Asantehene of Asante, who retained a great deal of prestige in the eyes of Africans, but they had no power to act outside the narrow boundaries laid down by colonialism, lest they would have found themselves in the Seychelles Islands as 'guests of His Majesty's

Government.' In as much as colonialism limited Africans' political freedom by entrenching foreign rule, discrimination and subservience (buttressed by an array of acts such as the Master and Servant Act), it was an anti-thesis of development and militated against African innovation, ingenuity and initiatives, and therefore fostered underdevelopment.

It was the systematic expropriation of the Africans and their consequent status of rightlessness that impelled them to their risings against Portuguese, Germany and British imperialism. In response, colonial post-pacification witnessed the brutal suppression of African risings, death of many Africans, dispossession of Africans of their land and cattle, and colonially induced starvation. Drechsler (1966) has traced the underdevelopment of Namibia to German colonial genocidal suppression of the Nama-Herero rising of 1904-1907 and subsequent dispossession as an essential prerequisite for reducing these people to a status of rightless, wage labourers. A situation of hopelessness, poverty and destitution ensued and even continued under British rule from 1918. Iliffe (1994: 168-202) has shown how brutal suppression of the Maji Maji rising in colonial Tanganyika was a source of underdevelopment as 250,000-300,000 died (one-third of the total population), starvation and famine became widespread as the old and infirm remaining population was not able to tap and harness resources for development. Iliffe further posits that the famine reduced the average fertility of the surviving women by over 25 percent. Arguably, the people of southern Tanganyika sank deeper into underdevelopment as they lost not only a hope of regaining freedom but also lost a battle in their long war with nature. The Shona and Ndebele were no exceptions in colonial Zimbabwe, as the British brutally suppressed the First Chimurenga, destroying crops and inducing starvation particularly in Mashonaland (Ranger, 1967). Conversely, colonialism led to political subjugation and economic disarticulation that generated poverty and underdevelopment in Africa.

One of the political consequences of colonialism was the creation of arbitrary boundaries. The boundaries of new states that emerged from partition cut across pre-existing ethnic groups, states and kingdoms. Previous groups were disrupted, through a forced partition that allocated the same ethnic group to two or more countries (Asiwaju, 1984). Strained relations continue to characterise interactions among countries because of competing claims to territories or people. Examples include the tension between Nigeria and Cameron over a number of groups on the southern frontier, South Africa and Botswana over the Tswana, Ghana and Togo over the Ewe, Nigeria and the Republic of Benin over the Yoruba, Senegal and Gambia over the Wolof, Kenya, Ethiopia and Somalia over the Somali (Falola, 1996: 10). Zhou (2017) has shown the effects of arbitrary boundaries in Southern Africa reflecting how the Subia ethnic group, *inter-alia*, suffered the greatest fragmentation as it was partitioned into four countries, *viz*, Botswana (11%), Namibia (30%), Zambia (53%) and Zimbabwe (6%). Indeed, it is too late to reunify divided groups, but frontier tensions will continue as long as different countries pursue policies that disregard the fact that these groups were previously members of the same nation. It is noteworthy that competing imperialism added to the gulfs created by the partition. Bujra (2002: 5) asserts that although the Organisation of African Union (OAU) declared artificial boundaries in Africa inviolable in 1963, conflict have flared up from time to time on account of territorial claims and counter claims. Arguably, the reprehensible colonial borders led to ethnic fragmentation and struggles, patronage politics, civil conflict, loss of life, inequality, underdevelopment and poverty.

Economically, colonialism meant a great intensification of exploitation of Africa – to a level much higher than previously in existence under communalism or feudal-type African societies. Simultaneously, it entailed the export of that surplus in massive proportions, and this subsequently led to shocking levels of poverty and underdevelopment. The combination of being oppressed, being exploited, and being disregarded is best illustrated by the pattern of the economic infrastructure of African colonies: notably their roads and railways. These had a clear geographical distribution according to the extent to which particular regions needed to be opened up to import/export activities. Where exports were not available, roads and railways had no place. The only exception is that certain roads and railways were built to move troops and make conquest and oppression easier. Indeed colonial powers put considerable resources into building infrastructure to service the colonial enclave economies. According to Tidy and Lemming (1987: 156-57), in East Africa the colonialists constructed the Uganda Railway line, better known as the 'Lunatic Express' - 1700 km line from Mombasa to Kisumu at the coast of £5.5 million in the period 1895-1901, which would be £9.4 million today. The period 1880-1914 was the great age of railway building in West Africa. The railways were built primarily to facilitate the export of cash crops and minerals. No clearer evidence of this can be found than in German Togo where the lines were actually named after the products they were built to carry: iron line, palm oil line, cotton line and coconut line. In colonial Zambia and Congo, railways were largely constructed to facilitate the exportation of copper, while in colonial Zimbabwe they exported coal, iron ore, asbestos, tin, chrome and tobacco (Yaniki, 1990: 173-185; Zhou, 2012: 152, 209, 249). Colonial infrastructural development was designed to maximise exploitation and greatly contributed to poverty and underdevelopment in Africa.

The roads and railways were not constructed in the colonial period so as to facilitate free movement of Africans in visiting their friends. More importantly, they were not constructed to promote internal trade in African commodities. Noteworthy is the fact that there were no roads connecting different colonies and different parts of the same colony in a manner that made sense with regard to Africa's needs and development. Colonial transport network was, therefore, tailor made to siphon raw materials from the periphery (colony) to the metropolis (coloniser) and this ensured that it was impossible to develop an integrated transport system for Africa. As propounded by Rodney (1972: 252), "the most outstanding characteristic of the transportation system of Africa is the comparative isolation in which they have developed within the confines of individual countries and territories. This is reflected in the lack of links between countries and territories within the same geographical sub-region." The colonial legacy is still felt in the 21st century, with production and export of commodities geared towards the needs of the former colonial powers - not value addition. Even the substantial modernisation and enlargement of harbours in Africa from 1900 was not so much of development in Africa as of enabling them to handle the increased volume of produce brought by the railways. Any benefits that accrued to Africans were incidental to their exploitative design and underdevelopment framework.

One feature of the colonial state was its direct engagement in the economic exploitation and impoverishment of Africa. The hegemonic tendencies of the colonial state entailed that it redistributed land and determined who produced what and how. Moyana (2002) and Muzaale (1987: 80) assert that in Central and Southern Africa, lands of high agricultural potential were annexed and made available to European settlers for plantation agriculture while natives were pushed to geographically isolated marginal land and unable to produce enough food for their consumption. Plaatje (2007) argues that the Native Land Act of 1913 which set aside 7 percent of Agricultural land as reserves for 67 percent of Blacks in South Africa engineered the poverty of Black South Africans and laid the groundwork of the apartheid system introduced later in 1948. As such, the cycle of poverty which is still prevalent in South Africa today, is traceable to the legacy of socio-economic injustice emanating from the land dispossession and apartheid during the colonial period. Similarly, whites got the lion's share of both quantity and quality of land through the Land Apportionment Act of 1930 in Southern Rhodesia, even reserving land for their unborn white children. By 1939, the hitherto self-sufficient agricultural economy of the Shona and Ndebele, like that of the Kikuyu in Kenya, had been greatly undermined by land dispossession (Palmer 1977). Mosley (1963) and Odhiambo (2006: 2) condemn the whites' land grab in East Africa and posit that it robbed Africans of their livelihoods and security. Indeed, Bundy (1979), Mosley (1983) and Palmer and Parsons (1977), have traced the roots of rural poverty and underdevelopment in Central, Southern and East Africa, to land dispossession. It is their argument that the major means of production for Africans was the land. Once dispossessed of their fertile land and pushed into rocky, infertile and inadequate reserves, Africans were economically disarticulated, impoverished and vulnerable to the caprices of the monetary economy in order to supplement their now riddled agricultural economy. Overcrowding of both people and animals caused soil erosion and land degradation, which further aggravated food shortages with the consequent creation of a vicious circle of poverty.

The appropriation and expropriation of African lands by colonial governments achieved two things simultaneously. They satisfied their own citizens (who wanted mining concessions or farming land) and they created the conditions whereby landless Africans had to work not just to pay taxes but also to survive. This motive tended to be the norm across the African continent as epitomised by the words of Sidney Sheppard (the Chairperson of the British Bechuanaland Land Commission) when he wrote to his superiors in the colonial office that:

> Strict adherence to the limits of the Reserve fixed by the Land Commission may also be regarded as desirable in the best interests of the natives themselves in as much as it must have a direct tendency to compel the surplus native population – instead of leading a life of degrading idleness on the Reserve – to earn money for themselves by working at the Diamond Fields or Gold Mines or the European farms (Quoted in Jacobs, 2003: 87).

In settler areas such as Kenya and Rhodesia the colonial government also prevented Africans from growing cash crops so that their labour would be readily available for the whites. According to Ake (1996: 2), in Kenya the Coffee Plantation Registration Ordinance of 1918 forbade the growing of coffee, the country's most profitable commodity, by Africans. One of Kenya white settlers, Colonel Grogan, put it bluntly when he stated of the Kikuyu: "We have stolen his land. Now we must steal his limbs. Compulsory labour is the corollary of our occupation of the country" (Rodney, 1972: 180). Conversely, the colonialists made sure that there was steady flow of African labour by stifling any African initiative and taking over control of the means of production, especially control over land. In areas of the continent where land remained in the hands of Africans (West Africa and some parts of East Africa), colonial governments forced Africans to produce cash crops no matter how low the prices were. According to Iliffe (1994) and Settles (1996: 8), colonial

49

authorities in Tanganyika shifted labour from food production and attempted to create a surplus of a labour intensive, non-food cash crop, cotton. It is noteworthy that forced labour was reintroduced in Kenya and Tanganyika to keep settler plantations functioning during the Second World War.

From the infancy of colonial rule, taxation was introduced by colonialists not only as an indicator that Africans had lost independence but also to force Africans into the monetary economy. Money taxes were imposed on numerous items such as cattle, land, houses, dogs and the people themselves. Money to pay taxes was acquired by growing cash crops or working on European farms and mines. In French Equatorial Africa, the French officials banned the Mandja people (now in Congo Brazzaville) from hunting, so that they would engage solely in cotton cultivation (Rodney, 1972: 181). The French enforced the ban although there was little livestock in the area and hunting was the main source of meat in the people's diet. It is clear, therefore, that colonialism was largely interested in profit making at the expense of the poverty and misery of African communities. Not surprisingly, colonial powers even resorted widely to the physical coercion of labour – backed up of course by legal sanctions, since anything which the colonial government chose to do was deemed 'legal'. It is Yaniki (1990), Mosley (1983) and Iliffe's (1994) argument that the laws and by-laws by which peasants in British East Africa were required to maintain minimum acreage of cash-crops like cotton and groundnuts were in effect forms of coercion by the colonial state, although they were not normally considered under the heading of 'forced labour'.

Perhaps the worst case of abuse of forced and slave labour was the shipping of thousands of Angolan Africans to the cocoa-producing islands of Sao Tome and Principe. These contract workers were actually captured by the Portuguese in the interior of Angola, brought in chains down to Benguela, registered as contract workers, and sent to the islands from where they never returned (Tidy and Leeming, 1987: 150-151). In the moist and malaria infested islands, these workers were exposed to long working hours, poor diet, brutal treatment and high mortality rate. The Portuguese, therefore, robbed Angola of its virile population, leaving the old and infirm incapable of tapping and harnessing natural resources for the development of Angola. Isaacman and Isaacman (1983) have shown how the Portuguese ruled with an iron rod in Mozambique, and how production of cotton and forced labour greatly contributed to poverty and underdevelopment in the country. Recruitment of miners for the Transvaal was entrusted to the Witwatersrand Labour Association (WNLA). As propounded by Coquery-Vidrovitch (1990: 167), the "average between 1913 and 1930 was 50 000 emigrants per year, or a total of 900,000 of whom 35,000 died and only 740,000 returned in satisfactory health." A great deal of forced labour also went into construction of roads, railway and ports to provide the infrastructure for private capitalist investment and to facilitate the export of cash crops. The hard work and appalling conditions led to the death of a large number of those engaged in work on the railway, thereby robbing Africa of her young population capital needed to foster development. In the British territories this kind of forced labour (including juvenile labour) was widespread enough to call forth in 1923 a 'Native Authority Ordinance' restricting the use of compulsory labour for porterage, railway and road building (Grier, 2005; Zhou, 2012: 161-163). However, the restrictions were never seriously enforced. Van Onselen (1976) has shown how forced labour (*chibbaro*), which he erroneously called *chibaro*, was the crux of primitive accumulation of capital by colonialists in mines and farms of colonial South Africa and Zimbabwe, with the subsequent increased poverty, disease, immiseration and underdevelopment of Africans, stretchable beyond the colonial period.

A brief examination of the colonial economy of Belgian Congo, particularly focusing on forced labour and taxation, reflects the exploitative nature of colonialism and its generation of poverty and underdevelopment among Africans. Congo was considered as personal colony of King Leopold of Belgium. Given the fact that he had no money, he parcelled out large tracts of African land to companies in order to spearhead 'development' on a profit-sharing between him and companies, and at the expense of the suffering of Africans. The only way the companies and Leopold could make profit was to force the Africans to work for them. Consequently, Africans were forced to give European agents rubber or ivory as a levy or tax. Wild rubber in the Congo brought enormous profits for European companies. According to Tidy and Leeming (1987: 146), Leopold made a profit on rubber alone of over £3 million between 1896 and 1905. Concessionaire Company started with a paid-up capital of £9,280 yet made a net profit in six years of £720,000. Tidy and Leeming further reflect that another company, the concessionary, working in Kasai region with a paid up capital of £40,200 made a profit of £736,680 in four years. Paradoxically, Africans received very small rewards for tapping rubber and handing it over to European agents. As the rubber was usually taken as tax, Africans were hardly paid for their work. Indeed, Africans suffered far more than mere financial loss. Failure to deliver the levy in rubber, food or by unpaid labour was punishable by flogging, chaining, mutilation, imprisonment, the burning of villages and even death. As an American Missionary, Reverend John B. Murphy outlined in 1895:

Each town in the district is forced to bring a certain quantity of rubber to the headquarters of the commissaire every Sunday. It is collected by force. The soldiers drive the people into the bush. If they will not go they are shot down, and their left hands cut off and taken as trophies to the commissaire. The soldiers do not care who they shoot down, and more often they shoot the poor helpless women and harmless children. These hands, the hands of men, women and children, are placed in rows before the commissaire, who counts them to see that the soldiers have not wasted the cartridges (*The Times*, 18 November 1895).

As such, in their quest for profit making, colonialists engaged in plunder, barbarity and atrocities. They had very little regard for Africans' dignity and rights.

Boahen (1990: 162-170) argues that faced with the demand to collect rubber or hunt ivory and pay it as tax, the Africans of the Congo had insufficient time to cope with the major task of cultivating food and fishing, and of continuously fighting the forest to prevent it winning back cleared land. African farmers were forced to abandon villages and flee into the forest to escape from company agents and punitive expeditions. Conversely, the neglect of farming and fishing led to starvation, famine and depopulation. Above all, the Belgians and companies plundered Congo's natural resources, such as land, rubber, elephants and copper at the expense of the poverty and underdevelopment of Congo. Such plunder and brutality in Belgian Congo is partly to blame for the perilous state of the population and parlous state of the Democratic Republic of Congo today.

As much as the presence of industry in Europe fostered and multiplied scientific techniques, colonialism ensured that no industry developed in colonies, and therefore there was no generation of skills. There were no processing industries in Africa. Even in the mining industry, colonialism ensured that the most valuable labour was done outside Africa. In light of the fact that the industries using African raw materials were located outside Africa there was no beneficial backward and forward linkages inside Africa. This confirms Ross (1999: 301-302)'s assertion that:

> ... resource industries were unlikely to stimulate growth in the rest of the economy, particularly if foreign multinationals dominated resource extraction and were allowed to repatriate their profits instead of investing them locally. Resource exporters would be left with booming resource enclaves that produced few 'forward' and 'backward' linkages to other parts of the economy.

Arguably, with the mining companies simply exporting raw materials during the colonial period, colonialists lost an opportunity to add value to the locality by creating finished products, which could have provided more jobs and revenue for the benefit of Africans. Seidman and Seidman (1984: 45) state that the limited pattern of accumulation and reinvestment of capital in African countries did not stimulate a multiplier effect to spread productive employment and higher living standards throughout the African economies because the Africans continued to produce primarily crude agricultural products while the whites transformed these into sophisticated manufactured goods which raised the living standards of people in developed countries. This therefore confirms the authenticity of Baran (1973) Frank (1971, 1972), Furtado (1973) and Rodney (1972) that the less developed countries should be fully comprehended as the periphery of the developed countries (centre).The underdevelopment of the periphery was an inevitable reflection of the development of the core. As such, the development of Europe and underdevelopment of Africa are two sides of the same coin.

It is a historical fact that shareholders of mining companies (who remained in Europe and North America) collected fabulous dividends from gold, diamonds, manganese, uranium, emeralds, asbestos, iron ore, copper and other minerals which were brought out from African soils by African labour (Kaniki, 1990: 178-180; Kassab, 1990: 189; Zhou 2012: 1-16). From the very beginning of the scramble for Africa, huge fortunes were made from gold and diamonds by colonialists. Copper became Africa's chief export in the 20th century because of its importance in the capitalist electrical industry. It is conceivable that while the Industrial Revolution in Europe during the 18th and 19th centuries was the Age of Steam, the colonial epoch was the Age of Electricity. As much as vital copper exports from Congo, Northern Rhodesia and other parts of Africa contributed to the leading sector of European technology, the respective African countries remained poor and underdeveloped. Such underdevelopment and resource plunder is epitomised by the swift mining of gold by the British in south Tanganyika from 1933 onwards at a place called Chunya. By 1953, they had gobbled it all up and exported it abroad. Rodney (1972: 239) argues that, "By the end of the colonial period, Chunya was one of the most backward spots in the whole of Tanganyika, which was itself known as the poor Cinderella of East Africa." Kaniki (1990: 178) argues that "... the colonial administrations deliberately and systematically excluded Africans from the mineral resources of their country." Conversely, most countries abounded in incredible mineral resources during the colonial period, such as Angola, Congo, Ghana, Ivory Coast, Zimbabwe, Zambia Sierra Leone, and many others, had nothing to show for such wealth except scars, land degradation, poverty, environmental damage and diseases, by the end of the colonial period. Arguably, this overwhelming negative environmental impact of mining upholds the validity of the 'resource curse' (paradox of plenty) thesis and the role of racial capitalism in the production of disease in Africa. As such, even after the demise of colonialism, African economies have struggled to move away from the poverty and underdevelopment trenches created by colonial governments.

The most decisive letdown of colonialism in Africa was its failure to change the technology of agricultural production. The most convincing evidence as to the superficiality of the talk about colonialism having 'modernised' Africa is the fact that the vast majority of Africans went into colonialism with a hoe and came out with a hoe. As much as some capitalist plantations introduced agricultural machinery, and the odd tractor found its way into the hands of African farmers, the hoe remained the overwhelming dominant agricultural implement (Rodney, 1972: 239). Conversely, while capitalism revolutionised agriculture in Europe through intensive application of scientific principles to irrigation, fertilisers, tools, crop selection, stock breeding and others, it could not do the same for Africa. At any rate, capitalism brought about technological backwardness in agriculture. As already noted above, on the reserves of Southern Africa, far too many Africans were crowded on to inadequate land, and were forced to engage in intensive farming using techniques that were suitable only to what was once loosely termed 'shifting cultivation', but which Allan (1965: 5-6) rightfully calls 'land rotation cultivation.' In practice, that was a form of technical retrogression, because the land yielded less and less and became destroyed in the process. Wherever Africans were hampered in their use of their ancestral lands on a wide-ranging land rotation basis, the same negative effect was to be found. It is noteworthy that in pre-colonial Africa, sustainable indigenous land and water management systems were used. In Southern Africa cultivation involved making planting pits and thus minimum tillage of the land which in essence limited soil erosion. Similarly, the *Zai* system from West Africa involved digging planting holes on the soil where organic materials were added, and rainfall water was trapped with the consequent guarantee of good harvests (Danjuma and Mohammed, 2015). It, therefore, allowed farmers to concentrate both fertility and moisture close to crop roots and, in so doing, addressed some of the major challenges to crop production. Sadly, the use of the plough during the colonial period as opposed to indigenous knowledge pit systems previously common in Southern Africa, and were a variation on the *Zai* pit system from West Africa, left the land susceptible to soil erosion and degradation, and was worse off than indigenous conservation farming technology (Mazvimavi, *et al.* 2007). Above all, some of the new cash-crops like groundnuts and cotton were very demanding on the soil. In countries like Senegal, Niger and Chad, which were already on the edge of the desert, the steady cultivation led to soil impoverishment and encroachment of the desert.

A major source of exploitation and underdevelopment of Africa foreign governments since the colonial period has been trade. The terms of trade were set up by the developed countries in a manner entirely advantageous to them and detrimental to Africans. The export of agricultural produce from Africa and the import of manufactured goods into Africa from Europe, North America and Japan were advantageous to Western countries. The big nations established (and have continued to establish to present day) the price of the agricultural and mineral products and subjected (still subject) these prices to frequent reductions. At the same time the price of manufactured goods is also set by them, along with the freight rates necessary for trade in the ships of those nations. As put forward by Ocheni and Nwankwo, (2012: 46), this long history of exploitative trading patterns where the African colonies were viewed as consumers of Western finished goods created the present primary role of African states in the international world economy as the dominant source of raw materials and major consumers of finished products from their former colonial masters. Onuoha (2012: 19) argues that colonial ties cemented Africa's dependence on traditional markets and reinforced her static comparative advantage in primary products rather than ensuring their transformation into value added products. As such, upon attainment of independence by most African countries from their colonial overlords, it was extremely difficult to disentangle from the colonial economy and the intrinsic tying of the same with the external economy of the colonisers. It is this dependency syndrome that killed Africa's initiative and militated against progress or development in the continent. Under such conditions, African poverty increased by the passing of each day as African governments sought to service the debts created by unbalanced trading patterns. Arguably, the whole import/export relationship between Africa and its trading partners is one of unequal exchange and exploitation with the consequent entrenchment of underdevelopment and poverty in the continent.

More far-reaching than just trade is the actual ownership of the means of production in Africa by foreigners. The most direct way of sucking the African continent, is the ownership of land and the mines of Africa by citizens of Europe. Under colonialism, the ownership was complete and backed by military domination (Rodney, 1972: 175). Foreign ownership is still present in some African countries, long after the armies and flags of foreign powers have been removed. As long as foreigners solely own land, mines, factories, banks, insurance companies, means of transportation, power stations and others, then the wealth of Africa will continue to flow outwards into the hands of those elements. Conversely, in the absence of direct political control, foreign investment ensures that the natural resources and the labour of Africa produce economic value which is lost to the continent, with the consequent growth of poverty and underdevelopment. What the colonialists dubbed 'the development of Africa' was a cynical short-hand expression for the intensification of colonial exploitation in Africa to develop capitalist Europe.

Colonialism was a negation of freedom and development. Previous African development was blunted, halted and turned back. Indeed, nothing of compensatory value was introduced in place of that interruption and blockade. As reflected above, during the centuries of pre-colonial trade, some control over social, political and economic life was retained in Africa, in spite of the disadvantageous commerce with Europeans. That little control over internal markets disappeared under colonialism. Colonialism was much further than trade as it entailed a tendency towards direct appropriation by Europeans of the social institutions within Africa. Africans ceased to set indigenous cultural goals and standards, and lost full command of training young members of the society. These were undoubtedly major steps backwards, and ramifications of such bastardisation, moral decadence, social decay, and corrosion of African cultural heritage are felt to the present day. As put forward by Memmi (1965: 135), "the most serious blow suffered by the colonised is being removed from history and from the community. Colonialism usurps any free role in either war or peace, every decision contributing to his destiny and that of the world, and all cultural and social responsibilities." The removal from history followed logically from the loss of power and interruption of their development which colonialism represented. Fanon (1963) and Cabral (1969) argue that colonialism made Africans into objects of history. Khapoya (2013: 135) posits that the destruction of African culture and values through the imposition of alien religious and the relentless attack on African values mounted by mission schools contributed to a mentality of ennui and dependency. It also resulted in the Africans losing confidence in themselves, their institutions and their heritage. Arguably, colonialism ensured that Africans were no more makers of history than objects that could be pushed around into positions which suited European interests and damaging to the African continent and its peoples.

While it is a fact that pre-colonial trade had started the trend of the disintegration of African economies and technological impoverishment, it was colonial rule that speeded up that trend. They had undergone no technological advance and they had not expanded, but they had survived. It is Boahen (1990: 332)'s conviction that the mass production of capitalism virtually obliterated African industries such as cloth, salt, soap, beads, iron and even pottery making. Had pre-colonial manufacturers been encouraged and promoted through the modernisation of productive techniques, as was done in India between 1920 and 1945, Africa not only could have increased her output but could also have steadily improved her technology. Colonialism induced African ironworker to abandon the process of extracting iron from the soil and to concentrate instead on working scraps of metal imported from Europe. Conversely, the non-industrialisation of Africa was not left to chance. It was deliberately enforced by stopping the transfer to Africa of machinery and skills which could have given competition to European industry during the colonial period. All in all, colonialism halted African technological development, and it was never resumed until after independence. It is for this reason that Rodney (1972: 239) dismisses the modernisation rhetoric of such scholars as Gann and Duignan (1969, 1970) arguing that Africans could have been better off in the bush.

Indeed the colonial period was a period of ruthless economic exploitation rather than of economic development in Africa.

Instead of speeding up growth, colonial activities such as mining and cash-crop farming speeded up the decay of 'traditional' African life. In many parts of Africa, vital aspects of culture were adversely affected, nothing better was substituted, and only a lifeless shell was left. As already reflected by Kakini (1990), Van Onselen (1976) and Isaacman and Isaacman (1983), the capitalist forces behind colonialism were interested in little more than the exploitation of labour. Consequently, even areas that were not directly involved in money economy exported labour. In extracting that labour, they tampered with the factor that was the very buttress of the society, for African traditional life when deprived of its customary labour force was no longer traditional. Coquery-Vidrovitch (1990) and Isaacman and Isaacman (1983: 49-59) have shown how the impact of colonialism left so many villages deserted and starving, because able-bodied males had gone off to labour elsewhere. Isaacman and Isaacman (1983) trace the roots of the current backwardness, poverty and underdevelopment in Mozambique to colonial cash crop production and labour migration of several people to South Africa. Indeed, several communities deprived of their effective labouring population during the colonial period failed to develop.

The character of growth in Africa under colonialism was that it did not constitute development as it did not enlarge the capacity of the society to deal with the natural environment, to adjudicate relations between members of the society, and to protect the population from external forces. Indeed, in colonial (just as in post-colonial) Africa, a pattern of growth without development emerged. As much as there was growth in terms of volume of raw materials exported and manufactured goods imported, the profit went abroad, and the economy of Africa became more and more a dependency of the metropolis. According to Rodney (1972: 276), "in no African colony was there economic integration, or any provision for making the economy self-sustained and geared to its own local goals." By and large, there was growth of the enclave import/export sector, but the only things which developed were dependency and underdevelopment. A further revelation of growth without development under colonialism was the overdependence on one or two exports. In the agricultural sector, Liberia was a monoculture dependent on rubber, Gold Coast on cocoa, Dahomey and South-East Nigeria on palm produce, Sudan on cotton, Tanganyika on coffee and sisal, and Uganda on cotton (Boahen, 1990: 332). In Senegal and Gambia, groundnuts accounted for 85% to 90% of money earnings. Diversified agriculture was within African tradition, whereas monoculture was a colonialist invention with many harmful effects.

Sometimes, cash crops were grown to the exclusion of staple foods thereby causing famines. Rodney (1972: 257) has shown how Gambia rice farming was so popular before the colonial era, and how so much of the best land was transferred to groundnuts that rice had to be imported on a large scale to try and counter the fact that famine was becoming endemic. Similarly, the concentration on cocoa production in Asante, raised fears of famine in a region previously famous for yam and other foodstuff. Arguably, such growth in cash crop production diverted Africans from their traditional diversified agricultural practices which ensured food security, and left African communities, starving, poverty stricken and underdeveloped. Yet the threat of famine was a small disadvantage in comparison to the extreme vulnerability and insecurity of monoculture. When the crop was affected by internal factors such as disease, an overwhelming disaster ensued, as in the case of Gold Coast cocoa when it was hit by swollen-shoot disease in the 1940s. Above all, at all times the prices fluctuations (which were externally controlled) left the African producer helpless in the face of capitalist manoeuvres. After being compelled to ignore the production of food for their own consumption, Africans were forced to buy imported food at exorbitant prices in order to survive. Thus, under the colonial system, Africans were in most cases made to produce what they did not consume and to consume what they did not produce, clear evidence of a lopsided and exploitative nature of the colonial economy. In fact, the factor of dependency made its impact felt in every aspect of life of the colonies, and can be regarded as the crowning vice among the negative social, political and economic consequences of colonialism in Africa, being primarily responsible for the perpetuation of the colonial relationship into the epoch of neo-colonialism. Colonialism also had a stunting effect on Africans as a physical species. It created conditions which led not only to periodic famine, but also to chronic undernourishment, malnutrition and deterioration in the physique of the African people. Evidence provided in this chapter convincingly indicates that African diet was previously more varied, being based on a more diversified agriculture than was possible under colonialism.

A highly regrettable social impact of colonialism was the deterioration that it caused in the status of women in Africa. Subsequent to the advent of colonialism, the pre-colonial social, religious, constitutional and political privileges and rights of women disappeared, while their economic exploitation was intensified because the division of labour according to sex was frequently disrupted. Isaacman and Stephen (1984: 11-12), and Zhou (2012: 48-55) argue that traditionally, African men did the heavy labour of felling trees, clearing the land, building houses and others, apart from conducting warfare and hunting. When the men were required to leave their farms to seek employment, women remained behind burdened with every task necessary for the survival of themselves, the children and even the men as far as food-stuffs were concerned. Above all, men entered the monetary economy more easily and in greater numbers than women, thereby rendering women work greatly inferior to that of men. As propounded by Rodney (1972: 248), within the new value system of colonialism, men's work was 'modern' and women's was 'traditional' and 'backward'. Boahen (1990: 336) posits that "women were inhibited from joining most of the activities introduced or intensified by colonialism such as Western education, cash-crop farming in some parts of Africa, and many of the professions such as law and medicine." As such, the colonial world was indeed a man's world, and women were not encouraged to play any meaningful role in it. Therefore, the deterioration in the status of women was bound up with the loss of political power by African society as a whole and with the consequent loss of right to set indigenous standards of what work had merit and what did not.

As much as we acknowledge some seemingly positive effects, such as the introduction of western technology, medicine and currency, it is our argument that colonialism underdeveloped Africa and helped immensely in the creation of poverty and inequality. Politically it led to destructive wars of conquest, African loss of independence, sovereignty and freedom. A permanent political cancer in Africa that emanated from colonialism was the arbitrary border designs that have led to ethnic fragmentation and struggles, patronage politics, civil conflict, inequality, underdevelopment and poverty. Economically, colonialism led to the destruction of pre-colonial progress and industries through flooding African markets with European manufactured goods, entrenchment of 'robbery' colonial economy, excessive exploitation, unequal trade and underdevelopment. According to Harper and Rajan (2004: 4) "since the beginning of colonialism, Asia, Africa, and the Americas were seen by the colonizers as a source of natural wealth to be exploited for short-term gains ... Five centuries later, mineral extraction and agribusiness continue to play important roles in North-South trade, with grave ... consequences." Socially, colonialism obliterated Africans from history, intensified oppression of women, entrenched racism, moral decadence and social decay. As much as colonialism is a contested terrain, we argue that it led to political subjugation of Africans, economic disarticulation and marginalisation, destruction of inherent social cohesion, and reduced Africa into perpetual penury. As such, while acknowledging some positive results that emanated from colonialism, on a balance sheet, we argue that these were incidental by-products of colonialism's never ending pursuit of exploitation, underdevelopment, plunder, wrecking and siphoning of African resources by this extenuating phenomenon in the history of Africa.

African Development beyond Colonialism

This section provides a balance sheet that takes cognisance of both external (shown above) and internal factors behind poverty and underdevelopment in Africa. It, therefore, goes beyond dependency theorists, Afro-centric scholars, and African rulers' reductionist and mono-casual theory rooted in colonialism as the Alpha and Omega of poverty, underdevelopment and inequality in Africa. According to

Ekwo (2012: 12), Africa is endowed with dynamic human resources as well as natural resources. Indeed, Africa is a continent with immense untapped mineral wealth and millions upon millions of acres of untilled land. The enormous tourism potential characterised by unrivalled wild, scenic grandeur and pristine ecology constitute Africa's third great natural resource after agriculture and mineral wealth. The challenge is how to utilise these resources more effectively through increased participation of citizens. Africa cannot afford to continue making reference to the external factors of colonialism and neo-colonialism for her woes several decades after attaining independence. Focus should be on the internal dynamics in Africa that may spearhead development. Indeed, there are various issues internal to Africa which have worked, and continue to work, against the development of the continent. Such issues to do with leadership, democracy, good governance, respect of human rights, corporate governance, regional integration, African industrialisation and intra-state trade that is less exploitative, among others, need to be interrogated.

It is a historical fact that colonialism did not bequeath much to Africa. When Tanzania gained independence in 1961, it only had 16 university graduates to run the country. Zambia was a little luckier, as it had 100 university graduates, 1500 dropouts with full secondary education, and 6000 with two years at secondary schools in a country of 4 million (Ayittey, 1999: 41). Paradoxically, both Tanzania and Zambia after independence opted for state planning and development – an economic system that made heavy demands on skilled bureaucrats, the very inputs they lacked. At the end of the 500 years of shouldering the 'white man's burden' of civilising the 'African natives', the Portuguese had not managed to train a single African doctor in Mozambique, and the life expectancy in Angola was less than 30 years. According to Lamb (1983: 5), what the Portuguese in Guinea-Bissau left after 300 years of colonial rule was pitiful: "14 university graduates, an illiteracy rate of 97% and 267 miles of paved roads in an area twice the size of New Jersey. There was only one modern plant in Guinea-Bissau in 1974 – it produced beer for the Portuguese troops – and as a final gesture before leaving, the Portuguese destroyed the national archives." Arguably, colonialism left a litany of baneful destruction and poverty in Africa. On the eve of African independence, the Portuguese colonialists even sabotaged whatever incidental development that had ensued as a by-product of their never ending pursuit of exploitation during the colonial period.

Yet sound as this may appear, it is noteworthy that in many African countries, the leadership could not maintain, let alone augment, the little that was inherited from colonialism. In fact they destroyed it. The inherited infrastructure – roads, bridges, schools, universities, hospitals, telephones, and even the civil service machinery – are now in shambles. When Zaire (now DRC) attained its independence in 1960, it had 31,000 miles of macadamised roads (Ayittey, 1999: 42). Today less than 2,500 miles remain usable. In Ghana and Zimbabwe, transport-network infrastructural development has been neglected since independence, and the colonial roads are now strewn with yawning potholes. While roads have been declared a state of disaster in 2017 in Zimbabwe, there is very little effort to transform their current status. Officials in Ghana and Zimbabwe even insist that it is the vehicle owners who must obtain 'road-worthiness certificates' for their vehicles and not the roads that must be made 'vehicle worthy.' In the 1950s Makerere University in Kampala, Uganda, used to be proudly dubbed 'the Harvard of Africa.' Today, it is in a state of dilapidation and several universities in Africa are in a similar state. Bridges built by colonialists are now falling apart for want of repairs. Railways and other infrastructural facilities are in various states of decay. Such a state of affairs must squarely be blamed on incompetent African leaders rather than the colonialists.

For decades, the externalists' position held sway, attributing the causes of almost every African problem to such external factors as Western colonialism and imperialism, the pernicious effects of the slave trade, racist conspiracy plots, exploitation by avaricious multi-national corporations, an unjust international system, inadequate flows of foreign aid, and deteriorating terms of trade. African scholar and historian, Professor Ali Mazrui (1986) claims that almost everything that has gone wrong in Africa is a fault of Western colonialism and imperialism. Even bribery and corruption, according to Mazrui (1986: 241), was the fault of colonialism and the "coming of new institutions such as Western-style banks, with their new rules and new values." Mobutu offered a more dramatic elucidation of the emergence of corruption in Zaire, retorting that "European businessmen were the ones who said, 'I sell you this thing for $1 000, but $200 will be for your [Swiss bank] account'" (*New Africa*, 1988: 25). Mazrui's condemnation of Western colonialism resonates with dependency theorists, such as Baran (1973), Frank (1972), Furtado (1973) and Rodney (1972), who argue that the underdevelopment of Africa is a direct result of colonialism and neo-colonialism. Rodney's book title, *How Europe underdeveloped Africa*, captures vividly the externalist argument. However, the constant wailing over colonial legacies is at best disingenuous and attributing Africa's underdevelopment, poverty and inequality to external factors *per se*, is intellectually deficient.

Indeed, when Africa gained independence from colonial rule in the 1960s, the euphoria that swept across the continent was infectious. Almost everywhere, this independence euphoria was accompanied by expectation of freedom and development. It was best evinced by the late Dr Kwame Nkrumah the first black president of Ghana. Nkrumah (1957: 34) exuberantly remarked, "We shall achieve in a decade what it took others a century ... and we shall not rest until we demolish these miserable colonial structures and erect in their place a veritable paradise." However, for many Africans, the paradise promised then turned out to be a starvation diet, unemployment, and a gun to the head. According to Falola (1996: 11), "in most of the African countries the inheritors of power became like the new lords presiding over the feudal estates with reckless abandon and without regard for accountability or respect for their 'tenants.'" As such, independence did not become a revolution, only a change of rulers: the colonial machinery of government was inherited and its symbols of power and authority were retained in most countries. After independence, why was it that true freedom never came to much of Africa nor did development? Such an investigation cannot find answers by looking into the arena of colonialism but rather by going beyond colonialism and neo-colonialism.

Ake (1996) argues that the African leaders proclaimed the need for development and made development the new ideology without necessarily translating it into a program of societal transformation. They did so not because they were uninterested in societal transformation but because their minds were absorbed in the struggle for power and survival. Africa's underdevelopment can be partly blamed on the political interests of its leaders who fail to take into account the aspirations of the general populace. In this regard, political interests of most African leaders conceive development as an autonomous process that is independent of politics, culture and institutional framework. Ake (1996) further asserts that conceiving development in this way allowed African leadership unrestricted liberties. They could appropriate selectively from African institutions and culture, using what served them best, to maintain and exploit power and discarding the rest. Thus, they used traditional institutions and notions of consensus to justify one party system without drawing attention to the traditional processes of consultation and participation that produced this consensus.

In the process, Africa was gripped by a wave of dictatorship just after attainment of independence. The leaders were pampered with praises for their role in liberating their respective countries to an extent that some ended up taking awe-inspiring epithets for themselves. Kwame Nkrumah of Ghana was "Osagyefo" (The Redeemer), Julius Nyerere was "Mwalimu" (The Teacher), Felix Houphouet-Boigny of Ivory Coast was "Le Vieux" (The Seer), Mobutu Sese Seko of Zaire (DRC) changed his name to "Sese Seko Kuku Ngbendu WaZaBanga" which, in the local Lingala language, meant "The rooster who leaves no chicken untouched" and Idi Amin called himself "The Conqueror of the British Empire" (Nyawo *et al.*, 2014: 338). Similarly, during his reign, Sekou Toure of the Republic of Guinea took for himself a wide variety of titles designed to enhance his own personality cult. He was referred to as the 'Faithful and Supreme Servant of the People', the 'Doctor of Revolutionary Sciences', and the 'Liberator of Oppressed Peoples" (Toure, 1963: 11-16). The African leaders used their parliamentary majorities to subvert their constitutions, outlaw opposition parties, and declare their countries one-party states and themselves presidents-for-life. As

Ayittey (1999: 93) posits, after independence most African leaders "dismissed the concept of democracy as alien, claiming that multiparty democracy was a Western thing, a luxury Africa could not afford .... Others claimed that Africa had no democratic culture, and too many feuding tribes make democracy a risky venture." Ayittey further asserts that Presidents Paul Biya of Cameroon and Daniel Arap Moi of Kenya vehemently opposed multiparty democracy on the grounds that it would degenerate into destructive tribal politics. In Ghana, Nkrumah (1968: 8) denounced it as an "imperialist dogma." It was the conviction of Mobuto Sese Seko of Zaire (now DRC) that: "Democracy is not for Africa. There was only one African chief and he ruled for life. Here in Zaire we must make unity." It is largely because of such defective political sultanism and personal rule that African leaders have failed to harness both human and natural resources for development in post-independent Africa.

As much as African leaders inherited an authoritarian colonial state at independence, responsible and astute leaders could have dismantled it and returned Africa to its democratic pre-colonial roots. Surprisingly, African leaders strengthened the unitary colonial state apparatus and expanded its scope enormously – especially the military. Even the repressive colonial measures used to quell black aspirations for freedom were retained. Within a year of Ghana's independence in 1957, Nkrumah introduced the Preventive Detention Bill of July 1958, which gave the government sweeping powers to imprison without trial any person suspected of activities prejudicial to the state's security. While apologetics of Nkrumah often point to the fear of the former coloniser's secret hand in undermining his leadership as one of the reasons for the detention bill (Nkrumah, 1957), that many of Nkrumah's victims were those who had fought alongside him for Ghana's independence expose a more selfish motive. The revolution lost its way and ended up eating its own 'fathers', as Nkrumah destroyed the basis for every hope for democracy in Ghana. In Zambia, the state of emergency, used to crush black aspirations for freedom, was continued by President Kenneth Kaunda for 20 years and used by him to arrest and jail many of his opponents. Zhou and Makahamadze (2012: 71-72) have shown how President Robert Mugabe in Zimbabwe similarly kept the state of emergency in effect in the period 1980-1990, as well as the price and exchange controls former white supremacist leaders Ian Smith had introduced to fight off sanctions after his 1965 Unilateral Declaration of Independence from Britain. Arguably, the modern African states have exhibited political lapses and failings. In the first place, government and leadership have failed to acquire credibility, and in most cases the basis of power legitimation lies in violence. Although most African governments began with huge support in the first few years of independence, the promise of mass-based political parties quickly degenerated to one-party authoritarian state with the consequent sink of the states into poverty, underdevelopment and inequality. Conversely, dictators in Africa ruined their respective countries after inheriting them from the colonial masters in a better position. Socialism which many African countries such as Ghana, Guinea, Mali, Libya, Ethiopia, Sudan, Algeria, Angola, Zambia and Zimbabwe (just to mention a few) adopted at independence became an ideology for the systematic exploitation and oppression of people thereby militating against sustainable development.

Indeed, African leaders proceeded to set up autocratic, one party systems that bore no affinity to their own indigenous systems. In country after country, heads of state filled important positions in key institutions (such as the civil service, the military, and the judiciary) and surrounded themselves with members of their own ethnic group: the late Samuel Doe of Liberia with the Krahn; Moi of Kenya with the Kalenjin; Biya of Cameroon with the Beti; Eyadema of Togo with the Kabye; Rawlings of Ghana with the Ewe; Mugabe of Zimbabwe with the Zezuru; and so on. As noted by Wanyande (1988: 74), "In African one party states, the rulers have tended to use their power and the institutions they control not only to promote their own individual and group interests as rulers – and in some cases sectional as opposed to national interests – but also to manipulate and undermine the rights and freedom of the rest of society." Personal rule has prevailed in most African countries over much of the post-colonial period. Giving a composite portrait of the typical African tyrant and how he rules, Sandbrook (1993: 90) remarked:

The strongman, usually the president, occupies the centre of political life. Front and centre stage, he is the centrifugal force around which all else revolves. Not only the ceremonial head of state, the president is also the chief political, military and cultural figure: head of government, commander-in-chief of the armed forces, head of the governing party (if there is one) and even chancellor of the local university. His aim is typically to identify his person with the 'nation.

In most cases, Africa has been rocked by civil wars such that development processes failed in those countries that experienced these civil wars. Civil wars have caused considerable damage and destruction, and in most cases development projects are suspended in those areas heavily affected. According to Bujra (2002: 1), during the four decades between the 1960s and the 1990s, there have been about 80 violent changes of governments in 48 sub-Saharan African countries. During the same period, many countries experienced different types of civil strife, conflicts and wars. At the beginning of the new millennium, there were eighteen countries facing armed rebellion and eleven facing severe political crises. Areas that have faced worrisome explosive conflicts recently include Eritrea and Ethiopia, DRC, Rwanda, Uganda, Namibia, Sudan, South Sudan, Somalia, Burundi, Guinea Bissau, Central Africa Republic, Nigeria, Lesotho, Ivory Coast, Tunisia and Libya. Other conflicts were in the form of secessionist rebellions and the most spectacular secessionist war was that of the Biafra in Nigeria (1966-1970) that ended in catastrophic failure. Kabinda (1975-2002), Katanga (1960-1965) and Southern Sudan (1983-2011), were other examples. Bujra (2002: 8) argues that despite the limited success of secessionist rebellions, they have nevertheless caused considerable damage and destruction, much to the detriment of development. By and large, there are cases where civil wars have led collapse of states with the consequent increased poverty and underdevelopment such as Somalia from the early 1990s to the present, Sierra Leone (1991-2000), and Libya (from 2011 to the present). Democratic institutions and processes were corroded due to a systematic redistribution of power, wealth and status to military actors thereby generating lawlessness, atrocities, poverty and development of underdevelopment.

According to Alemu (2014: 145), the 1983-2005 war that ultimately led to secession of South Sudan in 2011 left 2 million people killed, 42,000 refuges, and 4million displaced. West Africa has had a fair share of these conflicts in the form of coups. Beginning with a coup in Togo in January 1963, West African states by the end of 2004 had experienced 44 successful military coups, 43 bloody failed coup attempts, 82 reported coup plots and as many as 7 terrible civil wars (Atuobi, 2007: 13). As such, energy that could have been used for productive work was wasted in useless civil wars, coups and destruction, thereby retarding development, and generating poverty and misery. In Southern Africa, Zimbabwe was rocked by a civil war in the period 1982-1987, while Angola experienced civil war from 1975 to 2002. In most cases these wars were home grown and the Africans should shoulder the blame for the effects of these wars on the development of Africa as leaders tried to elbow one another out of power through conflicts or wars. However, despite the internal origination of the wars, external factors have in some cases exacerbated the conflicts. The proliferation of arms from countries such as America, France, Russia, and China has aggravated conflict in some African countries such as Angola, Democratic Republic of Congo, Sudan, South Sudan and Libya. As such, by sponsoring military machinery the developed countries have in some way aggravated conflict and underdevelopment in Africa.

While it is a historical fact that artificial colonial borders contributed to the Ethiopian-Eritrean war of 1998-2000 and North-South Sudan war of 1983-2011 it is noteworthy that the artificial borders are not the tape-root of conflict in Africa. People of Africa traditionally have paid little attention to borders. They move when the need arises, border or no border, as attested to by the movement of refugees. Despite the creation of artificial colonial borders, Zhou (2017) unravels corridors of opportunities that emerged in times of war and crises whereby ethnic brotherhood/sisterhood was mutually beneficial to the fragmented groups. Somalia, though ethnically homogenous, collapsed in 1991 because of Said Barre's defective political system of sultanism. Above all, lamenting over artificial colonial borders that Organisation of African Union (OAU) - now African Union (AU) – accepted is illusory. Only African governments – the same members of AU – pay much attention to borders for the collection of import duties by official and unofficial personnel. The politics of exclusion has been the source of Africa's chronic political instability, civil strife, wars and chaos. Where the ruling elites had the foresight and wisdom to agree to and implement real democratic reform and power sharing, they saved not only themselves but their countries as well. Examples of such cases include Benin, Malawi, Mali, and South Africa. But where benighted rulers and hardliners refused to share or relinquish power, those excluded had no choice but to seek to overthrow the system or to secede. Either course of action resulted in violence, carnage, destruction and poverty, as evidenced by Burundi, Ethiopia, Liberia, Rwanda, Somalia, DRC and Southern Sudan. It can, therefore, be argued that internal factors such as poverty of leadership, poor governance and parochialism have far more contributed to political instability, wars, destruction, poverty and underdevelopment than the external factor of artificial borders.

Two factors underlie Africa's never-ending political violence and civil wars: the absence of mechanisms for peaceful transfer of political power, and for the resolution of conflicts. As shown above, carnage and chaos often result from a mad grab for power centralised at the capital. The long-term solution would involve the decentralisation or diffusion of power and the adoption of power-sharing arrangements, namely democratic pluralism. Indeed, there are too many dictators in Africa and this has affected development in the continent. The democratic reform process, which gathered momentum after the collapse of communism in 1989, has stalled. According to Ayittey (1999: 75), the number of democratic countries grew from 4 in 1990 to 14 in 1996 (Botswana, Benin, Cape Verde Islands, Central Africa Republic, Madagascar, Malawi, Mali, Mauritius, Namibia, Sao Tome & Principe, Senegal, Seychelles, Sierra Leone, South Africa, and Zambia). However, political tyranny is still the order of the day in Africa, and some of the countries dubbed as democratic in the past, such as Central Africa Republic, have relapsed into dictatorship and worsened poverty and underdevelopment through wars. Wily autocrats quickly learned new tricks to beat back the democratic challenge by inflating voter rolls, manipulating the electoral rules, and holding fraudulent elections to keep themselves in power, as in Algeria, Angola, Burundi Cameroon, Congo, DRC, Egypt, Kenya, Mozambique, Sudan, Uganda, and Zimbabwe. Arguably, very few countries have given their people the right to change leaders through the ballot box. Only seven leaders are known to have voluntarily relinquished power until 2016 and with the exception of Nelson Mandela of South Africa, Olusegun Obasanjo of Nigeria and Abdul al Dahab of Sudan, the rest did so after spending many years in office (Siaka Stevens of Sierra Leone, Leopold Senghor of Senegal, Julius Nyerere of Tanzania, and Ahmadou Ahidjo of Cameroon). Falola (1996: 13) has vividly captured how African leaders are a stumbling block to development. "There is no effective way of changing regimes. Rulers refuse to relinquish power and the military uses violence to perpetuate itself. Political coercion and repression replace democracy. Life presidents have emerged, with a notion that a leader should possess a state and government", he stated. Rather than wailing over the effects of colonialism and imperialism, Africa must rid itself of dictatorial, egocentric and one armed bandit leaders so as to foster sustainable development.

The most lethal practice of African leaders is the propensity to perpetually hold onto power. The fatality of an iron grip on power has been demonstrated several times in African politics. From Burundi's Pierre Nkurunziza, Cameroon's Paul Biya, Rwanda's Paul Kagame, the DRC's Joseph Kabila, Zimbabwe's Robert Mugabe, Uganda's Yoweri Museveni, Gabon's Bongo dynasty, Angola's Eduardo Do Santos, to Gambia's Yahya Jammeh. While there was emerging ray of hope in Rwanda, Kagame pulled a shocker when he went on to amend the constitution (following a referendum in December 2015) to facilitate another term from 2017, against the dictates of the supreme law (*Daily News*, 2015). In Burundi, Nkurunziza worked hard in 2015 after the expiry of the two terms, unashamedly forcing himself into power and plunging Burundi into conflict and underdevelopment. Similarly, after tampering with the constitution, Museveni was able to contest and win elections in Uganda thereby extending his 30-year iron grip on power (*News Day*, 2016). Matyszak (2010) has shown that though Mugabe lost elections in March 2008 and failed to gain credibility through his defective and violence riddled June 2008 victory, his mastery of politics of staying in power enabled him to regain his legitimacy through an inclusive government from 2009 to 2013, after which he extended his grip on power for 37 years by 2017. The more than 80% unemployment rate, rampant corruption, collapse of industries and reduction of Zimbabweans into vending, is evidence of what a continued reign by a single leader can do. The democratisation process in Zimbabwe, as in many African countries, has stalled through political chicanery and strong-arm tactics.

The script is hardly different in DRC, where Kabila's term of office lapsed in December 2016, but has made attempts to either unlawfully extend it beyond 2018 on the pretext that the country has no money to conduct elections or change the constitution to allow him to run for a third term. His actions have ignited ugly protests and systematic killing of innocent civilians by the army (*Daily News*, 2016). While some African states (such as Botswana and Ghana) practice some acceptable forms of democracy with leaders accepting defeat after losing in an election, there are several cases where leaders either refuse to go or prepare their relatives (wives and children) to take over after their reign. In Gabon, Omar Bongo's grip on power stretched from 1967 until his death in 2009. His son and successor, Ali Bongo has been on the steering wheel since 2009 thereby entrenching Bongo dynastic rule in the country. Indeed western liberal system has its weaknesses and limitations in international power relations, but it certainly promotes some semblance of acceptable internal democracy based on specified limited term of office of a ruler and free and fair elections. On the contrary, only a few of the 55 African countries are democratic, and political tyranny remains the order of the day. After initially conceding defeat on 1 December 2016, Jammeh a week later rejected presidential election results and called for fresh vote thereby plunging Gambia into chaos and uncertainty (*The Standard*, 2016: 10). It was only the intervention of Economic Community of West African States (ECOWAS) forces that forced Jammeh out of power in January 2017, with his consequent settlement in exile in Equatorial Guinea. Evidently, African leadership is squarely to blame for the stagnation, decay and backwardness in the continent. With a continued hold on power, leaders start to get a false sense of ownership of a nation, while in reality they are just but citizens mandated with a term to govern a country. Ekwo (2012: 13) argues that democracy based on freedom of expression, freedom of the press, open government, transparency, accountability and genuine commitment to change will guarantee Africa's growth and development. Above all, the exercise of democratic rights is supportive to economic objectives through revealing where remedial action is needed, thereby applying pressure on government to swiftly respond (Dziva *et al.*, 2013: 84). Sadly, those in power in Africa are at best prepared to be accountable only to themselves and care little about the notion of popular democracy (Nyawo *et al.*, 2014: 341). Over-centralisation of decision making processes facilitates fraud, which affects not only the governance of the state but the management of the country's entire economy. Unless leaders become democratic and acquaint themselves with the realities of economic dynamics, most African states will remain locked in situations far worse than the colonial period.

Economically, two models were followed by African countries after independence with disastrous effects. According to Falola (1996: 12), many countries like Nigeria, Liberia, Kenya and Ivory Coast adopted a capitalist path of private ownership and private management of the economy, allowing the state to interfere in those areas that required financial commitments beyond the rich of the private sector. He further asserts that other countries such as Tanzania, Guinea, and for a while Egypt and Mali took a socialist path of state control and ownership of industries. In Southern Africa, Zambia, and later Angola, Zimbabwe and Namibia, also pursued the socialist route from the infancy of their independence. In both models results were disappointing, and by the 1970s there was need for re-assessment. In the capitalist countries, indigenous private companies collaborated with external forces to milk the state. In the socialist ones, the state was a poor economic manager, never to be trusted. In the words of Falola (1996: 12), "the countries saw economic stagnation, a worsening balance of payments, deteriorating terms of trade, wealth transfer, mass poverty, and decline in agricultural production." By the 1980s, the conclusion was that past policies had failed, and ideologies were seriously questioned. The need for economic diversification and foreign investments became too paramount solutions in all countries, even in a few that still claimed to be socialists (Voss, 1973: 10).

Ayittey (1999: 40) asserts that the African region suffers from a long-standing economic crisis rooted in low productivity, limited capacity for adjustment, government policies which have long emphasised intervention and control and overlooked incentives, and an international economy characterised by weak demand for Africa's exports, high interest rates, and stagnating resource flows. While external factors have played a determining role in present economic difficulties, internal policy failures are also to blame as reflected above by the defective economic policy of statism. As such, the overall direction of change must be towards more market freedom, more emphasis on producer incentives, as well as reform of the public sector to ensure greater profitability.

Greater profitability has been hard to achieve in Africa because of high profile corruption that has become routine rather than episodic, thereby entrenching poverty underdevelopment and inequality. Power has been used primarily to steal from the state. Political leadership in Africa is characterised by corruption and mismanagement. Built strongly on clientelism and cronyism, political leaders reward their supporters with positions and money. As Falola (1996: 13) posits, corruption of such extensive magnitude "compromises the management of the state, destroy morale, and wrecks the fabric of society." Because the private gains to be made from state power are enormous, competition to control the state is fierce and brutal. Ultimately, the end justifies the means; the winner takes all, and does everything to perpetuate himself. Corruption is admittedly, a global cancer, but it is its high profile and routine nature, rather than episodic, that has worsened the plight of Africa. Africa is awash with examples of corrupt leaders, whose corruption brought their respective countries to ground. Mawere and Tandi (2017) argue that Mobutu Sese Seko, Zaire (now DRC)'s president allegedly stole at least US$5 billion from Zaire. Ayittey (1999: 24) estimates Mobutu's personal fortune in Swiss bank accounts to have been as high as US$10 billion. In contrast to such opulent riches and externalisation, the Congolese were left greatly impoverished and underdeveloped with the lowest Human Development Index as it was ranked 187 out of 187 countries with a low life expectancy at birth of 45.7 years in 1997 (UNDP, *Human Development Report*, 2011:

2-5). Mobutu bequeathed DRC successive leaders with this resource plunder propensity that has reduced mineral wealth eastern DRC to a conflict war zone between 1996 and 2016, and left the generality of the people deeply entrenched in poverty and misery. Hastings Kamuzu Banda of Malawi was a typical post-colonial leader whose thirty year regime was characterised by widespread corruption which was never publicly discussed before his democratic deposition in 1994 (Hall-Mathews, 2007: 78). According to Hall-Mathews (2007: 79), Banda's successor, Bakili Muluzi, was guilty of embezzlement with the National Audit Office report for the 2002-2003 financial year revealing huge volumes of unrecovered dubious payments for goods, services, salaries and allowances which almost entirely accounted for a budget overspend of K346.4 million (£1.732 million). This was made possible through over 3000 bank accounts which were opened and run by government ministries without the Accountant General's knowledge.

Daniel Arap Moi of Kenya was no exception to looting state resources by African leaders in post-colonial Africa. During his 24 years in power, his government embezzled and stole an estimated US$3 billion to US$4 billion (Ayodele *et al.*, 2005: 3). The country's central bank was looted. The money was stolen by making fictitious payments of foreign debts; kickbacks were collected on all public contracts, and when that didn't supply enough cash, politicians awarded themselves fake contracts. A Report by Kenya's 21st century created Anti-Corruption Commission estimates that up to US$3 billion of the missing money was stashed overseas. Ayodele *et al.* (2005: 3) argue that after Moi left office, he and his family were among the wealthiest people in Kenya, with seven big homes and connections to at least 30 major business firms. Yet, in contrast to his personal life and riches, he left behind an economy crippled with foreign debt, collapsed infrastructure, unemployment hovering at 70%, and nearly two-thirds of the population living under the poverty line.

Sierra Leone typifies people living in poverty, slavery and limited liberty in a resource rich country. At independence in 1961, the country's development prospects looked encouraging. The country had a renowned educational system; a rich and diversified natural resource base comprising diamonds and other minerals, and abundant agricultural and marine resources; tourist attractions; and a seemingly stable democracy. However, diamond, gold and rutile mining have raised only a few people's living standards, resulted in modern day slavery and massive environmental damage. Since the departure of colonial rule, successive governments have been corrupt and extremely incompetent in the provision of most basic needs. As pointed by Ridell (2005: 126), Sierra Leoneans "were not just neglected, uninvolved, or would catch up later in the nation's development. They were actively exploited or 'ripped off', and had been for roughly a hundred years – first by colonialism and then by the policies, plans, and programmes of the government of independent Sierra Leone." The regime of the first president of Sierra Leone, Siaka Stevens, was infamous for its inordinate level of corruption. He appropriated a vast amount of government revenue for his personal gain, and along with fellow government officials, lived in luxury while the people went hungry. As Ridell (2005: 118-119) further argues, he used up most of the financial resources that were meant for his state and people with the effect that poverty and underdevelopment reigned, and has continued within Sierra Leone. Due to such consistent corruption within government, Sierra Leone is embroiled in poverty and has one of the lowest GDP figures: as of 2010, it was $900, even less than previously war-torn countries such as Rwanda (Central Intelligence Agency, 2010).

The diamond industry, one of the main sources of revenue for the Sierra Leonean government, has brought significant income to the country, but the top-down effect is virtually non-existent; lower class and rural citizens still experience exploitative labour relations, environmental terrorism and persistent poverty within mining communities (Le Billion and Levin, 2009: 695). The contrast between the supposed right to health and actual exploitation is particularly stark in the diamond-rich Kono District around the regional capital of Koidu. As Le Billio and Levin further argue, Kono is both the richest and poorest (pollution and disease infested) part of Sierra Leone. The external factors such as a decreased demand for diamonds worldwide has thrown many Sierra Leoneans out of jobs into poverty. Brown (2005) has estimated that Government elites have earned personal revenue of about US$7.5 billion. Such money could have been judiciously used to alleviate poverty in a corruption free society, rather than enriching the rich.

Nigeria is no exception to the general trend of corruption revealed above. For six years, 1988-1994, Nigeria's military rulers squandered US$12.4 billion in oil revenue, estimated to be a third of the nation's foreign debt (Ayittey, 1999: 35). Ayittey further asserts that most Nigerians collapsed into hysterical laughter when they heard their late head of state, General San Abacha, had launched a war on corruption, because they knew that several of his cronies, active or retired, were millionaires and no military men involved in the banking scandal (that cost the country US$180 million) had been touched. As succinctly put forward by a civil rights lawyer, "When the soldiers have eaten enough, he retires them" (*The Economist* (1996: 48). Ayodele *et al.* (2005: 2) remarked that, "... individual Nigerians are currently lodging US$170 billion in foreign banks – far more than Nigeria's foreign debt of US$35 billion." Goodspeed (2005: A1) argues that a succession of military dictators in Nigeria stole or squandered US$500 billion – equivalent to all Western aid to Africa in the period 1965-2005. Even when the loot is recovered, it is quickly re-looted. Of the recovered US$983 million loot by the former president Sani Abacha and his henchmen only US$12 million was found in the Central Bank of Nigeria by the Senate Public Accounts Committee (Ayittey, 2005: 439). Corruption in Africa has, therefore, become an endemic disease that fraudulently benefits some vandals in leadership and their lackeys. It has subverted or diminished the capacity of legitimate authorities to provide fully for the material and spiritual wellbeing of members of society in a just and equitable manner. Conversely, African politicians have been lining their pockets while Africa has remained underdeveloped and desperately poor.

Conflict has escalated in the Niger Delta area because of corruption by both federal and states government, and their insensitivity to the poverty stricken locals and indigenes. The governor of Central Bank of Nigeria, Chukwuma Soludo, disclosed in 2007 that "Nigeria has since the discovery of crude oil in 1959 earned a total of US$350 billion from sale of the natural resources, yet the crude oil has remained a curse for Nigeria as we are worse now than where we were" (Udeze, 2009: 351). As much as in the creeks and swamps of the Niger Delta is located one of the biggest reserves of oil on the planet with 35 billion barrel of black gold, the region is also home to some of its worst environmental destruction. There are villages without power, water, health clinics or schools; pipelines that scar the earth; oil slicks that shimmer on rivers; flares that blaze bright and loud, burning off the gas that gushes to the surface along the sweet crude. It is within this context of living a life of perpetual poverty in a resource rich area that the conflict of the people of Niger Delta with both federal and state governments must be fully comprehended. In light of the above internal factors characterised by systematic corruption, capital flight and economic mismanagement, the attribution of Africa's poverty, underdevelopment and inequality solely to external factors is intellectually deficient.

There are cases where internal and external factors have worked together to contribute to the poverty and underdevelopment of Africa. A case in point is the nexus of corruption, externalisation and foreign aid. The record of Western aid to Africa is one of abysmal failure. Yet we continue to have many African leaders stampeding for it from Western donors. More than US$500 billion of foreign aid – the equivalent of four Marshal Aid Plan – was pumped into Africa between 1960 and 1997 (Ayodele *et al.*, 2005: 1). The ultimate result of pouring such aid in Africa has been the lowering of standard of living and increased dependency. Former Senegalese president, Aboulaye Wade, vividly captured the impact of aid when he remarked: "I've never seen a country develop itself through aid or credit. Countries that have developed – in Europe, America, Japan, Asian countries like Taiwan, Korea and Singapore – have all believed in free markets. There is no mystery there. Africa took the wrong road after independence" (Onishi, 2002: A3). Much of the aid has simply been looted by African leaders. A free market economist, Douglas Casey, also remarked: "Foreign aid might be defined as a transfer from poor people in rich countries to rich people in poor countries" (Udeze, 2009: 348). Easterly (2003) has shown how the Global North therapy of aid has failed to uplift the Global South and how the Global North has continued to administer the same medicine over decades without learning from the past mistakes. Not surprisingly, of the 29 countries to which World Bank provided more than US$20 billion in structural adjustment loans between 1981-1991 only five (Burkina Faso, Ghana, Tanzania, Lesotho and Guinea) were still considered as success stories by the beginning of the 21st century (Udeze, 2009: 348). The disturbing reality is that no African country had achieved a sound macro-economic stance. Indeed, aid is a special kind of umbilical cord which ties Africa to the metropolitan Global North, distorts their economies and integrates them externally with the consequent entrenchment of dependency. It has led to a situation where Africa has failed to set its own pace and direction of development free of external interference.

Speaking at the New Partnership for Africa Development (NEPAD) in Nigeria in 2003, former British Secretary of State for International Development, Lynda Chalker, noted that 40% of the wealth created in Africa is invested outside the continent. "If you can get your kith and kin to bring the funds back and have it invested in infrastructure, the economies of African countries would be much better than what they are today", she remarked (Ayittey, 2005: 324). A United Nations Report, *Illicit Financial Flows* (2015: 1) reflects that "Africa lost about US $854 billion in IFFs over the period 1970-2008, which corresponds on average to US $22 billion per year." This sum is nearly equivalent to all the Official Development Assistance (ODA) received by Africa over that time frame and only a third of it would have been enough to fully cover the continent's external debt which reached US $279 billion in 2008. Tandi and Mawere (2017) argue that corruption is costing the continent of Africa US$150 billion a year. Considering the missing billions in export earnings from oil, gas, diamonds, platinum, gold and other minerals that are not openly accounted for, it is a paradox that Africa suffers from a poverty trap. It is also because of such corruption that foreign aid to African nations to support reforms has been largely unsuccessful, apart from it being a wrong prescription for the disease of poverty and underdevelopment. It is also noteworthy that the amount of capital that is siphoned out of Africa by the elites (capital flight) exceeds the amount that comes in by way of foreign aid and investment. Arguably, it would be more judicious to remove the environmental factor that exacerbates the capital shortage problem than to seek the infusion of more capital into Africa. That this has not been the case is entirely the fault of African leaders who have conditioned themselves to foreign aid because of high prospects for looting or lining their pockets.

By and large, the evidence provided in this chapter has shown that Africa cannot continue to blame colonialism and neo-colonialism several decades after attaining independence. As much as colonialism generated poverty and underdevelopment through integrating African economies into the exploitative global economy, care must be taken to focus on internal dynamics of Africa that have perpetuated poverty, underdevelopment and inequality in independent Africa. Such factors include, among others, poverty of leadership, political tyranny, senseless civil wars, military vandalism, and absence of mechanism for transfer of political power, lack of corporate governance, systemic corruption, capital flight, economic mismanagement, and flagrant violations of human rights. At any rate, external factors are beyond the control or manipulation of most African countries on an individual basis. Even if possible, any effort to alter external environment is likely to be protracted, taking decades. On the contrary, internal factors are mostly man-made or artificial and are therefore more amenable to change or correction by African governments than external factors. No matter how much colonialism is abhorred, that artefact of history cannot be undone or re-written; it must be seen as a given. Additionally, the stress to external factors presupposes that the solutions have to come from external sources; hence the repeated appeals to the international community. However, this approach, as reflected in the case of foreign aid, has proved disastrous. Foreign solutions have not worked well in Africa because they do not fit into its unique socio-cultural milieu. The continent is a graveyard littered with a multitude of failed imported schemes of systems. Falola (1996: 3) aptly captures the root of Africa's poverty and underdevelopment by stating that:

> Some people will blame our colonial oppressors. Well in some
> cases part of it is true but a whole lot of the blame should be put

squarely on our shoulders ... Independence was thought to be the beginning of the golden era where political freedom and expression, freedom of association, free enterprise, economic prosperity, less ethnocentricism, responsibility and accountability of each and every one prevailed. These loft ideas never happened because we replaced white imperialism with the black one.

Envisaged African Development path in the 21st century

As has been demonstrated in this chapter, many of the gains of independence in Africa have now been lost. Millions of people in Africa live below the poverty level in most countries, as leaders are unable to put a place and sustain policies and institutions that would allow them to measure up with the middle-income and developed countries. Debt, drought, the fall in living standards, and wars are now the major issues. Political dictatorship and military rule have become common place, and many talented intellectuals and skilled professionals migrate to the West. The modern African state has failed to move beyond the imperial doctrine of exploitation. As Falola (1996: 14) puts it, "The legacy of African leadership, revealed in this chapter, is brutalising and chaotic: fear, poverty, drought, warfare, theft, refugees and human rights abuse are commonplace." Capital income has fallen dramatically, and as was the case during the colonial period, growth without development has ensued in most cases in Africa. Agriculture is declining, famine is reported in many places, and expenditure on welfare and social services has declined. Although a few countries like Ghana and Botswana have been used as examples of foreign assistance success, structural adjustment has been a colossal failure, and the expected gains have not accrued to the majority of the African population. Indeed, Africa is now the poorest continent, in spite of being endowed with dynamic human resources as well as natural resources. There is therefore need for a political, economic and social paradigm shift in Africa in order to foster sustainable development.

It is within the above framework that African leaders must judiciously revert to appropriate use of traditional processes of consultation and participation that produced consensus to entrench democracy, good governance, accountability, transparency, equity and respect for human rights. Indeed, there is need for political reform to ensure peaceful transfer of political power and peaceful resolution of conflicts. As noted in this chapter, the absence of these two has caused political violence and civil wars in Africa. Peace should, therefore, be the best preventive measure for conflicts in the 21st century, as it paves the way for dialogue, cooperation and compromise, ultimately making it the best framework for sustainable development in Africa. Sustainable development would also generate employment, improve livelihood, and create a basis for durable peace and stability. It follows that there is no development without peace, and there is no peace without all-inclusive growth and raising quality of living for all.

Long term development in the 21st century will not be achieved in the absence of security, and short term security operations will not bring about sustainable benefits if they would not be coordinated with long term development efforts. It is therefore critical, in the 21st century African development agenda, to consolidate peace and stability, promote poverty reduction, rule of law and good governance, extend legitimate state authority, and prevent countries from relapsing into conflict in order to enhance economic growth and sustainable development (Zhou, 2016). Admittedly, good governance is crucial for sustained and inclusive economic growth and building capable states in Africa. By and large, the 21st century African development agenda should be punctuated by conflict-sensitive development or the conflict-sensitive approach to development and assistance in which sustainable development is connected to durable peace and stability. This will hopefully result in a comprehensive approach to development that can provide better answers to complex needs of fragile environments where poverty and conflict in Africa will be addressed simultaneously. Peace and development in Africa will in turn promote global peace and sustainable development. As Zhou (2016) argues, peace is the essential prerequisite of cooperation, inclusiveness and social equity necessary to solve global challenges, let alone empower the international institutions needed to regulate the challenges.

The chapter also revealed that abundant natural resources available in Africa, which should be a blessing to enhance the economies and social status in most cases, are the leading factor that makes them poor and poorer people. As reflected in the chapter, resources wealth has ignited conflict and wars with the consequent loss of lives and properties, thereby aggravating poverty and underdevelopment. Resource wealth and weak governments in Africa have enticed external powers to intervene in the internal affairs of African states thereby disturbing peace, stability and good governance. Governments in Africa must take actions to combat civil wars. This can be done by making greater efforts to adopt economic policies and institutions that can stimulate growth and reduce poverty, improve governance and transparency, and redress reasonable grievances among aggrieved parties and stakeholders. At any rate, rebel movements, particularly those seeking to secede on the threshold of natural resources, are greatly bolstered by the presence of corrupt elite and politicians that siphon off the revenues, rather than a government that spends them prudently and transparently, to enhance living standards across the board. There is need for leaders to improve on prudence, transparency, efficiency, and equity in order to ensure that local people in particular (and other citizens in general) benefit from resources accruing in their area. Above all, building a more peaceful and friendly world is not limited to encouraging tolerance and consensus. It is encompassing, involving a practical agenda for economic development and the effective global governance of the markets that facilitate rebellion and corrupt governance.

After independence African leaders did not only prove to be crocodile liberators, quack revolutionaries and grasping kleptocrats, but also Swiss bank socialist who plundered African resources and stashed several billions in foreign accounts. Therefore, mandatory regulations ensuring that African leaders and the ruling elite invest in their respective countries must be put in place. This would generate enough capital that can be invested in development and African countries can make do without foreign aid that so far has proved to be acidic by supplanting local capacity, undermining local knowledge and institutions and rendering recipient African countries more vulnerable and dependent on aid by cultivating dependency syndrome (Mawere and Tandi, 2017).

Despite colonial and neo-colonial plunder, Africa is still endowed with large amounts of natural wealth. There are numerous opportunities for investment in mining and oil industries so that the raw materials are processed locally into mineral, petroleum and chemical products. This will surely ensure value addition, best revenue and beneficiation. It is, therefore, envisaged that in the 21st century era of growing scarcity, resource-rich Africa will shift away from being a marginal supplier of raw materials, to tap and harness the full potential of its natural resources by diversifying into greater value addition, through processing and marketing. At any rate, even the argument by externalists that dependence on primary products condemns countries to underdevelopment is no longer tenable. Australia, New Zealand and Canada were all colonies built on exporting products back to the industrial core, but by the 1950s all were firmly established as part of the developed world (Zhou, 2012: 21). In Australia, India and Asia, internal reforms allowed the benefits of economic growth to be shared more widely, despite continued dependence on international economy. As such, at worst Africa's lucrative natural resources should be tapped and harnessed for a win-win situation with the developed countries, and at best, should be processed locally in order to maximise benefits.

Indeed, pre-colonial economy was diversified and was only emasculated by colonialists who invented monoculture in order to entrench African cash crop production and dependency. This was part of a large scale concept of orienting African economies to the export of raw materials. As such, one obvious way to reduce African nations' total dependency on natural resources is to help them diversify their economies and also fight corruption. As Udeze (2009: 349) asserts, countries with more diverse base of exports are better protected from the adverse effects of price fluctuations and less prone to the resource curse. On average, developing countries' exports in other continents are no longer predominantly primary commodities; therefore, African countries should not be an exception.

As colonialism fostered underdevelopment by deliberately failing to industrialise or transfer technology to Africa, and entrenched unequal trade that has continued even in post-colonial period, one major way to foster African development in the 21st century is industrialisation fostered, *inter-alia*, by agricultural development, regional and continental integration, and peace and stability. Africa should hasten the depth and pace of regional incorporation in order to facilitate greater levels of trade, boost diversification and sustainable growth, create large markets, pool human capital and natural resources, and leverage the different comparative advantages of African countries for the achievement of the continent's industrialisation goal. Rather than tie their economies to the industrialised North which offer no promise of serving as growth engine, African countries should rely on one another. South-South relations can be built on financial co-operation, complementarity in trade, promotion of joint ventures, and other means that can do away with exploitation of one country by another. As Falola (1996: 16) puts it, "Africa, as part of an integrated Third World market, would benefit from economies of scale, enhance its bargaining power by reducing its dependence on the West, and increase its productive capacity." Nevertheless, effective participation in these regional and global value chains requires investment in human capital (skills), transparent regulatory and business environments and effective hard and soft infrastructure including a steady source of reliable energy generation, transportation systems and information and communication technologies (ICT), which Africa must strive to achieve. Kanyenze *et al.*, (2006), have suggested that African countries should trade with the North as a block in order to minimise exploitation.

Since colonialism neglected agriculture, generated poor farming methods and intensified the exploitation of women, African countries must use their rich indigenous knowledge systems in order to enhance productivity and food security. There is also need to empower women to become drivers of continental development, prosperity and renaissance. Undoubtedly, more concrete steps need to be taken to ensure success or to foster women empowerment outside the informal sector. As more than two thirds of Africans

86

(mostly women) depend on agriculture for their livelihoods, investing in and boosting this sector is an effective strategy to reduce poverty and inequality. African countries can end hunger and malnutrition and become major players in global food market in the 21st century by investing in agriculture. The evidence provided in this chapter also reflected colonial infrastructural inadequacy, which calls for infrastructural development (roads, railway lines, energy, information and communication technology and ICT) in order to enhance national, regional and continental trade and development.

Conclusion

Africa's underdevelopment has been a topical issue for quite a long time with various causative explanations being put forward, both external and internal. A more accurate judgement in our view is not that colonialism did not do anything positive for Africa, but that given its opportunities and its resources and the power and influence it wielded in Africa at the time, it could and should have done far more than it did. Above all, the element of economic exploitation during the whole period of colonialism was very far in excess of that of economic development. On balance, therefore, the colonial era will go down in history as a period of growth without development, a period of lost opportunities and of the humiliation of the peoples of Africa. It is within this framework that in the peak days of the dependency theory in the 1970s, colonialism and Western imperialism as external factors were among the most respectable explanation for the underdevelopment and poverty in Africa. No one must ever discount this factor, in light of the political subjugation, economic disarticulation and marginalisation, social bastardisation and pauperisation of Africans consequent of the effects of colonialism. However, in comparison with internal factors such as poverty of leadership, political tyranny, senseless civil wars, military vandalism, systemic corruption, capital flight, economic mismanagement, and flagrant violations of human rights, external factors pale into obscurity, more so in light of several years that have ensued after independence. Arguably, it is grossly misleading to ignore or understate the internal factors: for instance, the troubles within the continent, generated by a leadership that victimises its own people, takes positions that cannot bring credit to the continent, and squanders and mismanages collective resources. There is virtually no aspect of African society that does not require reform: politics must move away from dictatorship to mass participation; the role of the state as a predator must change to that of an agency to serve people; the international community must back off from supporting illegitimate (those whose mandate to rule has expired), rebel and brutal political leaders to assist the people to gain freedom and enhance their living standards. The poverty of the people contrasts with the richness of the continent. The empowerment of the people, to allow mass participation in politics and to take charge of their own lives, has become more necessary than ever before. By and large, after independence, African nationalists and elites abjured their own indigenous institutions and rushed to blindly copy foreign systems they did not understand. Had they looked in their own backyard, they would have found the solutions to Africa's poverty, underdevelopment and inequality.

References

Afigbo, A.E. *et al.* 1992. *The Making of Modern Africa: The twentieth century*, Vol. 2, Longman: London.

Ake, C. 1996. *Democracy and Development in Africa*, The Bookings Institution: Washington D.C.

Allan, W. 1965. *The African Husbandman*, Oxford University Press, Oxford.

Alemu, S.K. 2014. 'The Horn of Africa: Some Explanations for Poverty and Conflicts', *Ethiopia Renaissance Journal of Social Science and the Humanities*, 1(1): 141-168.

Asiwaju, A.I. 1984. (Ed.), *Partitioned Africans*, University of Lagos Press: Lagos.

Atuobi, S. M. December 2007. 'Corruption and State Instability in West Africa: An Examination of Policy Options', *Kofi Annan International Peace Keeping Training Centre (KAIPTC)*, Occasional Paper, (21): 1-24.

Ayittey, G.B.N. 1999. *Africa in Chaos*, St Martin's Griffin: New York.

Ayittey, G.B.N. 2005. *Africa Unchained*, Palgrave Macmillan: New York.

Ayodele, T. *et al.* 2005. 'African Perspectives on Aid: Foreign assistance will not pull Africa out of poverty', *CATO Institute Economic Development Bulletin*, No. 2, 14 September.

Baran, P. 1973. *The Political Economy of Growth*, Penguin: Harmondsworth.

Blanton, R. Mason, T.D. and Athow, B. 2001. 'Colonial style and post-colonial ethnic conflict in Africa', *Journal of Peace Research*, 38 (4): 473-491.

Boahen, A.A. *et al.* 1986, *Topics in West African History*, Longman: London.

Boahen, A.A. (Ed.), 1990. *General History of Africa: Africa under Colonial Domination*, V11, James Currey: London.

Boahen, A.A. 1990. 'Colonialism in Africa: its impact and significance', In Boahen, A.A. (Ed.), 1990. *General History of Africa: Africa under Colonial Domination*, V11, James Currey: London: 327-339.

Bohannan, P. 1964. *Africa and Africans*, Natural History Press: New York.

Brown, P. P. 2005. 'Sierra Leone: Blood Diamonds', http://www.worldpress.org/Africa/2193 .cfm. Accessed 10 December 2016.

Bujra, A. 2002. 'African Conflicts: Their Causes and their political and social environment', *Development Policy Management Forum (DPMF)*, Occasional Paper, No. 4.

Bundy, C. 1979. *The Rise and Fall of the South African Peasantry*, Longman: London.

Cabral, A. 1969. *Revolution in Guinea: Selected Texts*, Monthly Review Press: New York.

Casley, H.J.E. 1911. *Gold Coast Native Institutions: With Thoughts upon a Health Imperial Policy for the Gold Coast and Ashanti*, Sweet and Maxwell Ltd: London.

Central Intelligence Agency, 2010. 'The World Facebook – Country Comparison: GDP Per Capita (PPP)', *CIA The World Facebook*.

Cobbing, J.R.D. 1976. 'The Ndebele under the Khumalos', *PhD Thesis*, University of Lancaster.

Coquery-Vidrovitch, C. 1990. 'The Colonia Economy of the former French, Belgian and Portuguese zones, 1914-1935', In Boahen, A.A. (Ed.), 1990. *General History of Africa: Africa under Colonial Domination*, V11, James Currey: London: 162-172.

Daily News, 2015. 20 December.

Daily News, 2016. 16 November.

Danjuma, M.N. and Mohammed, S. 2015. 'Zai Pits System: A Catalyst for Restoration in the Dry Lands', *Journal of Agriculture and Veterinary Science*, 8(2): 1-4.

Drechsler, H. 1966. *Let Us Die Fighting*, Akademie-Verlag: Berlin.

Ekwo, E. 2012. 'Media, Governance and Africa's Agenda for Development', *The Global African Diaspora Parliamentary Summit*, May 22-23, Pan African Parliament: Johannesburg: 1-14.

Gann, L.H. and Duignan, P. 1969. (Ed), *Colonialism in Africa, 1870-1960*, Vol. 1, Cambridge University Press: Cambridge.

Gann, L.H. and Duignan, P. 1970. (Ed), *The History and Politics of Colonialism*, 1914-1960 Vol. 2, Cambridge University Press: Cambridge.

Goodspeed, P. 2005. 'Corruption's Take: $148B', *National Post*, (Canada), 4 July.

Falola, T. 1996. 'Africa in Perspective', In Ellis, S. (Ed), *Africa Now: Peoples, Policies and Institutions*, James Currey Ltd: London: 3-19.

Falola, T. 2003. *The Power of African Cultures*, University of Rochester Press: Rochester.

Fanon, F. 1963. *The Wretched of the Earth*, Grove Press: New York.

Frank, A.G. 1971. *Capitalism and Underdevelopment in Latin America*, Penguin: Harmondsworth.

Frank, A.G. *et al.* 1972. *Dependence and Underdevelopment in Latin America*: Anchor: New York.

Furtado, C. 1973. 'The Concept of External Dependence in the Study of Underdevelopment', in

Wilber, C.K. (Ed.), *The Political Economy of Development and Underdevelopment*, Random House: New York.

Hall-Mathews, D. 2007. 'Tickling Donors and Tackling Opponents: The Anti-Corruption Campaign in Malawi', In Bracking S. (Ed.)

Corruption and Development. The Anti-Corruption Campaign, Palgrave Macmillan: New York.

Harper, K. and Ravi Rajan, S. 2004. 'International Environmental Justice: Building the Natural Assets of the World's Poor', Political Economy Research Institute, Working Paper Number 87, University of Massachusetts.

Hrituleac, A., 2011. 'The effects of colonialism on African Development: A comparative analysis between Ethiopia, Senegal and Uganda' *MSc in International Economic Consulting Thesis*, Aarhus University, Business and social sciences.

Hull, R.W. 1981. *Southern Africa Civilisations in Turmoil*, New York University: New York.

Iliffe, J. 1994. *A Modern History of Tanganyika*, Cambridge University Press: Cambridge.

Isaacman, A. and Isaacman B. 1983. *Mozambique: From Colonialism to Revolution*, Zimbabwe Publishing House: Harare.

Isaacman, B. and Stephen, J. 1980. *Mozambique, Women, the Law and Agrarian Reform*, Addis Ababa University Press: Addis Ababa.

Jacobs, N. J. 2003. *Environment, Power and Injustice: A South African History*, Cambridge University Press: New York.

James, T.G.H. 1986. *An Introduction to Ancient Egypt*, British Museum Publications Ltd: London.

Kaniki, M.H.Y. 1990. 'The Colonial Economy: the former British zones', In: Boahen, A.A. (Ed.), 1990. *General History of Africa: Africa under Colonial Domination*, V11, James Currey: London: 173-185.

Kanyenze, G. *et al.* (Eds.), 2006. *The Search for Sustainable Human Development in Southern Africa*, ANSA: Harare.

Kassab, A. 1990. 'The Colonial Economy: North Africa' In: Boahen, A.A. (Ed.), 1990. *General History of Africa: Africa under Colonial Domination*, V11, James Currey: London: 186-199.

Khapoya, V. B. 2013. *The African Experience: An Introduction*, 4th Ed, Peachpit Press.

Ki-Zerbo, J. and Niane, D.T. (Eds), 1997. *General History of Africa: Africa from the Twelfth to the Sixteenth Century*, 1V, James Currey Publishers: Oxford.

Lamb, D. 1983. *The Africans*, Random House: New York.

Matyszak, D. 2010. *Law, Politics and Zimbabwe's 'Unity' Government*, Research and Advocate Unit: Harare.

Matyszak, D. 2014. 'Madness and Indigenisation: A History of Insanity in the Age of Lawlessness', Paper prepared for Research and Advocacy Unit, June, Harare.

Mawere, M & Tandi, C. 2017. "Messianic resuscitation or foreign implantation of the seed of underdevelopment?' Interrogating foreign aid in Africa's development politics", In: Mawere, M. (Ed.), *Development Perspectives from the South: Troubling the Metrics of [under-]development in Africa*, Langaa Research & Publishing CIG: Bamenda.

Mazrui, A. 1986. *The Africans*, BBC Publications: London.

Mazvimavi, K. *et al.* 2007. *An Assessment of Sustainable Uptake of Conservation Farming in Zimbabwe*, Global Theme on Agro-ecosystems Report No. 39, International Crop Research Institute for the Semi-Arid Tropics (ICRISAT): Bulawayo.

Memmi, A. 1965. *The Coloniser and the Colonised*, Beacon Press.

Mosley, P. 1983. *The Settler Economies. Studies in the Economic History of Kenya and Southern Rhodesia 1900-1963*, Cambridge University Press: Cambridge.

Moyana, H.V. 2002. *The Political Economy of Land in Zimbabwe*, 2nd Ed, Mambo Press: Gweru.

Muzaale, P. J. 1987. Rural poverty, social development and their implications for fieldwork practice, *Journal of social development in Africa*, 2: 75-85

Narayan, D. *et al.* 2000. *Voices of the Poor: Can Anyone Hear Us?* Oxford University Press: New York.

New Africa, 1988. July.

News Day, 2016. 4 October.

Nkrumah, K. 1957. *Ghana: An Autobiography*, Nelson: London.

Nkrumah, K. 1968. *Handbook for Revolutionary Warfare*, Panaf Publishers: London.

Nyawo, V. Z. *et.al*, 2014. 'Vanguard Parties and Governance in Africa: Dimensions of Battling for States', *Sociology Study*, 4 (4): 334-347.

Ocheni, S. and Nwankwo, B. C. 2012. 'Analysis of colonialism and its impact in Africa', *Cross-Cultural Communication*, 8 (3): 46-54.

Odhiambo, O. 2006. 'Improving tenure security for the rural poor. Kenya, Tanzania and Uganda – Case Study. Formalisation and its prospects', *Legal Empowerment of the Poor (LEP) Working Paper #3*, Workshop for Sub-Saharan Africa, for Food and Agriculture Organisation of the United Nations.

Oliver, R. and Fage J.D. 1962. *A Short History of Africa*, Penguin Books: Baltimore.

Onishi, N. 2002. 'Senegalese Loner Works to Build Africa His Way', *New York Times*, 10 April.

Onuoha, G. 2012. 'Africa and twenty-first century development challenges. The north-south development agenda reconsidered', In *The Wilson Center's Africa program and leadership project*, Southern Voices in the Northern Policy Debate Initiative.

Palmer, R. 1977. *Land and Racial Domination in Rhodesia*, Heinemann: London.

Palmer, R. and Parsons, N. (Eds), 1977. *The Roots of Rural Poverty in Central and Southern Africa*, Heinemann: London.

Plaatje, S.T. 2007. *Native Life in South Africa: Before and since the European War and the Boer Rebellion*, 4th Ed, Picador Africa.

Ramlogan, R. 2004. *The Developing World and the Environment: Making the case for Effective Protection of the Global Environment*, University Press of America: New York.

Ranger, T.O. 1967. *Revolt in Southern Rhodesia*, Heinemann: London.

Riddell, B. 2005. 'Sierra Leone: Urban-Elite Bias, Atrocity and Debt', *Review of African Political Economy*, 32 (103): 115-125.

Rodney, W. 1972. *How Europe Underdeveloped Africa*, Zimbabwe Publishing House: Harare.

Seers, D. 1969. 'The meaning of development', *International Development Review*, 11 (4), 2-6.

Sandbrook, R. 1993. *The Politics of Africa's Stagnation*, Cambridge University Press: New York.

Seidman, A. and Seidman, R. B. 1984. 'The Political Economy of Customary Law in the Former British Territories of Africa', *Journal of African Law*, 28 (1 /2): 44-55.

Settles J. D., 1996. 'The impact of colonialism on African Economic development' *University of Tennessee Honors Thesis Projects*.

http://trace.tennessee.edu/utk_chanhoproj /182, accessed 12 December 2016.

The Economist, 1996. 8 June.

The Standard, 2016. 18 December.

The Times, 1895. UK, 18 November.

Tidy, M. and Leeming, D. 1987. *A History of Africa, 1840-1880*, Vol. 1, Hodder and Stoughton: London.

Tidy, M. and Leeming, D. 1987. *A History of Africa, 1880-1914*, Vol. 2, Hodder and Stoughton: London.

Todaro, M.P. 1992. Economics for Developing World: An Introduction to Principles, Problems and Policies for Development, 3rd Ed, Longman: New York.

Toure, S. 1963. *Guinea Revolution and Social Progress*, Republic of Guinea: Conakry.

Udeze, B. 2009. *Why Africa?: A Continent in Dilemma of Unanswered Questions*, Xlibris Corporation.

UN. 2015. *Illicit Financial Flows and Development Financing in Africa*, UN: New York.

UNDP. 2011. *Human Development Report, DRC.*

Van Onselen, C. 1976. *Chibaro: African Labour in Southern Rhodesia, 1900-1933*, Pluto Press: London.

Voss, J. 1973. (Ed.), *Development Policy in Africa*, Verlag Neue Gesellschaft.

Wanyande, P. 1988. 'Democracy and the One-Party State: The African Experience', In: Oyugi, W.O. *et al.* (Eds.), *Democratic Theory and Practice in Africa*, Heinemann: Portsmouth.

Webster, J.B. *et al.* 1990. *The Growth of African Civilisation: The Revolutionary Years, West Africa since 1800*, Longman: London.

Zhou, T.M. 2012. 'Environmental Impact of Mining in Colonial Zimbabwe: A Case Study of Mberengwa District, 1894-198', *D.Phil. Thesis*, History Department, University of Zimbabwe.

Zhou, T. M. and Makahamadze, T. 2012. *Asset or Liability? The Leadership of Mugabe in Independent Zimbabwe*, Lambert Academic Publishing: Saarbrucken.

Zhou, T.M. 2013. *An Analysis of the History Curricula in Zimbabwe*, Progressive Teachers' Union of Zimbabwe: Harare.

Zhou, T.M. 2016. 'Envisaged Trends in Post-2016 African Development Agenda and their Impact on World Economic System', In: Marongwe and Mawere (eds), *Politics, Violence and Conflict Management in Africa: Envisioning Transformation, Peace and Unity in the Twenty-First Century,* Langaa Research & Publishing CIG: Bamenda: 199-232.

Zhou, T.M. (2017). 'Partition of Africa and impact of borders on African societies in colonial Zimbabwe' In: Duri, F. *et al.* (Eds) *Restrictive mechanisms or corridors of opportunity? A social history of Zimbabwean borderlands since the colonial period,* Book Love Publishers.

Chapter Four

The Resilience and Challenges of Yoruba Religious Worship in Modern Context

Raymond Ogunade

Introduction

Worship is the centre of life in Yoruba Religion. By Yoruba Religion, we mean the indigenous faith of the Yoruba which was passed down from the genesis of their generation through oral traditions, art, crafts, liturgies, pithy sayings, proverbs, folklores, stories, songs and wise sayings to the present "modern age. It has no founder like Jesus in Christianity and Mohammed in Islam; no scriptures and does not possess zeal for membership drive. It has a natural appeal and most of the adherents are born into it. Over the years, some non- Yoruba have taken to Yoruba Religion. For example we have a place in North Carolina, USA, called Oyotunji dedicated to Yoruba language and culture. Most of the White American dwellers, living there have adopted Yoruba names and culture. In this chapter, we have attempted to create an acronym for Yoruba Religion, which is "Yorel". These are the first two letters "Yo" from the word Yoruba and the first three letters "Rel" from Religion. The combination of the two forms Yorel (Ogunade 2005: 54).

The adherents are referred to (in this chapter) as Yorelians. These are the adherents of Yoruba Religion – just like we have Christians from Christianity, Muslims from Islam; Afrel (Dopamu 1993: 188) from African Religion and the adherents of Afrel are referred to as Afrelist (Ogunade 2005: 30). The adherents of Yoruba Religion are also qualified to be called Yorelians. The Yorelians "are everything religious" (Idowu 1962: 41).

Yorel is rich and enduring. It is being embraced and practiced in most parts of the world, like in the rest of Africa, Europe, America, and Cuba. It is dynamic and very much alive. It is flexible, accommodative and creates a lot of succor for the adherents. This is the major reason why it cannot die or be phased out. *Olodumare* (God) is its central theme. Idowu (1962: 44), Awolalu (1981: 10-16) and Dopamu (Awolalu and Dopamu, 2005: 36-64) have all researched so much into the supremacy, names, place and integrity of *Olodumare* among the Yorelians.

This chapter gives attention to worship, as the essence and rhythm of life of the Yoruba people in all spheres of life. By worship, we do not mean the limited area of rituals and liturgies alone, but also the totality of the people's relation to the supernatural order of the deities, Chief of who is Olodumare (the Supreme God). The Yoruba people of homeland in Nigeria and of the Diaspora in foreign countries such as Brazil, Cuba, Republic of Benin, Togo, United Kingdom, France, India, Japan, and United States of America continue to practice their indigenous religious faith despite the challenges of modernity and foreign religions, especially Christianity and Islam. Hence, this chapter demonstrates the resilience and adaptation of Yoruba Religious Worship for relevance in the global context. It also shows that instead of being overwhelmed by Christianity, Islam and Westernisation the religion is getting stronger.

Methodologically, this chapter includes the phenomenological, descriptive and historical approaches, with interviews as tools of research. Overall, the chapter advances the argument that the challenges from Christianity and Islam have helped Yoruba Religion to deploy some of the modern media of propagation to enhance her reputation and population growth.

Elements of Worship in Yorel

Worship, is understood by the Yorelians, as a total response to *Olodumare* (Awolalu, 1981: 99) not just in words but in action as well. These words and deeds normally take the form of ceremonies and rites, which may include silent meditation, praying, prostration, invoking and hailing the spirits of the objects of worship, dancing, clapping, making offerings and sacrifices, sounding the bell or gong, drumming and singing, as determined by the situation. This may be private, by an individual in any convenient place; or it may be collective by the whole family. It can even be corporate by the whole community. The important thing is that it must be done in reverence and in an appropriate conduct and mood, if the desired result must be achieved (Awolalu 1981: 99).

In addition, the Yorelians take worship into their day to day life. Virtually all their daily activities are done with the consciousness of the ever – watching eyes of the invisible presence of the ancestors, spirits, divinities, and of course *Olodumare*. With this in mind, they conduct their deeds and affairs with one another and the environment in mutual respect and selflessness. The typical Yorelian life can be said to be a life of constant worship. Worship to the Yorelians has become a way of life.

Every major event in their lives is attended by elaborate worship. For example, in a typical formal worship libation is poured to open up the earth for the spirit beings to attend to the worship; invocation of esoteric names and praises which attracts the beings of worship, and divination, by which means the message and revelations of the Being of Worship are made known to the people. Worship is given its character also, in sacrifices (of animals and in the past, of human being* - Elebuibon, 2000: 101). There are different types of sacrifices in Yorel. They include propitiation *Ebo Etutu* (prevention), *Ebo Ogunkoja* (Votive), and *Ebo Eje* (substitution).

The liturgy also features prayer, music and dances (Idowu 1962: 113-128). Elements of the liturgy above are still in practice today. For instance *Ifa* is consulted regularly in the people's bid to find solutions to their problems and anxieties – to understand the knotty, unravel the mysterious, reveal the past and predict the future in advance of possible occurrences in line with predestination. From the *Ifa* corpus and based on interpretation of the *opele*, it can be said that *Ifa* recommends sacrifices that people have to make in worshipping respective divinities depending on the situation which worried the consultee (Bascom 1969: 277-411). It is for this vital role that Wande Abimbola describes *Ifa* as the only active mouthpiece of Yoruba Religion taken as a whole. In fact according to him, *Ifa* serves to popularize and to immortalize them (Abimbola 1997: 85-87).

A typical act of worship will include virtually all aspects of the liturgy if we go by Idowu's description of the act of worship of *Olodumare* at Ile – Ife:

The worshipper makes a circle of ashes or white chalk;
within the circle, which is a symbol of eternity, he pours
a libation of cold water, and in the centre he places his
kolanut, splits it and holding the valves firmly
between the hollow of his palm, he stretches them
up and prays to Olodumare, offering the kolanut;
then he casts the valves within the circle. Often,
a white fowl is offered in the same way (Idowu 1962: 142).

The act of worship in the cult of divinities is usually more elaborate. However, it is noteworthy that an important aspect of worship is the responsive use of *ase* (may it be sanctioned). Implying that the ultimate sanction of *Olodumare* is sought as a precondition to the granting of petitions made to the divinities. This singular factor supports the Yoruba argument of their 'monotheistic' theology.

Apart from formal prayers, the Yoruba engage extensively in ejaculatory and extempore prayers which can rightly be termed religious worship. They approach God directly in times of emergency, need, joy and distress. Ejaculatory prayers are made to Him in normal praise, thanksgiving conversation and He is called upon as witness to oaths and covenants as well as to render benevolence and blessing for a new venture be it personal matters such as commercial investment; traveling on a journey, naming a newly born baby, celebrating puberty, solemnising marriage, writing examination and taking a new job.

It is perhaps for this all-encompassing involvement of God in the lives of Yorelians that Idowu described them as being "… in all things religious". More often one hears the Yoruba say, *Olorun o!* (Oh God), *Olorun gba mi* (save me O God), *Modupe lowo Olorun* (I thank God), *Olorun yio see* (God will do it), and *Mo fi oruko Olorun bura* (I swear in God's name). Yoruba system of naming is also reflective of the providential attributes of God, for example *Oluwaseun* (God has done something good), *Oluwadare* (God vindicates), *Oluwatoyin* (God is praiseworthy), *Ifabunmi* (gift of Ifa), and *Ogunlaja* (ogun settles quarrels). Indeed the Yoruba religious worship (in belief and act) is very unique.

100

Conflicts and Compromise in Yoruba Religious Worship

A. Modern Challenges to Yoruba Indigenous Worship

i). Modernism and Pluralism

The Yoruba people prior to the advent of Western civilisation and religion could be said to be homogenous, particularly in their tradition and culture. It was the norm for virtually every member of the community under the king or chief to participate in the traditional religious worship. The traditional religious myths, moral taboos and injunctions held sway over the life of the people.

However, with the coming of the 'white man' with his so–called Western education, healthcare system and colonial social structure, there began a gradual process of demythologising the Yoruba indigenous faith which was soon dismissed by European settlers with obnoxious terminologies such as 'pagan', 'heathen' and 'idol'. The traditional taboo became less relevant in the face of scientific revolutions. As the Yoruba became assimilated in the Western systems, ambitions, cultures and mannerisms, the Yoruba 'new breed' began to drift away from the traditional rural setting to urban areas and cities with attendant vices characteristic of modern city-life. Therefore, the quest for westernisation based on Western civilisation posed the first major challenge to the development of Yoruba religious worship.

There was also the factor of pluralism in modern Yoruba societies. As mentioned earlier, before the efforts of the British Colonialists, the Yoruba people were homogenous – their social structure as diagrammed (below) by Awolalu presents a cultural indigenous independence and harmonious relationship (Awolalu 1987: 9-14) undisturbed by cultural conflicts from other non – Yoruba.

Political Hierarchy (top to bottom) in Pre – Colonial Yoruba Society

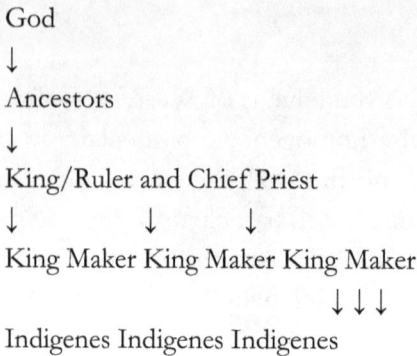

God
↓
Ancestors
↓
King/Ruler and Chief Priest
↓   ↓   ↓
King Maker King Maker King Maker
↓ ↓ ↓
Indigenes Indigenes Indigenes

The above situation has changed in the modern day due chiefly to the incorporation, interaction and assimilation of the Yoruba people with people of different tribes, cultures, and languages. There was the first effect following the slave trade whereby multitudes of Yoruba people were captured and taken to foreign nations where they served and resided with non-Yoruba, such as we find in United States of America, Britain, Brazil and Cuba.

Secondly, the scramble for Africa by European powers led to divisions among the Yoruba people. For instance, the British colonized Nigeria while the French took charge of Republic of Benin. This was responsible for separation between the Nigerian Yoruba and the Yoruba of Dahomey (in present day Republic of Benin).

Thirdly, the forging of the Federal Republic of Nigeria was done through the incorporation of several groupings of distinct cultural and linguistic identities. This included principally the Yoruba, Igbo, and Hausa. Apart from these major three, it is known that there are numerous other peoples and tribes in their distinct cultural and linguistic identities. The implication of this is that it became politically and socially expedient and inevitable for the Yoruba to share the destiny of the federation in conjunction with other peoples. This necessitated interaction and resulted into cross-cultural marriages, inter-tribal political associations and government.

Most vital to this study is the religious factor. The Yoruba though granted their freedom of worship, they still have to contend with the freedom of worship of other religions and cultures whose beliefs and interest were, more often than not, challenging to the age long Yorel.

ii). Christianity and Islam

Both Christianity and Islam are foreign to the Yoruba. Christianity was introduced to Yorubaland in 1842 via the southern coast. It was first preached at Badagry and then it moved on to Abeokuta where it settled properly. Islam penetrated Yorubaland via the North Western part due to contact with the Muslims from the Northern part of what is now known as Nigeria. Islam settled among the Yoruba before Christianity:

> *Aye la ba Ifa*
> *Imole tele*
> *Osan ganagan ni igbagbo wole de*
> We met *Ifa* in the World
> Islam followed it
> Christianity arrived late in the day (Ayandele 1987: 193; Omoyajowo 1989: 56; Dopamu 1992: 9).

When the two new religions arrived, the Yoruba in the usual cordial and accommodating hospitality welcomed them. It was the general belief that the Yoruba King has to be a patron to every religion embraced by his subjects (Ayandele 1987: 28-30). Moreover, a respected parable of harmonious relationship has it that:

> *Oju orun to eye fo*
> *Laifara kanra*
> The sky is wide enough to accommodate
> Flying birds without physical clash.

Therefore, there was sufficient room to accommodate different religions in the Yoruba compound which in itself was pluralistic in character – provided the new religions were ready to play religious game according to comfortable rules which guaranteed peace, harmonious relationship, love and tolerance.

Christianity and Islam (both of whom are essentially opposed to each other), soon proved jointly antagonistic towards Yoruba Religion, which they described as pagan, idolatry, etc.; terminologies which Yoruba scholars from Bolaji Idowu to the present day have vigorously condemned (Idowu 1973: 108-136). On a number of occasions, physical clashes were recorded between Christians and devotees of Yoruba Religion such as was recorded to have occurred at Ikenne sometime ago as recalled by late Asiwaju of Yorubaland, Chief Obafemi Awolowo in his Autobiography (Awolowo 1960: 10ff).

There were similar clashes at Abeokuta in the house breaking (*ifole*) incident (Ade-Ajayi 1965: 201-203); at Kudeti, Ibadan in the threat of destruction to the Christians (Oduyoye 1972: 272); at Ogbomoso in the persecution of Christians (Aiyegboyin 1983: 42); and at Ijebu-Remo in the humiliation of Christians (Olusola 1975: 76).

However, perhaps due to the high propagational zeal of both Christianity and Islam and the considerable lack of it in Yorel and definitely due to government patronage, social attractions and quest for modernity or change, large populations of Yoruba people converted to either of the two 'stranger' religions. This trend has become very widespread so much that viewed *prima facie* one may be tempted to expect the ultimate extinction of Yorel. However, this situation is not likely to occur, as would be examined later in this chapter.

Judging by 2006 Nigerian census, more than four-fifths, that is, 80% of the population of the Yoruba provinces was either Christian or Muslim (Ekpu 2006: 3). The above statistics may seem shocking or indeed taken as being too sweeping or exaggerated. It, for instance, depends on the reliability and accuracy of the said census which definitely cannot be said to represent the exact figure today for apparent reasons – there has been a consistent population growth in Nigeria from 2006 to the present. Also, one unfortunate observation about censuses in Nigeria is that they lack the required general acceptability. This notwithstanding, the figure of the census may be taken as approximately correct. At least it shows an undisputed reality of a massive influx from Yorel to Christianity and Islam. The religious phenomenon in Yoruba-land has not shown any drastic reversal of this trend.

One other consideration about the population of Yoruba people belonging to other religions is that no specific figure can be given decisively. This is because of the syncretic characteristic of many people who though claiming to belong to Christianity or Islam, still actively (albeit secretly) patronize cults, priests and functionaries of Yorel. Such people, when afflicted with 'spiritual' problems or during traditional festivals, partake in Yoruba religious worship. More so, the lack of propagational zeal of Yorel coupled with the lack of cohesion of its adherents who are devoted to different divinities, make it difficult to classify them under a collective population.

Also, it takes courageous pride for some Yorelians today to claim outright devotion to Yorel because of the derogatory attitude of some sectors of the society. Hence, active adherents may be inclined to use Christianity and Islam simply as cover. Thus, the population classification of the different religions may be perpetually unreliable.

It is helpful to take a quick glance at similarities between Yorel, on one hand and Christianity and Islam on the other hand. Early Christians adopted Yoruba religious names of God such as 'Olorun' and 'Olodumare'. Prayer, song, music, baptism, intercession and life after death, are concepts similar to Christianity and Islam. Yet, Christianity repels in Yorel the following: idolatry, polygamy, divination, wearing of amulets, incantations, practice of witchcraft and superstitions (Oladoja 1980: 81). In the case of Islam, it share similarities with Yorel in the areas of polygamy, divination, wearing of amulets, magic, pilgrimages to sacred sites and offering of sacrifices (Oladoja 1980: 82). Despite the above, Islam finds repugnant the many divinities of Yorel who serve as intermediaries between Yorelians and God. To Muslims, the Quran (Sura 112) regards as *shirk* (aberration), association of partnership with Allah. Only *kafirs* (unbelievers) commit such grave 'sin' of polytheism. Yorelians on the other hand, would not take kindly to the offensive label of being called *kafirs*. From the above, the religious scenes in Yoruba-land present us with conflicts of religious beliefs and interests but also compromises, as well, as will be observed in Yorel responses to the challenges posed by the factors treated above.

B. Yoruba Response to Contemporary Challenges

i). Protests and Adaptations

The responses of Yoruba people to contemporary challenges are twofold. Negative-by way of protests from committed adherents, and positive - by way of adaptation between Yorel and the foreign religions. This is different from syncretism in that while syncretism means outright indulgence of a person or a group of persons in more than one religion at the same time, adaptation refers to a situation whereby an adherent of a given religion modifies or changes its beliefs and practices to meet with challenges of another religious system, or faith.

When it became convincingly apparent that Yoruba traditions and religion were being threatened by Christianity, Islam and modern social systems there began to rise an instinctive protest by committed Yorelians. This was due more to provocation from the two new religions rather than to the loss of adherents of Yorel to the new religions. It soon became clear that if the conservative Yoruba in their usual tolerant disposition remained in defensive of their faith, it would soon be reduced to irrelevance and disrespect. Thus, arose a protest and cultural resurgence of the people's beliefs and lifestyles. Soon, traditional rituals and religious worship were being conducted openly with pride. Adherents began to clamour for equal rights from government (Dopamu 1993: 20).

The impacts of the protests by Yorelians can be felt in the Nigerian society today. For instance, Oaths can now be taken in law courts by adherents of Yorel, using (for example) a piece of iron symbolising the Yoruba god of iron – Ogun. The former practice was the recognition of only the Bible for Christians and the Quran for Muslims as oath – administering tools (Dopamu 1993: 21).

The recurrent theological argument especially in academic and enlightened circles that all religions lead to the worship of one and the same God, but in different ways is another logical basis for adherents of Yorel to insist on being given full recognition rather than being pestered with appeal to convert to either of the foreign religions. In this sense, there exists an instinctive desire for the

106

Yoruba to prize highest, their indigenous ways of life over and above that of any foreign system.

It is noted that in the modern day, the affairs of Yoruba societies are conducted in recognition of the indispensable roles of traditional priests and rulers. These see to aspects of rituals in times of need or emergency, such as drought, flood (the *Ogunpa* episode in Ibadan some time ago was a case in point), epidemic and land or border disputes. It is also known that members of the society are compelled to abide by rules (mostly of confinement) governing the performance of some Yoruba religious rituals such as the *Oro* masquerade which must not be physically witnessed by females in the communities. Also, the Chieftaincy (honorary and functional) institution for which the Yoruba have great respect (except that there are now trends of commercialising the process of its award), subjects deserving Yoruba citizens of either Christian or Muslim persuasions to undergo rituals which fall within the context of Yoruba religious worship.

Another way of impressing Yoruba religious values on the society can be seen in the continued naming of some of the days in a week. The days: *Ojo Aje* (Monday), *Ojo Ru* (Wednesday), *Ojo Bo* (Thursday), *Ojo Eti* (Friday), *Ojo Abameta* (Saturday), *Ojo Aiku* (Sunday) and *Ojo Isegun* (Tuesday) are derived from the Yoruba story of *Ela*. This story is similar to the Christian story of Jesus Christ, as we shall see shortly, the story reveals an episode of adaptation but it cannot be proved conclusively whether the myth is indebted to Christianity because it appears to have for long existed among the Yoruba especially as it occupies a prominent place in the *Ifa* Corpus.

The story is that of *Ela* the son of *Olodumare* who was sent to the human world to transform the decadent society. He was challenged by the opposing patron of evil (*Esu*) who, after protracted struggle (*Eti*) succeeded in killing *Ela*. However as decreed, *Ela* was to resurrect on the third day and ascend to heaven. *Esu* and his clique bound themselves with a tripartite oath (*Abameta*) of seeing to the death of *Ela*, preventing his resurrection and if it eventually occurs, debar him from ascending to heaven. However, their plans were brought to naught as *Ela* resurrected and was divinely aided to ascend into Heaven. The eulogy in honour of *Ela* is that the human world would not know perfect peace until *Ela* comes back to the world the second time to once and for all defeat *Esu* and establish the Kingdom of *Olodumare* on earth. This can be seen, as similar to the incarnation, mission, crucifixion, resurrection, ascension and expected *parousia* (second coming) of Jesus Christ in Christianity. By the *Ela* myth, Yorel challenges the faithful to adopt in its religious doctrine and practices similar concepts which could have attracted them to other (foreign) religions. In fact, some African theologians are currently engrossed in such spirit of contextualizing foreign concepts or religions in African background which will make such messages better appreciated by the Africans. Contextualization and its appendage – indigenization in the Yoruba context has been taken to a level of practical implementation.

The first half of the 20th century was particularly beneficial to Yoruba – land as far as indigenous religious movements were concerned. It was the period when indigenous (Yoruba) Christian churches broke away (independence) from the so-called 'imperialist' mission churches. For example, the African Church (incorporated), when it began, reformed the elements of colonialism in the Church practices and doctrines replacing them with Yoruba substitutes; for example, praying for the *Oba* (kings) and Chiefs in their prayer-book instead of praying for the Queen of England (Awolalu 1987: 14).

Also, the Church permitted the practice of polygamy and the taking of chieftaincy titles by its members. It would be recalled that the early Christian missionaries engaged in excommunicating polygamists from the Church and rather demanded that they divorce all but their first wife, as precondition for baptism. This phenomenon not only led to loss of membership from the Christian faith on the one hand, and for those who complied with the demand, it caused emotional frustration, family disunity, unhappiness and prostitution (of divorced wives) on the other hand (Ayandele 1987: 18).

This was also the era of 'Ethiopianism' which witnessed the amalgam of Church and State in struggling for cultural independence of Africa. It was in this spirit that prominent Yoruba citizens such as Jeremiah Obafemi Awolowo dropped their Christian names (in preference of the traditional) from public usage (Ayandele 1987: 71). Therefore, we begin to witness the movement of Yoruba religious worship to modifications of instructionalised religious system and organisations.

From the 1930s, some Yoruba Christians shifted base from Christianity and moved in close contact with Yorel. For example, in 1934, Mr. A.O. Oshiga founded the *Ijo Orunmila Adulawo* (African Congregation of Orunmila devotees). The hymn book and prayer-book of this Yoruba religious organisation were composed of elements from the *Ifa* Corpus. From this, lessons were read, songs rendered and sermons preached during congregational worship (Johnson 1975: 3-6).

It is, however, unfortunate that this organisation which still operates in Lagos lacks steady growth in membership, remarkable zeal of propagation and a distinct and original system of liturgy, yet their philosophy and efforts remain commendable. A similar type of organisation – 'The Reformed Ogboni Fraternity' which had on its roll notable Christians cannot be discussed in depth here because of the esoteric characteristics of Ogboni cults in Yorubaland.

The birth and rise of Pentecostal Indigenous Churches called *Aladura* (Praying ones) presents an interesting episode of protest and adaptation. The Churches were started or led by charismatic leaders of Yoruba descent (such as Moses Orimolade, Emmanuel Akinsowon and Joseph Babalola) who were aflame with desire to put into practice the saving and healing powers of God over people particularly in the superstition, poverty and disease – ridden societies as found in Yorubaland. Some of these Churches which started since the 1920s included 'Christ Apostolic Church' 'Church of the Lord' and 'Celestial Church of Christ'. These churches are largely Yoruba in character and population, although non-Yoruba are also many. What interests us here is that some practices of the *Aladura* are indeed indebted to Yorel. Such examples include the songs, music, dancing, proverbs, rituals (such as offerings, sacrifices, burning of candles and incense, and invocation). Though the *Aladura* have been attacked due to this indulgence, it still provided an outlet for the person interested in enjoying some elements of Yorel within the confines of Christianity, provided there is no compromise on the uniqueness of Jesus Christ (Oladoja 1980: 22).

We can thus see that in modern times, the Yoruba are making frantic efforts to salvage and protect their cultural values and particularly their religious worship from threats of other religions as well as from modern challenges. This effort sometimes in form of protest still continues today. For example, the Nigerian Inter Religious Council (NIREC) which was set up by government of General Olusegun Obasanjo (Rtd) did not include any representatives of Nigeria's traditional religions. Rather, it was composed of Christians and Muslims.

ii). Syncretism

Two major types of syncretic attitude can be observed among the Yoruba. Firstly, due to the pluralistic orientation of the people, it has become common to find some of them strongly committed to the belief and practice of more than one religious faith at the same time. Some do not regard it as sacrilegious to be a Christian or Muslim and at the same time partake in rituals of Yoruba or in times of personal emergency. *Ona kan ko woja* (A market does not have only one entrance) is a ready slogan on the lips of the syncretistic Yoruba Obas, who for example are either Christians or Muslims, yet they are Chief Priests (by tradition) of Yorel. This type of syncretism is simply systematic and attitudinal.

The second type is more interesting. It is found among the Yoruba of the Diaspora. It is an outright identification of Yoruba deities with some selected Roman Catholic Christian Saints. It would be recalled that as a result of slave trade, numerous Yoruba were taken to foreigner's homes as servants. Large concentration of the people can be found most particularly in Brazil (especially in cities such as Bahia, Rio de Janeiro and Pernambuco) and Cuba (especially Havana) and it is the phenomenon in these places that we wish to examine here.

The Yoruba people in these cities enjoyed considerable freedom of worship even though they were converted and baptised into Roman Catholicism which was dominant in the two countries under study. The Yoruba slaves did not forget their root and in order to perpetuate the worship of their indigenous ancestral deities, they found the easy way out, by identifying some of these deities with

110

Roman Catholic Saints. They in actual practice engaged in the pure worship of Yoruba deities. This syncretic attitude provided the slaves cover as they readily informed their masters (when challenged), that they were worshipping the Roman Catholic Saints in Yoruba ways. We may take a cursory glance at some of the identifications below.

Brazil

Yoruba Deity	Roman Catholic Saint
Yemoja	- Virgin of the Immaculate Conception
Ogun	- St. Anthony
Obaluwa ye (Sanponna)	- St. Lazarus
Sango	- St. Jerome
Osun	- Our Lady of Candlemas
Obatala	- Christ of Bumfin
Osumare	- St. Batholomew
Oshosi	- St. George

Cuba

Yoruba Deity	Roman Catholic Saint
Shango	- St. Barbara (a Lady)
Orisa Nla (Virgin of Mercy)	- Virgin de la meroco
Osun Cobre	- Virgin de caridad de (Virgin of Charity)
Yemoja	- Virgin de Regla (Virgin of Order)
Obaluwaye	- St. Lazarus
Ogun	- St. John the Baptist
Osonyin	- St. Raphael
Ifa	- St. Francis of Assisi

(Sosa 2008: 394-395).

Some of these identifications had basis for comparison, for example, Yemoja (mother of the Orisas) can be related to virgin of the Immaculate Conception in the area of divine conception and reproductions. Also, Osun (Sea goddess of Charity) finds perfect type in *Virgen de la Caridad de Cobre* (Virgin of Charity).

The danger with the foregoing is that though the syncretism was called for by the desire of the Yoruba of the *Diaspora* to save themselves from cultural extinction, it appears that the practice has become so imbedded in the people's beliefs and actions. It is hoped that the syncretic attitude of the Yoruba of the *Diaspora* will be placed in their original context and a reversal of the practice will be advocated and accomplished by the present generation of the Yoruba people as necessary step to facilitating genuine Yoruba religious worship.

iii). Cultural Resurgence

a). Scholarship
Yoruba indigenous scholars have contributed immensely to the promotion of Yorel and African culture after a long time of literacy abandonment. These contributions can be seen in two ways – defensive and expositional. Idowu (1962: 45), Awolalu and Dopamu (2005: 27) in their various publications not only challenged and dismissed the bias and misconceptions of foreigners about Yorel. They also vigorously researched into the values and ingredients of the indigenous faith-making it presentable to the outside world and even to educate the young Yoruba who incidentally are born and raised in the atmosphere of scientific advancement and westernisation rather than get to grips with the traditional base of their places of origin.

The contributions of Yoruba scholars have yielded so much fruits, that degrees can now be obtained in African Religion with specialty in Yoruba Religion, and Yoruba Language and Culture (up to doctorate level). Conferences are regularly organised to discuss themes which border on promotion of Yorel and African culture.

b). Creative and Performing Arts
Yorel has received a great boost from the creative and performing artistes. On the one hand are the Mass Media that

promote aspects of the religion on Radio, Television and Newspaper. An example is the Nigerian Television Authority (NTA) Ibadan programme – *Ifa Olokun Asorodayo*. On the other hand, there is the performing artiste of different categories. The Yoruba participants in Nigeria's occasional Festival of Arts and Culture often reveal and refresh in one's mind the rich religious values of the people such as, for example, the practice of libation, invocation, divination and masquerading during their performances. We also have the principal artists such as late Hubert Ogunde (in his films – *'Aiye'* and *'Jaiyesimi'*), Jimoh Aliu (in his drama presentation of Fagunwa's 'Igbo Olodumare') and late Duro Ladipo (in his drama – *'Oba Koso'*) and many others. Without doubt, the performances of some of these artistes often involve the use of magic and invocations of the supernatural within the context of Yoruba religious worship. In addition to these, Yoruba drama and movies are watched in homes both locally and internationally, to the point that performances outside Nigeria at shooting locations features non-Yoruba actors and actresses taking their lines in Yoruba language, performing traditional dances on stage, adorned in traditional costumes, and thereby promoting the Yoruba cultural heritage.

c). Yoruba Religious Worship Today

In spite of modern challenges to Yorel, the faith is not dead. In fact, it is current, present and active in the minds of individuals and "in collective relationship … whether they are believers or non – believers, whether they practice their religion or not…" (Awolalu & Dopamu 2005: 331). Religion is inherent in the personality of the Yoruba. Even those who belong to either Christianity or Islam, distinguish themselves in their levels of commitment. This sometimes border on fanaticism and extremism, which unfortunately polarise the Yoruba on ground of religious differences.

However, Yorel is still waxing strong among the people (openly or secretly). The spiritually afflicted persons, the barren females, the ambitious civil servant or military officer who wants protection, the student who is anxious to pass an examination, the fearful traveller who wants assurance of safe journey or deliverance in case of accident (for example *egbe***) and the bothered husband who wishes to guarantee the fidelity of his wife (for example *magun****) all these find cause to patronize priests of Yorel and undergo rituals preceding their treatment or procurements, such as medicinal incisions, portions of charms and pieces of amulets, etc. There are reports that even some Christian and Muslim priests also seek spiritual support from priests of Yorel (Chief Fatuyirele 20-10-2014). Some are said to even belong to secret societies such as the *Ogboni*. It should be noted that majority of Yoruba people still live in the rural areas where their traditions and culture still operate and prevail. These people have not been fully affected by the influence of modernism as is the case in the cities and towns. This is not to say however that many of them are not active Christians or Muslims. The point being made is that their environment still affords them the indispensable impetus to perpetuate their traditional religion whether fully or partly.

The gods and goddesses in Yoruba pantheon still receive active worship today. The major ones among them have devotees in virtually all parts of Yorubaland. However, some of them are limited to certain areas which facilitate their worship. For example, Olokun can only be worshipped in a riverine area because she is a sea goddess. Some of the deities have particular places of popularity; Osun (Osogbo), Ogun (Ondo), Ayelala (Okitipupa), Sango (Oyo), Moremi (Offa), Olumo (Abeokuta), Orosun (Idanre) and Obatala (Ile Ife). The worship and consultation of Ifa through the Babalawo is practiced everywhere in Yorubaland. The same goes for the Oro festival. This is the revered masquerade which comes into town at night to deliver messages from deities to the people. Sometimes they reveal or expose names of diabolical persons who wreak or intend to wreak havoc on the community. They may also recommend rituals and sacrifices which the people must make to the gods to ensure peace, health and progress of the community. Females are not allowed to see the *Oro*. If they do – as often happens accidentally, calamity befalls the victim. This is one aspect of the tradition which the Yoruba may need to change in line with realities of the modern day, where persons of various origins live in another town, unfamiliar with all the norms and timing of the practice of festivals; and a situation where night shifts exist for female workers such as Nurses.

In further identifying devotion to the deities, one notes that Yoruba professionals still actively invoke and worship their patron deities, for example, those who work with iron and steel, such as hunters (Olayemi 1975: 957-970), drivers of motor vehicles and, smithsmen, all actively patronise Ogun, while health workers consult Osanyin from time to time. Virtually, every Yoruba relate to Olodumare in all spheres of life in one way or another. In all the above, all elements of liturgy are actively practiced (Olupona & Rey 2008: 233-238). It is not unusual to still find sacrifices (Ebo) placed along footpaths or road intersections today.

Also, libation is brought into play when the Yoruba is dedicating his newly purchased motor vehicle or opening a newly built house or celebrating freedom from learning a trade or in solemnising matrimony. It is believed that the liquid poured into the ground softens the way to invite the easy attendance at the ceremony of the invoked spirit or deity. Invocation is often in the form of *Ofo* (incantation). The song, music and proverbs identified with Yoruba religious worship have been modified into modern music and poetry such as Juju, Apala, Sakara, Ewi and Fuji by Yoruba musicians such as Ebenezer Obey, Sunny Ade, Dele Abiodun, late Haruna Ishola, late Ayinla Omowura, late Yusuf Olatunji, late Kayode Fashola, Olanrewaju Adepoju, Oladapo Olatunbosun, late Sikiru Ayinde Barrister, Ayinla Kollington, late Herbert Ogunde and Israel Kehinde Dairo, and others. Yet the modifications and adaptations by these musicians do not erode the religious basis or flavour of such songs, music and sayings. It must be emphasized however that although the Yoruba deities still receive popular worship, they must not be seen as being perfect like the Christian and Islamic conception of their deities, as Awolalu and Dopamu put it, the Yoruba divinities have moral and functional weaknesses (Awolalu & Dopamu 2005: 126).

Yoruba religious and moral values still hold sway over the people. Despite the growth of corruption and moral decadence in Nigeria, the traditional Yoruba still recognizes and obeys the moral values of honesty, dedication, hard work, truthfulness, marriage fidelity, and respect to elders, faithfulness to Oaths, interpersonal love, peace, and progress. The Yoruba religious taboos regarding health, sanity, spiritual discipline and maintenance of the social order are also being obeyed. The passages of life among the Yoruba is characterized by the religious activities – birth, naming of the child, celebration of puberty, marriage solemnization and death and burial, all involve religious worship ceremonies.

Notable Yoruba religious sites are fast becoming tourists' attractions. In recent times, some Yoruba populations of the *Diaspora* have made pilgrimages to these in their continued zeal to identify with their roots. This trend has not just begun. In fact after the emancipation of Yoruba slaves in America, many of them returned to their fatherland, disembarking in either the Dahomeyan ports or the Lagos port being gateways to Yorubaland. Some of these returnee slaves continued the practice of Yorel. For example, the Brazilian influence on Lagos can be seen not only in the architectural structures of houses and in the habits and names of some families, but also in such religious activities as the Easter masquerade (*carreta*) being a synthesis of Yoruba traditional religious practice into Christian celebration. This is not surprising since majority of the returnee Yoruba slaves were Catholic Christians and Yorelians at the same time.

However, the recent pilgrimages to Yoruba religious sites became more popular during and after the Festival of Arts and Culture (FESTAC) of 1977. Thenceforth, individuals and groups of Yoruba of the *Diaspora* had to visit Ile – Ife (ancestral home of the Yoruba), Osogbo (site of Osun Shrine – which has been much studied especially its benevolence to worshippers (mostly barren women) during her annual festival), Esie (where stones images suggested to be of Dahomean origin (Ogunade 2004: 182), are mythologised as being transformations of a set of Yoruba ancestors), and Oyo (the ancient political headquarters of Yorubaland, the seat of the Alaafins, the fourth of which was the deified 'Sango').

There is a particular case that is worth mentioning here. It is that of a Yoruba community in United States of America. In the early 1960s, a group of Yoruba people established a Yoruba settlement called *Oyotunji* (Oyo resuscitated) in Beaufort Country in Carolina. This community renounced Western civilization and set up a model Yoruba village with an Oba, Priests, Chiefs and other traditional functionaries. They were bound to speak Yoruba language most of

116

the times of the day. They also actively practiced the libations, rituals and sacrifices of Yoruba religious worship. A school, the 'Yoruba Academy' sees to the task of inculcating in their young ones the values of Yoruba tradition, culture and religion (Clarke 2004: 157-161). One of their leaders, Chief Osaijefe Odefunmi visited Nigeria in 1972 on pilgrimage and in further search of knowledge of Yorel.

We can see therefore that there is a current drive for the resuscitation and perpetuation of Yoruba Religious Worship both by the Yoruba of the homeland and the Yoruba of the Diaspora. In the case of the homeland, the continued institution of Obaship (for example Oni of Ile – Ife, Alaafin of Oyo, Alake of Egba, Owa of Ijesha, Awujale of Ijebu and Olujumu of Ijumu), the conferment and operation of chieftaincy titles as well as the active role of Priests in the social life of the Yoruba portray the fact that the foundation of Yoruba religious worship remains solid and can only be built upon as time goes on.

Conclusion

Yorel is rich! Worship forms the centre of the life of the Yoruba people in all ramifications. By worship, we do not refer to the limited area of rituals alone, but also the totality of the people's relation to the supernatural order of the deities, chief of whom is Olodumare (the Supreme God). The Yoruba people of the homeland in Nigeria and of the *Diaspora* in foreign countries such as Brazil, Cuba, Republic of Benin, Togo and United States of America continue to practice their traditional religious faith despite the challenges of modernity and foreign religions, especially Christianity and Islam. It must be accepted that these religions have strongly affected the reputation and population growth of the Yoruba Religion.

The current efforts by Yoruba scholars, artistes and the people in general to perpetuate Yorel can be said to be yielding positive fruits although the religion is currently not being accorded the respect it deserves by the successive Nigeria governments. Up to the present day, National Public holidays are not declared in honour of traditional festival. So also are their prayers not called for at public functions and ceremonies. They are not even represented at commissions on inter – religious peace and dialogue such as the recently set – up Nigerian Inter–Religious Council. Perhaps the lack of propagational zeal as well as syncretic attitude of the Yoruba people does not compel them to make a vigorous demand for rights given to the foreign religions. Whether the governments will assent if they do, is subject to debate. By and large, Yoruba Religious Worship being an inherent part of the Yoruba people continues today in belief, reverence and practice, even if it has been subjected to series of challenges and modifications. That the religion still exists actively is commendable and provides impetus for the further promotion of this aspect of life of the Yoruba. The supreme challenge of Yoruba religious worship to the contemporary societies is in its tolerance of religious pluralism. This is a lesson for Nigeria in particular and the rest of the world in general in the quest for inter–religious peace and harmony which in recent times have been put to test.

References and notes

Abimbola, W. 1977. *Ifa Will Mend Our Broken World*, Aim Books: Massachusetts.

Ade – Ajayi, J. F. 1965. *Christian Missions in Nigeria 1841 – 1891*, Longman: London.

Aiyegboyin, D. 1983. Baptist Missions Enterprises in Ogbomosho – 1855 – 1975, *M.A. Dissertation*, Department of Religious Studies: University of Ibadan.

Atanda, J. A. 1972. *Clark's Travels and Explorations in Yorubaland*, University Press: Ibadan.

Awolalu, J. O & Adelumo Dopamu, P. 2005. *West African Traditional Religion*, Revised Edition, Macmillan Nig. Publishers: Ibadan.

Awolalu, J. O. 1987. "Christianity in a new Political Order" in S.A. Adewale (ed.), *Christianity and Socio – Political Order in Nigeria*, N.A.C.S: Ibadan.

Awolalu, J. O. 1981. *Yoruba Beliefs and Sacrificial Rites*, Longman: London.

Awolowo, O. 1960. *The Autobiography of Chief Obafemi Awolowo*, University Press: Cambridge.

Ayandele, E. A. 1987. "Traditional Rulers and Missionaries in Pre – Colonial West African" in *Tarikh*, Vol. 3/1.

Bascom, W. 1969. *Sixteen Cowries – Yoruba Divination from Africa to the New World*, Indiana University Press: London.

Clarke, K. M. 2004. *Mapping Yoruba Networks, London*: Dukc University Press.

Dopamu, P. A. 1993. "A Religion in a Secular State: Problems and Possibilities within the Nigerian Context" in *Indo – British Review: A Journal of History*, Vol. xx No 1.

Ekpu, R. 2006. "Reflections on the Nigerian Census", in *Newswatch Magazine*, Newswatch Publications: Nigeria.

Elebuibon, Y. 2000. *The Healing Power of Sacrifice*, Athelia Henrietta Press: New York.

Fatuyirele, A.O. Oral interview, 46 Owatunmise Street, Ilepa, Ikare Akoko, 82 years old, 20-10-2014.

Idowu, E. B. 1962. *Olodumare: God in Yoruba Belief*, Longman: London.

Johnson, J. 1975. Missionary Travels in Ijebuland in J.O. Olusola, *Two Missionary Visits in Ijebuland*, Daystar Publishers: Ibadan.

Johnson, S. 1975. *The History of the Yoruba*, CSS: Lagos.

Lloyd, P. C. 1965. "The Yoruba of Nigeria," In: J. L. Gibbs, *Peoples of Africa*, Holt Rinehart & Winston: Germany.

Oduyoye, M. 1972. *The Planting of Christianity in Yorubaland*, Daystar Publishers: Ibadan.

Ogunade, R. 2005. "A Comparative Study of the Concept of the Will of God in Yoruba Religion and Christianity", *An unpublished PhD thesis*, University of Ilorin: Department of Religions.

Ogunade, R. 2004. "Environmental Issues in Yoruba Religion: Implications for Leadership and Society in Nigeria," In: *ALORE: Ilorin Journal of the Humanities* Vol. 14. University of Ilorin: Faculty of Arts.

Oladoja, J. O. 1980. "African Response to Christianity: The Yoruba Episode," In: S.B. Mala and Z.I. Oseni, (Eds). *NASR Conference Papers,* Ibadan: NASR.

Olayemi, V. 1975. "The Supernatural in Yoruba Folktale", In: Wande Abimbola, (Ed), *Yoruba Oral Tradition,* University Press: Ibadan.

119

Olupona, J. K and Terry Rey. 2008. *Orisa Devotion As World Religion*, Wisconsin University Press.

Sosa, J. J. 2008. "La Santeria: An Integrating, Mythological Worldview in a Disintegrating Society," In: Jacob, K. Olupona and Terry Rey, (Eds.) *Orisa Devotion As World Religion*, Wisconsin: University Press.

*The common explanation for the rationale for practice of Human sacrifice is the desire of the people to give to God as offering, what they consider the most precious which is human life. This still does not justify the practice and it remains condemnable.

** *Egbe*, literally means "carry me" or that which "lifts me". A strong and very reliable Yoruba, magic which insures and protects a frequent traveller by instantly and supernaturally removing or taking him/her away from the accident in the process of occurrence. It is usually used by Yoruba commercial drivers of inter – state motor vehicles.

****Magun*, meaning "do not climb". This is a Yoruba magical preparation that is employed by some Yoruba husbands who do not trust the fidelity of their wives. This magic is secretly placed on such women and any Man apart from their husband that attempt to have sex with them will die in the process.

Chapter Five

On the Philosophy and Historicity of the Development Agenda: Problematising African Nationalism in the Context of Zimbabwe's Land Question since the Colonial Period

Fidelis P.T. Duri

Introduction

This chapter problematises African nationalism as a philosophy in the context of development discourses in general and the land question in particular in Zimbabwean history since the colonial period. It interrogates a repertoire of ambiguities such as continuities and discontinuities, consistencies and inconsistencies as well as synergies and dissonances in the application of the philosophy of African nationalism to the land question during the anti-colonial struggle up to the attainment of independence in 1980, and in the post-independence development agenda.

In Zimbabwe, as was the case in other parts of Africa, African nationalism was the guiding philosophy of the anti-colonial struggle and the development discourse after independence. In colonial Zimbabwe, African nationalism was a philosophy of unity, independence, freedom, social equality, equal opportunities in development, and economic prosperity. Even though African nationalism in Zimbabwe's struggle for independence had its own cleavages characteristic of other movements, it was relatively more cohesive and inclusive than the post-independence one. Its foundations lay in the desire of oppressed Africans, both indigenous and non-indigenous; and other liberal sections of the white community, to end various forms of colonial abuses and exploitation to which the nationalist leaders elevated land deprivation above other grievances in an attempt to mobilise the majority of the population.

The attainment of independence in 1980 heralded the triumph of African nationalism as a philosophy and there was unprecedented optimism across all sections of the Zimbabwean population of a just social order characterised by, among other things, social equality; equal access to resources, particularly land; prosperity; and a sustainable economic dispensation for the majority of the citizens. Lamentably, this was not to be. The nationalist philosophy of the pre-independence period was shattered particularly from the year 2000 when the Zimbabwe African National Union Patriotic Front (ZANU-PF) government led by President Robert Mugabe embarked on a violent land reform programme. On 26 February 2000, the government-sponsored invasions of commercial farms, mostly white-owned, and redistributing them to 'blacks,' began in Zimbabwe under the nationalist rhetoric of retrieving 'stolen lands.' This was part of the ruling ZANU-PF party's desperate attempts to restore its waning legitimacy ahead of local government, parliamentary and presidential elections that were due later during the year (Duri, 2010; Hill, 2003; Masunungure, 2004).

ZANU-PF's popularity had considerably slumped during the 1990s when various sections of the population, particularly the workers, were discontented by the government's implementation of the Economic Structural Adjustment Programme (ESAP) recommended by the World Bank and International Monetary Fund (Duri, 2010; Hill, 2003; Masunungure, 2004). The programme slashed state expenditure on social services, scrapped off state subsidies on basic goods, deregulated consumer prices resulting in high cost of living, and escalated unemployment levels through job cuts (Bond and Manyanya, 2001; Hill, 2003). In this dispensation of extreme disillusionment, the opposition Movement for Democratic Change (MDC) was formed on 11 September 1999 largely through the efforts of workers' unions and civil organisations with financial backing from local commercial white farmers and international donors (Masunungure, 2004; Meredith, 2002). In an attempt to cling to power, ZANU-PF authorised and sponsored the violent seizure of commercial farms, most of which were white-owned, and redistributed them to 'blacks' (Duri, 2012; Meredith, 2002). In an effort to speed up the process, the Fast-Track Land Reform

Programme, also known as the Accelerated Land Reform and Resettlement Implementation Plan (Moyo, 2001), was officially launched in July 2000 when about 3000 white commercial farms were targeted for compulsory acquisition. The seized land was apportioned in two models: A1, for small-scale farmers, and A2, for the new commercial farmers (Amnesty International, February 2004). On the average, AI plots were six hectares of arable land and between 50 and 60 hectares of communal grazing land in extent. A2 farms were medium-sized commercial farming units ranging from 300 hectares with no communal pastures (Goulding and Mutopo, 21 August 2012).

According to the ZANU-PF government, the repossession of land on a grand scale epitomised the triumph of nationalism. To the contrary, this chapter argues that the land seizures and the subsequent reallocation process were often executed selectively and exclusively in a way that othered significant sections of the population thereby undermining the nationalist philosophy and the development agenda in a number of ways. Discourses on citizenship were deliberately tapered and deflated during contestations for land; nationalism was re-delimited and the nation was severely bifurcated along racial, ethnic, political, class and gender dimensions, and generated a surfeit of intense struggles after the struggle.

Thus, with particular reference to the land question in Zimbabwe since the colonial period, this chapter unpacks African nationalism as a philosophy loaded with contestations and ambiguities, and one that is vulnerable to manipulations and reconfigurations by the elite in order to suit the dictates of the moment in history. This does not, in any way, imply that African nationalism lacks well-laid principles, but that the elite often apply the philosophy inconsistently in order to promote and safeguard their class and other interests. Indeed, such manipulations and reconfigurations constitute some of the major stumbling blocks to the development trajectory in independent Zimbabwe.

Conceptualising nationalism as a philosophy

The term nationalism was first used in the year 1409 at Leipzig University in Germany to refer to unity of purpose in various political, economic and socio-cultural aspects of life (Kecmanovic, 1996). It is undisputable that nationalism is a belief, creed or ideology that involves an individual or group identifying with a nation in pursuit of socio-economic and political goals (Rothi, 2005). Politically, it involves self-determination, self-rule, and loyalty to a nation (Graham and Newham, 1998; Hauss, 2003; Metcalf, 2003). In social terms, it involves identifying with each other as members of a nation in a manner that transcends discrimination based on various divisive micro-identities such as race, class, ethnicity, religion and language (Collier, 10 March 2015). The economic dimensions of nationalism encompass access to national resources in an inclusive manner devoid of favouritism and exploitation (Kecmanovic, 1996).

There is a very close relationship between the philosophies of nationalism and Ubuntu, commonly known in Zimbabwe as Hunhu by the Shona and Vumunhu by the Shangani. Ubuntu/ Hunhu is an indigenous African philosophical concept that placed the community ahead of individual interests. Like African nationalism, this ethical concept emphasised unity and altruism (Gade, 2011, 2012; Samkange and Samkange, 1980; Swanson, 2015). Ubuntu/ Hunhu/ Vumunhu was popularised by African nationalist leaders as a philosophy of decolonisation in Southern Africa, particularly in colonial Zimbabwe and Apartheid South Africa (Samkange and Samkange, 1980). Among other issues, the philosophy advocated for the interaction and unity of purpose between indigenous and non-indigenous communities (Samkange and Samkange, 1980). According to Eze (2010: 190-191), unity was the core attribute of Ubuntu/ Hunhu/Vumunhu; thus he argues:

> (Ubuntu)…is a demand for a creative intersubjective formation in which the 'other' becomes a mirror (but only a mirror) for my subjectivity. This idealism suggests to us that humanity is not embedded in my person solely as an individual; my humanity is co-substantively bestowed upon the other and me. Humanity is a quality

124

we owe to each other. We create each other and need to sustain this otherness creation. And if we belong to each other, we participate in our creations: we are because you are, and since you are, definitely I am. The 'I am' is not a rigid subject, but a dynamic self-constitution dependent on this otherness creation of relation and distance.

It can be noted that, in terms of development discourses, there is also a close relationship between the philosophies of Ubuntu/Hunhu/Vumunhu and African nationalism. Besides being communitarian in nature, both philosophies are opposed to uneven development, exploitative tendencies and instrumentalist interactions, and advocate for equal access to resources in order to attain a social order that is economically and environmentally sustainable (Samkange and Samkange, 1980).

There are two dominant theories on the origins and dynamics of nationalism. These are primordial (perennialism) and modernist (constructivism).The primordial school contends that nationalism is inherent in human beings (Hobsbawm and Ranger, 1983; Smith, 1971). To the primordialists, nationalism is an ancient phenomenon that emerges naturally from a pre-existing community sharing similar cultural traits. This theory does not insist that all members should be completely similar; they do not necessarily have to be alike but need to share a connection of solidarity and empathy towards other members of the nation (Bozhinov, 5 July 2012).

On the other hand, the modernists argue that nationalism is a modern phenomenon that is invented by the elite in order to fulfil their socio-economic and political aspirations. In other words, it is an artificial construct (Bozhinov, 5 July 2012). Hobsbawm and Ranger (1983), for example, assert that nationalism is constructed; it can be borrowed, added to, or invented, and can be sustained by myths. Gellner (2006) reiterates that nationalism is neither self-generating nor self-evident but is primarily programmed by the elite. According to Faber (2011), nationalism is not natural, it has not existed forever, and it does not happen automatically but is a socio-political reaction to a specific dispensation. He further asserts that it is a tool used to create collective entities in order to fulfil specific goals such as: to overcome socio-cultural, political and economic hegemonic forces;

to achieve self-determination and liberty; and to secure recognition on the international arena by formulating self-justifying narratives. A nationalist agenda, he argues, usually manipulates the past to invent mutual identity. To Benedict Anderson (1991: 7), nationalism is "an imagined community – a cultural logic that conceives of the nation as a deep, horizontal comradeship, a belonging to a territorially delimited, sovereign state."

Antony Smith (1971) proposes a synthesis of primordial and modernist theories of nationalism. He argues that nationalism is a modern construct but it capitalises on pre-existing history and traditions of a group and manipulates them to cultivate a sense of common identity and shared history. He notes that nationalism is often sustained by historically inaccurate interpretations of the past and tends to overemphasise minor and faulty parts of history to accomplish a specific agenda. Nationalism, according to Smith (1971), does not demand that members of the nation be alike, but they should feel attached and committed to, and identify with, each other.

This chapter is more inclined towards the modernist approach but, like Antony Smith (1971), it contends that nationalism is an opportunistic construct whose elite leaders capitalise on pre-existing shared identities and prevailing dispensations to forge unity of purpose in pursuit of a defined agenda. It argues that African nationalist leaders in Zimbabwe's struggle for independence exploited the shared primordial African identities such as race and cultural affinities, and the relatively common experiences of colonial subjugation to mobilise people. During the anti-colonial struggle, Africans of foreign origin and liberal whites were taken on board. After the attainment of national independence, the nationalist project was redefined by the ruling Zimbabwean elite to exclude certain constituencies in the utilisation of natural resources such as land.

Historical background: Land annexation in colonial Zimbabwe from 1890

The white settlers, under the administration of the British South Africa Company (BSAC), began to allocate themselves large tracts of

126

land after invading Southern Rhodesia (colonial Zimbabwe) in 1890. After defeating the Ndebele in 1894, the BSAC dispossessed them from their land and forcibly resettled them into two reserves, Gwaai and Shangani, which were infertile, semi-arid and tsetse-infested (Palmer, 1977). The Southern Rhodesia Order-in-Council of 1898 approved the annexation of land by white farmers and miners and also provided for the creation of African reserves throughout the country in the most unproductive areas (Bratton, 1978). By 1905, there were about 60 African reserves covering about 22% of the country in which nearly 50% of the African population of 700 000 lived. The rest of the African population lived outside the reserves in the urban areas, or as tenants on land annexed by the BSAC and white settlers (Rolin, 1978). With the appointment of the Native Reserves Commission in 1914, more reserves totalling about 87 400 hectares were set aside for the forced resettlement of Africans (Haw, 1965). By 1920, African reserves covered an area of 8.7 million hectares (Rolin, 1978). At this time, the number of white commercial farms numbered 2 500 with a cumulative extent of 15 million hectares in the most fertile and well-watered parts of the country (Palmer, 1977). By 1927, 64% of the African population was confined to the increasingly overcrowded reserves in the largely semi-arid and virtually unproductive rural areas (Astrow, 1983).

The Land Apportionment Act of 1931 institutionalised the racial allocation of land. The Act subdivided land into white settler areas (50.8%); African Reserves (22.4%); African Purchase Areas (7.7%); Forest Areas (0.6%); Unassigned Area (18.4%); and Undetermined Area (0.1%) (Astrow, 1983). The period 1935-1955 witnessed the forced eviction of 67 000 African families from their lands (Chitiyo, 29 April 2007). The Native Land Husbandry Act of 1951 sought to decongest African reserves, unsuccessfully though, by, among other things, limiting the number of domestic animals one could own, rearrangement of African households in linear order, and the reallocation of farming and grazing lands (Murray, 1977; Palmer, 1977). African grazing areas were drastically reduced in size owing to the limited number of livestock that had been prescribed for them (Weitzer, 1990). The Land Tenure Act of 1969 again confirmed the racial division of land but this time, on a 50-50 basis between the whites and the blacks in view of the overcrowded conditions in the reserves which had caused serious environmental degradation. The majority of Africans, however, were settled in the most unproductive lands (Chitiyo, 29 April 2007).

In early 1998, some 18 years after independence, white commercial farmers possessed 15.5 million hectares of land which constituted 39% of Zimbabwean land while 8500 African small-scale farmers occupied 1.4 million hectares, about 4%. At this time, about 700 000 African households in the communal areas occupied 16.4 million hectares (42%) in the most arid and least productive areas of the country (Sachikonye, 2002). Government statistics of late 1998 indicated that 4000 white commercial farmers possessed 28% of the land, about 11.2 million hectares, while more than one million African households in the rural areas owned 42 %, constituting about 16.3 million hectares. About 70 000 African rural households had been resettled on about 2 million hectares, around 9%, since independence in 1980 (Stoneman, 2002). In 1999, 11 million hectares of the most fertile land was still in the hands of about 4500 commercial farmers, mostly whites (Commercial Farmers Union, 19 October 2001).

Land policies in colonial Zimbabwe were racially-skewed to the disadvantage of the black majority. For the greater part of the colonial era and the first decade of the post-colonial period, the whites had a monopoly over land both in terms of extent and quality. This severely crippled the productive capacities of significant numbers of blacks in agriculture and other land-based economic activities of survival. The African people's attachment to land lay not only in its economic productivity, but also in its psycho-spiritual significance as the historical abode of the ancestors. Among other critical grievances, colonial land seizures provoked strong collective reaction from Africans against British colonialism (Mupfuvi, 2014).

Nationalism and the land question during Zimbabwe's liberation struggle

Various scholars and activists have articulated the close relationship between land and nationalism. Graham (2006), for example, noted that land, nationhood and nationalism are closely related. According to Malcolm X, quoted by Foner (1970: 1), "Land is the basis of all independence." Echoing similar sentiments, Turner, quoted by Foner (1970: 1), stated: "Without control over land, resources and production, there can be no self-determination for a people." Foner (1970: 1) reiterated: "A real nationalism is based on the relationship of a people to a land." While the importance of the land issue in Zimbabwe's struggle for independence should not be underestimated, it was not the only critical grievance. The land question was magnified by the nationalist leaders to supersede other grievances for purposes of mobilisation and giving impetus to the liberation movement.

The Southern Rhodesia African National Congress (SRANC) was perhaps Zimbabwe's first nationalist party which was formed in September 1957 after the merging of the Bulawayo-based African National Congress and the Salisbury-based City Youth League (Astrow, 1983). The SRANC, which lasted until 1959, was largely an urban-based party. Initially, it focused on seeking redress to the problems faced by Africans in colonial urban centres such as rising unemployment and inadequate housing (Weitzer, 1990). It also demanded political power for the blacks and later penetrated into the rural areas where it capitalised on land hunger to get massive support. In the countryside, as James Chikerema, its Vice-President, acknowledged, the party became very popular for vilifying the Land Husbandry Act of 1951: "The Land Husbandry Act has been the best recruiter Congress ever had" (O'Meara, 1975: 100).

The National Democratic Party (NDP) was founded in 1960 as a successor to the SRANC which had been banned. It did not specifically focus on the land question but on majority rule based on universal adult suffrage, higher wages for Africans, improvements in African education and the abolition of racial discrimination in all spheres of life (Ntungakwa, 21 September 2014; Weitzer, 1990). The Zimbabwe African People's Union (ZAPU) was formed in 1961 soon after the NDP had been proscribed by the colonial government. It advocated for an armed struggle to bring about majority rule (Ntungakwa, 21 September 2014).

It was the Zimbabwe African National Union (ZANU), formed in 1963 after breaking away from ZAPU, which elevated the land issue above other African grievances in the nationalist project in order to canvass grassroots support from the rural areas. During Zimbabwe's liberation war from the late 1960s until the late 1970s, "*mwana wevhu*", in Shona, and "*umtwana womhlabati*", in Ndebele (meaning child of the soil) became the nationalist rallying point for the Zimbabwe African National Liberation Army (ZANLA), ZANU's military wing (O'Meara, 1975: 1). In Zimbabwe's armed struggle, as Chitiyo (29 April 2007: 5) noted:

> Land became one of the rallying cries of peasant conscientisation as peasants were well aware of the local land grievances. The guerrillas' task was to elevate the personal and local discontent of the peasants to a national level, and to make them aware that the war was being fought to redress the historical experience of land dispossession.

According to Ranger (1985), most peasants were mobilised to support Zimbabwe's armed struggle because of grievances over land. "Land ranked highest among the grievances that motivated the indigenous black majority to launch the Second *Chimurenga/ Imfazwe* to free the country from colonial expression" (Embassy of Zimbabwe in Stockholm, March 2009: 1). In his speech during a trip to Australia in 1973, Herbert Chitepo, the Chairman of ZANU, said:

> I could go into the whole theories of discrimination in legislation, in residency, in economic opportunities, in education. I could go into that, but I will restrict myself to the question of land because I think this is very basic. To us, the essence of white domination is domination over land. That is the real issue (Embassy of Zimbabwe in Stockholm, March 2009: 1).

In 1978, Henry Hamadziripi, a senior ZANU official, proclaimed that all white commercial farms would be nationalised after independence under the collective ownership of black workers with the former owners being given positions in their management (Embassy of Zimbabwe in Stockholm, March 2009). During the same year, these sentiments were reiterated in an official ZANU publication:

> On the land question, ZANU has stated repeatedly that all natural resources- land, minerals, water, flora and fauna- belong to the people of Zimbabwe as a whole in perpetuity. No person has right of private ownership of land and minerals. Land hunger was one of the main objectives of the freedom struggle, and certainly is the inspiration of peasants who have rallied behind the movement…We are compelled to state categorically that ZANU would dismantle the white farms and base its effort for increased production on an entirely new socialist arrangement (Astrow, 1983: 140).

Mugabe added weight to this stance at the Lancaster House Conference in October 1979:

> Land is the main reason we went to war: to regain what was taken 89 years ago. There are 6 000 farmers owning seven million black people's rights…We have a right to pass that land on to the people. It is a life and death matter (Astrow, 1983: 140).

It is historically inaccurate to single out the land question as the sole grievance for African participation in the struggle for independence. What is needed is a holistic approach that considers colonial abuses and exploitation in various aspects of life because some grievances tended to be more profound in specific settings than in others. It should be noted, however, that the elevation of the land issue was an important mobilisation strategy in the pre-independence nationalist project. During the post-colonial period, Zimbabweans waited in anticipation for the anti-colonial nationalist agenda, dominated by development discourses around land, to be accomplished.

Land invasions, the collapse of African nationalism and the derailment of the development agenda from the year 2000

The land reform programme from the year 2000, also known in ZANU-PF circles as the 'Third *Chimurenga*,' was largely regarded as the war of economic liberation (Mugabe, 2001). Border Gezi, the Governor of Mashonaland Central Province declared the land invasions as "The Third Liberation" or "The Third *Chimurenga*," thereby positioning them in a sequence of violent struggles against colonial rule dating back to the 1890s (Alexander, 2003: 101). In an attempt to legitimise the land invasions to the international community, the Zimbabwean Embassy in Sweden issued a statement in 2007: "The land question has always been and remains at the core of Zimbabwe's political, economic and social development. Indeed now as in the past, it remains the root of the political tension within the country and with the former colonial power, Britain" (Embassy of Zimbabwe in Stockholm, March 2009: 1). Through the land invasions, ZANU-PF also portrayed itself as an architect of militant African nationalism and economic empowerment in the wake of globalisation in the post-colonial era (Moyo and Yeros, 2007).

Alienation of the white population

The land reform programme from the year 2000 was deeply divisive by being rooted in racially-defined liberation politics and exclusive Black Nationalism. The issue of race was used to politically mobilise people to support the land programme and its gross human rights violations (Muzondidya, 2010; Scarnecchea, 2006). The land invasions were ushered under the nationalist rhetoric of reclaiming lands lost to the whites and "reverse the colonial legacy of racialised land economic inequalities" (Hammar and Raftopoulos, 2003: 11).

The racial tirade that typified the land project deliberately overlooked the role played by some whites during the Zimbabwean liberation struggle, and that a significant number were Zimbabwean citizens. Terence Ranger, a white lecturer from England, for example, was deported from Rhodesia in 1963 for participating in African nationalist politics (Raftopoulos, 1999). Guy Clutton Brock, a British missionary, was also a white man who played a prominent role in the anti-colonial struggle. He arrived in colonial Zimbabwe in 1949 and worked for 10 years at St. Faith's Mission farm where he became friends with future ZANU veteran nationalists, Didymus Mutasa and Maurice Nyagumbo. He was involved in the formation of the SRANC in 1957 (Clutton Brock, 1969). He was detained during the late 1950s for his involvement in African nationalist activities (Fisher, 2010). During the 1960s, he helped the Tangwena people in north-eastern Zimbabwe to resist eviction from their land by white settlers (Clutton Brock, 1969). He was also actively involved in establishing two multi-racial farming cooperative schemes at Nyafaru in north-eastern Zimbabwe and Cold Comfort near Harare (Fisher, 2010). He was deported from the country in 1971 and when he died in 1995, his ashes were scattered at the National Heroes' Acre (Commonwealth Histories, 11 January 2015; Fisher 2010).

The Lancaster House Conference of 1979, which negotiated Zimbabwe's independence, and was attended by the nationalist leaders such as Mugabe, acknowledged that a significant number of whites were Zimbabwean citizens and this is largely why 20 parliamentary seats were reserved for them in the new government. In addition, the conference resolved that legislation pertaining to the equitable redistribution of land could only be effected after 10 years but meanwhile, the government could purchase land from willing white farmers (Astrow, 1983). Soon after independence, the government proclaimed the policy of reconciliation in which whites and blacks would coexist peacefully. General Peter Walls, the former commander of the colonial armed forces retained his post. Mugabe, the new Prime Minister, appointed two white ministers in his new cabinet: David Smith (Commerce and Industry) and Dennis Norman (Agriculture) (Astrow, 1983). Mugabe allayed the fears held by many whites of a backlash from the blacks when he said in August 1980: "Those who talked about the possibility of personal and other properties being nationalised, being seized, have not read us correctly" (Astrow, 1983: 101). This evidence indicates that the new Zimbabwean government recognised significant sections of the white population as legitimate citizens and equal partners in developing the country.

The ZANU-PF government changed goalposts from the year 2000 in the wake of its waning popularity emanating from socio-economic hardships caused by the Economic Structural Adjustment Programme (ESAP), and the increasing challenge from the opposition MDC, which enjoyed considerable support from the white population. In a move reminiscent of Idi Amin's racial cleansing of Asians in Uganda in 1973 (Young, 2004), the government launched a violent onslaught on the white community. In its campaign message prior to the 2000 presidential elections, the ruling party announced: "ZANU-PF has decided that 20 years is long enough to be polite to white farmers and Britain and has now started taking back your land" (*Zimbabwe Independent*, 9 January 2004: 1). Government-sponsored land invasions targeting white commercial farms began on 26 February 2000. By 8 March 2000, about 400 farms had been seized (Meredith, 2002). The presence, or existence, of the whites in Zimbabwe increasingly became awkwardly perceived as an affront to sovereignty. Mugabe chastised the whites for supporting the MDC and seeking to reverse the gains of independence by abandoning ZANU-PF, a party that had played a prominent role in the liberation struggle. He mobilised war veterans and civilians to target white commercial farms for seizure. The farm invasions were often done violently in line with Mugabe's instructions: "Our party must continue to strike fear in the heart of the white man, who is the real enemy" (Masunungure, 2004: 176). Dispossessed white farmers who took the government to court were castigated by Mugabe in April 2000 as "our enemies, not just political enemies, but definite enemies in wanting to reverse our revolution and our independence" (Alexander, 2003: 103).

The number of farms confiscated rose to 1 500 by June 2000 (Alexander, 2003). At the end of June 2000, the Commercial Farmers Union reported that 1 525 farms had been grabbed (Pilossof, 1 December 2010). The year 2000 saw more than 1 600 commercial white farms being seized (Moyo, September 2000). Between 2000 and 2001, around 3 000 white farmers were evicted from their farms (Chibber, 26 July 2014). By the end of 2002, 11.5 million hectares of land had been seized inside the space of 36 months (Sachikonye, 2003). The farm invasions reduced the number of commercial farmers in the country from 4 500 to only 450 by February 2004 (Cross, 4 February 2004). By 2007, more than 4 000 farms had been confiscated (Duri, 2014; *Financial Gazette*, 26 July- 1 August 2007). Land invasions continued after the setting up of the Government of National Unity (GNU) in February 2009 soon after which the General Agriculture and Plantation Workers Union of Zimbabwe (GAPWUZ) estimated that around 225 farms were seized (Zimbabwe Human Rights NGO Forum, 2010). By 31 December 2009, far less than 300 white commercial farmers remained on their farms (*Voice of America*, 31 December 2009). The Internal Displacement Monitoring Centre approximated that more than 3 000 white commercial farmers were evicted during the period 2000-2010 (Zimbabwe Human Rights NGO Forum, 2010).

While considerable numbers of displaced white farmers either relocated to their remaining premises within the country or fled abroad to reunite with their families or ventured into other businesses, others became destitute in Zimbabwe. A white beggar at the corner of Leopold Takawira and Robert Mugabe Streets in Bulawayo, Zimbabwe's second largest city, told the *Zimbabwean* that he began panhandling in 2007 after his grandfather's farm in Shangani had been seized by the government (Sithole, 28 March 2012).

Clashes were common between white farmers and incoming occupiers during the land reform programme. At Virginia Farm in Mazowe District in 2000, a white farmer reportedly locked his gates and electrified the fence to deny the newly-resettled farmers access to their fields. At Msonendi Farm in Mvurwi during the same year, a white farmer allegedly tilled the fields and uprooted the crops of the newly-resettled people. At Chirobi Farm in Mazowe District, again in 2000, there were several confrontations between war veterans and civilian occupiers on the one hand and the white commercial farmer and his workers on the other (Marongwe, 2003). In April 2000, two white farmers were shot dead by war veterans after trying to remove them from their land (Chitiyo, 29 April 2007). From mid-February to June 2000, a total of six white farmers were killed (Mamdani, 2008). As Bond and Manyanya accurately put it, the land reform programme was an economic disaster that derailed the development agenda by employing a divisive and exhausted brand of racial nationalism in which the ZANU-PF government mostly targeted the whites, some of who were Zimbabwean citizens, when seizing commercial farms (Bond and Manyanya, 2001).

In the selective redistribution of land, as Dore (2 October 2013: 1) succinctly summarised the situation, many white farmers were stripped of their Zimbabwean citizenship thereby narrowing the confines of African nationalism in the country along racial lines and jeopardising the development agenda by eliminating the most experienced and productive elements of the commercial farming community:

> White farmers are not Rhodesians, but Zimbabweans, in every sense of the word. Unlike many of their erstwhile Rhodesian compatriots who left Zimbabwe to settle in other countries, many whites chose to live and work in Zimbabwe's nationalist government, took out Zimbabwean citizenship, and hold Zimbabwean IDs and passports. Many had opposed the Smith regime and welcomed the opportunity to contribute to building a progressive and non-racial society...

It is to demonise and discriminate against a class of Zimbabwean citizens- white farmers- not on the basis of any wrongdoing, but by associating them with deeds done by others of the same race, in another era, and by another government...It is to punish the children and grandchildren for the deeds of their mothers, fathers and grandparents...

Exclusion and pauperisation of farm workers

ZANU-PF officials accused farm workers of sympathising with their displaced white employers. Consequently, most of them were ostracised from the nationalist land project through violent onslaughts, displacement and deliberate acts of sinking them into profound poverty and destitution.

The land seizures impoverished many former farm workers after the new owners failed to reemploy them. This was partly because some new farmers either lacked the technical skills for both intensive and extensive commercial farming, or were not interested at all, while others did not have the financial resources to pay workers. In 2005, for example, more than 50% of the seized farms were not being utilised (Duri, 2014). At Stockdale Farm near the town of Chegutu, for example, its 78 former white owners employed more than 60 000 workers but less than 50% of the workforce was retained by the new owner, Edna Madzongwe, a senior ZANU-PF official and President of Senate (Chikwanha, 4 May 2014). Charleswood Farm in the Chimanimani District used to employ more than 1 000 workers but when Zimbabwean soldiers took over in April 2004, they engaged only 100 workers (Wasosa, 28 January 2005). More than 20 000 workers lost their jobs when Kondozi Farm in the Mutare District of Manicaland Province was seized by riot police and ZANU-PF supporters on 19 July 2005 (Poverty Reduction Forum Trust, 2013).

The national unemployment levels among former farm workers clearly illustrate the ruinous impact of the evictions in alienating some sections of the population from the so-called nationalist land project. GAPWUZ stated that employment for its members decreased from 500 000 in 2000 to 200 000 in 2008. As a result, the Union's membership declined to 25 000 in 2008 from 150 000 before the land seizures (Chikwanha, 4 May 2014). The Internal Displacement Monitoring Centre, based in Geneva, estimated that about 1 million farm workers lost their jobs from farm invasions during the period 2000-2010 (Zimbabwe Human Rights NGO Forum, 2010). Over 50% of the permanent female farm workers lost their jobs while 60% of the seasonal female workers became jobless and 30% and 33% of their male counterparts, respectively, lost their jobs. This also left between 1.8 million and 2 million (approximately 20% of the total population of Zimbabwe) dependants of former farm workers destitute (Sachikonye, 2003).

It should be noted, however, that this sad picture is characteristic of most revolutions. As revolutionaries struggle to achieve their goals, it becomes inevitable that some sections of the society, mostly the subaltern, incur more losses as compared to the others. This is what happened during Zimbabwe's armed struggle for independence when many lives were lost. Similarly, during the so-called Third *Chimurenga*, many farm workers lost their jobs. Thus, every revolution has its own victims. This analysis, however, is not an attempt to absolve the architects and implementers of the Land Reform Programme of blame for the suffering and marginalisation of some sections of the population. With proper planning, such hardships could have been mitigated.

In addition to losing their jobs, most former farm workers were left homeless together with their dependants. There were Zimbabweans who had been born and bred at the farms where they worked and had no close family members and relatives to accommodate them. In July 2001, GAPWUZ claimed that over 40 000 farm workers in the Mashonaland provinces had been displaced to shack settlements around the towns of Chinhoyi, Centenary and Rusape (Alexander, 2003). During an incident of 23 July 2002, Caleb Chikwamba and 200 other workers at Leopard Vlei Farm in Mashonaland Central Province were evicted by Reward Marufu, the brother of the First Lady, Grace Mugabe. The farm had been offered to Marufu by the government under the A2 scheme. "Marufu first told us that everyone was fired", Chikwamba stated, "...He came back later with several of his guards and known ZANU-PF youths and set ablaze our huts" (Worby, 2003: 52).

In February 2003, more than 150 000 displaced farm labourers and their families were homeless (Watson, 1 March 2003). By 2004, between 45 000 and 70 000 permanent farm workers had been displaced with nowhere to go (Chambati and Moyo, 2004). When Kondozi Farm in Manicaland Province was seized in July 2005, scores of displaced workers who included women, children and the elderly were stranded along the road outside the farm with their life-long belongings while others congregated at nearby business centres. On 21 July, a 70-member delegation comprising chiefs and headmen from the surrounding Marange Rural Area, most of whose subjects had been employed at the farm, approached Vice President Joseph Msika seeking a reversal of the evictions (Kahiya and Mukaro, 22 July 2005). Their pleas fell on deaf ears and a "humanitarian crisis" set in (Kahiya and Mukaro, 22 July 2005: 1).

Most of the evictions were carried out violently resulting in the death of 11 black farm workers countrywide during the period from mid-February to June 2000 alone (Mamdani, 2008). To aggravate the plight of evicted workers, most of them were not allocated land. Only less than 5% of the displaced farm workers received land under the government's land redistribution exercise countrywide by May 2003 (Sachikonye, 2003).

Xenophobic practices were also employed to elbow out farm workers of foreign origin, most of who had become Zimbabwean citizens by birth or naturalisation, from struggles over land. Nearly 20% of the displaced farm workers were foreigners who had taken up permanent residence at their workplaces (Mamdani, 2008). At a campaign rally in 2000, President Mugabe lambasted farm workers of Malawian and Zambian origin for supporting the MDC and referred to them as *mabwidi* or *mabhurandaya* (derogatory reference to foreigners mostly from Malawi, Mozambique and Zambia) and "totem-less Africans" who should go back to their countries (Zvomuya, 23 May 2008: 1). At the height of land invasions in 2000, some ZANU-PF supporters told displaced farm workers that they did not qualify as recipients of land because most of them were of foreign origin (Rutherford, 2003). Such xenophobic pronouncements were also made by several government officials (Bond and Manyanya, 2001).

By implication, such hypocritical tendencies distorted history by diminishing, or deliberately overlooking, the role played by foreign Africans in the liberation of Zimbabwe. African countries such as Mozambique, Zambia, Tanzania and Algeria provided bases for military training during Zimbabwe's armed struggle. Mozambican forces assisted ZANU guerrillas while Umkhonto weSizwe, the military wing of the South African National Congress, fought alongside ZAPU militants on the battlefront (Baxter, 18 December 2011; Mbofana, 16 November 2007). Some labour migrants from Malawi, Zambia and Mozambique and their descendants, were actively involved in anti-colonial movements in Rhodesian urban areas (Raftopoulos, 1999). Simon Chimbetu, a prominent musician who died in 2005 and was declared a Zimbabwe Liberation War Hero, was born in Zimbabwe from Malawian parents. Although his parents were foreign migrant workers, he got involved in Zimbabwe's liberation struggle by joining ZANU and at some point

139

played music to entertain and boost the morale of ZANLA combatants in Tanzania (Ruwende, 12 August 2012).

The process of land grabbing and redistribution was therefore characterised by "authoritarian nationalism" and "selective citizenship" (Raftopoulos, 2003: 217). Thus, according to Boas (2009: 19), there is "a direct link between contested citizenship and land rights." In 2003, these developments made Eric Worby (2003: 52) to question the authenticity of ZANU-PF's post-colonial nationalist agenda:

> Two decades after achieving independence, Zimbabwe's rulers present an apparent paradox for any theory of post-colonial politics. How can one explain a government's relentless effort to elevate the principle of national sovereignty over the survival of the very people…who seem to constitute its mass public?

Selective land redistribution along political party lines

The land reform programme witnessed widespread discrimination on political grounds. The majority of the land seizures were perpetrated by ZANU-PF supporters who largely used political muscle to monopolise economic space (Chitiyo, 29 April 2007). Significant numbers of war veterans, under the orders of the state, initiated the land invasions in February 2000. The veterans politicised the land question and any anti-ZANU-PF elements were accused of being against the land reform exercise. Judges who outlawed land seizures and ruled in favour of evicted commercial farmers were castigated as enemies of the nationalist revolution (Alexander, 2003).

Some farms were specifically targeted because their white owners were alleged to be MDC supporters. Makay Farm in Mashonaland Central Province, for example, was seized after its owner was accused of providing MDC supporters with space for military training and being found in possession of MDC regalia and membership cards. Penrose Farm in Mashonaland West Province was also invaded after its owner had availed his premises to train MDC militants. Landscape Farm in Mashonaland West was grabbed following the discovery of MDC regalia and cards at the farm. Barria Farm in Mashonaland Central Province was forcibly occupied after the owner, who had been found with MDC shirts and cards, had influenced his workers to attend the opposition party's campaign rallies (Marongwe, 2003).

Most MDC supporters were left out and some were even forbidden to apply for land (Human Rights Watch, March 2002). The violent land invasions also targeted MDC supporters and sympathisers who the ZANU-PF government labelled as traitors who sided with the white enemy to sabotage 'the final phase of the nationalist, anti-colonial revolution, the so-called Third *Chimurenga*' which sought to redistribute land to the 'blacks.' In Mutoko District during October 2000, war veterans threatened to evict new farm occupants accused of supporting the MDC. In Masvingo, the ZANU-PF Provincial Political Commissar ordered that MDC supporters be removed from their newly-occupied land. There were numerous reports throughout 2000 that war veterans and ZANU-PF card-holding members were the chief recipients of the land grabbed from the whites (Alexander, 2003).

District and Provincial Committees that allocated the seized land were comprised of ZANU-PF functionaries such as Provincial Governors and Administrators, District Administrators, war veterans, ZANU-PF officials and some traditional leaders. In August 2000, the then Provincial Governor of Matabeleland North declared that only ZANU-PF members and war veterans would be considered in the allocation of land. War veterans in the land committees chased away civil servants, such as the Gwanda District Administrator, and the Matabeleland South Provincial Administrator in late 2000, after accusing them of being sympathetic to the MDC (Alexander, 2003). In 2002, the 70 000-hectare Hippo Valley Estate (Meldrum, 4 February 2004), the country's biggest sugar producer comprising 49 plantations and owned by the South African Anglo-American Corporation, was seized (Kahiya and Mukaro, 22 July 2005). Close to 180 new farmers subdivided among themselves part of the estate into plots ranging from 20 to 60 hectares in size while 140 others, most of who were connected to the ruling ZANU-PF party, took over privately-owned plots within and around the sugar plantations (*Zimbabwe Independent*, 20 March 2006).

It is now apparent that the parameters of citizenship were shifted during the contestations over land. Issues of sovereignty were "turned inward and used to construct internal enemies accused of allying with neo-colonial and imperial interests" and the war veterans and ZANU-PF militia came to be regarded as "super citizens" who legitimately promoted and safeguarded Zimbabwean independence (Hammar and Raftopoulos, 2003: 27). Jocelyn Alexander (2003: 103) also noted: "In the new nationalist vision, veterans were the legitimate liberators of the land from whites seen as too slow to change and a former colonial power now cast more vehemently than ever as the major obstacle to 'real' decolonisation." Thus, Henning Melber (2002: 3) noted "the mystification of liberators" that culminated in the criteria of "liberation war credentials" in the allocation of resources and positions of power in Zimbabwe.

The law-enforcement agents were also actively involved in the land invasions by providing food, vehicles and other forms of support (Alexander, 2003). The Central Intelligence Organisation, Zimbabwe's spy agency, was also involved in directing the war veterans to invade specific farms from March 2000 (Alexander and McGregor, 2001). The alliance involving law-enforcement agents, security details, politicians and war veterans, Alexander (2003: 102) argued, "increasingly divided the state in a new relationship with (civilian) occupiers as well as commercial farmers. This largely marked the collapse of inclusive nationalism preached during the anti-colonial struggle and at independence which encompassed various sections of society regardless various divisive affiliations, and paved way for an exclusivist form of nationalism based on loyalty and attachment to the ruling ZANU-PF party (Hammar and Raftopoulos, 2003). George Ayittey (1998: 152) lamented how most African political leaders have betrayed the nationalist cause and ruined their countries' economies by taking advantage of their power positions to amass wealth with impunity and with the full protection of law-enforcement agents:

> In case after case, African government officials get rich by misusing their positions. Faithful only to their foreign bank accounts, these official buccaneers have no sense of morality, justice, or even patriotism...The inviolate ethic of the vampire elite is self-aggrandisement and self-perpetuation in power...Of course, Africa has

a police force and judiciary system to catch and prosecute the thieves. But the police are themselves highway robbers, under orders to protect the looters, and many of the judges are themselves crooks. As a result, there are no checks against brigandage.

The preference given to ZANU-PF supporters in the allocation of land antagonised the othered sections of the Zimbabwean population and confuted the authenticity of the proposed nationalist agenda. About 900 villagers from Mvuma and Chirumhanzu who were resettled on the 65 000-hectare Sebakwe North Farm under the Fast Track Programme early in August 2000 were kicked out by war veterans in late November during the same year. They petitioned Ignatius Chombo, the then Minister of Local Government, and complained that the land redistribution exercise was only benefitting war veterans and politicians (*Daily News*, 5 December 2000). In December 2002, some villagers who had been evicted by the war veterans from a farm they had occupied in the Midlands Province complained to Chombo that the land reform programme was not being conducted in a transparent manner (Alexander, 2003). Scoones Marongwe, Mavedzenge, Mahenehene, Marimbarimba and Sukume (2010: 252) acknowledge that land became a key source of political patronage in Zimbabwe that "undermined the land reform programme's credibility and legitimacy both nationally and internationally."

It should be noted, therefore, that the rhetoric of political sovereignty, sloganeering, and the often coercive attempts to cultivate fanatic adherence to ZANU-PF as a political party that had participated in the anti-colonial struggle in the context of the land reform programme from 2000, failed to sustain the nationalist agenda. Lamentably, significant sections of society were eviscerated from the promissory nationalist land project. The programme was indeed a corrosive dynamic to the proclaimed nationalist trajectory of freedom, equal access to resources and prosperity for Zimbabweans.

Intra-political party class and ethnic cleavages

Struggles over land also erupted at various levels within the ZANU-PF constituency itself thereby scuttling the nationalist project further. Class conflicts emerged where the subordinate communities accused the elite of privileging themselves with the most extensive and productive farms, sometimes after evicting earlier occupiers. Multiple farm ownership by the high-ranking officials was another cause for concern among the subaltern. At times, the ZANU-PF elite clashed within their ranks over certain tracts of land. In addition, the land wrangles sometimes assumed ethnic dimensions after some communities blocked incomers from being resettled in areas where they had ancestral claims.

Typical of Mobutu's 'Zairenisation' edicts in the Congo during 1973 and 1974 (Young, 2004), high-ranking politicians parcelled out large tracts of land to their cronies and reserved for themselves, the largest and most fertile ones. Preferential treatment for the ZANU-PF elite in the allocation of land was rampant, resulting in discontentment even among the ordinary supporters of the party. In February 2001, some newly-resettled farmers alleged that senior politicians and war veterans, as well as high-ranking civil servants were being given land with better facilities such as farmhouses (Alexander, 2003). In 2004, Amnesty International also noted that there was corruption in the redistribution of land resulting in the best commercial farmlands being given to influential political cronies while the relatively poor land was issued to small-scale farmers (Amnesty International, February 2004). Boas (2009: 19) rightly stated that "citizenship does not automatically entitle all people to land: Citizenship itself does not secure access to land, but at the very least it allows those with status a legitimate entry to the competition for land." In July 2012, for instance, it was reported that President Mugabe, top ZANU-PF politicians, senior government officials, high-ranking military personnel and judges had benefitted the most with 5 million hectares of land among them. About 2 200 politically-connected elite Zimbabweans owned more than 50% of the most fertile land seized from white commercial farmers (*Zimbabwe Online Press*, 16 July 2012).

Multiple farm ownership also characterised the predatory instincts and extreme self-aggrandisement on the part of the political elite. In 2005, the Ministry of Lands ordered senior government officials to adhere to the One-Person-One-Farm Policy and give up extra farms without success. A committee appointed to investigate multiple farm ownership noted that 13 cabinet ministers and four provincial governors had more than one farm (Phiri, 21 April 2006). In 2012, President Mugabe and his wife, Grace, were reportedly owning 14 farms, about 16 000 hectares in extent. The First Vice-President, Joyce Mujuru, and her husband, together with their relatives, were alleged to be in possession of more than 25 farms with a combined area of 105 000 hectares. The Second Vice-President, John Nkomo, was also reported to be a multiple farm owner. One of his farms was the Jijima Wildlife Sanctuary which he allegedly seized from a black commercial farmer. By contrast, only 150 000 ordinary Zimbabweans had benefitted from the land redistribution exercise by July 2012 and most of them had each received plots of land ranging from 10 to 50 hectares (*Zimbabwe Online Press*, 16 July 2012).

Table1: Farms allegedly owned by President Robert Mugabe and his wife, 2012 (Source: *Zimbabwe Online Press*, 16 July 2012)

Name of farm	Location	Area in hectares
Gushungo Estate	Darwendale	4046
Gushungo Dairies	Mazowe	1000
Mazowe Iron Mask	Mazowe	1046
Mazowe Sigaru	Mazowe	873
Mazowe Gwebi Wood	Mazowe	1200
Mazowe Gwina	Mazowe	1445

Banket Leverdale	Mazowe	1488
Mazowe Highfield	Norton	445
Norton Cressydale Estate	Norton	676
Norton Tanktara	Norton	575
Norton Clifford	Norton	1050
John O'Groat	Norton	760
Bassiville	Mazowe	1200

Thus, one of the major obstacles to socio-economic development in independent Africa is the existence of "predatory governments" dominated by a "cabal of looters" (Ayittey, 1998: 21) "driven by self-interest, so excessive that their people's interests are forgotten- hardly different from the colonial masters" (Ayittey, 1998: 47-48). After independence, in most African countries, as Ayittey (1998: 7) points out, "...the freedom and development promised by...African nationalists transmogrified into a melodramatic nightmare. In many countries, these nationalist leaders soon turned out to be crocodile liberators, Swiss bank socialists, quack revolutionaries, and grasping kleptocrats." Consequently,

> The African state has been reduced to a mafia-like bazaar, where anyone with an official designation can pillage at will. In effect, it is a "state" that has been hijacked by gangsters, crooks and scoundrels. They have seized and monopolised both political and economic power to advance their own selfish and criminal interests, not to develop their economies. Their overarching obsession is to amass personal wealth, gaudily displayed in flashy automobiles, fabulous mansions and a bevy of fawning women. Helping the poor, promoting economic growth or improving the standard of living of their people is anathema to the ruling elites. "Food for the people!" "People's power!" "Houses for the

masses!" are simply empty slogans that are designed to fool the people and the international community (Ayittey, 1998: 151-152).

On a number of occasions, the ordinary people registered their discontentment pertaining to the disparities in the redistribution of land to the authorities most of whom, ironically, were the very major beneficiaries of the programme. On 28 May 2015, for example, Douglas Mombeshora, the Minister of Lands and Resettlement, acknowledged that there were complaints from the general public that President Mugabe and his wife possessed vast pieces of land. He, however, retorted that the members of the First Family actually deserved more since they were using their farms productively (Ncube, 29 May 2015).

In some instances, the subaltern embarked on open resistance. As a few examples illustrate, these class struggles over land clearly manifested the collapse of the nationalist project and rendered it an illusion. In April 2002, war veterans and other civilian settlers were evicted from Maganga Farm near the town of Marondera which they had occupied in order to pave way for Sydney Sekeramayi, the Minister of Defence. The 80 settlers attempted to resist and appealed to the Provincial Governor but were evicted by the anti-riot police (Business Highbeam, 12 April 2002). In January 2006, Stan Mudenge, a cabinet minister, was involved in a wrangle with war veterans over a former white commercial farm, Chikore, south of the town of Masvingo. Mudenge was alleged to have encouraged war veterans to take over the farm from its white owner in 2004. He later obtained an offer letter from the Ministry of Lands authorising him to take over the farm but the war veterans refused to vacate (*Zimbabwe Online Press*, 21 January 2006). In 2010, the settlers were arrested for staying on gazetted land. Early in 2011, the court convicted them for illegally staying on the minister's farm (Tukutuku, 17 October 2012). In January 2013, a group of war veterans appealed to President Mugabe to intervene after Willard Chiwewe, the Masvingo Provincial Governor and Resident Minister, had sought to evict them from Allanvale Farm in Chiredzi District which they had occupied since 2000 (*Zimbabwean*, 23 January 2013). During mid-November 2014, another group of war veterans in Chiredzi District accused their

ZANU-PF Member of Parliament of receiving bribes from white farmers to block their takeover of Tongaat Hullet Sugar Estate (*All Africa*, 16 November 2014).

The nationalist cause was also dented by intra-elite struggles over land. In October 2012, ZANU- PF senior politicians: Ignatius Chombo, Minister of Local Government; Herbert Murerwa, Lands and Resettlement Minister; and Martin Bimha, the Governor of Mashonaland Central Province, reportedly clashed over the ownership of Marimambada Citrus Farm in Guruve District (Chitemba, 26 October 2012). In March 2015, two ZANU-PF ministers clashed over the 370-hectare Barquest Farm in Masvingo Province. Shuwai Mahofa, the Masvingo Resident Minister, blocked Walter Mzembi, the Minister of Tourism, from taking over the farm from a white woman on grounds that it was strategic to the province's poultry needs (Maponga, 14 March 2015).

Patrimonial aggrandisement by the elite in the allocation of land sometimes faced fierce resistance from subordinate communities. In January 2015, for example, attempts by Edwin Chinotimba, the son of a senior ZANU-PF official and Member of Parliament, Joseph Chinotimba, to grab the 164- hectare Chihoza Farm near the town of Chipinge were blocked by angry villagers, including women, youths, and war veterans (Mapepa, 9 January 2015). Unlike its pre-independence predecessor, as Ibbo Mandaza observed, post-colonial nationalism failed to adequately disguise class differentials and related struggles within African societies (Mandaza, 1986).

The divisive nature of the land reform programme sometimes assumed ethnic dimensions when some social groups clashed within their ranks over certain tracts of land. During September and October 2000, villagers from Gutu, Mwenezi, Bikita and Chivi Districts in Masvingo Province fought over certain farms with rival parties claiming preference based on ancestral claims and history of occupation (Alexander, 2003). Some politicians and politically-connected traditional leaders became ethnic entrepreneurs who blocked other citizens from being resettled in certain parts of the country. From 2008 to 2013, war veterans resettled in farms near the town of Norton were engaged in a bitter wrangle with Claudius Mandaza Nyamweda, the local chief, who was pushing for their eviction because they had no ancestral claim to the Mhondoro Rural Area (Kwaramba, 11 February 2013).

What now prevailed can be likened to autochthony: a flattened, narrowed and selective form of nationalism for the sake of self-aggrandisement. Under such circumstances in the struggle for resources, autochthony "links the individual, territory and group in such a way that shared culture/descent follow from the place of birth/residence" (Zenker, 2011: 63). In this way, the land reform programme had a demobilising effect to the nationalist cause of unity and development by de-essentialising some sections of the society along ethnic lines. The so-called nationalist land revolution therefore caused "extreme divisions within the state" (Alexander, 2003: 113). As Marongwe (2003: 155) rightly observed:

When people hear of land conflicts in Zimbabwe, they normally think of the colonial injustices that divided the country into fertile large-scale commercial farms for whites and semi-arid and infertile communal areas for blacks...There are many other struggles over land...taking place elsewhere, with varying degrees of intensity, such as in state lands and in both communal and resettlement areas.

Table 2: Farms allegedly owned by top government officials, 2012 (**Source**: *Zimbabwe Online Press*, 16 July 2012)

Name of official	Rank	Name of farm/s	Location of farm/s	Area in hectares
Solomon and Joyce Mujuru	Former army commander and his wife, First Vice President, respectively	Alameia	Beatrice	1300
John Nkomo	Second Vice President	Jijima	Hwange	Not stated
Simon Khaya Moyo	ZANU-PF chairman	Marula Block 36	Bulilimamangwe	2034
Joseph Made	Cabinet minister	Tara	Odzi	840
Emmerson Mnangagwa	Cabinet minister	Sherwood	Kwekwe	1600
Francis Nhema	Cabinet minister	Nyamandla	Karoi	1000
Stan Mudenge	Cabinet minister	Chikore	Masvingo	760
Kembo Mohadi	Cabinet minister	Jopembe Block Benlynian Range	Beitbridge Beitbridge	3000 3200

Patrick Chinamasa	Cabinet minister	Tsukamai Nyamajura	Headlands Odzi	800 1260
Herbert Murerwa	Cabinet minister	Rise Holm	Acturus	1100
Ignatius Chombo	Cabinet minister	Allan Grange Oldham Shingwiri	Banket Chegutu Chegutu	3000 400 1600
Webster Shamu	Cabinet minister	Lambourne Tobacco Estate	Selous Chegutu	1340 900
Obert Mpofu	Cabinet minister	Young Umguza Blocks 39-41 Auchenberg	Nyamandlovu Umguza Nyamandlovu	2300 6200 1026
Walter Mzembi	Cabinet minister	BW farm	Masvingo	720
Nicholas Goche	Cabinet minister	Ceres	Shamva	Not stated
Savior Kasukuwere	Cabinet minister	Conucorpu Harmony	Mazowe Mazowe	100 500
Sydney Sekeramayi	Cabinet minister	Maganga	Marondera	620
Edna Madzongwe	Cabinet minister	Atape Coburn Estates Plot 13A Bourne Mpofu Stockdale Reyden	Chegutu Chegutu Chegutu Chegutu Chegutu Chegutu	2000 560 445 1200 750 1340

Table 3: Top military officials and the farms they allegedly possessed, 2012 (Source: *Zimbabwe Online Press,* 16 July 2012)

Name of official	Name of farm	Location	Area in hectares
Constantine Chiwenga	Chikoma Estates	Goromonzi	1276
Perence Shiri	Bamboo Creek Erin	Shamva Marondera	1950 1460
Augustine Chihuri	Woodlands	Shamva	Not stated
Paradzayi Zimondi	Upton	Goromonzi	1029

Table 4: Top ZANU-PF and government officials and the farms they allegedly owned, 2012 (Source: *Zimbabwe Online Press,* 16 July 2012)

Name of official	Name of farm	Location	Area in hectares
Reward Marufu (Also brother of the First Lady Grace Mugabe)	Leopard Vlei Kachere	Glendale Mazowe	1294 880

Sabina Mugabe (Also sister of President Mugabe)	Mlembwe	Makonde	1037
	Longwood	Makonde	924
	Gowrie	Norton	430
Leo Mugabe (Also nephew of President Mugabe)	Diandra	Darwendale	815
	Nangadza	Mhangura	1200
	Journey's End	Makonde	3000
Patrick Zhuwao (Also nephew of President Mugabe)	Marivale	Mazowe	244
George Charamba	Battlefields 02	Kwekwe	1572
Nathan Shamuyarira	Mount Carmel	Chegutu	No figures
Bright Matonga	Lion's Vlei	Chegutu	2000
Dick Mafios	Insingizi	Bindura	1100
Joseph Chinotimba	Watakai	Mazowe	1240
Happison Muchechetere	Burry Hill Estate	Makonde	617
Tobaiwa Mudede	Ballineety	Nyabira	3147
Austin Zvoma	Chinomwe Estates	Makonde	1432
Mariyawanda Nzuwah	Stella Burton	Mazowe	425
David Parirenyatwa	Rudolphia	Murewa	802
Charles Utete	Rudzimi	Lomagundi	3350
Paddy Zhanda	Chipfumbi Meadows	Goromonzi	1364

Table 5: Top judges and the farms they reportedly owned, 2012
(**Source**: *Zimbabwe Online Press,* 16 July 2012)

Name of judge	Name of farm	Location	Area in hectares
Godfrey Chidyausiku	Estes Park	Concession	895
Luke Malaba	Marula Block 35	Bulilimamangwe	1866
Paddington Garwe	Faun	Chegutu	760
Antonia Guvava	Harndale	Chegutu	1000
Mafios Cheda	Marula Block 37	Bulilimamangwe	3039
Ben Hlatshwayo	Kent Estate	Norton	800
Charles Hungwe	Little England	Makonde	6956
Alfias Chitakunye	The Grange	Chegutu	1300

Table 6: Provincial governors and the farms they possessed, 2012 (**Source**: *Zimbabwe Online Press,* 16 July 2012)

Name of provincial governor	Name of farm	Location	Area in hectares
David Karimanzira	Arcadia	Marondera	1300
Cain Mathema	Gwayi Ranch	Gwayi	4600
	Umguza Block	Umguza	3700
Christopher Mushohwe	Kondozi	Odzi	400
Titus Maluleke	Clipshap	Masvingo	3000
Thokozile Matutu	Dete	Dete	2800
	Antonia Extension	Umguza	500

151

| Angeline Masuku | Wollendale | Gwanda | 3000 |
| Cephas Msipa | Chershire | Gweru | 2100 |

It should be noted that the Land Reform Programme shattered the nationalist project and the development agenda in a number of ways. It is against this background that Brian Raftopoulos (2006: 219) argued that the manner in which the Land Reform Programme was implemented from 2000, under the guise of African nationalism, was mere political expediency that had disastrous implications as far as Zimbabwe's prospects of development were concerned:

> ...This embattled nationalism (around land) is channelled against the citizens of our states, and the nationalism that presents itself as the nation's shield is often the suffocating embrace of murderous regimes. We need to find new collective discourses that build on a broad participation...For Zimbabweans, this challenge is more urgent than ever as divisions...continue to deepen.

Alexander (2003: 99) reiterated:

> ZANU-PF in 2000 promised the land, but at the price of an extreme and violent political intolerance that severely undermined the long-standing popular aspirations for a 'good' state, and labelled as enemies a range of social groups that had once been included in the nationalist constituency. It was not a revived pre-independence nationalism that lay behind the wave of occupations in 2000, but a far narrower one.

Ndlovu-Gatsheni (2008) rightly observed that with the end of colonialism in 1980, Zimbabwe was born as a successor to the Rhodesian colonial state rather than an alternative to it. In most independent African countries, as Crawford Young (2004: 32) noted, "formal sovereignty and the anti-colonial struggle gradually became less salient as defining attributes than the colonial origins of the African state; more crucially the wholesale importation of the routines, practices, and mentalities of the African colonial state into its post-colonial successor became evident."

This section has unpacked the ambiguities and dissonances in the land reform programme from 2000 which contradicted the very nationalist ideology which ZANU-PF purported to be pursuing. The claims of pursuing a nationalist agenda guided by the values of Ubuntu/ Hunhu (freedom, unity, selflessness, equal access to resources, prosperity and development), it has been proved, constituted grandstanding manoeuvres to accumulate wealth under the guise of land reform. The inter-class, intra-class and ethnic cleavages that emerged during struggles over land attest to this.

Gender discrimination in the allocation of land

The Land Reform Programme failed to surmount gender inequalities in the allocation of land. The number of women allocated land under the Fast Track Land Reform Programme was dismally low countrywide. In December 2002, according to government statistics, only 16% of the land redistributed since 2000 went to women (*Irin News*, 4 December 2002). In 2003, women headed about 30% of the households in Zimbabwe. Lamentably, only 18% of the beneficiaries of the new small-scale farms and 12% in the A2 farms were women-headed households (Zimbabwe Government, 2003). In 2010, Ghosh (21 June 2010) lamented that women made up 51% of Zimbabwe's population yet very little was mentioned about them during the land redistribution exercise. She maintains that patriarchal dominance in pre-colonial and colonial Zimbabwean society permeated into the post-colonial era and largely accounts for the side-lining of women in the redistribution of land.

In May 2010, Dominic Pasura, a Research Fellow in the Department of Geography at the University College of London, moaned: "According to the government, land redistribution has been completed and yet most women failed to get access to land" (Ghosh, 21 June 2010: 1). In May 2013, Adelaide Rutendo Mazwarira (7 May 2013: 1) expressed concern that only 20% of the female population in Zimbabwe had got land: "Despite women's central role in farming, their subordinate position mediated by cultural and social expectation often inhibits their ability to own land. In a culture that privileges men, it is no surprise that women's entitlement to land comes through marriage." In 2014, according to Scoones (14 October

153

2014), between 15 and 20% of A1 plots were recorded as having been allocated to women. The pattern was more skewed in favour of men in A2 farms where only 10% were owned by women.

Women's groups in Zimbabwe expressed their concerns over the issue. As early as 2000, the Women and Land Lobby Group, for example, unsuccessfully pressured the government to give more land to women. When asked during a news interview in the same year why few women got land, Joseph Msika, the then Vice-President of Zimbabwe, bluntly retorted: "Because I would have my head cut off if I gave women land...Men would turn against this government" (Ghosh, 21 June 2010: 1). In December 2002, Abby Mgugu, the Director of Women and Land in Zimbabwe, a lobby group, complained:

> We had lobbied the government to allocate us 35% but the figure was eventually reduced and we eventually settled for the 20% ...Women operate in an extremely hostile policy framework and they are treated as secondary citizens in a country where they play a very vital role (Alexander, 2003: 99).

The development agenda in general and the nationalist land project in particular in post-colonial Zimbabwe therefore had an uneven and differential presence (Raftopoulos, 1999). Gender disparities in the allocation of resources illuminate the de-unifying capacity of the land reform programme.

Conclusion

This chapter has contextualised the philosophy of African nationalism in the development discourse in general and Zimbabwe's land question in particular. Since the colonial period, African nationalism as a philosophy in Zimbabwe, as in many other parts of Africa, propagated the values of Ubuntu/ Hunhu/ Vumunhu. Lamentably, Zimbabwe's Land Reform Programme during the post-independence era was largely characterised by dissonances that conspicuously contradicted the philosophy of African nationalism and severely compromised the development agenda.

To a greater extent, the Land Reform Programme was implemented in a selective and exclusive manner that pitted many sections of the Zimbabwean population against each other. This chapter has noted the primacy and centrality of racism in the acquisition and redistribution of land which antagonised many white people, some of whom had played prominent roles during Zimbabwe's struggle for independence. Racial tension ensued thereby depriving the country of the societal unity of purpose that is critical for development.

The land redistribution exercise also shattered the nationalist dream by marginalising farm workers, most of whose former white employers had been evicted. A humanitarian catastrophe set in as most former farm workers lost their jobs and had nowhere to stay. To aggravate their plight, most of them did not benefit from the land redistribution exercise. Former farm workers of foreign origin, some of whom had been born and bred in Zimbabwe, became one of the most vulnerable and disillusioned section of the population. In addition to being left homeless and unemployed, they were ostracised by government officials. Such xenophobic tendencies militated against the values of African nationalism and destabilised the development trajectory.

Zimbabwe's post-independence development project was also derailed by the emergence of societal fissures that emanated from the selective redistribution of land along the lines of political affiliation. This chapter has illuminated how ZANU-PF officials presided over the land reallocation exercise. Consequently, most beneficiaries of the Land Reform Programme were supporters of the ruling ZANU-PF party, a considerable number of who lacked the technical and financial capacity to engage in productive commercial farming. Thus, in addition to polarising the nation along political party lines, the programme was largely a disaster in terms of socio-economic development.

Various struggles over land emerged within the ruling ZANU-PF party and the generality of the population. Class struggles, for example, erupted as the party elite grabbed the most extensive and productive pieces of land ahead of the ordinary supporters. Ethnic strife also ensued as some communities barred incomers from being allocated land where they had traditional entitlement. In addition, gender struggles were quite evident as men benefitted much more than women.

Nationalism, as noted earlier on in this chapter, is universally perceived to be both a doctrine and practice of enhancing the collective interests of a national or broader community above those of individuals, regions or other nations. ZANU-PF's Land Reform Programme from 2000 failed dismally in this regard. Nationalism remained a populist rhetoric that could not be realised in practical terms.

The Land Reform Programme did considerable harm than good to the cause of African nationalism and sustainable development in independent Zimbabwe. In Rhodesia, the colonial administration sought to undermine African nationalism in an effort to monopolise the utilisation of resources. Similarly, in post-colonial Zimbabwe, the African rulers derailed the nationalist cause and instituted selectivity in the allocation of resources such as land thereby compromising the development agenda.

References

Alexander, J. 2003. 'Squatters, veterans and the state in Zimbabwe,' In: A. Hammar, B. Raftopoulos and S. Jensen (Eds.) *Zimbabwe's unfinished business: Rethinking land, state and nation in the context of crisis*, Harare: Weaver Press, pp.83-118.

Alexander, J. and McGregor, J.A. 2001. 'Elections, land and the politics of opposition in Matebeleland,' In: *Journal of Agrarian Change*, Volume 1, Number 4, pp.510-533.

All Africa, 16 November 2014. 'Zimbabwe: War veterans, MPs fight over sugar estate,' available at: www.allafrica.com, Accessed 3 July 2015.

Amnesty International, February 2004. 'Zimbabwe: Power and hunger; violations of the right to food,' available at: www.amnesty.org, Accessed 9 October 2015.

Anderson, B. 1991. *Imagined communities*, London: Verso.

Astrow, A. 1983. *Zimbabwe: A revolution that lost its way?* London: Zed Press.

Ayittey, G.B.N. 1998. *Africa in chaos*, New York: St. Martin's Press.

Baxter, P. 18 December 2011. 'The emergence of the Zimbabwe liberation struggle,' available at: www.peterbaxterafrica.com, Accessed 23 March 2015.

Boas, M. 2009. '"New" nationalism and autochthony: Tales of origin as political cleavage,' in: *Africa Spectrum*, Volume 44, Number 1, pp.19-37.

Bond, P. and Manyanya, M. 2001. *Zimbabwe's plunge: Exhausted nationalism, neoliberalism and the search for social justice*, Asmara: Africa World Press.

Bozhinov, L.S. 5 July 2012. 'The origins of nationalism: Nationalism versus modernism,' available at: www.glipho.com, Accessed 8 July 2015.

Bratton, M. 1978. *From Rhodesia to Zimbabwe: Beyond community development*, Gwelo: Mambo Press.

Business Highbeam, 12 April 2002. 'War veterans clash with defence minister,' available at: www.business.highbeam.com, Accessed 10 September 2015.

Chambati, W. and Moyo, S. 2004. *Impacts of land reform on farm workers and farm labour processes*, Harare: African Institute for Agrarian Studies.

Chibber, K. 26 July 2014. 'Zimbabwe's economy needs stabilising,' available at: www.qz.com, Accessed 3 June 2015.

Chikwanha, T. 4 May 2014. 'Land seizures leave farm workers destitute,' available at: www.dailynews.co.zw, Accessed 2 June 2015.

Chitemba, B. 26 October 2012. 'ZANU-PF bigwigs fight over key citrus farms,' available at: www.theindependent.co.zw, Accessed 12 December 2015.

Chitiyo, T.K. 29 April 2007. 'Colonial legacy of Zimbabwe's land disputes: Reconceptualising Zimbabwe's land and war veterans' debate,' available at: www.africaresource.com, Accessed 6 October 2015.

Clutton Brock, G. 1969. *Rekayi Tangwena: Let Tangwena be*, Gwelo: Mambo Press.

Collier, P. 10 March 2015. 'Good and bad nationalism,' available at: www.socialeurope.eu, Accessed 9 June 2015.

Commercial Farmers Union, 19 October 2001. 'Statement of the Commercial Farmers Union,' available at: www.mweb.co.zw, Accessed 12 July 2015.

Commonwealth Histories, 11 January 2015. 'Commonwealth history project,' available at: www.commonwealthoralhistories.org, Accessed 13 December 2015.

Cross, E. 4 February 2004. 'Fat cats feed on Zimbabwe's misery,' available at: www.eddiecross.africahead.com, Accessed 28 July 2015.

Daily News, 5 December 2000. 'War veterans kick out resettled villagers,' available at: www.dailynews.co.zw, Accessed 4 March 2015.

Dore, D. 2 October 2013. 'Remaking history: Citizenship, power and the recasting of heroes and villains,' available at: www.sokwanele.com, Accessed 22 November 2015.

Duri, F. 2010. *The relentless governance by the sword: Situating Operation Murambatsvina in Zimbabwean history*, Saarbrucken: VDM Verlag.

Duri, F. 2012. 'Negotiating the Zimbabwe-Mozambique border: The pursuit of survival by Mutare's poor, 2000-2008,' in: S. Chiumbu and M. Musemwa (eds.) *Crisis! What crisis? The multiple dimensions of the Zimbabwean crisis*, Cape Town: Human Sciences Research Council, pp.122-142.

Duri, F.P.T. 2014. 'Linguistic innovations for survival: The case of illegal panning and smuggling of diamonds in Chiadzwa, Zimbabwe (2006-2012)' in: *Africana*, Volume 7, Number 1, pp.41-60.

Embassy of Zimbabwe in Stockholm, March 2009. 'Background to land reform in Zimbabwe,' available at: www.zimembassy.se, Accessed 3 May 2015.

Eze, M.O. 2010. *Intellectual history in contemporary South Africa*, London: Palgrave Macmillan.

Faber, P. 19 December 2011. 'Evolving ideas of nationalism,' in: *International Relations and Security Network*, available at: www.isn.ethz.ch, Accessed 13 June 2015.

Financial Gazette, 26 July- 1 August 2007. 'Price blitz devastates Zimbabwe's rural economy,' Harare: Zimbabwe.

Fisher, J.L. 2010. *Pioneers, settlers, and aliens, exiles: The decolonisation of white identity in Zimbabwe*, Canberra: Australian National University Press.

Foner, E. December 1970. 'Exchange of Black nationalism,' in: *The New York Review*, Issue 3.

Gade, C.B.N. 2011. 'The historical development of the written discourses in Ubuntu,' in: *South African Journal of Philosophy*, Volume 30, Number 3, pp.303-329.

Gade, C.B.N. 2012. 'What is Ubuntu? Different interpretations among South Africans of African descent,' in: *South African Journal of Philosophy*, Volume 31, Number 3, pp.484-503.

Gellner, E. 2006. *Nations and nationalism*, Oxford: Blackwell Publishing.

Ghosh, T. 21 June 2010. 'Zimbabwean women lose out in land reform,' available at: www.panos.org.uk, Accessed 10 May 2015.

Goulding, K. and Mutopo, P. 21 August 2012. 'Revisiting the role of women in Zimbabwe's agrarian structure in the aftermath of the Fast Track land reform programme,' available at: www.unrisdo.org, Accessed 6 March 2015.

Graham, E. and Newham, J. 1998. *Penguin dictionary of international relations*, London: Penguin.

Graham, J. 2006. 'Writing the land: Representations of the land and nationalism in Anglophone literature from South Africa and Zimbabwe, 1969-2002,' PhD thesis, Department of English, University of Warwick.

Hammar, A. and Raftopoulos, B. 2003. 'Zimbabwe's unfinished business: Rethinking land, state and nation,' in: A. Hammar, B. Raftopoulos and S. Jensen (eds.) *Zimbabwe's unfinished business: Rethinking land, state and nation in the context of crisis*, Harare: Weaver Press, pp.1-47.

Hauss, C. 2003. 'Nationalism: Beyond intractability,' in: G. Burgess and H. Burgess (eds.) *Conflict information consortium*, Boulder: University of Colorado.

Haw, R.C. 1965. *Land Apportionment Act in Rhodesia*, Information Paper Number 1, Salisbury: Rhodesia Information Service.

159

Hill, G. 2003. *The battle for Zimbabwe: The final countdown*, Cape Town: Zebra Press.

Hobsbawm, E. 1992. *Nations and nationalism since 1780: Programme, myth and reality*, Cambridge: Cambridge University Press.

Hobsbawm, E. and Ranger, T.O. (eds.) 1983. *The invention of tradition*, Cambridge: Cambridge University Press.

Human Rights Watch, March 2002. 'Fast Track Land Reform in Zimbabwe,' available at: www.hrw.org, Accessed 16 July 2015.

Irin News, 4 December 2002. 'Zimbabwe: Focus on women's lack of access to land,' available at: www.irinnews.org/report, Accessed 10 April 2015.

Kahiya, V. and Mukaro, A. 22 July 2005. 'Kondozi farm seized in latest farm raid,' available at: www.theindependent.co.zw, Accessed 9 June 2015.

Kecmanovic, D. 1996. 'What is nationalism?' in: *The mass psychology of ethno-nationalism*, Sydney: Springer, pp.15-78.

Kwaramba, F. 11 February 2013. 'Chiefs, war veterans clash over land,' available at: www.dailynews.co.zw, Accessed 4 April 2015.

Mamdani, M. 2008. 'Lessons from Zimbabwe,' in: *London Review of Books*, Volume 31, Number 23, pp.17-21.

Mandaza, I. 1986. 'Introduction,' in: I. Mandaza (ed.) *Zimbabwe: The political economy of transition, 1980-1986*, Dakar: CODESRIA.

Mapepa, L. 9 January 2015. 'Chinotimba's farm takeover resisted by villagers,' available at: www.harare24.com/index, Accessed 12 October 2015.

Maponga, G. 14 March 2015. 'Mahofa, Mzembi clash,' in: *Herald*, Harare: Zimbabwe.

Marongwe, N. 2003. 'Farm occupations and occupiers in the new politics of land in Zimbabwe.' in: A. Hammar, B. Raftopoulos and S. Jensen (eds.) *Zimbabwe's unfinished business: Rethinking land, state and nation in the context of crisis*, Harare: Weaver Press, pp.155-190.

Masunungure, E. 2004. 'Travails of opposition politics in Zimbabwe since independence,' in: D. Harold-Barry (ed.) *Zimbabwe: The past is the future: Rethinking land, state and nation in the context of crisis*, Harare: Weaver Press, pp.147-192.

Mazwarira, A.R. 7 May 2013. 'Remembering women in Zimbabwe's land reform programme,' available at: www.justassociates.org/en, Accessed 10 June 2015.

Mbofana, W. 16 November 2007. 'South Africa guided by self-interest on Zimbabwe,' in: *Zimbabwe Independent*, Harare: Zimbabwe.

Melber, H. 2002. 'From liberation movements to governments: On political culture in Southern Africa,' in: *African Sociological Review*, Volume 6, Number 1, pp.1-19.

Meldrum, A. 4 February 2004. 'Mugabe seizes largest sugar producer,' available at: www.theage.com.au, Accessed 14 May 2015.

Meredith, M. 2002. *Mugabe: Power and plunder in Zimbabwe*, New York: Public Affairs.

Metcalf, A. 2003. 'Nationalism and the nation state,' available at: www.regentsprep.org, Accessed 4 February 2015.

Moyo, S. September 2000. 'The interaction of market and compulsory land acquisition processes with social action in Zimbabwe's land reform,' Paper presented at SAPES Trust annual colloquium, Harare.

Moyo, S. 2001. 'The land occupations movement and democratisation in Zimbabwe: Contradictions of neoliberalism,' In: *Millennium Journal of International Studies*, Volume 30, Number 2, pp.311-330.

Moyo, S. and Yeros, P. 2007. 'The radicalised state: Zimbabwe's interrupted revolution,' in: *Review of African Political Economy*, Volume III, pp.103-121.

Mugabe, R. 2001. *Inside the Third Chimurenga*, Harare: Ministry of Information and Publicity.

Mupfuvi, B.M. 2014. 'Land to the people: Peasants and nationalism in the development of land ownership in Zimbabwe from pre-colonialism to the unilateral declaration of independence (UDI) period,' *PhD thesis*, University of Salford.

Murray, D.J. 1977. *The governmental system in Southern Rhodesia*, London: Heinemann.

Muzondidya, J. 2010. 'The Zimbabwean crisis and the unresolved conundrum of race in the post-colonial period,' in: *Journal of Developing Societies*, Volume 26, Number 1, pp.5-38.

Ncube, X. 29 May 2015. 'First family deserves more land,' in: *Newsday*, Harare: Zimbabwe.

Ndlovu-Gatsheni, S.J. 2008. 'Reaping the bitter fruits of Stalinist tendencies in Zimbabwe,' in: *Association of Concerned African Scholars Review, Special issue on the Zimbabwe crisis*, Bulletin 79.

Ntungakwa, J. 21 September 2014. 'Feature: Zimbabwean nationalism after the split of 1963,' in: *Sunday Mail*, Harare: Zimbabwe.

O'Meara, P. 1975. *Racial conflict or coexistence?* London: Cornell University Press.

Palmer, R. 1977. *Land and racial domination in Rhodesia*, London: Heinemann.

Phiri, G. 21 April 2006. 'Chefs ignore order to give up extra farms,' available at: www.theindependent.co.zw, Accessed 10 June 2015.

Pilossof, R. 1 December 2010. 'The Commercial Farmers Union of Zimbabwe and its politics after *Jambanja*,' available at: www.solidaritypeacetrust.org, Accessed 18 September 2015.

Poverty Reduction Forum Trust, 2013. 'Study of poverty in Manicaland: The case of Mutare rural,' Research paper, Harare: Poverty Reduction Forum Trust.

Raftopoulos, B. 1999. 'Problematising nationalism in Zimbabwe: A historiographical review,' in: *Zambezia*, Volume XXVI, Number ii, pp.115-134.

Raftopoulos, B. 2003. 'The state in crisis: Authoritarian nationalism, selective citizenship and distortions of democracy in Zimbabwe,' in: A. Hammar, B. Raftopoulos and S. Jensen (eds.) *Zimbabwe's unfinished business: Rethinking land, state and nation in the context of crisis*, Harare: Weaver Press, pp.217-241.

Raftopoulos, B. 2006. 'The Zimbabwean crisis and the challenge from the Left,' in: *Journal of Southern African Studies*, Volume 32, Number 2, pp.203-219.

Ranger, T.O. 1985. *Peasant consciousness and guerrilla warfare in Zimbabwe*, Oxford: James Currey.

Rolin, H. 1978. *Rolin's Rhodesia*, Bulawayo: Books of Rhodesia.

Rothi, D. 2005. 'National attachment and patriotism in a European nation: A British study,' in: *Political Psychology*, Volume 26, pp.135-155.

Rutherford, B. 2003. 'Belonging to the farm(er): Farm workers, farmers and the shifting politics of citizenship,' in: A. Hammar, B. Raftopoulos and S. Jensen (eds.) *Zimbabwe's unfinished business: Rethinking land, state and nation in the context of crisis*, Harare: Weaver Press, pp.191-216.

Ruwende, I. 12 August 2012. 'Dendera gala in Chinhoyi,' available at: www.herald.co.zw, Accessed 9 August 2015.

Sachikonye, L.M. May 2002. 'From "growth with equity" to "fast track" land reform: The discourse on Zimbabwe's land question,' Paper presented at the conference on peasants, liberation and socialism,' Leeds: Leeds University.

Sachikonye, L. 2003. 'The situation of commercial farm workers after land reform in Zimbabwe,' *Report prepared for the Farm Community Trust of Zimbabwe*, Farm Community Trust of Zimbabwe; Harare.

Samkange, S. and Samkange, T.M. 1980. *Hunhuism or Ubuntuism? A Zimbabwe indigenous political philosophy*, Salisbury: Graham Publishing.

Scarnecchea, T. 2006. 'The Fascist cycle in Zimbabwe, 2000-2005,' In: *Journal of Southern African Studies*, Volume 32, Number 2, pp.221-237.

Scoones, I. 14 October 2014. 'Gender relations and land reform in Zimbabwe,' available at: www.chronicle.co.zw, Accessed 12 September 2015.

Scoones, I. Marongwe, N. Mavedzenge, B. Mahenehene, J. Marimbarimba F. and Sukume, C. 2010. *Zimbabwe land reform programme: Myths and realities*, Woodbridge: James Currey.

Sithole, Z. 28 March 2012. 'Inflation, land seizures impoverish whites,' available at: www.thezimbabwean.co/news, Accessed 22 May 2015.

Smith, A.D. 1971. *Theory of nationalism*, London: Duckworth and Company Limited.

Smith, D. 7 February 2006. 'Nationalism,' available at: www.thecanadianencyclopaedia.ca.en, Accessed 12 June 2015.

Stoneman, C. 2002. 'Zimbabwe land policy and the land reform programme,' in: T.A.S. Bowyer-Bower and C. Stoneman (eds.) *Land reform in Zimbabwe: Constraints and prospects*, Aldershot: Ashgate.

Swanson, D.M. 2015. 'Frames of Ubuntu: (Re) framing an ethical education,' in H. Smits and R. Naqvi (eds.) *Framing peace: Thinking about and enacting curriculum as 'radical hope'*, New York: Peter Lang, pp.49-63.

Tukutuku, R. 17 October 2012. 'Not all mourn for Mudenge,' available at: www.thezimbabwean.co.uk, Accessed 10 July 2015.

Voice of America, 31 December 2009. 'Zimbabwe military deploys to remove country's remaining white farmers,' available at: www.voazimbabwe.com, Accessed 10 June 2015.

Wasosa, M. 28 January 2005. 'ZDI admits involvement in Charleswood seizure,' available at: www.theindependent.co.zw, Accessed 12 May 2015.

Watson, F. 1 March 2003. 'Understanding the food crisis in Zimbabwe,' available at: www.ennonline.net/fex, Accessed 3 April 2015.

Weitzer, R. 1990. *Transforming settler states: Communal conflict and internal security in Northern Ireland and Zimbabwe*, Berkeley: University of California Press.

Worby, E. 2003. 'The end of modernity in Zimbabwe? Passages from development to sovereignty,' in: A. Hammar, B. Raftopoulos and S. Jensen (eds.) *Zimbabwe's unfinished business: Rethinking land, state and nation in the context of crisis*, Harare: Weaver Press, pp.49-81.

Young, C. 2004. 'The end of the post-colonial state in Africa? Reflections on African post-colonial dynamics,' in: *African Affairs*, Volume 103, pp.23-49.

Zenker, O. 2011. 'Autochthony, ethnicity, indigeneity and nationalism: Time-honouring and state-oriented modes of rooting individual- territory- group triads in a globalizing world,' In: *Critique of Anthropology*, Volume 31, Number 1, pp.63-81.

Zimbabwe Government, 2003. 'Presidential land review committee: Report on the implementation of the Fast Track land reform programme,' Harare: Government Printer.

Zimbabwe Human Rights NGO Forum, 2010. *The land reform and property rights in Zimbabwe*, Volume 1, Zimbabwe Human Rights NGO Forum: Harare.

Zimbabwe Independent, 9 January 2004. 'Four years on, land reform still marred by chaos,' Harare: Zimbabwe.

Zimbabwe Independent, 20 March 2006. 'Sugar production hits new lows,' available at: www.theindependent.co.zw, Accessed 12 July 2015.

Zimbabwe Online Press, 21 January 2006. 'Zimbabwe government minister, war veterans clash over farm,' available at: www.reliefweb.in/report/zimbabwe, Accessed 2 July 2015.

Zimbabwe Online Press, 16 July 2012. 'Zimbabwe's Mugabe and cronies: Main beneficiaries of land reform,' available at: www.africagreed.blogspot.com, Accessed 4 July 2015.

Zimbabwean, 23 January 2013. 'Minister, war veterans, fight over farm,' available at: www.thezimbabwean.co.zw/news, Accessed 12 February 2015.

Zvomuya, P. 23 May 2008. 'Africans have never liked one another,' available at: www.mg.co.za/article, Accessed 10 July 2015.

Chapter Six

Indigenous Religion and Security Regimens in Africa: A Study of the Yoruba Vigilante Groups in Southwest Nigeria

Ogunbiyi Olatunde Oyewole

Introduction

Across Africa today, the security challenges bedevilling the continent are various and flekked. No part of the African land space escapes these threats to lives and property. Not so long ago, xenophobic challenges engulfed parts of South Africa and Zambia, while the war in Somalia and neighbouring areas is having untold hardship on the people of the horn of Africa. Religious and political crises are negatively impacting the lives of the people in Eritrea, Sudan of Northern Nigeria and adjourning nations of Cameroon, Chad Republic and the Niger Republic. Political upheavals in various countries of Africa are making a mockery of the ever increasing refugee camps spread across the landscape of the African. Socio-economic problems of inflation, joblessness and currency devaluation impinge upon the security challenge facing many governments of the nations of Africa. In addition to this plethora of challenges creating stress on the security to lives and property, are the various environmental challenges experienced in parts of Africa. This chapter will be incomplete if is just a few of the security challenges that the leaders of the African continent have to grapple with.

Nigeria is not an exception when it comes to the myriads of problems experienced in various parts of Africa. As a matter of fact, this nation has a peculiar share of the challenges the continent is confronted with. A cursory observation of media coverage on Nigeria has exposed issues that are related to crimes of a high intensity and in an uncommon dimension. The probing of public officers, for example, has revealed the quantum of financial improprieties that past regimes have plunged the nation into. Aside from this, ethnic rivalry and politically motivated killings are on the increase. The case of the Fulani cattle rustlers sacking villages across Nigeria is another dimension of the crimes in the score sheet of security issues facing the nation. On the socio-religious plane, the cacophony of crimes engendered across the nation abhors. A few of the crimes perpetrated include ritual killings, kidnappings, armed robbery, sexual slavery springing across the southwest, east and south east geopolitical regions. The case of Boko Haram in the North eastern Nigeria is no longer news and the egregious handlings of the kidnapped Chibok girls have since elicited worldwide attention.

What eventually coalesced into the Nigerian Police Force has been with the people before the formation of the territorial integrity called Nigeria. This force is saddled with the responsibilities of curbing internal security challenges facing the people of the nation. However, evidence in the mass media is indicating that they are inept in their attempts at curbing these crimes. The frequency and rapidity of crimes indicate that the Police Force though trying is incapable of addressing these security challenges. There is no unanimity among scholars, stakeholders and even community leaders about the effectiveness of the Nigerian Police's ability to address crime (see for example, Ikuteyiyo and Rotimi, 2010: Samuel, 2012; Nimbe and Bayo, 2011).Evidence abound that many apprehended criminals were often released after the police are bribed. These criminals not only go back to commit the crimes for which they were arrested for, but also boast of having the police on their payroll. Many of them are seen on the streets and inter-state routes collecting bribes from the motorists on the road without properly checking those who have given them tips. Being that as it were, the Police Force, despite their low level of financial, inadequate and improperly maintained vehicles, evidence abound to show that they still, to some extent, help to maintain law and order within the society.

The apparent reluctance of the Police Force to arrest the steady rise of crime across the geopolitical spaces of Nigeria have culminated into the search for an alternative crime control agencies that will be devoid of corruption, understand the terrain in which criminals operate and be within the ambit of the legal system operational in Nigeria. It is along this line that the vigilante groups of Yoruba land merits discussion. This chapter focuses on the use of indigenous vigilante in Africa, with particular reference to the Yoruba people of South-west Nigeria. This is considered in the light of the people's perception of the traditional religion of the Yoruba people. Three categories of vigilante groups were identified namely, the state-organised, community-organised, and private employed vigilante personnel. The chapter examines the prevailing values, beliefs, practices and the capability of the vigilante groups in providing community security. Field trips were conducted across Yoruba land regarding the activities and efficiency of these groups. For the purpose of this chapter, Yoruba land was divided into three zones. Vigilante groups were found to play remarkable roles in neighbourhood crime control as they enjoy state support, though sometimes acting in excess of the law. Result showed that indigenous resources are efficacious, to a large extent, in provision of security, but many of the vigilante groups need serious overhauling and sponsorship to effectively address the security challenges plaguing Africa.

Theoretical and Conceptual Framework

Vigilantism has been studied by several scholars over the past thirty years. Fourchard (2008) agrees to this when he opines that there is a new interest on vigilantism in literatures emanating from the African continent. In spite of this however, scholars are not unanimous about the meaning of the word. Vigilantism is a term that is difficult to define. Some definitions are positive while others are negative. The *Black Law Dictionary* (2004) for example defines vigilante as "a person who seeks to avenge a crime by taking the law into his or her own hands." This functional definition is hazy calling whoever takes revenge as a vigilante. *Random House Dictionary* further defines vigilante as action "done violently and summarily, without recourse to lawful procedures: vigilante justice." Again this definition is one that places premium on the illegality of the word. As a matter of fact, several synonyms of the word like 'informal Policing', ' everyday policing' have been arising in a bid to explain the word. Accordingly, Les Johnson (1996) is one of the earliest scholars to define the term vigilante. In his attempt at defining vigilantism, he came up with the constituents of vigilantism. These include:

i). It involves planning and premeditation by those engaging in it;

ii). Its participants are private citizens whose engagement is voluntary;

iii). It is a form of 'autonomous citizenship' and, as such constitutes a social movement;

iv). It uses or threatens the use of force;

v). It arises when an established order is under threat from the transgression, the potential transgression, or the imputed transgression of institutionalized norms;

vi). It aims to control crime and other social infractions by offering assurances (or 'guarantees') of security to participants and others (Johnston 1996: 220).

Johnston's submission above conceptualizes vigilantism as a reactive 'social movement'. Martin opines that this social movement places vigilantism in the context of its host community and suggests at least an undercurrent of grassroots appeal, participation or public support towards vigilante activity. (Martin 2012). Johnston's perception further broadens the scope of vigilante activities to cover not only offenders but also those who deviate from societal norms. This position is supported by other scholars commenting on similar issues in other climes Casey (2008: 94), Chavez (2008: 32) and Knox and Monaghan (2002).

An examination of the activities of the vigilante over the decades in Nigeria and their counterparts all over the world, it is apparent that they share some qualities which include the fact that the vigilantes are not secret societies; rather they are recognized by the community in which they serve. They oftentimes operate through the instrumentality of violence as they combine the functions of crime punishment and prevention. Their activities generate fear which is usually occasioned by the retributive justice they mete out to victims summarily.

Several theories have emerged over the years and from several scholars on the study of vigilantism. These theories are connected to crime and its resolution within the community. One theory that is will be used in this work is the theory of the Philosophy of Punishment propounded by Anthony Duff. Anthony Duff has made substantial contributions in philosophizing the idea of crime. In many of his contributions, Duff has devoted himself to such inquiries as punishment in so far as it relates to communication, the idea justification, what constitutes a crime or an attempt to commit a crime, when is an act a crime as opposed to an innocent act. Then he considers the philosophical questions of which a criminal is: 'what kind of punishment should be meted out on the offender and by who?' What endears Duff's theory to this work is the fact that it encapsulates the three important areas of focus of this work. These include the police force, the vigilante and the community, which is the nexus where the earlier two operate. In addition, Duff's effort is contemporaneous work that is apposite for the present times.

African Indigenous Religion (Yoruba Religious Beliefs) and Security Maintenance Strategy

In the psychology of the Yoruba of Southwest Nigeria, there is no dichotomy between religion and life as it is seen in western thoughts. Mbiti (1969: 262) encapsulates this when he said:

> ...religion, more than anything else, which colours their understanding of the universe and their empirical participation in that universe, making life a profoundly religious phenomenon. To be is to be religious in a religious universe. That is the philosophical understanding behind African myths, customs, traditions, beliefs, morals, actions and social relationships.

Idowu, who was also a Yoruba and scholar in African Religion, agrees with Mbiti when he concurs that in everything the Yoruba is religious. By extension they do not differentiate between the physical and the spiritual. They always have a religious explanation to everything that they do or all that is happening to them, both within and outside their communities. On the apex of the religious pedestal of the Yoruba is Olodumare who is the Creator and sustainer of the universe. He is over and above all the divinities that are created to serve in his theocratic governance of the world. The objective phenomenon of Yoruba religious belief is the divinities. These divinities are many numbering over a thousand but are in three categories. The primordial category consisting of the divinities that emanated from the Supreme Being. Closely following these are the deified ancestors. These were heroes who became deified at death. Some examples of this second category are Sango, the fourth Alafin of Oyo, Moremi and Ayelala to mention only a few. In the last category of the divinities are the personified spirits. These ones inhabit natural phenomena like rivers, trees or mountains. Aside from the divinities, the ancestor veneration among the Yoruba is active. The notion that the dead are actually still living gave birth the idea of life after death. These dead human beings are believed to still live within the compound and are interested in the affairs of family members. Yearly, they are venerated during festivals in order to allow for their protection and provision. Closely following the ancestors are the spirits who are believed to be powerful in mysterious powers. These spirits are believed to live in the bush are of different types. There are the ones called *iwin* who though invincible, live in the surrounding. Many of these creatures are believed to have several mysterious powers that those who know them can access these powers. Other spiritual creatures include abiku, emere and *akudaiya*. Worthy of mention here is the people's belief in mysterious powers. The Yoruba people hold that magic and medicines can be efficacious in the war against crime.

African Religion (Yoruba Traditional Beliefs) and Crime Control in Southwestern Nigeria

Commenting on the acceptability of the vigilante in Southwest Nigeria, Owumi and Ajayi (2013) insist that:

One of the key features of indigenous law enforcement is its wide acceptance by the citizens. Members of a society where traditional policing exists generally accept and participate in their indigenous system. In short, the community members own the indigenous system. Being part owners of the system, it is very unlikely that any significant part of the population will be excluded from the system or its mode of operation.

Adherents of African Religion (Yoruba extraction) are very strong believers in the efficacy of their magic and medicine. The appeal of the local vigilante groups is based on the people's confidence in the efficacy of their charms and the loss of confidence they have in the police force. The fear of the vigilantes was based on the belief that they had at their disposal magical forms of detection and protection, which would protect the innocent, a sentiment shared by other Nigerian communities (Harnisehfeger, 2003; Gore and Prattern, 2003; Omololu, 2003).

Divinities, Spirits and Security Challenges in South west Nigeria

The divinities are of three categories. There are the primordial divinities; those who emanated from Olodumare such as Obatala, Esu, Ogun and others. These have specialized responsibility in the smooth running of the universe. In the second category are the deified ancestors. In this category are such figures like Sango, Moremi, Ayelala while the third category encompass spirits inhabiting rocks, rivers, and trees. They are referred to as personification of natural phenomena. These divinities have roles to play in the security of Yoruba land. Each of these divinities is recipient of sacrifices not only for provisions but also for protection. When a particular community is plagued by the menace of crime, sacrifices are made and the divinities ensure that the culprits are caught. The Yoruba believe that one of the ways by which Sango protects his people is by hurling *edunara* (thunder stone) on evil people. These who are victims of this kind of punishment are not buried in the towns but are taken to the evil bush for burial. All their property are confiscated by the priests. Ayelala is a divinity that is given prominence among the Ilaje people, consulted all over Yoruba land. She is known to be a revealer of evil people, especially those who steal. When consulted, she is reputed to mention who the thief is and where the property stolen is hidden. It is worthy of addition here that there are divinities of justice in the religious consciousness of the Yoruba people. Ogun and Sango are prominent gods that can be involved to punish offenders and to take oath when a controversial issue has to be settled (Okunola and Ojo 2012: 1057-1076). However, apart from these deities, other deities can also be invoked to settle controversial matters among the Yoruba, through oath taking. One of these deities is Aje-Olokun which is acclaimed to be the deity of the ocean (Ojo 2014: 115-128). With AjeOlokun, swearing is done either by biting the smallest finger and uttering a curse or a coin is biting after swearing to an oath or denying an accusation. What the Yoruba do is to make a person swear and when he or she does this, the repercussions of suffering and dying an unnatural death follow if the person has told a lie. What evils are pronounced will automatically come upon the culprit.

Closely following the above is the spirits forces in the ontology of the Yoruba. These forces are numerous and pervade the Yoruba worldview. They are of different shapes and number. Some have nothing to do with security while others either support criminality or fight crimes within the community. In this category are Iwin. These spirit figures are known to have been contacted by powerful priests who have the formula to reach them. They in turn help by giving these priests, herbs and roots that can be used either to prevent criminals from operating in the community or to catch them when they are on their nefarious activities.

Ifa Priests and Fight against Crime

One very common area where the traditional priests especially the Ifa Priests fight crime is in the area of oracular consultation. Through divination, many things are revealed. The past is revealed as it influences the present and even prophecies for the future as given. When the priests are consulted, they are able to discover destinies that are bad and make correction based on the people's worldview.

174

Orunmila is believed to be *eleri-ipin* (witness to choice) *Obirikitiaji pa ojuiku da* (the Great one who changes the date of death). By this, the Yoruba believe that the evil destinies of a person can be changed by the divinity that was present when the person was making the choice. As herbalists, these men also assist in the preparation of charms that we deter criminals from entering the community.

Place of magic and medicine

Atolagbe (2011: 57-62) posits that Yoruba magic and medicine is predicated on a tripod of Oogun (charm as produced by the indigenous Pharmacist), the Babalawo (indigenous religious priest) and the Ifa oracle. While the *Onisegun* (Pharmacist) goes around getting the ingredients for the homoeopathic and contagious medicinal and magical products, he or she is guided by the Priest who in turn is guided by the oracular pronouncements concerning the person or community in need of a particular charm. He goes further to identify sixteen groups of charms that the Yoruba employ to defend themselves or insulate their property from those who wish to vandalize them. These include:

Prophecy laden or prophetic words (Àfòse or MápohuIdà), disarming or de-fetishing devices (Gbètugbètu), metal or iron/steel dispossession devices (Agbunrin), forgetfulness (Afòra), procrastinating devices (Etì), muscle stiffening devices (Àgbéró), disappearing devices (Àféèrî), the falling game (Subúsiré), debilitating devices (Àlùro or àlùwó), de-envisioning devices (Ìsújú), cut resistors (Òkígbé), and bullet proof devices (Ayeta), etc. a good number of which is often accompanied by incantations (Ofò or Ìgèdè).

It is noteworthy to say that these charms are used in the past but they have resurfaced when the modern policing system have not been able to safe communities from marauders who not only cart away properties but also kidnap whoever they wish. Those kidnapped are either released on the payment of a ransom or are killed by ritualists. The efficaciousness of the product is not in doubt as members of the OPC; politicians use them during electioneering campaigns. Those who possess these charms are often employed as guards by private organizations of communities. Ilorin for example, indigenes of a Sao town beside Sobi Military Cantonment on the way to Malete are believed to possess these charms. As a result of which many of them are employed as guards.

Ancestors and Crime Control in Yoruba land

The ancestors are venerated all over Yoruba land of South west, Nigeria. People usually take care to cherish their ancestors in order to be protected, to thank or to be forgiven. They are the living dead who still live among the people. It is believed that when they are venerated, the protections of the living family members are assured. These ancestors according to the Yoruba see beyond the living and are very interested in the affairs of the people. Consequently, they are venerated in annual festivals during which they return to bless their people. They not only bless people with children, land and prosperity, they are also believed to be protectors of the family land, homestead and also settle squabbles. By these they are able to shield their people from criminal acts. Besides, they correct family members thereby preventing them from destroying the family name.

Covenant Keeping Among Yoruba People

Covenants are agreement between two parties; usually of there are two types of covenants (Ogunleye 2013: 81-85). The first one is the covenant between equal partners and the second one is the covenant between unequal partners. The first one usually has to do with agreements either between relatives, about business, building houses or taking care of a farmland. Whoever violates this covenant will have the wrath of the gods to contend with. The Yoruba have a popular saying that says: "*eniba dale, abale lo*; whoever violates the covenant will have to die".

The other covenant, the one between two unequal partners is the one that subsists between man and the supernatural beings (divinities, spirits and ancestors). The supernatural beings are bound to provide security for the community they are in contract with in so far as the community provides the objects of sacrifice. In the light of this, when a community enters into an agreement with these spirit beings, they

176

will ensure that no evil befall that community. Usually, these communities are protected by them, often times warn them of impending danger and way be which these can be averted.

Vigilante Groups in Southwest Nigeria: A Historical Perspective

What eventually became the Vigilante Group of Nigeria is a phenomenon that goes far before the colonial era. Age group bodies in various communities across the geopolitical regions of what later became Nigeria were saddled with the responsibilities of providing securities for their various communities. Apart from these age groups there are various volunteers who traditionally existed that take care of the security challenges of the communities. In times of wars, loss of people in the community, saving drowning children from the rivers, attacking marauding beasts and driving nuisance from their environs, these community volunteers are relied upon to curb these crimes within the community. Whenever criminals are apprehended, these volunteers bring them to the councils for appropriate sanctions. Gradually, the challenges confronting the communities eventually allowed a metamorphosis of these age group and volunteers to what is now known as vigilantes groups. By the times of the military era the concepts have developed to the level of being seen as additions to the law enforcement agents. The reason for this is because the police force is understaffed, underequipped, misunderstood and above all do not have an understanding of the environment like the members of the communities. The dwindling fortunes of these groups soon brought positive dividends to the volunteer. The vigilante groups were included among the soldiers and policemen as anti-crime squad and they were armed. These squads were well known for their cruelty and extra-judicial killing of suspected criminals. The Vigilante Group of Nigeria exists with offices in all the state of the federation; they have a running battle with the Nigeria Police Force.

The position of the federal government towards armed vigilante groups remains unclear, since they are often regarded as an internal matter of the states and not as a federal issue. The police and the

Armed Forces (both under the responsibility of the federal government) have been accused of inaction and neglecting to investigate, and when required, arrest and prosecute members of armed vigilante groups. In February 2001, the Inspector General of the Nigeria Police Force, declared illegal the detention of suspected offenders by vigilance groups, and warned that individuals or groups who flouted the order would be prosecuted. In fact, although the police have arrested several members of vigilante armed- groups, the suspects are often released after a few months through the intervention of authorities of the state and their charges dropped before going through trial.

A few major regional vigilante groups have emerged over the years. Among the Yoruba there are is the Oodua People's Congress which was founded in 1994. There have been two factions of the group, the one that is headed by Fredrick Fasheun and Gani Adams. The faction of Gani Adams appears to be the most popular. Theirs is an organization that is devoted to stopping perceived political marginalization of the Yoruba ethnic group. Aside from this, members also perform other series of other security works that keep crime rate at a low ebb. On several occasions the group has been banned by government but they are irrepressible. Of late, the group has been most involved in politics. In the election of 2014, the group has solidly stood behind the ruling party (PDP) who lost the election to the ruling party (APC).

There exist numerous other vigilante groups that have emerged over the years among the Yoruba whose activities have assisted in reducing community crimes to appreciable level. These groups do not have the popularity enjoyed by the OPC nor the patronage and recognition of the government; nevertheless they exist and complement one another in the crime reduction of the geopolitical zone. These vigilante groups are usually State or community based vigilante outfits.

Data collection used in this work was both quantitative and qualitative. These methods of data collection were chosen so as to allow a thorough analysis of the subject matter. Field trips were conducted across Southwest Nigeria regarding the performance of these groups. For the purpose of this research, Southwest Nigeria was divided into three zones. Cross section survey design was used to generate quantitative data from 3,321 community members of 18 years and above, while in-depth interviews were conducted to stimulate qualitative data. On completion of the field work, closed focus-group discussions were held with some stakeholders, various representatives, and academics to inform the direction of the chapter's objectives. The data were analysed by zonal summaries, simple percentages and content analysis. The choice of this method was in consonance with the functional and control theories on which the study is hinged.

The study took place in the three zones across Nigeria. This first zone is the Southwestern Nigeria, covering the Lagos and Ogunstates; the second zone is Oyo and Osun states while the third zone covers Ekiti and Ondo states. It must be put on record here that the division is merely for the ease of research and that there are several other groups sub-summed in these three sub-divisions. A total of 3,500 community members of 18 years and above responded to the questionnaires but out of this number only 3,321 responded. Out of this number, 1113 were female equivalence of 36.9 %, while 2208 were male respondents. Most of the female respondents were relatives of victims of vigilante brutality, police women and market women. The male respondents include members of the vigilante groups across the zones, community leaders, employers of vigilante members, and members of the various communities across Nigeria. 18 research assistants were used to administer questionnaires and interviews at six per zone.

Criminal activities in Southwest Nigeria have gone from bad to worse over the years. In times past, the crimes that the traditional vigilante groups of different communities have to grapple with is petty stealing, witchcraft, wizardry and the like. Today however, the vigilante groups in the community have to be responsive to modern dynamisms of criminality across the three zones covered by this chapter. While these crimes still persist, it is worth mentioning that several other similar criminal attempts are on the increase. Today, several criminal hideouts are discovered. A case in point is the Soka House of Horror discovered in the precincts of Ibadan, where ritual killers carry out their nefarious activities. Reports of missing persons are awash in the mass media and the movie makers are cashing in on the opportunity to present movies to highlight the danger of the moment.

Research has shown that the Vigilante Groups of different categories have laboured assiduously to maintain the crime rate at a very low level. The consensus is that the vigilantes have actually reduced the scale of crimes in Nigeria. Most communities across the cities, towns and villages now have vigilantes patrolling the communities at night. Their whistle blowing at night, though disturbing, have come to raise the people's confidence and strike terror to the harbingers of crime among the Yoruba of South West Nigeria. However, in the execution of their objectives they have oftentimes embarked upon extra-judicial killings (Bakare 2014: 69-88). When thieves are caught, many are not often reported to the police who are licensed to reduce crime rates. Rather the some of the vigilantes use African indigenous charm prepared belts to whip these thieves who are left to go and die outside the community. These revelations are gotten from the focus interviews conducted after the field work.

Concerning the relationship between the Vigilante groups, the Police Force and the public, respondents have submitted that the relationship between the police and that of the vigilante is not so cordial. On the surface, there is cordiality. The vigilantes are seen manning the highways, the communities and industries working in conjunction and complimenting the effort of the Police. Though the public is given the impression that the police welcome the vigilante groups, they actually assume that they have come to usurp their responsibilities. When it became apparent that the vigilante and the community did not accept the corrupt tendencies of the Police Force the relationship became strained and really got bad when the vigilantes accuse them of releasing those in their custody after receive bribes. Conversely, the Force also accuses the Vigilante Groups of carrying out extra-judicial killing. In view of the inability of the Police to curb crime in the rural and urban communities, it is the general consensus of the people that the vigilante groups are a necessary intervention to stem the depth of the criminal activities in the community.

Recommendations

Based on the findings above, the researcher is making these some recommendations. Firstly, the Nigerian Police Force and the Civil Defence Corps of Nigeria need urgent overhauling in order to be relevant to modern standards. The Civil Defence Corps was established in response to the apparent ineptitude of the police force to arrest the growing trend in security. Since its establishment, evidence abound to show that the Civil Defence corps have contributed immensely to the safety of Nigerians but the increase in crime shows that the combination of the police force and the civil defence is weak in curbing security challenges. It is recommended that this twin policing should be sufficiently empowered with modern weapons and trained in the art of safety consciousness. Aside from this, steps must be urgently taken to rid the force of corrupt officer who pervert justice and put the name of the force in disrepute. The forces should be adequately funded so that they are able to recruit more staff especially to be posted to the rural places and crime endemic areas. Adequate sanctions are to be enacted to errant officers as deterrent to others.

Secondly, the vigilante groups of Southwest Nigeria should be given adequate recognition by state governments and should be well funded. It is clear that crime control cannot be left in the hands of the police force alone. The vigilantes are members of the community who know where the criminals hide and are also aware of their hideouts. Incidences of armed robbery on the highway are one issue that the vigilantes have been able to curb better than the police force. They should be trained, be equipped with utility vehicles, arms and ammunition to be able to accost criminals.

Thirdly and closely following the above is the need to enact laws that will curb the excess of the vigilante. Many of them in a bid to prove their effectiveness often commit extra-judicial killings. Oftentimes, family members of some of their victims often complain of the innocence of their family members that have been subjected to gruesome torture and death. The vigilantes should also be compelled to take those who are caught to the police rather than take the laws into their hands.

Conclusion

The main objective of this exercise is to study the impact of vigilante groups on security challenges confronting Southwest Nigeria with a view to using it as a template for curbing crime in Africa. The phenomenal growth of crime across the present day Nigeria and the proliferation of vigilante groups as a measure to assist the Nigeria Police Force necessitated this study. The data collected indicated that the Police Force for reasons of insufficient fund, staff low morale and corruption has made it impossible to control the skyrocketing criminalities in the communities. It was further revealed that the intervention of vigilante groups have stemmed the tide of crime across the nation. As a result of this, it is believed by the community members that crime control should not be left on the hands of the Nigerian Police Force alone but all hands should be on deck to stem the tide of crime in Nigeria and by extension, in Africa.

References

Atolagbe, A. M. O. 2011. Security Consciousness in Indigenous Nigerian Houses: A Preliminary Survey of Yoruba Ethno-medical Devices, *Ethno Med*, 5(1): 57-62.

Bakare, A. R. 2014. Rivalry or Partnership Policing? Harvesting the Gains of the State and Non- State Security Providers in Ilorin, Nigeria, *Centre Point Journal (Humanities Edition)* 17 (2): 69-88.

Casey, C. 2008. "Policing through violence: fear, vigilantism, and the politics of Islam in Northern Nigeria," In: Pratten, S. and Artyee, S. (Eds.), *Global Vigilantes*, Columbia: University Press, New York.

Chavez, L. 2008 Spectacle in the desert: The minuteman project on the Us-Mexico border', in Pratten, S. and Artyee, S. (Eds), *Global Vigilantes*, Columbia: University Press, New York

Duff, R. A. 1980. 'Legal Obligation and the Moral Nature of Law,' *Juridical Review*, 25: 61–87.

—— 1986. *Trials and Punishments*, Cambridge University Press: Cambridge.

—— 1990. *Intention, Agency and Criminal Liability: Philosophy of Action and the Criminal Law,* Basil Blackwell: Oxford.

—— 1996. *Criminal Attempts*, Oxford University Press: Oxford.

—— 2001. *Punishment, Communication, and Community.* Oxford University Press: Oxford.

—— 2002. Harms and Wrongs, *Buffalo Criminal Law Review*, 5: 13–46.

—— 2002. Crime Prohibition, and Punishment, *Journal of Applied Philosophy*, 19: 97–108.

—— 2004. Rethinking Justifications, *Tulsa Law Review*, 39: 829–50.

—— 2005.'Strict Liability, Legal Presumptions and the Presumption of Innocence', In: A. P. Simester (ed.), *Appraising Strict Liability*, Oxford University Press: Oxford, pp. 125–49.

—— 2007.*Answering for Crime: Responsibility and Liability in the Criminal Law*, Hart Publishing: Oxford.

—— 2007. The Intrusion of Mercy, *Ohio State Journal of Criminal Law*, 4: 361–87.

—— 2009. Philosophy and The Life of the Law, *Journal of Applied Philosophy*, 26: 245–58.

—— and Garland, David, (Eds) 1994. *A Reader on Punishment*, Oxford University Press: Oxford.

—— and Marshall, S. E. 2007. 'Criminal Responsibility and Public Reason', In: M. Freeman and R. Harrison (Eds), *Law and Philosophy*, Oxford University Press: Oxford.

—— Farmer, L., Marshall, S., and Tadros, V. (Eds) 2007. *The Trial on Trial Vol. 3: Towards a Normative Theory of the Criminal Trial.* Oxford: Hart Publishing.

Flexner, S. B. 1987. *Random House Dictionary* (2nd ed. 1987), London.

Fourchard, L. 2008 "A New Name for an Old Practice: Vigilante in South-western Nigeria," In: *Africa*, Cambridge University Press, 78 (1): 1-15.

Harnischfeger, J. 2003. The Bakassi Boys: fighting crime in Nigeria, *Journal of Modern African Studies* 41(1): 23-49.

Garner, A. B, (Ed). 2004. *Black's Law Dictionary*, Thomson West: Texas.

Gore, C. & Pratten, D. 2003. The Politics of Plunder: the Rhetorics of Order and Disorder in Southern Nigeria, *African Affairs* 102. 407.

183

Ikuteyiyo, L. and Rotimi, K. 2010. *Community Partnership in Policing: The Nigerian Experience,* Ile-Ife: Obafemi Awolowo University, Nigeria.

Johnston, L. 1996. 'What is Vigilantism?' *British Journal of Criminology,* 36 (2): 7-29.

Knox, C and Monaghan, R. 2002. *Informal Justice in Divided Societies: Northern Ireland and South Africa,* Palgrave Macmillan, Basingstoke.

Martin, J. R. 2012. 'The Community Will Kill You': Policing and Vigilantism in Zandspruit", *PhD dissertation submitted to the Department of Criminology,* Monash University.

Mbiti, John S. 1969. *African Religions and Philosophy,* Heinemann Educational Books Ltd: London.

Nimbe, E. and Bayo, O. 2011.Implications of State Police in a Fledgling Democracy, *European Journal of Social Science,* 22: 1.

Ogunleye, A. Richard. 2013. Covenant-Keeping among the Yoruba People: A Critique of Socio-Political Transformation in Nigeria, 3: 9

Ojo. M. O. D. 2014. Aje-Olokun as a Deity for Swearing among the Yoruba Natives *Antropologija* 14, sv. 1

Okunola, R. A and Ojo, A. M. O. 2012. Re-assessing the Relevance and Efficacy of Yoruba Gods as Agents of Punishment: A Study of Sango and Ogun, *Issues in Ethnology and Anthropology* 7 (4): 1057-1076.

Omololu, F.O. 2003. Public-private partnership in policing for crime prevention in Nigeria, *A concept chapter presented to Nigeria Institute of Social and Economic Research [NISER],* Ibadan.

Owumi, B. and Ajayi, J. O. 2013.Traditional Values, Beliefs and Reliance on Indigenous Resources for Crime Control in Modern Southwest Nigeria. *An International Multidisciplinary Journal, Ethiopia Vol. 7 (1), No. 28.*

Samuel, I. Z. 2012. Community Policing in Contemporary Nigeria: A Synthesis of Models. *Journal of Educational and Social Research,* 2(9): 132-139.

Chapter Seven

Epistemic (In-)justice and African (Under-) development

Ephraim Taurai Gwaravanda

Introduction

This chapter is rooted in the intersection of epistemology and ethics. It examines the influence of epistemic injustice on both African indigenous knowledge systems and African development. Firstly, it is argued in this chapter that colonialism, basing on its hegemonic tendency, unfairly dismissed, displaced and marginalised African indigenous knowledge systems on the basis of prejudice and sometimes out of ignorance. This means that Africans were deprived of their epistemological heritage such that it was difficult for them to appreciate and advance their worldviews after the creation of knowledge vacuum by colonialism. Meaningful development should respond to the problems and challenges of a given culture. In this view, it is argued that Africans have relied on the Western epistemological paradigm that has shown to be ill-suited for African developmental issues. Secondly, the chapter explores the historical epistemological vacuum and mental colonisation of Africans by Westerners. Mental colonisation resulted in the imposition of Western categories of thought and it supported systems of knowledge that justified Western thinking while casting doubt on the African indigenous knowledge systems. It is argued that Africans were made to think that their knowledge systems are inferior and subordinate to Western knowledge systems thereby creating uncertainties, dilemmas and paradoxes among Africans. It is further argued that mental colonisation has caused underdevelopment in Africa and genuine development can only be achieved after a rigorous mental decolonisation exercise that recognises the place and value of African indigenous knowledge systems.

Thirdly, the chapter maps out the way forward in terms of African development by defending the significance and centrality of the African epistemological paradigm as the foundation of African development. On this note, I advance that it is important for any society who want to proceed meaningfully in development to, first of all, take stock of its own identity by discovering its epistemological paradigm which is the lifeblood for any human community. It is only when the epistemological paradigm is identified that supplementary (or foreign) epistemological frameworks can be incorporated into the creation of a solid epistemic structure that can critique development issues relating to Africa. The opposite is reckless; one cannot make foreign epistemology the basis of his/her knowledge foundation, only to incorporate in them worthy home-grown epistemology as supplement. It is better to begin with knowledge that is proper to the person and community and then allowing for the possibilities to be enriched from outside so that epistemology becomes the basis of development.

Epistemic (In-)justice, Development and Knowledge: A Conceptual Analysis

The concept of epistemic justice is central to this chapter. Collste (2014: 387) understands the concept of epistemic justice globally and argues that it is broad enough to capture distribution, rectification and retribution. The first aspect which Collste identifies, "distributive justice" can be understood as a just arrangement in how goods are apportioned or spread within a given place (Allingham, 2016). Although Allingham refers to actual goods, the distribution of epistemic goods gives rise to "epistemic distributive justice." Epistemic resources from different cultures must be given equal weight and validity without unfair dismissal of their status. If one epistemological paradigm is seen to dominate globally in terms of knowledge contribution, then the idea of epistemic justice is negated. The second aspect, "rectification" is an improvement to replace a mistake (Mark, 2016). In the context of epistemic justice, it is important to revisit and correct the mistakes that dominant epistemology committed in sidelining other forms of knowledge as illegitimate and invalid. However, the problem which is likely to be faced is that if real goods are difficult to replace and correct, epistemic injustice is much more difficult to rectify since it involves mental conditions that may be difficult to undress. Mental reorientation is much more difficult to address compared to replacement of commodities such as land, minerals and infrastructure, for example, because it involves the change of one's mindset. The third aspect is retribution. "Retribution" becomes the act to correct a wrong doing. Global rectificatory justice takes the legacy of colonialism into account (Collste, 2010: 85). Taking colonialism into account helps to address current epistemological thinking and address the epistemological ills created by the colonisers. However, the thinking which dominated colonialism has taken new forms that are seen in epistemic racism, epistemic hegemony and epistemic dualism. While the Global South may see the need to correct and level the epistemic playing field, the Global North may negate efforts for dialogue and fruitful exchange of ideas because of its advantageous epistemic positioning. Such epistemic unwillingness gives rise to epistemic injustice as shown in the nest section.

Fricker (2007) exploits the intersection between epistemology and ethics and makes a distinction between two forms of epistemic injustice, namely, testimonial and hermeneutical injustice. With testimonial injustice, "speakers are, variously, thwarted in their claims to acknowledgment as subjects of knowledge, and thereby harmed in their self-development" (Fricker, 2007: 2). The harm of epistemic confidence followed by the harm to self-development both affect development in philosophy and science. With hermeneutical injustice, "speakers' knowledge claims fall into a blank gap in the available conceptual resources" (Fricker, 2007: 3). This blocks their capacity to understand, and hence to interpret their experiences. When such harms go deep, Fricker suggests, people are "prevented from becoming who they are" (Fricker, 2007: 5). The distinction is significant for this study because it addresses the harms caused by displacement or marginalisation of epistemic resources. This means that their identity is destroyed and they follow the identities of other people blindly without an appreciation of the epistemological justifications inherent in the identities.

Bhargava (2013: 413) defines epistemic injustice as "a form of cultural injustice that occurs when concepts and categories by which people understand themselves and their world is replaced or adversely affected by the concepts and categories of the colonisers." Bhargava brings out key issues that require attention. "Cultural injustice" is the unfairness that occurs when one culture uses its epistemic resources to dominate another culture. In Zimbabwe and other colonised spaces, indigenous knowledge systems that have been used in education, science, agriculture, philosophy, politics and law, among others, have been unfairly dismissed as non-knowledge by Western scholars during the colonial period. "Concepts and categories" are used for understanding and classifying things. Once people's concepts and categories are displaced and replaced by foreign ones, loss of epistemic confidence arises. African concepts of culture, community and the individual have been replaced by Eurocentric notions thereby blinding the contribution of Africa. "Replaced" entails displacement and marginalisation while substituting with a foreign epistemic framework leading to confusion and ignorance. The adverse effect of epistemic injustice is understanding oneself in foreign worldviews. Failure to fully understand oneself results in developmental failures in philosophy, history, and culture.

Keita (2011: 115) defines development etymologically as "expansion by a process of transformative growth' or 'growth and differentiation' of some entity along lines natural to its kind." This entails increase in quantity, quality or scope. Philosophically, there are problems in equating "growth" with "development" because interchangeable use of the two terms implies conceptually equating them (Gyekye, 2013: 32). "Growth" is a physical and sensory concept measured in quantitative terms while "development" is a behavioural concept. Such a comparison results in a conceptual confusion called a category mistake. Development goes beyond mere growth and it should be seen in terms of "adequate responses to the environment in all its complexities" (Ibid: 35). Development should be people centred and it should improve the livelihoods of people (Nyerere, 1968), reduce the gap between the rich and the poor (Mabogunje, 1980) enhance freedom and overcome hunger, famine, ignorance and unemployment (Sen, 1999). Adequate responses are inclusive of intellectual responses based on epistemic frameworks proper to a culture. Development is based on the exercise of rationality as "it is a directed and purposive activity" (Gyekye 2013: 41). Rational exercise depends on sound and tested epistemic responsibility and practice. It also implies the need for a human agent to do the development as such. The indicators of development such as high industrial output, high levels of food production, viable political systems and technological advancements are thought of, deliberated upon, planned and produced by human beings. Thinking, planning and deliberation are important for this chapter because they point to epistemic resources necessary for development to take place. This implies rationality and creativity of development. It involves the use of mental powers by human beings and the effective use of "strategies, methods and systems" (ibid: 42). Ideas begin with individuals but the participation of others brings the ideas to realisation. Political, economic and social institutions must be open and accessible to all members of the society. Development has an ethical character. Linked to the lexical definitions, development involves progress, advancement, forward movement. Each of the terms implies a goal or direction because one can only progress or advance towards a goal or direction. Development must be "guided and underpinned by a set of goals rationally and consciously defined" (Gyekye, 2013: 42). These goals are "values cherished by society" (Ibid: 42). The rational pursuit of a goal presupposes a value judgment because goals are judged to be worthwhile, valuable or desirable. The statement that 'a nation is developing' is a "concealed moral statement and derives from the moral appreciation or assessment of what may be seen as achievable regarding the conditions of people in society. The ultimate goal of the development of every human society is well-being, or satisfaction of the basic needs of its people. The purpose of development lies in improving human lives. The framework of development must be the culture of a people (Ibid: 44). This means that attitudes, habits, behaviour patterns, mental outlooks, values, institutions and social practices are important considerations in development. Development should fulfil the socio-cultural needs of individuals in society.

Wetmore and Theron (1998: 92) take human development to community level and argue that development should provide community capacity and empowerment in terms of self-reliance and control over economic resources. For development to be self-reliant and "ethically" controllable there must be an authentic epistemological paradigm that describes, justifies and evaluates the development process. Swanepoel and De Beer (2006: 26) identify epistemic resources as part of human development. Negation of people's epistemic resources such as concepts and categories retards well-being. For Todaro and Smith (2006: 17) development is a process meant for equitable social and economic transformation of the society through institutionalised social structures and people's positive attitudes for an accelerated and increased growth and poverty eradication. The institutionalised social structures must be based on strong epistemic foundations that are both authentic and liberating to the group of people concerned.

Development and epistemology are intertwined issues in the sense that any country uses its knowledge base as a foundation of economic, social, political and cultural progress. If the foundations of knowledge are destroyed, it becomes difficult or even impossible for meaningful development to take place. The destruction of knowledge which Ramose (1999) calls 'epistemicide' results in knowledge vacuum that is eventually filled by foreign knowledge systems that not only lack relevance but also cause confusion and obscurity. If a group of people is given the opportunity to explore its own epistemological resources, the results are not only authentic but they become part and parcel of the group of people in the sense of belonging. If knowledge is marginalised, as in the case of African knowledge systems following encounter with colonialism, the people whose knowledge is thrown in the peripheries see themselves as inferior and they lack confidence and courage to exploit and realise the potentialities of their knowledge system. Displacement of knowledge entails removing people's knowledge resources and replacing it with other systems of knowledge and this result in lack of confidence and trust in the new knowledge system. The scepticism tied to the new knowledge retards development in the sense that an obscure system of knowledge that is used is beyond the comprehension of many individuals. Subordination of knowledge (Hountondji, 2003) results in knowledge systems being 'placed under' other knowledge systems that are considered superior. This means that knowledge becomes managed and controlled by external forces. If knowledge is externally controlled, then it fails to meet developmental goals and objectives in the sense that it becomes a tool of controlling people rather than a liberating force. If the knowing subject is the point of reference around which all knowledge claims revolve, what happens when the subject has only an indirect and long-distance relationship to its own "here" and "now", or when it has an alienated account of its own reality? The result is that it can no longer serve as the reference point for knowledge, or judge the adequacy of claims of justification. It no longer knows (Alcoff 2007, 86). Knowledge that is externally guided fails to identify developmental problems and solutions to them. Hountondji (2002: 140) argues that the task facing Africa today consists in "constructing a new space of theoretical production, seeing to it that sub-Saharan Africa, which is marginal today in relation to Europe and the West in exchange of ideas, becomes fully autonomous, a centre in its turn, or its own centre". Sub-Saharan Africa should cultivate epistemic autonomy to facilitate development of other spheres of life such as philosophy, science and technology. Epistemic autonomy gives both the foundation and direction of development. The foundation of development becomes rooted in authentic and reliable knowledge that has been tested through time. The direction of development becomes clear because of the knowledge of the values that a given community prioritises. Eyong (2007) argues that conserving knowledge is a long term sustainability solution because future generation will benefit from centuries of experimentation and knowledge accumulation.

Impact of Western Epistemological Paradigm on African Epistemic Space

Pannikar (1979: 9) argues that Eurocentric epistemology crossed boundaries in a mistaken manner:

To cross the boundaries of one's culture without realising that the other person may have a radically different approach to reality today is no longer admissible. If still consciously done, it would be philosophically naive, politically outrageous and religiously sinful.

Three issues can be drawn from Panikkar's observation. Firstly, recognition of another culture's different approach to reality goes beyond mere epistemological tolerance but it involves some epistemological respect. Secondly, the philosophical naivety observed by Panikkar is a result of lack of facts while there is rashness predicated on prejudice. Thirdly, failure to realise other approaches to knowing is a result of assumed superiority that has no factual underpinnings. The three issues mentioned above characterise the act of epistemic colonisation which is more dangerous than physical and administrative colonisation because while colonisers have physically left their former colonial territories, intellectual colonisation still exists (in the minds of the colonised) in forms that are both entrenched and invisible.

Zea (1988: 36) acknowledges that the rationality and the very humanity of the people of the conquered world were put on trial and judged by the jury of its conquerors. The judgement was made, not on the basis of reasoned research and evidence, but merely on prejudice. Logically this is a fallacious procedure whose conclusions are based on false premises that have no factual basis. Paradoxically, Africans were not considered to be in a position to present their own epistemic credentials, much less to judge the Western European ones. As a result, there was no uniform epistemological platform but a one-sided analysis of the conquered by the conqueror and this indicates epistemic injustice. Although claims to objectivity were made by the Eurocentric thinkers, they used ethnic and racialised identity to judge the epistemic status of the indigenous people of Africa. This shows inconsistency in the claims of Eurocentric thinkers in that while they pretend to value investigation and objectivity, they go exactly the opposite direction in judging African epistemology.

Alcoff (2007: 80) notes that "the epistemic effects of colonisation are the most damaging, far-reaching and least understood." The damaging effect is seen in the destruction of mindsets, denial of one's own culture, uncertainties and contradictions that characterise colonised minds. The epistemic effects of colonialism are said to be far-reaching because they displace one's epistemological paradigm to the extent of disregarding one's indigenous forms of knowledge and think like the Eurocentric philosophers. The epistemic effects of colonialism are least understood because of the brain washing victimisation created by Eurocentric epistemology among Africans. As a result, individuals may fail to think outside the epistemological boxes created by colonisers. The task of decolonisation is to come up with an anti-colonial epistemic resistance (Alcoff, 2007: 80). One way of epistemic resistance is the construction of forms of knowledge based on an African epistemological paradigm.

Imposition of a foreign epistemological paradigm by the coloniser caused contradictions and dilemmas among the colonised (Ocitti, 1994: 69; Sall and Bangirana, 2010: 1; Lebakeng, 2010: 24; Grosfoguel, 2013: 74). The contradictions caused involve opposing views regarding knowledge claims with one group agreeing with the coloniser while the other group takes a radically opposite direction. This situation still exists today and some Africans believe in the validity of indigenous knowledge while others mistakenly describe it as non-knowledge, superstitious and illogical. The dilemmas lie in the practical level where decisions between Eurocentric epistemology and African knowledge systems have to be made. A worse-off effect is epistemicide which Santos (1998: 103) describes as "...the murder of knowledge." For Santos (1998: 103), unequal exchanges among cultures have always implied the death of the knowledge of the subordinated culture, and hence, the death of the social groups that possessed it. In the most extreme cases, as that of European expansion, epistemicide was one of the conditions of genocide. In the light of Santos' understanding of epistemicide, it can be noted that it was intended to destroy both the culture and the epistemological paradigm of the colonised. This move was of strategic importance in alienating the colonised people from their epistemological paradigm thereby making it easier for the colonisers to impose their own epistemological paradigm. Nyamnjoh (2012: 129) understands epistemicide as "...the decimation or near complete killing and replacement of endogenous epistemologies with the epistemological paradigm of the conqueror." Colonial epistemicide did not only partially destroy the epistemological paradigm of the colonised people. It also led to the partial destruction of their cultural experiences. This is so because knowledge is context-bound meaning to say that it is informed by a given cultural experience (Okere, 2005; 20-21; Okere, Njoku and Devisch, 2005: 3). The consequence of the said restrictions on African epistemic space is a proportional narrowness in conceptualising key pillars of development such as education, science and philosophy as shown in the next section.

Impediments to African Development

As pertaining to education wherein knowledge is produced, Nyamnjoh (2004) argues that a major impediment to development in Africa stems from the alienating effects of the colonial education to which Africans were subjected over many decades. For him, the paradigm of colonial education was one that was strictly empiricist and materialist in content, being modelled on modern science. This means that sense perception is seen as the basis of knowledge. He further argues that this approach is too epistemologically restricting, given its preoccupation with answering 'what' questions instead of 'why' questions. Nyamnjoh embarks on a set of critiques of the systems of Eurocentric education that still dot the African continent. His prescription is that genuine development would necessarily require serious paradigm changes in Africa's educational structures. The change should include an upside down approach to the current situation. Instead of using foreign culture as the foundation of knowledge and supplementing with local knowledge, it is important to use cultural knowledge systems as the base and supplement them with foreign ideas for the purpose of both richness and inclusivity. The richness of grounding knowledge on the African epistemological foundation is that it gives a deeper and wider understanding of knowledge which is based on a wealth accumulated experiential knowledge, experimentation, validation and justification. Inclusivity of education derives from the fact that indigenous knowledge

194

becomes integrated with other epistemic paradigms of knowledge while at the same time, it contributes a larger percentage of that knowledge.

The second main impediment to African development is science which involves methods of investigation in the production of knowledge. The colonialist presented their form of knowledge as scientific, objective, measurable, systematic, neutral, logical and advanced. The scientific nature referred to involves understanding science in the narrow sense (Okere 2001; Nyamnjoh 2004). The narrow conception of science leaves out a vast amount of knowledge as non-science and it also throws away practical issues that can solve problems affecting humanity. African categories of thought present a holistic epistemology that sees the metaphysical as intertwined with the physical; the natural as part and parcel of the supernatural and the dead as belonging to the same community with the departed. The holistic epistemology enables African categories of thought to unite the objective with the subjective, the emotional with the intellectual and the rational with the mythical. Distinctions made are only logical and thinkers do not face the problem of dualism. Non-dualistic thought is significant in African epistemology because it avoids divisions that retard progress in development. Indigenous conceptions of science are not narrow to focus on the empirical only but they consider reality in non-dualistic and comprehensive manner.

The above analysis entails the use of non-dualistic thinking because dualistic thinking contains the assumptions of scientific imperialism. Science must be decolonised of these assumptions. Knowledge must be disentangled from the snares of colonising assumptions to pave way for indigenous knowledge systems from all cultures of the world. According to Mignolo (2000: 93), border thinking is not aimed at normative epistemic concerns about justification and belief formulation, but it is focused on the way knowledge is normatively defined with reference to others. It specifies the location of subaltern knowledge as a border location rather than simply beyond Western knowledge. Situating knowers in a context is revolutionary in itself, going against the normal procedure of Western epistemology. Border thinking is seen as a double critique with a capacity to examine the thinking of both the

195

colonizer and the colonized. Border thinking implies the ability to think from both sides. It is dissolution of borders as opposed to border control. The task of border thinking is to unmask preconceptions about divisions.

The third impediment to African development is philosophy which is associated with evaluation of knowledge claims. Oyeshille (2008: 62) argues: "for anything to be philosophical it has to do with the reflection on the experience of a society, group or an individual." Drawing on Oyeshille's understanding of philosophy, there is no doubt that there is a triadic relationship between philosophy, society and development. It is from this understanding that I advance the argument that the reliance on philosophy that is based on a Eurocentric epistemological paradigm retards development because it fails to give the necessary critique and innovative hand tools to development. Yet, the content of philosophy should focus on past and present experience of Africans with a view of drawing directions for the future. This reflection should be based on two factors: it must be "…necessitated by wonders about some compelling problems of life and existence" (ibid). Kurasha (2016) locates African problems in three categories which include slavery, colonialism and existing problems such as mismanagement, disease, drought, wars, genocide and terrorism. While slavery and colonialism are external problems, Kurasha argues that genocide, wars and mismanagement are internal problems. The distinction between internal and external problems may not be very neat since wars and genocide may be found on the intersection between internal and external problems. This means that they have elements of both internal and external factors. The ideologies behind wars and genocides are external, yet the internal factors become the drivers of these problems. The task of philosophy is to unmask the root causes of these problems so that solutions are found.

Another important factor is that "such reflection must be critical and logical" (Oyeshille, 2008: 62). This requirement means that philosophy must examine problems in the most objective manner. For philosophy to be fully critical, it must be self-critical. This means philosophy should examine itself. Self-examination interrogates the questions of African identity, the meaning of Africanness and thinking about how Africans think so as to revise and improve ourselves philosophically. The logical part involves formulating arguments whose premises are based on African realities so as to draw conclusions relevant to the African situation. Reliance on external arguments fails to develop the thrust which is necessary for African development.

Towards an African Epistemological Paradigm

The first step towards an African epistemological paradigm is decolonisation. Wiredu (1998: 17) defines decolonisation as "divesting African philosophical thinking of all undue influences emanating from our colonial past." The word 'undue' is important because some aspects such as scientific advancements, technological innovations and medical developments of colonial past are beneficial to the colonised communities. However, a critical outlook reveals that Western epistemological categories are inconsistent with African thought patterns and development endeavours. Colonialism becomes an epistemological imposition when it uses its knowledge perspective to replace indigenous knowledge systems. Colonialism unjustly de-Africanised epistemic categories and replaced them with Western categories of thought. A good example to show this point is the contrast between the western and African understanding of development. The African understanding of development is modelled along the biological model which is holistic and comprehensive (Gyekye, 2013) while the Western model of development is linear and narrow. For a long time, development prescribed economic growth to African countries yet that conception of development failed to translate to the wellbeing of African people. Mawere (2017: 1) argues that "most theories and models (about development) imported from the Global North are either useless or limited when it comes to contexts such as those in Africa." The limitation arises because "they principally reflect the thinking and objectives of those who coin them together with their unique circumstances and experiences" (Ibid). Failure to develop other aspects of development such as cultural, moral and spiritual aspects results in half backed personnel that channel the fruits of economic development to egocentric needs through corruption, nepotism, tribalism and regionalism, to mention a few ills. Development should therefore be grounded on a critical outlook that takes positive aspects from diverse cultures while being rooted on a firm African bedrock that provides both the vision and guidance for present and future development goals.

While reinforcing the point of a critical outlook, Grosfoguel (2011: 13) makes an important distinction between colonisation and coloniality. For Grosfoguel, colonisation allows us to think of the continuity of other forms of domination after colonial administration. Coloniality addresses present forms of situations in racist culture and the ideological strategies used by Western Europe. It involves rethinking the modern colonial world from the colonial difference point of view. Thinking from a colonial difference point of view allows us to modify important assumptions of our paradigms. Grosfoguel's line of thought gives room to rebut the false assumptions of Eurocentric thinking and validate and legitimise development projections based on an African epistemological paradigm.

The second step consists in using the African epistemological paradigm as the foundation of development. Makumba (2007: 128) argues that it is important for any society who wants to proceed meaningfully in development to, first of all, take stock of its own identity by discovering its own values which are the lifeblood for any human community. The values are normally expressed in beliefs and thinking about the human person, community, authority and the world (ibid: 129). It is only when these values are identified that supplementary (or foreign) values can be incorporated into the creation of a solid developmental structure (Ibid). The opposite is reckless; one cannot make foreign values the basis of one's development, only to incorporate in them worthy home-grown values as supplement. It is not only better but wiser to begin with what is proper to the person and community and then allowing for developmental possibilities to be enriched from outside (Ibid). The individual is never defined in isolation but in relationship to the other individuals within the community (Ibid). Despite the communitarian sense of African communities, individual talents and contributions are recognised (ibid: 130). Development initiatives that benefit the community are preferred in the African setting because such steps are consistent with community wellbeing. Development that is grounded on African knowledge becomes crucial because it is through the epistemological paradigm that values are known, recognised and enhanced.

The third step is to take stock of African intellectual resources as the centre of philosophical and developmental analysis through recentring. The intellectual dominance of the Western model of knowledge has derived not from its inherent unequivocal superiority but rather from the political dominance of those who believe in its superiority (Banuri, 2011: 30). Banuri's point is that the political privileging of Western thought allows it to dictate its intellectual influence across the globe. Tied to the intellectual influence, Western thinking also dominates in terms of economics, culture, science, technology and development. Western models of development have been seen to be both inconsistent and unsuitable for African needs. Critics have argued that "there is nothing inherently superior in the epistemology of our time" (Mungwini, 2016: 527). Superiority is rather imagined and inferred from prejudice as opposed to facts. With the democratisation of knowledge, it is important to recognise plurality of epistemological frameworks rather than taking a narrow view. Recentring Africa entails "to centre again" and demarginalise it presupposes the act of restoring it to the position it once occupied before the historical upheaval (ibid). African underdevelopment in the field of knowledge should be characterised by the same way as economic underdevelopment whereby African knowledge was subordinated to the world market of ideas and concepts from other regions. According to Ramose (2000: 53), the African experience should be the primary source from which to draw concepts to understand and interpret politics, history and philosophy. If the African experience is used as the basis of knowledge, there is a wider participation of African people in the contribution to knowledge and hence development. On the contrary, reliance on foreign models of knowledge is exclusive because only those who have been schooled in the coloniser's politics, history and philosophy will be able to follow development debates.

Mungwini (2016: 528) argues that recentring derives from a set of important ontological, epistemological and ethical considerations. The ontological assumptions entail "knowing who we are" (ibid). Self-knowledge is important because it is a product of self-evaluation or self-criticism. Self-examination becomes a critical exercise that offers an objective picture of own weaknesses and strengths. In the context of development, understanding oneself as an African ontologically gives a firm foundation of paving way for developmental needs that are both relevant and appropriate for Africa. African identity, though it is difficult to pin down at least in contemporary times, is shaped by African history, culture and philosophy. Meaningful African development should be premised on a sound understanding of African history, culture and philosophy because these critique the factors that hinder or foster development. Historically, the wealth of African experiential knowledge should be used as the basis to foster development and at the same time, African development should both be critical and corrective of historical circumstances that shaped development especially during the colonial era. While mindful of the overall epistemological goal, the ethical consideration consists in challenging the foundations of epistemic marginalisation (ibid). The ethical dimension creates new conditions necessary for mutual respect and dialogue across all knowledge traditions. Justice then takes the direction of fairness in knowledge and knowledge claims. The epistemological consideration involves the 'rebirth' of the African knowing subject and Africa has to be fully autonomous in knowledge production and direction for its own development.

Conclusion

This chapter has explored the intersection of epistemology and ethics to locate an African and authentic development framework. It has been argued that epistemology and development are closely linked because the accumulated knowledge and experience is the basis of meaningful and relevant development for Africa. The chapter has examined the impact of Western hegemonic and positivistic epistemology on African epistemic space as evidenced by marginalisation, displacement and epistemicide. The colonisers have imposed Eurocentric education, science and philosophy upon the colonised and this has blinded critiques of development for Africa while justifying colonial thinking patterns. To overcome the problems, this chapter has suggested decolonisation as the first step towards mental liberation that is necessary for African progress and development. The second stage consists in locating development needs in the African epistemological paradigm that takes local knowledge and values into account before supplementing with external ideas so as to provide both authenticity and identity to African development. The third stage, which can be simultaneous with the second, involves recentring African epistemology by challenging the basis of marginalisation while taking into account African identity into the African development debate.

References

Alcoff, L. 2007. Mignolo's epistemology of coloniality. *Continental Review, Vol.7, No.3* , 79-101

Banuri, T. 2011. "Development and the politics of knowledge: A critical interpretation of the social role of modernisation theories in the development of the third world," Oxford Scholarship Online. www.oxfordscholaship.com.

Bhargava, R. 2013. Overcoming the Epistemic Injustice of Colonialism. *Global Policy,* 4 (4): 413-417.

Collste, G. 2014. Epistemic Injustice and Global Justice: A Response to "Overcoming the Epistemic Injustice of Colonialism". *Global Policy, Vol.5, Issue 3,* , 386-387.

Collste, G. 2010. 'Restoring the Dignity of the Victims' Is Global Rectificatory Justice Feasible? *Ethics and Global Politics,* 3 (2): 85-99.

Eyong, C.T., 2007. *Tribes and Tribals,* Special Volume, No.1, pp.121-139.

Fricker, M. 2007. *Epistemic Injustice: Power and the Ethics of Knowin,* Oxforf University Press: Oxford.

Gyekye, K., 2013. Philosophy, Culture and Vision: African Perspectives, Selected Essays. Accra: Sub-Saharan Publishers.

Grosfoguel, R. 2010. Epistemic Islamophobia and Colonial Social Sciences, *Human Architecture: Journal of the Sociology of Self-Knowledge*, Vol.8, No.2, pp. 29-38.

Grosfoguel, R. 2011. Decolonising Post-Colonial Studies and Paradigms of Political Economy: Transmodernity, Decolonial Thinking and Global Coloniality, *Transmodernity: Journal of Peripheral Cultural Production of the Luso-Hispanic World*, 1(1): 1-36.

Grosfoguel, R., 2012. Decolonizing Western Uni-versalisms: Decolonial Pluri-versalism from Aimé Césaire to the Zapatistas *Transmodernity: Journal of Peripheral Cultural Production of the Luso-Hispanic World*, 1(3): 88-104.

Grosfoguel, R. 2013. The Structure of Knowledge in Westernized Universities: Epistemic Racism/Sexism and the Four Genocides/Epistemicides of the Long 16th Century, *Human Architecture: Journal of the Sociology of Self-Knowledge*, 11(1): 73-90.

Hountondji, J. 2002. *The Struggle for Meaning: Reflections on Philosophy, Culture, and Democracy*, Ohio University: Ohio Center of International Studies.

Keita, L. 2011. Philosophy and Development: On Problematic African Development-A Diachronic Analysis, In: L. Keita, *Philosophy and African Development: Theory and Practice* (pp. 115-138), Dakar: CODESRIA.

Kurasha, J. 2016. Philosophical Reflections on the Integration of Africa, *Dzimbahwe Arts Festival*, Masvingo: Great Zimbabwe University.

Lebakeng, T. J. 2010. Discourse on Indigenous Knowledge Systems, Sustainable Socioeconomic Development and the Challenge of the Academy in Africa, *CODESRIA Bulletin*, Nos. 1 & 2, pp. 24-29.

Mabogunje, A. 1980. *The Development Process: A Spatial Perspective*, Cape Town: Hutchinson and Company.

Makumba, M.M. 2007. *An Introduction to African Philosophy: Past and Present*, Nairobi: Paulines Publications Africa.

Mawere, M. 2017. *Theorising Development in Africa: Towards Building an African Framework of Development*, Bamenda, Langaa Publications.

Mungwini P. 2016. The Question of Recentring Africa: Thoughts and Issues from the Global South, *South African Journal of Philosophy*, 35 (4): 523-536.

Okere, T. 2005. Is There One Science, Western Science? *Africa Development*, XXX (3): 20-34.

Okere, T., Njoku, C. A. & Devisch, R. 2005. All Knowledge Is First of all Local Knowledge: An Introduction, *Africa Development*, Vol. XXX (3): 1-19.

Ocitti, J. P. 1994. *An Introduction to Indigenous Education in East Africa*, Bonn: DVV.

Oyeshile, O. A. 2008. On Defining African Philosophy: History, Challenges and Perspectives, *Humanity and Social Science Journal*, 57-64.

Nyamnjoh, F. B. 2012. 'Potted Plants in Greenhouses': A Critical Reflection on the Resilience of Colonial Education in Africa, *Journal of Asian and African Studies*, 47 (2): 129–154.

Nyerere, J. 1968. *Freedom and Socialism: A Selection from Writings and Speeches 1965-1967*, Oxford University Press: Oxford.

Panikkar, R. (1979) *Myth, Faith and Hermeneutics*, Paulist Press: New York.

Ramose, M. B. 2000. "'African renaissance': A northbound gaze," *Politeia* 19 (3): 47–61.

Todaro, M.P. and Smith, S.C., 2006. *Economic Development*, Harlow: Pearson Addison Wesley.

Sall, E. and Bangirana, A. 2010. Africa at 50: Looking to the Future. *CODESRIA Bulletin*, Nos. 1 & 2, pp. 1-2.

Santos, B. D. S. 2006. *The Rise of the Global left: The World Social Forum and Beyond*. London and New York: Zed Books.

Sen, A. 1999. *Development as Freedom*, New York: Oxford University Press.

Swanepoel, H., and De Beer, F., 2006. Community Development: Breaking the Cycle of Poverty, Kenwyn: Juta.

Wetmore, S., and Theron, F. 1997. Participatory Learning and Action: Methodology for the New Development Vision, in *Participatory Development Management and the RDP*, edited by S Liebenberg & P Stwart . Kenwyn: Juta.

Wiredu, K., 1995. *Conceptual Decolonization in African Philosophy: Four Essays*, Ibadan:
Hope Publications.
Zea, L., 1988. Identity: A Latin American Philosophical Problem, *The Philosophical Forum* XX, Nos 1-2 Fall, Winter, pp. 33-42.

Chapter Eight

Markets and Indigenous Technology in Ilorin Emirate before 1900: A Hermeneutical and Historical Analysis

Ibrahim Bashir Olaitan

Introduction

This chapter attempts to show the technological dynamic and commercial capabilities as exhibited by the people of Ilorin Emirate before 1900. It is noteworthy that the general economy of Ilorin and its environ as in other African societies before 1900 was very active, contrary to rather dormant and totally unimpressive picture painted by people like high Trevor- Ropers, that Africans have no past and therefore no history. A cursory look at the pre-colonial economic activities in Ilorin shows that both males and females in the town were highly enterprising. Apart from farming in which both sexes jointly practice, especially at the harvest stage, there were some specific crafts which were regarded as exclusively preserved for women or men as the case might be.

The reason for this could partly be explained by the peoples' culture which regarded women as a weaker sex with fragile feminine frame. Thus, they were not allowed to engage in energy sapling vacations but be treated kindly (Quran4, 9). Men often placed the responsibility of preparation for sale of some portion of their farm produce to their women, because the men were busier on the farm. These responsibilities, however, gave the women folks intricate knowledge of markets and indirectly opened them up to marketing. That was why women were the most noticed in the pre-colonial Ilorin market. Markets served other purposes in Ilorin as in other African countries. They served as social and religious forum like place to court and meet lovers. It also served as religious link since central mosques were located close to the markets and for communication purposes beside buying and selling.

Thus before 1900, the economic activities of Ilorin Emirate exceeded the subsistence level to a commercial level. As indicated in the work, the markets in the villages were well attended with supply of products while those in the bigger towns enjoyed national and international patronages. For instance, Alapa, Afon and Megida as well as some courters in Oke Imale and Magaji Ngeri markets supplied items to the principal markets in Ilorin which attracted customers from distant places (Asude, 2017).

The Establishment of Ilorin Emirate

The close of the 18th century signalled the gradual disintegration of the old Oyo Empire largely due to intense political crisis which rocked the empire. The crisis that engulfed old Oyo initially had the character of rivalry among the leading chiefs in the empire, especially between the *Oyomesi* (Council of Ministers) and the *Alafin*. But it soon degenerated into an outright conflict of immense magnitude between the capital and its dependencies. The mounting political tension in the capital weakened old Oyo's hold on its provincial territories and in effect, such colonies declared their independence which included Ilorin (Atanda, 1971: 56-89).

Perhaps the leading event in the politics of the Yoruba country in the early decades of the 19th century was the rapid growth of Ilorin from a provincial territory of old Oyo to an imperial power in Yoruba land. It is obvious that the emergence of Ilorin as an Emirate in the Yoruba country was a product of the disintegration of old Oyo as from the close of the 18th century and the spread of the Fulani Jihad to the region in the early 19th century.

Afonja around this period invited Alimi an itinerant Fulani Muslim preacher that had earlier passed through the town back to Ilorin for him to achieve his goal of making Ilorin independent of old Oyo. This request, coincide with the ambition of the Fulani to spread the *Jihad* to Yoruba land haven noticed that Islam was not well grounded in the town. Since *Afonja's* calculation was to use Alimi to achieve his political goal, he was not against the different types of people, including slaves that followed Alimi to Ilorin. In fact, *Afonja* thought that such slaves would probably be useful as soldiers to strengthen his power and consolidate his authority. In this circumstance, Ilorin attracted groups like slaves, marauders, travellers, traders, Islamic scholars, and other migrants who later became useful in state affairs. By C. 1823 when the Emirate was formed, Ilorin had emerged as a potential imperial power in Yoruba land. Between 1823 and 1835, Ilorin raided several old Oyo tributaries, and gradually prepared itself for a grand imperial task in 19th century Yoruba land. The success of Alimi in receiving the support of the Sokoto leaders authorized him and his supporters to launch the Jihad in Ilorin (Danmole, 1980: 54-68). Although Alimi did not ascend the throne (for he died in 1823), his son, Abdul Salam, was proclaimed the *Emir* of Ilorin in 1823 (Balogun 1978, 13).

The political circumstance which led to the foundation of Ilorin Emirate naturally put the Emirate in a difficult position as regards her southern neighbours. Therefore, immediately the nascent Emirate was established, the most fundamental problem it had to grapple with was that of survival in the midst of rival Yoruba powers. It thus became incumbent on the leaders of this frontier Emirate to work out strategies that would guarantee the survival of the Emirates. And the strategy of course was to put up a good economic structure which is our concern in this exercise.

Survey of Ilorin Economy Before 1900

It is noteworthy that the general economy of Ilorin Emirate before 1900 was very active, contrary to the rather dormant and totally unimpressive picture painted as said before that Africans have no past and therefore no history (Hugh, 1963: 869-871). A good look at the pre-colonial economic activities in Ilorin Emirate, show that both male and female were highly enterprising. Apart from farming in which both sexes jointly practiced, especially at the harvesting stage, there was specialization of trade and division of labour in the practices of indigenous industries and crafts between the men and the women (Ann, 1981: 56-77), which indicated how serious the people of Ilorin were economically.

After the interruption caused by Ilorin wars with her neighbours which involved mostly men of the Emirate, like all other parts of

Yoruba land, Ilorin Emirate was able to once again settled back to their normal economic and commercial activities. Women became more noticeable earlier in commercial activities because, the men folk concentrated on the act of defence and farming throughout the period before 1900 and could also be explained by the religion doctrine which regarded women as a weaker sex with fragile feminine 'frame' and delicate object to be spared (Paul, 1971: 153-159). That was why it was only during the harvesting stage that women were invited to render help on the farm. Thus, Men often pushed the responsibility of the preparation for sale of some portions of their farm produce to their women. Such responsibilities gave the women folk's intricate knowledge of markets and indirectly opened them up to marketing and trading techniques.

Ilorin Emirate indigenous technology before 1900

Technology can simply be defined as the technique employed to aid the production processes or production made easier by applying the basic concept of 'science'. Thus, technology could be said to have begun with man's ability to conquer his environment in order to cater for his basic needs of feeding, clothing and shelter (Olaoye, 1993: 54-99). Indigenous technology thus, entails the process or methods of production as practiced in the "local and traditional" society before the European's cultural contact. Indigenous technology covers a wide range of crafts and industries that deals with daily life of farming, building construction, food processing, preparation of bodily decorations, cloth wearing, wood carving, basket-making, herbal medicine, drinks, among others (Jimoh, 1994: 115). As noted, there were separations and specializations in the male and females' mode of handling their indigenous technological activities in Ilorin Emirate. That is why this paper examines those handled by men and women separately to show the distinct in the modes employed as well as the raw materials used in their production processes before the final products were taken to the market by the women and men back to the farm to cultivate food for the family.

Men's crafts

Farming

Ilorin people were predominantly farmers. This is not to suggest that they do not practice some other vocational crafts and industries. Their involvement in vocational crafts and industries were undertaken side by side with farming. Farming was done individually with every human-being responsible first for his family's needs, after which excesses were sold off. The women and the children gave helping hands during planting and harvesting season as observed by Lloyd (1953: 30-44).

Evidence of technology involved in farming was the admirable display of foresight. For instance, both slashing and burning have to be done well in advance, followed by ridging before the end of raining season in October /November. Due to the natural factor of weather –rainfall and sunshine -farming activities, though long and cumbersome, have to be done in anticipation of a favourable weather (Abdulkareem 2016). This was why the operations for the planting of yam, usually started from about –August. Selected yams are cut into required sizes to make yam-sets; which after a period of five to seven days (to enable the wounds to heal up) are kept in the soil until the new piece of land being cultivated was ready. This was then followed by planting and mulching which were done simultaneously. The usual farming tools are the hoe and cutlass, fashioned by the local traditional blacksmiths. The storage aspect was another area where technological skill was displayed. Surplus yams are preserved in the barn where it could later be removed for either sale or consumption. Yams are therefore preserved by tying firmly, piece by piece, in rows on sticks, with ropes, usually in a well shaded area (Hopkin, 1973: 23-65).

Blacksmithing

This was another prominent occupation common in the emirate and practiced by both Hausa and Yoruba men. It was not certain who between the two sides introduced it to the other, since each tribes claimed independent of the other (Oliver, 1975: 183-189). Some profession is lineage or tribe based but some are not. This explains why Hausa and Yoruba engaged in blacksmithing because they both have the knowledge of iron working. The blacksmith specialized in the manufacturing of various objects like hoes, cutlasses, padlocks, keys, traps, house utensils and other materials needed by other craft men, hunters and soldiers (Woru, 2016). Apart from the fact that the profession promoted intergroup relations among Hausa and Yoruba it laid the foundation for modern technology in the Emirate.

Carving

Carving is a craft which epitomized the richness of people cultural skilled. Carvers were abound in Oloje and Okelele areas of Ilorin as well as Shao, Megida, and many towns of the Emirate. Secular or religious objects carved were adored. They were held in high esteem, as god's special creation and therefore they signified wealth and prosperity. Carving also had much to do with the masquerades festivals in Shao, Megida, Oloworu, Alapa, and other villages that bounded the town (Woru 2016). The significance of carving comes to play with the mask and head load of the masquerades *Egungun* (ancestors- on visit) used to case-their faces, heads and other costumes. These costumes which "blow up" their normal (life) size (to mystify as spirits would) were made by carvers. However there were architectural carvings for posts of verandahs of palaces, rich men's houses, pillars and richly decorated doors (Ibrahim, 2006: 126-132). This further enhanced the popularity of the Emirate to outside world as the wood works of the Emirate were preferred to those of other places.

There were also carved utensils for everyday use, such as bowls, dishes, *Ayo* boards, and stools, pulleys for weaver's loons, mortals, pestles and wooden spoon. Also included were carved hollow wood for building different types of drums *Gangan, Dundun, Bata, Gudugudu* and so on. There were also carved handles knives, cutlasses and hoes. Large scale production of carved decorations for marketing purposes in Ilorin Emirate was not common; requests for calabash carvings were often few and far between, usually from rich individuals, chiefs and royal families. Markets for carved spoons, dishes, and bowls were scattered all over the emirate from pre entry to daily markets. The material for carving was a specially carved knife. Carving techniques were to first cut the masses and hollows with axe and assize, then smoothing the forms with chisel and knife, and lastly cut details and pattern (Macfies, 1913). The carvings depicted the experiences of individual carvers as well as the happening in the societal life. Thus, it was another source of historical documentation.

Leather processing

Leather workers in the Emirate obtained their raw materials from reputable hunters in the Emirate or imported. Only leather of wild animals is mostly useful for leather works. Therefore, there was a link between a leather worker and a hunter. Like other indigenous industry in the town, there was specialisation in leather works. This was why the hunter leaves the art of leather working to those who were very versed and skilful in processing leathers, for shoes, shippers, bags, drums, medical straps and bolts (Macfies,1913).The interconnectivity between leather workers and hunters was inseparable. While the hunters provided leathers for the workers in exchange for money, the leather workers also helped hunters used in keeping their hunting charms. This included *onde* (worn round waist) and *Ifunpa* (armlets), among other things.

For each of the above items the method of production differed. For example, leather prepared for drums were distended and large as against those for medicinal fetes and straps which were physically thicker and narrower. Markets for leather works in the Emirate were very popular in Gambari, Emir; Alanamu and Idiape markets in Ilorin Township. The wards and daily markets that spread across the Emirate also paraded finished leather works that attract customers from far and near (Woru, 2016). To date the leader works persists and continue as major items that can be found in Gambari courter of Ilorin.

Herbal/Religious Medicine

Herbal medicine deals with the indigenous medical science whereby healing is achieved through spiritual force and the use of medicine extracted from plants. The technique was to collect specified leaves, shrubs and bark of woods, put them together and boil or grinded. These concoctions were renowned for their

211

efficiency in aborting ailment such as malaria, bone fracture and internal disorders among others.

The masterpiece in this home technology could be seen in the initiatives taken to test and the ability to identify leaves, roots, shrubs, and barks which possessed high chemical compounds and properties. Raw materials for the production of herbal medicine were available at the Alanamu, Gambari Oja-Gboro and in some markets across the Emirate where these raw materials (roots, shrubs, bark and alligator pepper) were stocked in a well-preserved form (Olaoye, 1993: 34).

The Emirate being an Islamic environment also paraded special Islamic religious medicinal method. Endowed Islamic clerics extract portion of the Holy Quran and other Islamic write- up to cure ailments of all kinds. Some of these extracts might be written in pieces of leaves or paper to be hanged in houses or swallowed to cure some illness. Also extracts might be written in a slate, washed and drank just like the traditional concoction. In the same vein, some of the extracts might be written in a paper or leather to be hanged on neck or as bolts *Onde* by the Emirate soldiers and other individuals. Some portion of the Holy Quran may only just be recited in a room or house with the belief that it would cure or prevent calamity and thee like (Woru.2016). The fact that this age long tradition still persists, then some kinds of benefits are attached.

Architecture

The Emirate people were resourceful as uniquely displayed in the construction of their modest houses and huts. The construction of houses was painstakingly designed and executed to reflect a measure of rudimentary technological and architectural (skills the raw materials included local mud with thatched leaves for roofing. The frame for the roof was usually made of raffia palm and trees before covered with long grasses, perfectly arranged to drain rainfall to achieve some cooling effects from the scorching tropical sun, the room was usually screened with mats and often specious. On the other hand, huts built on the farms displayed some architectural design to withstand and protect against successive heavy rainfall and sunshine (Afolabi 1966, 28-35).The use of grasses was the common phenomenon. The style differed from one tribe to another, for example, Hausa-Fulani and Yoruba. The type you see may also tell of the affluence or other wise of the occupants. However, the grasses were replaced seasonally and during dry season then were prone to fire disaster.

Basketry

Among the weaving crafts (as practiced by men) in Ilorin Emirate included basket weaving, rope weaving, mat weaving and cloth weaving as shall be discussed in the sections below. Basket is fashioned from palm fronds and canes which were carefully and neatly pealed into long stands. These stands were then closely knitted to a desired shape of basket: round, square or conical. Ganmo, Igbo Owu, Reke, Ogbondoroko villages and Yoruba quarters of Alanamu, Oloje, Okelele of Ilorin and many other villages that bounded the city, were part of the areas where basket weaving were common. Basket was the means by which agricultural products were carried from one place to another (head potentate) (Abeni, 2015). The raw material was obtained often from the palm tree. There were no special markets for the product, because every market had a fair display of the big or small basket for sale. The conical shaped basket were used for keeping chicken, ducks and fowls while the ordinary ones were used for carriage and storage (Johnson, 1921: 34-60).

Rope weaving

Weaving was very common among the Hausa and the Fulani quarters in Ilorin Township, perhaps due to their influx from the northern parts where the craft originated from. The raw material for rope making were not only consumed locally but made available in markets. These products were carried by agents to towns within the Emirate and far (Ibrahim 1986, 23-44). The material is derived from a special tree called 'Sisal hemp' (*Iko*) in Yoruba. The bark of which is peeled and sun-dried before weaving began. The uses of ropes were for tying roofing poles of buildings and huts, as well as for tying animal down among others (Ilorprof, 5. Amuda 2016).

Cloth weaving

Men weaved cloths of narrow breaths about 51/2 inches wide called *Alawe*. Yarn was the principal raw materials used for weaving which could be gotten from cotton seeds that were grown locally by the Ilorin farmers. Ilorin cloth was woven on the loom *Aso Ofi*. The cloth was very rich in texture and celebrated in many other places (Olaoye, 1993: 50). Cloth weaving was not only men's job women also weave but different type and for different purposes. While men looms were outside, those of women were within the compounds. Women cloth products were used as *Ipele* (muffler), *Oja* (used to hold a backed baby).

Mats and hats weaving

Mats and Hats were woven from grass and plant fibers. Mat wearing was a very popular industry in Ilorin, Malete, Alapa, Megida, Afon and Bode-Saadu. The various types produced include *Eni Alini*, *Eni Sana Eni Ore* among others. Mat weavers attracted buyers from far and near especially from the southern Yoruba towns and villages. Some mats were often finely coloured and soft thus suitable as bed spread. Some were for packing, some as drying for produce, partitioning of sleeping rooms and sitting rooms among others (Abdulkareem 1985). The craft strengthened rural urban relations because the grasses were gotten from the distant villages and were brought to the city to weave. The different sizes and types of mats also explained volume about the social strata in the society, i e the rich and the poor, the old and the young, literate and the illiterate.

Women's craft

Weaving

Weaving as practiced among the people of Ilorin was an occupation engaged in by both men and women as discussed but with differences in the processes, types and methods adopted. Preparation of cotton meant to be weaved after harvesting started by separating the cotton from the seed. Here, some sort of technology came into play as the seeds (gosypium barbadenesss) were removed from the coat by placing it in between a smooth slog of wood and a piece of finely polished won. This would be followed by spinning done by weighing this rod of about twelve inches with a small ball of clay attached to one end before making it into a fluff by attaching it into the string. This is followed by final spinning and carding before it is dyed in to desired colour (Ann, 1981: 67). This made the material to be preferred in the town and even outsiders for important ceremonies to the present time. The wearing proper was then done by women in sitting position, hand-woven on vertical or up right loom. The strip of cloth produced was about twenty- one inches in width called *Kutupu*. The weaving industry fully enhanced the indigenous artistic mastery because all the materials used were all locally sourced. Marketing of the woven textile was done by making it available in all the markets in and around the emirate headquarter Ilorin where buyers trooped to for their purchases as observed by Clarke (1972: 30-45). Ilorin cloth therefore competed with similar clothes produced in other Yoruba towns such as Iseyin, Iwo and Ikirun among other.

Pottery

Pottery was another woman industry whose raw materials were obtained within the Emirate. Pot making was usually done where the best clay could be found. Such locations, as it was in the case with Okelele dada pottery centre. The mode of production was by taking the required quantity of day soil to the pot industry called *Ebu*, mixed with water and then pounded with motor and pestle to solidify and stricken it. This was followed by moulding, scraping and smothering the day into different objects and shapes before it is designed (Ann 1981: 67). The marketing of the products was always done in the period before 1900 by displaying it at the centre of production or carried to the markets nearer to the place of production. Though, some of the products found their ways to places outside the town of production. But this was in low quantity because it was not mentioned as an article of long distance trade (Krapt.1969: 103-109).

Dyeing

Dyeing was also an important occupation in Ilorin that was purely practised by women. It was prominent among the folks of

Agbaji, Okelele and Masingba areas of Ilorin as well as other villages across the Emirate. Dyeing was however a family occupation passed from mother to daughter with few outsiders allowed learning the craft. Dye-making typified the indigenous technology whereby environmental resources were maximally tapped and optimally utilized. Indigo leaves *Elu* were collected from indigo era and then pounded in a mortar, rolled into balls to sun dried, then mixed three different concoctions of *Ayin, Emi* and *Igbaluwere* to produce the needed chemical *Ilaru* that produced the desired colour. Marketing of *Elu* and *Ilaru* cut across the Emirate in the period before 1900. The patronizes were mostly weavers who dyed the yarn needed for weaving into various colours (Saka 1985: 18-33).This occupation is among those crafts that refused to bow out for imported materials and continue to wax stronger in the Emirate..

Locust (Iru) making

Iru making was made from locust beans which have been boiled and fermented. This indigenous craft was illustrative of the advantageous exploitation of environment resources by the people. Locust bean tree was widely grown all over the Emirate. The process is not farfetched. The long parkia seed *Igba* was harvested and the fleshy yellowish part washed away to get the nut. The nut is sun dried before cooked for a whole day to ensure it softness. The soft inner seed is removed washed, covered for three days for fermentation and ready to be added to soup and vegetables as flavour. It was an indispensable cooking ingredient for all classes of soup in the society (Oliver 1975: 179-180). This product is still an occupation to be reckoned with in Ilorin and it does environ till the present time.

Bead making

Bead making otherwise known as Lantana work was another important indigenous industry among the women folk. The raw material needed for this industry was said to have come from the Old Oyo area and near Illo in the neighbouring of the Gwandu Emirate. The stone is rough and coral coloured. Ilorin beads were very popular and widely used among the indigenous. The stone could be made into necklace, waist bead. (That could be used for adoring newly wedded brides during marriage ceremonies). An Ilorin bead was not only a local material but traded to Warri, Ibo, Igbomian and Ekiti towns among other places (Ibrahim, 1986: 34-35). The chiefs in these areas used them for their crowns, wristband and necklaces. Others used it for their children during marriages and as presents, and the Benin exchanged it for slaves.

Body decorations cosmetics

Body decorations cosmetics product devices produced in pre-colonial Ilorin were mostly done by women in an elaborate preparations as well as application of some indigenous technical devices. For example, *tiro* application on eye-lashes and eye brow to make the eyes aesthetically satisfying and to reinforce the frames of the eyes (Ibrahim, 2006: 130). In the same manner were some traditional body lotions like coconut oil *adin agbon*: Palm kernel jelly *adi* sheer –butter pomade *ori* and *osun* and *Laali* believed to be efficient in smoothing the body. For example, *osun* prepared from cordwood (petrocarpus), (i) as made into pomade: mixed with water, coconut oil palm kernel jelly and used to redden the skin and newly born baby. *Laali* was for body adornment. In the same vein was indigenous black soap *Ose dudu* made from palm kernel jelly (Elaies Guinesis) ashes of cordwood and husks of the palm tree, all mixed and burnt together. The ashes were then shifted and the liquid collected and reheated to sticker it and cut to sale in all markets within the Emirate (Sanusi, 2016).The usage of some of these items still continue but in a well packaged container to make it attractive.

Ilorin Emirate markets before 1900

The Emirate paraded a unique marketing system before 1900. There were three market structures in Ilorin. The first was the pre-entry market, the second being the wards markets and the principal markets (Ibrahim, 2006: 128).

The Ward Markets

Ilorin Township was divided into five wards for administrative convenience under the four Baloguns and Magajin Gari. Each ward had markets that served its immediate people. The villages and other towns that later made up the Emirate equally had markets that served its immediate people. These markets were often established by the ward or village heads to facilitate easy marketing system for immediate needs of the people. For example, there were ward markets in Oja Iya, Ita Kure, Oni Tanganran Alapata, Eruda, Oloje, Megida, Alapa, Ajikobi, Eji Dongari and in other towns and villages.

The Pre-Entry Markets

The pre-entry markets were occasional markets that took place at the gate that entered Ilorin Township. The markets were situated at the Gbagba, Ondoko and Foma among other gates that surrounded the town. Traders from the wards and the principal markets moved to the toll gates where most of the markets were situated to meet the villagers. There, they will buy their commodities to be re-sold at the wards or any of the principal markets. The villagers would therefore return to their respective villages without coming into Ilorin town with the commodities they bought to be resold in their villages and towns. The goods bought at the pre-entry markets were regarded as cheaper than when the village traders brought them to the markets. The intended buyers would therefore buy the goods, and in turn re-sold them to the final buyers or consumers. The pre-entry market has been reformed now re-named *Ajapa* (Those engaging it are called *Alajapa*). The traders however now move beyond the vicinity of Ilorin and actually go to the villages to buy these commodities.

The Principal Markets

The pre entry and the ward markets described above served as tributaries for the principal markets in Ilorin. The Emir market (Oja Oba) was one of the principal markets. The market was often conducted at night, but by the middle of the twentieth century, it had become both day and night market. Almost anything could be obtained in these markets. The origin of the Emir's market was obscured, but *Magaji* Are maintained that similar markets were common in all other Yoruba town including Offa, Ijebu, Abeokuta, Ibadan, Ijaye, Ile-Ife among others (Ibrahim 1986, 20-24). The location of this market made the Emir and his agents to monitor activities in the market and by extension the whole Emirate.

The second principal market and the most viable in the nineteenths century Ilorin was the Gambari (Hausa). The market was the largest market in Ilorin from the middle of nineteenth century to the middle of twentieth century. Clarke said of the market.

Where all goods such as saddles, silk-sash, raw silk, trona, and many other articles brought by interior traders are deposited, is at the international markets situated in Gambari quarter. There the northern caravans discharged their goods. These they found the lodging, house, keepers, the brokers, the dealers and Islamic scholars who would see to their wants, direct them to buyers (Hodder 1965: 15).

Also the southern traders patronized the Gambari market than did the Emirs market. It should be further stated that, the pre-entry and the ward markets dealt with the local commodities (Ann, 1981, 15). However, the two principal markets in Ilorin had international recognition. At the Emir's market almost every commodities were sold there. Villages and the ward markets traders patronized it for goods that could not be obtained at their various markets. The Gambari market on the other hand was a bit special. It was there the northern caravan traders discharged their wares either for sale or rebound them for onward journey to the south. Some traders as a result of frequent visit stayed permanently in Ilorin partly because of the warm reception accorded them by the local inhabitants, or buoyant sale made at the market (Ann1981, 65-90).

Conclusion

This chapter analyses the various indigenous industries and their technological modes that were popular among Ilorin people before 1900. It has been argued that the ready markets for the various indigenous goods meant a high "demand" which of course, had to be met with a correspondingly active "supply" system. In addition, the various types and functions of the indigenous markets in the pre-colonial Ilorin have been highlighted: from the purely social and economic ones to a highly cultural and ritualistic one. For instance, the Oja-oba market in front of the Emir's market hosts the Fulani once annually during Eid Adha (kabir) festival. It is my personal conviction that Nigeria has genuine technological and industrial take-off, has in realistically reassessing and rehearsing our numerous but rich indigenous technological base. Adequate tapping (where necessary) should follow the reassessment, for the industrial and economic benefits of the nation.

References

Abdulkareem L G. (Late) 1985. Oral Interview, C.72. Ilorin.

Abdulkareem O. 2016. Oral Interview. C.66 Ilorin.

Abeni-Eleni O. 2015. Oral Interview, C60. Ilorin.

Afolabi Ojo, G. J. 1966. *Yoruba Palaces: A Geographical Analysis*, University of Ife and London Press: Ife.

Ali A.N. 1968. *The Holy Qur'an Text Translation Commentary, Surat Nisa' The Woman vs.8- 9* Beirut Press.

Amuda, O. 2016. Oral Interview, C.70 Ilorin

Ann, O. 1981. "Economic History of Ilorin in the 19th and 20th Centuries", Ph.D. Thesis, Centre for West African Studies, University of Birmingham.

Asude, M. 2017, Oral Interview, C.66 Alapa.

Atanda, J.A. 1971, "The Fall of the Old Oyo Empire: A Reconsideration of its Causes," *Journal of Historical Society of Nigeria. (JHSN). Vol.5.No4.*

Balogun, S. A.1978. "Historical Significance of Ilorin: A Preliminary Survey" *Confluence.No.1.* Vol.1Clarke, W.H. 1972, *Travel and Exploration in Yoruba Land 1854-1658*. Ibadan, University Press.

Danmole H. O. 1980. The Frontier Emirate: A History of Islam in Ilorin, *Ph. D Thesis*, University of Birmingham.

Hodder, B. W. and Ukwu, U. I. 1969. *Markets in West Africa*, University Press: Ibadan. Hopkin, A.G.1972. *An Economic History of West Africa*, Longman: Essex.

Hugh, T. R 1963. The Rise of Chirotian Europe in *The Listener*. See also West Africa No.2433, also Akintoye, S.A. "Nigeria

Contribution to Black History" in *Nigeria Magazine, Festival* Issue/ Nos. 115-116

Ibrahim, B.O. 1986. "A History of Ilorin Trade Network 1830-1950," *B.A. Dissertation*, University of Ilorin.

Jimoh, L.A.K. 1994. *Ilorin The Journey So Far*, Atoto Press Limited: Illorin.

Johnson, S. *A*. 1921. *History of the Yoruba*, Lagos, CMS Bookshop.

Krapt-Askari, E. 1969 *Yoruba Towns and Cities*, Oxford University Press: London.

Lloyd, P.C. 1953. "Crafts Organisation in Yoruba Towns," *Africa* Vol. 23.

Macfies, S. 1913. "The Pottery Industry in Ilorin Northern Nigeria," *Bulleting of the Imperia Institutes,* Vol.11.

National Achieve Kaduna. Ilorprof. (Assessment Report). 1012/1013, National Achieve Kaduna.Ilorprof.22QT: Touring by Industrial Promotion Division, 1964-66. 2015.

National Achieve Kaduna.Ilorprof, 5, 3685: Local Industries-Order.

Olaoye, R.A. *Ilorin Textile Industry 1850-1900: A Case Study in the History of Technology,* PhD Thesis, University of Ilorin, 1993. pp. 54-99.

Oliver and Forgan, 1975. *Africa in Iron Age*, Cambridge University Press: London.

Paul, B. A. and Philip C. (eds.) 1971. *Africa and Africans,* National History Press: New York.

Sanusi A. 2016. C.64 Oral Interview, Ilorin.

Saka, A.D. 1985. *The Weaving Industry in Ilorin*, B.A. Dissertation, University of Ibadan: Ibadan.

Woru, M. 2016. *Magaji Nda of Ilorin*, Oral Interview, C71, Ilorin.

Chapter Nine

Interrogating the Role of Non-state Actors in the Development Agenda of the Global South

Munyaradzi Mawere & Costain Tandi

"They do not have the interests of the countries they are operating in at heart and, therefore, assisting these countries to overcome their economic challenges is none of their business" (Clark, 2010: 32).

Introduction

This chapter examines the role of Non-state Actors (NSAs) in the development process and agenda of Africa. NSAs include Non-Governmental Organisations (NGOs), Transnational Corporations (TNCs) Civil Society Organisations (CSOs), to mention only but a few. The chapter seeks to provide a better understanding of the role that NSAs are currently playing in the context of development in the Global South. The motivation to carry out this research stemmed out of the realisation that there is dearth of systematic research on this important area of scientific inquiry, yet the role and activities of NSAs has increasingly become so controversial and questionable in many parts of the Global South. Of those who have contributed to the debate on NSAs, two distinct intellectual camps have tussled against each other, with some scholars arguing that the activities of NSAs are beneficial to developing host economies while others conclude that their activities are detrimental to the developmental processes and efforts of the Global South. The latter intellectual camp has posited that Africa has been so thoroughly plundered by NSAs, as to be desolate in all respects, to the extent that it becomes an oxymoron or rather a misnomer to argue that Africa was largely underdeveloped and not overexploited.

In this chapter, we argue that with reference to Africa, the activities of NSAs have, more often than not, been identified as questionable or sometimes unethical because of the harms they have inflicted on the people and their environs. Owing to their formidable resource base, some NSAs have allegedly tended to dominate the economies of the Global South, straddling and strangling the indigenous entrepreneur while creating monopoly in the process. The uncertainties associated with these activities are an obvious reason for further analysis on the subject. In this endeavour, the present chapter contributes to the scientific understanding of the often taken for granted relationship between NSAs from the Global North and economies of the Global South. Specifically, it critically questions whether NSAs are serving as agents of imperialism in the various countries they operate in.

While the debate rages on, the fact remains that the so-called Third World countries are in need of economic growth and transformation to fight the running away poverty levels affecting their economies. In fact, Africa's poverty level is accelerating at a sporadic pace. This is, however, a paradox given that the Global South has plenty of natural endowments to take herself out of poverty (Mawere 2014; 2016; 2017; Andebo 2014a). It is piteous to note that most countries in the Global South lack the necessary technology to fully exploit their natural resources. Resultantly, the continent relies more on the investments done by the TNCs, mainly in the area of resource extraction and NGOs especially in areas to do with the so-called humanitarian aid. Nevertheless, this has had disappointing outcomes in the continent's efforts to reduce poverty through natural resources utilisation. It is now known that many NSAs in general and TNCs in particular, have their bases in the Global North where they repatriate their profits. Sadly, they exploit the legal structures and policies of taxation to deny developing countries the revenue they deserve from the business of resource extraction. This precipitates the Global South's economic instability.

That said, the present chapter critically interrogates the role of NSAs, particularly the NGOs and Transnational Corporations in view of the development agenda of the Global South such as Africa.

Perspectives on Non-state Actors

The conceptualisation of NSAs is highly contested in academic circles such that it remains difficult to pin down with precision the universal definition of the concept. The way the concept of NSAs is applied remains context-specific and therefore varies from one situation to another. This resonates with Blamey's (2001) observation that the membership of non-state actors depends on the definition of the concept and therefore varies from place to place and according to the context in which it is used. Blamey (2001) equates delineation of the boundary for non-state actors' membership to "drawing a line on sand". In this chapter, we adopt the working definition of non-state actors as enunciated during the Partnership Agreement between the European Union (EU) and the African, Caribbean and Pacific Rim (ACP) countries signed in Cotonou, Benin, in June 2000 thus:

> NSAs are the private sector, the social and economic partners, includes trade union organisations, and the civil society in all its diversity. NSAs can include a wide range of actors such as non-governmental organisations (NGOs), trade unions, employers' organisations, private businesses, consumer organisations, academic and research organisations, church and religious associations and communities, independent foundations, organisations representing indigenous peoples, organisations representing national and/or ethnic minorities, organisations representing economic and social interests, organisations fighting corruption, and fraud and promoting good governance, civil rights organisations and organisations fighting discrimination, local organisations involved in decentralised regional cooperation and integration, cultural research and scientific organisations, the media and others (Kironde, 2007: 45).

From the foregoing, we note that non-state actors are "an heterogeneous set of non-sovereign entities ("for-profit" and "not-for-profit"; formal or informal) including the private sector and the civil society in all its diversity" (Ibid). These include: Non-governmental organisations (NGOs), Community-Based Organisations (CBOs), Community-Based Associations (CBAs),

Faith-Based Organisations (FBOs), Business Management Organisations (BMOs), Trusts, women groups, Youth groups, Community Forest Associations (CFAs), and Resource User Associations (RUAs), and Beach Management Units, among others. Owing to the ubiquity of NSAs, this chapter will focus on the role of NGOs and TNCs in the development agenda of the Global South.

Role of Non-State Actors: A Case of NGOs

The role of non-state actors in development has continued to receive increasing space both an alternative route to poverty alleviation and as an area of scientific inquiry in the academy. Owing to the increasing development crisis globally, there is an explosive growth in the presence of NSAs and other privately funded charitable organisations in the Global South. Interestingly, the term "NSA" itself and the activities associated with them remain controversial. This is chiefly because of the fact that in reality most of the NSAs from the Global North receive their funding from a multitude of imperialist agencies and governments. The imperialist governments and agents in turn manipulate and direct the operations of many NSAs such that the latter are widely understood as vehicles which carry interests of the imperial powers. NGOs are perhaps the most common example of non-state actors since they operate at global, regional (for instance, Africa, East Africa), national, sub-national and local levels.

Although on paper the main aim of most NSAs is to alleviate poverty in the developing world, the effectiveness of their mission, in fact, remains dependent on the framework of neoliberalism. Porter and Craig (2004) opine that, the global economic system of neoliberalism is not geared towards bridging socio-economic inequality but oriented to protecting existing property rights and providing for their expansion as well. It is against this background that it remains difficult to view the work of Non State Actors in general and NGOs in particular as anything more than short-term and ineffective band-aid solution to Africa's development challenges.

If we are to go by this observation, there is need, therefore, for development practitioners especially in the South, to question whether the recent upsurge of development initiatives by NSAs is a genuine call for development or just a tactical manoeuvre that favours the Global North at the expense of the Global South. Besides, there is also need to subject under scrutiny the Poverty Reduction Strategy Papers (PRSPS) and the subsequent Millennium Development Goals (MDGs), which have been used as the most recent frames of reference for multi-lateral development interventions in the Global South. We advance that it is our legitimate right to question whether these development policies, infused with a politicised language that everyone agrees with, will offer any real hope for a poverty free world. Although the United Nations (1992) strongly recommends that NGOs should foster cooperation and communication to reinforce their effectiveness as actors in implementation of sustainable development, this chapter audaciously interrogate the genuineness of development agencies mushroomed in many countries of the Global South.

TNCs' role in the development of the Global South

Besides NGOs, transnational corporations are also one of the most common variant of NSAs active in the Global South. The term "Transnational corporation" (TNC) can be defined from different perspectives and on a number of various levels theoretically and discipline-wise, as it straddles areas such as law, sociology, history, and strategic planning as well as from the perspectives of business ethics and society (Owenyuchi & Obmneke 2013; Henmart 2008). Dunning (1992: 3) opines that "a multinational or transnational enterprise is an enterprise that engages in foreign direct investment (FDI) and owns or controls value-adding activities in more than one country." While this definition captures the inherent attributes of TNCs, it excluded share of assets. For this reason, a definition which is now widely accepted by the United Nations Conference on Trade and Development (UNCTAD) includes a specific requirement regarding the share of assets controlled by the parent enterprise. UNCTAD (2002b: 291), thus, conceptualises TNCs as:

Transnational corporations are incorporated or unincorporated enterprises comprising parent enterprises and their foreign affiliates. A parent enterprise is defined as an enterprise that controls assets of other entities in countries other than its home country, usually by owning a certain equity capital stake. An equity capital stake of 10% or more of the ordinary shares or voting power for an incorporated enterprise, or its equivalent for an unincorporated enterprise, is normally considered as a threshold for the control of assets.

From the foregoing, it can be noted that TNCs are companies which seek to operate strategically on a global scale. We, thus, define a transnational corporation as a company, firm or enterprise that operates worldwide with its headquarters in a metropolitan or developed country. However, certain features of TNCs should be identified from the outset since they serve, in part, as their defining features. Often referred to as "multinational enterprises," in some early documents of the United Nations, TNCs are called "Multinational Organisations." This connotes that TNCs are usually very large corporate entities that while having their base of operations in one nation—the "home nation"—carry out and conduct business in at least one other, but usually many nations, in what are called the "host nations" (cf. Heindeinreich 2012; Owenyuchi & Obmneke 2013; Eluku *et-al* 2016). It is from this understanding that Eluku *et-al's* (2016: 61) also understands TNC as "a corporation that has its management headquarters in one country, known as the home country, and operates in several other countries, known as host countries". The operations outside the company's home country may be linked to the parent by merger, operated as subsidiaries, or have considerable autonomy. TNCs usually engage in multiple economic activities across national boundaries, while much of the cross border markets are internalised, that is, they are transacting the goods and services internally. This distinguishes TNCs from other transnational institutions like large Non-Government Organisations (NGOs) or international organisations. Most TNCs are nationally controlled, but internationally owned and, their control is based on a hierarchical order and centralised system.

The industrialised or imperialist nations use their TNCs (Transnational Corporations) to further plunder the resources of the Global South till today. It can be noted, for instance, that North-America and European corporations have acquired control of more than two thirds of the known mineral resources of Asia, Africa and Latin America. This means that their TNCs normally invest in countries with cheaper labour markets, hence the reason why many critics consider most of these corporations as imperialistic and parasitic in nature. We advance that TNCs have developed a global production line, which is detrimental and exploitative of the Global South. It is arguably true that, today, by controlling the substructure of the Global South, the imperialists who could be in more recent terms called neo-imperialists or super-colonialists, control the substructure of the world economy and as such control the superstructure of the Third World countries. This owes to the fact that at global level, major economic decisions are being made by the developed countries, who by virtue of their technological and economic influence in the developed world, tend to produce more goods for exportation to the Global South. On the other hand, the Global South is relegated to the background in the international division of labour, by just producing raw materials which is a very primary stage of production and economic development. This situation makes the Global South run at a deficit balance of payment because they buy more than what they sell. Also, the situation brings about dependency on the Global North for even local businesses.

Taking it from the above, we argue that TNCs are a creation of the so-called Empire or Global North imperialists who at root are indeed exploiters of resources of the Global South. It is worth noting that, today the Global South is not being controlled directly like in the colonial period. Yet, while the control over the Global South is indirect through the TNCs, and sometimes the media for indirect psychological control of the Third-World, such control is even more dangerous than the direct one. This is because indirect control catches people of the Global South unaware the same way animals are caught by traps.

Such indirect control is further aggravated by the metropolitan bourgeoisie of the Global North who plunder the resources of the

229

Global South with the aid of the comprador bourgeoisie. In Zimbabwe today as elsewhere in the Global South the situation is not different. During colonialism, Europe featured prominently in the exploitation of the Global South. Europe exploited the Global South directly by way of physical presence in the form of civil administration while America exploited them indirectly through the activities of their TNCs. It is in this view that Gilpin (1987) along with Owenyuchi & Obmneke (2013) opine that the term multinational corporation for a long time was largely a euphemism for the foreign expansion of America's giant oligopolistic corporations. This means America took the lead in this neo-colonialism (or rather super-colonialism) of Africa in the form of TNCs. Nevertheless, Japan and China of late have posed the greatest challenge to America. It can be noted that, Japanese and Chinese TNCs especially in the Global South countries, are merely for the purpose of amassing raw materials or low-cost components to the international markets. This is one reason why it is very rare to see any Japanese or Chinese TNCs venturing into manufacture investment in the Global South.

Further, TNCs can be regarded as a vehicle or agent of neo-colonialism, when considering the type of relationship that exists between the TNCs and their home governments. Taking America as an example, one can easily deduce that there is complementarity of interest between the TNCs in the Global South and the United States government. This explains why United States policies have continued to encourage corporate expansion abroad and not only that but offered protection to them. An example of this is the stand of the American government any time there is conflict between the youths of the Niger-Delta and the oil companies of United States nationality in Nigeria (cf. Owenyuchi & Obmneke, 2013; Ozoigbo & Chukuezi, 2011).

Besides, American TNCs are playing a pivotal role in stabilising the United States of America balance of payments. Equally vital in this regard is the fact that TNCs are the most veritable mechanism to spread abroad the United States of America ideologies especially that of free enterprises system. It can, therefore, be noted that the mother countries of the TNCs are doing indirectly what the Empire did directly during the colonial era namely, the exploitation and the oppression of their periphery states by milking them of their all-important raw materials and transferring the same to their respective nations for economic development and thereby systematically under-developing the Global South.

With regard to operations in the Global South and Nigeria in particular, most economists have come to believe that the TNCs are exploitative of natural resources found in the Global South countries despite the rhetoric call of the Global North to meet the Global Millennium Goals. This is observable in the American TNCs' gesture towards the de-capitalisation of the economy in form of profit repatriation (Owenyuchi & Obmneke, 2013). It is for the same reason that Ozoigbo and Chukuezi (2011), in full support of the claim above, argue with reference to TNCs that the idea of investing in foreign land is not to better the lot of the host nation but to exploit as much as possible in order to develop the home country. This resonates with Ugwu's (2010) argument when he posits that TNC enterprises have been used as a foreign policy instrument of their home governments, to the disadvantage of host country's economic development. The TNCs are often accused of destructive activities such as damaging of the environment, complicity in human rights abuses, involvement in corruption and stifling of infant industries autonomy, and above all involvement in the expatriation of profits and looting of natural resources from their host countries. Thus, corporations have siphoned the Global South by sending bulk of their profits to their home countries which they could have invested to develop the continent, thereby, subjecting Africans to the whims and caprices of underdevelopment. Consequently, the royalties or pittance paid to the Global South governments by these TNCs are so inconsequential that they cannot be invested into heavy industrial projects. Today, Africa is suffering from economic underdevelopment partly because of capital flight.

Clark (2010: 32) has summarised the impact on the indigenous economies and politics of TNCs operating in the Global South as follows:

- They do not have the interests of the countries they are operating at heart and therefore assisting these countries to overcome their economic challenges is none of their business.
- They promote and encourage more of commercial activities than productive activities. Therefore the Global South countries are turned into trading output.
- They discourage indigenous production activities.
- They deceive Global South governments into giving them concession enabling them to repatriate huge sums of profits.
- The money made from host nations are not used to develop them.
- They shift and take control of the more profitable sector of the economy like petroleum or diamond mining for instance in Zimbabwe and the Democratic Republic of Congo.
- They compound the developmental problems of Global South countries by sending them over-priced obsolete equipment like vehicles, computers and many others.
- They retard the progressive government of Global South countries through blackmail and sabotage.
- They engage in monopolistic capitalism for instance Coca-Cola Company that do not want any other foreign or indigenous soft drink company in African nations where they operate.
- They encourage members of host countries to patronise their products in lieu of indigenous products which they brand inferior.
- They encourage privatisation of indigenous enterprises and buy the larger shares in such privatised enterprises.

In addition to what Clark gives us, Langdon (1981) has observed that TNCs repatriate their profits and move large amounts of currencies across borders especially in the event of a relocation of plant for various reasons. This reverberates with Abdulla's (1997: 43) argument that "MNCs have cast the stigma which characterises their predecessors associated with colonialism." Contrary to the expectations of most countries of the Global South, research has it that the TNCs' transfer of technology is of no significant economic benefit to the host state. Ake (2002) points out that what passes as technology transfer is not that the technology transferred is appropriate but that it is available. The technology so transferred is often obsolete, archaic, expensive and often unsuited to the application and demands of the host state. The TNCs have in many instances, for example, transferred obsolete technology to developing countries such as expired pharmaceuticals, radioactive goods such as union carbides toxic products, and the dangerous DDT. Hahlo *et al* (1997) establishes that an average TNC welds more economic power twice or thrice than that of the nation state in which it operates. Over two decades ago, the annual turnover of General Motors' Corporations, for instance, was equal to the GNP of Switzerland, Pakistan and South Africa combined (Tirimba & Machaira 2014).

Worse still, many TNCs make huge profits through unscrupulous means. Studies of the drug industries in several countries show that TNCs make huge profits at the home base by raising the cost of materials supplied from abroad and services rendered to their subsidiary companies (Hahlo *et al* 1997; Langton 1991). This is transfer pricing. Tirimba & Machaira (2014) note with concern that transfer pricing is a problem in Kenya. A subsidiary of a large textile firm in Kenya purchased all inputs from the parent company until recently at much higher than competitive prices. On this note, Tirimba & Machaira (2014) invite Silberztein (2008) to argue that transfer pricing is a challenge for developing countries. Unfortunately, the problem of transfer pricing by TNCs seems to be receiving very little attention. We, therefore, argue that debate on TNCs should not only focus on revenue leakage reduction through tax evasion by corporations operating in developing countries, but on transfer pricing which continue soaring day by day.

According to Tirimba & Macharira (2014: 4):

> a study to determine the TNCs perpetuation of poverty that was held in the cities of Kenya indicated the prevalence of poverty by regions. National percentage stood at 52%. Urban prevalence of absolute poverty is overwhelming despite the fact that TNCs operate in major urban centres. Kisumu has the highest percentage of absolute poverty, food poverty and hard core poverty respectively. Urban food poverty stood at an average of 35% while overall poverty stood at 45%.

This means that almost half of the urban population of Kenya lived below the absolute poverty line. How this is possible in the presence of TNCs, one wonders. We argue that the wealth of a nation and living standards are a direct reflection of the performance of the economy. The activities of the TNC in Kenya as elsewhere in the Global South, thus, directly affect the growth of the economies of the host states.

The working relations between NSAs and national governments in Africa

Chukwaemeka *et al* (2011) argue that Africa, apart from being the cradle of the human race, compared to the rest of the world, is one of the best endowed with the richest natural resources the world has ever seen. Africa has a landmass several times the size of Europe with rich deposits of oil, gold, diamond, iron, copper, and various types of wildlife and wood, among other valuable resources (Aja, 2009; Mawere 2014). Since time immemorial, Africa has been involved in developing an economy enabling her to produce its own food and its own tools, including weapons. It is against this background that since their contact with Africa, NSAs realised they had found the right niche for themselves in the social life of the nations of the Global South. Since then, NSAs have cunningly used cultural imperialism to destroy the psyche and value system of the new states. The result is that cultural heritage of the Global South has either been destabilised or thrown to the winds in favour of Western styled culture. It is quite authentic to say, the increase in the activities of NSAs in the Global South has not been accompanied by the development in good governance and economic growth. This has attracted widespread condemnation from Afrocentric scholars as well as other critical social commentators who continue to question what NSAs are really doing in the Global South.

NSAs, for instance NGOs, have been accused of worsening economic problems in the developing countries although they preach that more aid, fair trade as well as debt forgiveness is a panacea to the African development jam. Sadly, even though they have been involved in African affairs since many centuries ago, they continue to produce harrowing pictures of a continent gravely stricken by poverty and disease. The multi-million dollar question is whether Africa should de-link in order to develop, discard the NSAs or whether NSAs operating in the continent should be more grassroots-centred in order to achieve desired results. One wonders how NSAs can be a panacea to the development jam of the Global South. We argue that the mandate of NSAs in Africa should be shifted from a conduit for advocating good governance and disseminating Western aid to economic empowerment of African communities.

Besides, NSAs such as TNCs, equally contributed either to the emergence or perpetuation of social class structure in their host states. Some schools of thought argue that the existence of these oligopolies led to a change in economic base and structure of nations of the Global South. It has been argued a numberless time that owing to the size of TNCs, they could be used to undermine the sovereignty of states through political manipulations (Mcphail, 1988). The proponents of this view argue that TNCs could be used as a foreign policy instrument of its home government. This is already a reality if we are to consider the fact that Transnational Corporations such as the United African Company (UAC), Toyota motors, Coca-Cola, Lever brothers, Mobil oil, Shell BP and many others, dominate the landscape of the Global South. These corporations are very rich in all respects because of the profit they make in the Global South. Over the years, TNCs have been a source of controversy with some scholars arguing that, in the context of globalisation the Global South requires their investment to improve its competitive edge and to facilitate micro-level structural changes required for alleviating poverty and reducing its riskiness for investment (Kingsly 2014).

Contrary to Kingsly's thinking, some scholars have however argued that TNCs transfer technologies, capital and the culture of entrepreneurship to the Global South. For these scholars, TNCs, in fact, increase investment levels and income in the host countries; they promote improvement in their immediate environment; create access to high quality managerial skills; improve the balance of payment of host countries by increasing exports and decreasing imports; and help to equalise the costs of factors of production. As Onyewuchi & Obmneke (2013) note, many pro-TNCs argue that the latter stimulate domestic production and enhance efficiency and effectiveness in the production process; they stimulate positive responses from local operators. We, however, advance the argument that the major objective of TNCs is maximisation of profit at the lowest possible cost. Profit maximisation is actually the feature that gave rise to TNCs. In other words, the idea of investing in the Global South is not to better the lot of the host nations but to exploit and plunder as much as possible in order to develop the home country (Ozoigbo and Chukuezi, 2011). It is quite convincing, therefore, to say that activities of the TNCs in the Global South have generated a repulsive reaction from many economic theorists (Onimode 1982).

In Onomode's (Ibid) view, TNCs, for instance, are monsters that have consistently and systematically stultified economic development in various parts of the world in general and the Global South in particular. The question of NSAs precipitating the Global South's underdevelopment is not a mirage but a reality. In fact, it is an existential reality confronting resident humanity in the continent. It is real and not a myth that "the countries of Africa are underdeveloped today (and) their rate of economic growth has been far lower than that in the Western world" as a result of the activities of NSAs such as TNCs (Seligson, 1993: 52). This problem of underdevelopment in Africa, whose effects continue to reflect in the day to day quality of life of Africans, has generated responses or reactions intellectually and pragmatically in terms of government policies and practices among Africans and non-Africans within and outside the continent. Some of these reactions and responses can be traced to as far as the colonial era such that it is safe to argue NSAs are agents of international capital for the re-colonisation of the Global South. They are believed to be on the political agenda of paving way for the penetration of imperialist capital and for creating fertile ground for the smooth operation of capital and extension of the market, which will for many years to come guarantee the perpetuation of super-colonialism. It is now widely believed by many critics that in order to introduce market relations, the NSAs in general and NGOs in particular choose or select the so-called "backward communities" for their work in the guise of community development projects (cf. Mawere 2014; Nhemachena 2017). Thus, NSAs especially NGOs, are actively involved in so-called community development projects in almost all corners of the Global South not principally for humanitarian reasons but for reasons of advancing the interests of the imperialists.

Debating the existence of NSAs in Africa through Marxism

Marxist scholars believe that the NSAs represent merely the latest expression of capitalist exploitation and imperialism. For them, NSAs are held by their home countries as instruments of the inter-national class struggle supplanting the bourgeoisie nation-state precisely owing to the fact that they are a more efficient means by which the capitalistic economies can dominate and exploit the Global South economies. It is again important to note that the major criticism of NSAs is that their huge roles in Africa have failed to significantly improve the lots of Africans. Despite their activities in the continent, Africa still posts a disheartening picture of economic stagnation, poverty and underdevelopment. Thus, the role of NSAs in Africa is being viewed with suspicion and has been likened to that of early missionaries to Africa who, as claimed by critics, were used as instruments of subjugation by colonial masters.

It remains questionable how much NSAs have contributed to economic growth and development in the Global South. Their efforts at rehabilitating local services, for instance, only survive as long as they are on the ground, the reason being that most international NSAs working in Africa do not put much effort into capacity development, grassroots mobilisation, and empowerment. Rather, they concentrate on disseminating information and dubious aid. Many Western NSAs operating in Africa also fail to build strong partnerships with the local communities and the local governments, whose activities affect the life of the people. They are the servants of imperialist capital. Almost all the NSAs are directed by the invisible hand of the imperialists who set them up or fund them in accordance with their strategic goals. Huge funds are thus poured into the coffers of the NSAs in the name of development, social justice, human rights, grassroots democracy, and so on.

Marxist scholars further advance that besides, NSAs serve as ideologues for imperialism by justifying the penetration of imperialist capital into the countries of the Global South, and promote the vice-like grip of the imperialists over the economies of these countries. That is why the imperialists, selfish blood-suckers as they are, pour in huge amounts to form and nurture these organisations. Ford Foundation, Rockefeller Foundation, Carnegie Foundation, Heinrich Boll Foundation, and a host of other imperialist institutions pump in millions of dollars every year to maintain these NSAs in their respective areas in the Global South. They fund every type of project, institute, and research as long as they are supported by the imperial countries. For instance, the Ford Foundation has granted funds to numerous organisations and projects in almost every country in the world that had reached an astronomical figure of $ 8 billion since its formation in 1936. It has commissioned research scholars and intellectuals to undertake studies on subjects that are of relevance for the imperialists. Without a consistent and relentless struggle against these disguised imperialist agents and apologists, revolutionaries cannot bring the masses out of reformist and constitutional illusions. Meaningful and sustainable contributions to Africa's development are not possible without strong and deliberate investment into the lives of local Africans. We, thus, insist that the emphasis has to shift from doing it for Africans to teaching Africans how to do it for themselves.

Overcoming the problem

Owing to the problems highlighted in this chapter in view of NSAs operations and activities in Africa, we propose the following solutions to easy the tapestry of Africa's political and socio-economic problems:

- The Global South should delink from the world's capitalist system (see Frank 2005; Matunhu 2011).
- There is need for a fundamental structural transformation of the Global South economies. It should mean the transformation of production that will be devoid of imperialism. Walter Rodney (1972: 108), the chief

critic of underdevelopment of Africa, throws light on how structural transformation in Africa could be achieved when he notes that "to achieve economic development, one essential condition is to make maximum use of the country's labour and natural resources" through peaceful means.

- The problems of social infrastructure such as power, telecommunications, manpower, development and so forth should be adequately addressed if the Global South is to move forward and take advantage of the trends of globalisation.
- The on-going asymmetrical relationship between most governments of the Global South and trans-national enterprises including World Bank and IMF should be discouraged and re-assessed to the advantage of both the developed world and the third world countries.
- Governments of the Global South should emphasise the training of their nationals in some professionally skilled areas such as oil sector which is currently the exclusive sector of the NSAs, and in many others such as mineral processing and manufacturing.
- Host states should encourage the appointment and promotion of their own citizens to the real policy making positions of trans-national enterprises to ensure that NSAs policies are all-inclusive.
- Legislative incentives should be used to direct foreign investment to manufacturing sub-sector of the Global South and such industries should be capable of using local inputs for its operations. We, therefore, argue that the aspirations of the host nations to welcome the NSAs with the hope of drawing technology from them has failed to yield expected results.

Conclusion

In light of the above analysis, it is logical to conclude that the underdevelopment of the Global South can be partly attributed to their continued interaction and unequal encounter with international capitalism. The interaction which has always been based on unequal relationship, has distorted the underdevelopment of the Global South and at the same time stagnated the development of the South. It is unfortunate that even after independence from colonialism, this asymmetrical relationship has continued unabated. On the basis of facts presented in this chapter, the NSAs have outlived its usefulness as a development agent. The role of NSAs should be redefined in the context of the African nations in which they operate. The chapter also concludes that the over-dependence on these NSAs should be avoided at all costs.

References

Ake, C. A. 2002. *A political economy of Africa,* Longman: London.

Abdullah F. A. 1997. *Financial management for the multinational firm,* Prentice Hall, London.

Aja, E. 2009. The evil consequences of trans-national corporations, *International Journal of Politics,* 4(4): 45-50.

Andebo, P. 2014a. *African intergenerational and international issues in the light of Catholic Social Teaching: Demographic transition & Social Security – Environment & Resource Exploitation - Aid, Debt & Public Dependency on External Financing.* Retrieved from http://www.taxjustice-andpoverty.org/fileadmin/Dateien/Taxjustice_and_Poverty/Et hics_and_Religion/topical/Topical_01.pdf.

Blamey, R. K. 2001. 'Principles of Ecotourism,' In: Weaver, D. B. (Ed). *The Encyclopedia of Ecotourism,* CABI Publishing: New York & Oxon UK.

Bornschier, Volker and Christopher Chase-Dunn. 1985. *Transnational Corporations and Underdevelopment,* New York: Praeger.

Chukwuemeka, E. Anazondo, R. Nzewi, H.N. 2011. African underdevelopment and the Multinationals-A political commentary, *Journal of sustainable development,* Vol, 4 No 4, August 2011.

Clark, E. 2010. *Understanding African Economy,* Vinez Publishers: Lagos.

Dunning, J. H. 1992. *Multinational Enterprises and the Global Economy,* Wokinham: Addison Wesley.

Eluku, J, *et-al.* 2016. Multinational Corporations and their effects on the Nigerian economy, *European Journal of Business and Management,* 9(4): 61-75.

Frank, A. G. 2005. 'The Development of Underdevelopment,' In: *Development: Critical Concepts in the Social Sciences,* Washington DC: USA.

Ghasemi, M. & Hamzah, A. 2011. *An Evaluation of the Role and Performance of NGOs in Community- Based Ecotourism at Ulu Geroh, Malasyia*, Centre for Innovative Planning and Development, Monograph No. 9 (2011), Faculty of Built Environment, University Technology, Malasyia.

Hahlo, H.R. *et al.* 1997. *Naturalism and the multinational enterprise*, Oceania publication Inc: New York.

Heidenreich, M. 2012. The social embeddedness of multinational companies: A literature review, *Socio- Economic Review*, 549–579.

Hennart, J. F. 2008. The *Future of Multinational Enterprise*: *Academy of Management Annual Meetings*, Netherland.

Kingsley, A. O. 2015. The paradox of corporate social responsibility in Africa, Case of French Multinational Corporations, *International Journal of Knowledge and innovation in Business*, 2 (1): 39-77.

Kironde, J. M. L .2007. 'The role of non-state actors in enhancing participatory governance and local development,' *Paper presented at the African Local Government Action Forum Phase VII: Enhancing Participatory Governance and Local Development,* 1st June, 2007.

Langdon, S. 1991. *Multinational Corporation in the political economy of Kenya*, Macmillan Press: London.

Mawere, M. 2014. *Divining the Future of Africa: Healing the Wounds, Restoring Dignity and Fostering Development,* Langaa RPCIG: Bamenda.

Mawere, M. 2016. *Development Perspectives from the South: Troubling the Metrics of [Under-]development in Africa,* Langaa RPCIG: Bamenda.

Mawere, M. 2017. *Theorising Development in Africa: Towards Building an African Framework of Development*, Langaa RPCIG: Bamenda.

Matunhu, J. 2011. A critique of modernisation and dependency theories in Africa, *African Journal of History and Culture*, 3 (5): 65-72.

Mcphail, E. 1988. *British Colonial Objectives in Africa: The Roots of Underdevelopment,* McGraw Hill: New York.

241

Nhemachena, A. 2016. Post-development and the Social Production of Ignorance: Farming Ignorance in 21st Century Africa,' In: Mawere, M. 2016. *Development Perspectives from the South: Troubling the Metrics of [Under-]development in Africa,* Langaa Publishers: Bamenda, pp.77-117.

Onimode, B. 1982. *Imperialism and underdevelopment in Nigeria: the dialectics of* mass *poverty,* Zed Books: London.

Onyewuchi, O. G. & Obmneke, E. 2013. Multinational Corporations and the Nigerian economy, *International Journal of Academic research in Business and Social Sciences,* 3 (4): ISSN 2222-69990.

Ozoigbo, B. I. & Chukuezi, C. O. 2011. 'The Impact of Multinational Corporations on the Nigerian Economy', *European Journal of Social Sciences* – Volume 19, Number 3.

Porter, D. & Craig, D. 2004. The Third Way and the Third World: Poverty Reduction and Social Inclusion in the Rise of 'Inclusive' Liberalism, *Review of International Political Economy,* 11 (2): 387-423.

Rodney, W. 1972. *How Europe underdeveloped Africa,* University of Dar Es Salaam, Tanzania.

Tirimba, O. I. & Macharira, G. M. 2014. Economic impact of MNCs on development of developing nations, *International Journal of Scientific Research publications,* Vol 4, Issue 9, September 2014.

Seligson M. A. 1993. "The Dual Gaps: An Overview of Theory and Research," In: Seligson, M.A. & Passe-Smith, J.T. (eds.), *Development and Underdevelopment: The Political Economy of Inequality,* Lynne Reinner Publishers: Colorado.

Ugwu, B. 2010. Can African survive? International Journal of Sustainable Development, 5(5): 40-48.

UNCTAD. 1992. *World Investment Report 1992 - Transnational Corporations as Engines of Growth,* United Nations, Geneva.

United Nations. 1992. United Nations Sustainable Development (Agenda 21), *United Nations Conference on Environment and Development,* Rio de Janeiro Brazil 3 to 14 June 1992.

Chapter Ten

Servant Leadership and the Paradox of Africa's [Under-]development Predicament

Fortune Sibanda

Introduction

Today, Africa is a subject that has attracted different perspectives in society. For some, Africa is synonymous with strife, hunger, corruption, and human rights abuses. For Ngambi (2014), Africa presents a paradox in that it is the richest continent in natural resources, but yet is the poorest and most underdeveloped. In addition, some also regard Africa as being synonymous to mass victimisation, exploitation and plunders caused by slavery, colonialism, neo-colonialism, capitalism and despotism. This makes Africa a typical paradox and a 'continent in crisis' (Jackson 2002), notwithstanding that the fact that this predicament is attributed to an admixture of both internal and external factors. Because of the crisis, Africa is on the brink of cultural, economic and political collapse, which has far reaching implications to development and human progress on the continent. Apparently, development is a multidimensional phenomenon, which can be perceived from many points of view (Hallencreutz 1987). For instance, the fact that the majority of the people on the continent are living below the poverty datum line and exposed to hunger, famine, diseases and poor governance is a sad reality that calls for remedies from among Africans to realise some form of human development. Africa is poor on the socio-economic, political and leadership indicators (Ngambi 2014). Along these lines, although external factors such as the legacy of colonialism, globalisation and neo-colonialism are blameworthy for Africa's underdevelopment (Mawere 2016), there also exists poor, incompetent and "toxic" leadership, which are causes partly to blame for the continent's misery as they escalate the problems of disease, poverty and corruption. As such, postcolonial African political and

243

religious leaders to a certain extent should be held accountable and responsible for the dilemmas facing the African continent in their full gaze.

At the backdrop of all these problems bedevilling Africa, this chapter focuses on servant leadership as a remedy for underdevelopment in Africa in general and Zimbabwe, in particular. Anchored in the discipline of Religious Studies, it is posited that servant leadership, expressed in the biblical teaching of Jesus Christ on leadership and captured in the African leadership philosophy of *Ubuntu/Unhu* (humanness) is quintessential in reinventing the past for sustainable development for 21st century Africa in general and Zimbabwe, in particular. It is further argued that harnessing servant leadership could resolve problems in the socio-economic and political spheres provided they successfully build people, networks and relationships on the basis of being, *inter alia*, responsible, accountable, relevant and ethical in order to develop and transform Zimbabwe. Of late, African academics, journalists and many other stakeholders have expressed concern on leadership failures and corruption for reducing Zimbabwe to poor economic backwater (Hungwe 2016; Muleya 2016). This has stimulated a study of this kind at a time when Zimbabwe, though not a failed state, has been described as a 'strong but reluctant state', which is in a 'fragile situation' (Hungwe 2016). As Hungwe (2016) further observes, "Fragility applies to a state that demonstrates inability or unwillingness to deliver the core functions to the majority of the population. It's normally characterised by weak governance, policies and institutions". This shows how important it is to evaluate the contribution of the existing form of leadership in light of the socio-economic and political problems in Zimbabwe through the lens of Religious Studies. The role of religion in society is attached to the long history of its ambivalence in matters of development and public policy. On one hand, the positive role of religion has been noted in the moral leadership espousing peace, unity, economic justice, good governance and development as demonstrated by Mahatma Gandhi, Pope John Paul II, Archbishop Desmond Tutu, Dalai Lama, among other religious leaders. Conversely, the negative role of religion in the history of different nations has been recorded in the rise of different forms of say, Christian and Islamic fundamentalism that resulted in war, violence and destruction of great scale (Kaulemu 2006: vii). On this basis, the late and former President of Zimbabwe, Canaan Banana, a theologian in his own right, rightly pointed that "religion is a basic reality in any African society and has as such to be considered in any development strategy relevant to Africa" (Hallencreutz 1987: 7). This explains why a religious lens is also necessary in understanding leadership in matters of [under]development in Zimbabwe.

Theoretical Framework

The study was guided by the Afrocentric theory as a tool for understanding leadership and development in the African context. At the backdrop of the long history of slavery and colonialism that affected Africa and the Africans, the Afrocentric theory becomes handy for providing an "epistemological vigilance" (Mudimbe 1998) on matters of leadership and development, which enable African people to develop the necessary decolonised mind-set that rejects the enslavement of the western cultural logic camouflaged as the standard for all cultures to follow. Among scholars who popularised the Afrocentric theory is Molefi Kete Asante who refers to alternative terms used for this paradigm such as Africology, Afrology and Afrocentricity (Asante 1998). Essentially, the Afrocentric theory arose as a counter ideology to Eurocentricity that claimed to possess a universal command in intercultural communication, rhetoric, philosophy, linguistics, psychology, education, anthropology and history (Asante 1998). In this way, Afrocentricity was a corrective to the western meta-paradigm, which denied and marginalised the agency and action of the African people. A philosophy of the centre and periphery was developed as a product of 'racial mythology' in which western culture was deemed superior and core whilst African heritage was made inferior and situated in the doldrums.

The Afrocentric theory is significant in African studies because it "stands as both a corrective and a critique" (Asante 2007: 27). As a corrective, it seeks to address the biases, myths, misconceptions and actions by the westerners about the folly of African leadership,

245

Indigenous Knowledge System and [under]development by promoting the African agency, action and liberation in contemporary society. Through Afrocentricity, Africans can unravel the development traps that have been laid by colonialists to expropriate African resources in the name of 'development'. In addition, the western philosophies and models cannot be universalised in the context of leadership and development. Apparently, as a strong corrective measure, the Afrocentric theory could advocate the application of the African leadership philosophy, which stresses the concept of *Ubuntu* to attain the African Renaissance ahead of western borrowed concept of democracy. As Kondlo (2014: 9) rightly observes, "Liberal democracy [in Africa] is a borrowed concept; for that matter it is not democracy in the fullest truest sense." Like 'borrowed robes' which Africa must take off and dress up in her own, the corrective step from Afrocentricity must see Africa breaking this dependence and generate new thought leadership consistent with the uniqueness of Africa's experience. In this way, the Afrocentric paradigm would resituate the African people in expressing their agency by prioritising the domestic ahead of the international models of leadership and development.

The Afrocentric theory also serves as a critique to some of the African systems of leadership that end up thwarting the hopes for Africa's renewal and development. Although the weight of priority on models of leadership and development should be guided by the African philosophy of *Ubuntu* that is largely people-centred, history has shown that some African 'great men' in society have been immoral due to corruption of power and indulgence to satisfy their self-centred interests (Mawere 2016: 1). In other words, in African authoritarian systems, individual interests trump public interests where leaders become *kleptocrats* that debauch key government institutions and protect fraudsters. A case in point is Mobuto Seseko's Zairean monstrous leadership that benefited his selfish interests. Hence, the Afrocentric theory has the merit of being African-based and suitable to address African issues and problems better, but at the same time caution must be exercised to strike a balance when utilising it in some African contexts of leadership and development. This justifies the advocacy for servant leadership to spear-head Africa's sustainable development.

Cartography of Leadership

The very definition of 'leadership' is contested (Anderson 2014). However, leadership has certain properties that seem necessary and indispensable for it to exist at all and to be what leadership is. Ladkin (2010) defines leadership in terms of action and behaviour. In this way, leadership is a function and leader or manager is a position in an organisation. In addition, Ladkin (2010) says that the phenomenon of leadership can be studied through the lens of philosophy given that this discipline teaches how to live with uncertainty by asking questions. In this study, questions on the moral implications of leadership and its impact are raised in the social, political and religious contexts of Zimbabwe. For instance, to what extent does this leadership promote the goals of sustainable development in Africa? Although 'greatness comes through leadership' (Kamwendo 2016), today's challenge is that some of the religious and political leadership is interested in its own gains and personal conveniences, notwithstanding that the call for leadership is service.

In the discipline of Religious Studies, all the political and religious leaders are sacred practitioners with positions of responsibility in society. The religious functionaries in African Indigenous Religion include the chief, headman, elders and *n'anga* (traditional diviner-healer) whilst in Christianity there is the priest, prophet and bishop, among others who are sometimes referred to as 'men of God'. As leaders in privileged positions, they are expected to be highly responsible people guided by the philosophy of *Ubuntu* (communal love). In principle, the same demand for moral and spiritual integrity also applies to those who hold public offices in the government and other institutions, who ideally in Zimbabwe are sworn into office holding the Holy Bible. This brings an aura of spirituality to leadership showing that in principle, the government, church and traditional setup provide moral leadership to attain economic justice, good governance, peace, development and public policy.

Writing with reference to leadership in The Sunday Mail, a weekly local newspaper, Milton Kamwendo, a Zimbabwean motivational columnist, identified leadership as more of a spirit than things as testified by the life of the Indian leader, Mahatma Gandhi who provided moral leadership of all time. However, the leadership field is not level due to 'misleadership' (Rayment and Smith 2010). This shows that for whatever reason, leadership can mislead. Kamwendo (2016) identifies 'seven social sins' that Mahatma Gandhi taught. It is these 'social sins' that Kamwendo (2016) applied to the leadership plane to develop 'seven leadership sins'. These are presented in Table 1 below:

Table 1: Social Sins Juxtaposed to Leadership Sins

Seven Social Sins	Seven Leadership Sins
• Politics without principles	• Leadership without principles
• Wealth without work	• Leadership without work
• Pleasure without conscience	• Leadership without conscience
• Knowledge without character	• Leadership without character
• Commerce without morality	• Leadership without morality
• Science without humanity	• Leadership without humanity
• Worship without sacrifice	• Leadership without sacrifice

Source: *The Sunday Mail*, 5 June 2016, p. B12.

The Table above is significant in showing how the seven social sins affect the leadership plane. All citizens in their day-to-day lives are called to be responsible and accountable for their actions. Yet, leadership is dysfunctional where the leadership sins thrive. This diabolical leadership becomes 'misleadership', which lacks leadership values such as principles, work, conscience, character, morality, humanity and sacrifice. The presence of such leadership values results in a globally fit leadership called servant leadership, which is explored in the next section.

A Kaleidoscope of Servant Leadership

The term 'servant-leadership' was first coined and introduced in 1970 in an essay by the Indiana-born businessman and thinker, Robert K. Greenleaf (1904-1990), which was entitled 'The Servant as Leader'. The traditional approach to leadership in which people were viewed as objects or as cogs in a machine was transformed through the efforts of people like Greenleaf, Margret Wheatley, Stephen Covey, among others who suggested a team-oriented approach to leadership and management (Spears 1999). In 'servant-leadership' there is the juxtaposition of the words "servant" and "leader". The words servant and leader have been brought together to create a paradoxical idea of servant-leadership. In other words, the servant-leader concept merges servanthood into leadership and vice-versa in a continuous and fluid pattern. Some of the attributes of a servant-leader include listening, empathy, healing, awareness, persuasion, conceptualization, foresight, stewardship, commitment to the growth of people and building the community.

In his works, Greenleaf proposed a new kind of leadership model which prioritises "increased service to others; a holistic approach to work; promoting a sense of community; and a deepening understanding of spirit in the workplace" (Spears 1999: 10). Therefore, behind servant leadership is service. Referring to the responsibilities of a servant leader, Greenleaf (1977: 27) cited in McVay (2014: 111) once asked: "Do they, while being served, become healthier, wiser, freer, more autonomous, more likely themselves to become servants? And [sic], what is the effect on the least privileged in society? Will they benefit, or at least, not be further deprived?" This shows that a servant leader strives to involve the whole community and not just the elites and seeks to improve the lives of others through self-sacrifice. It is an institutional philosophy and model that is replacing the old hierarchical models of leadership. Spears and SanFacon (2008: 4) cited in McVay (2014: 108) observe that "at its core, servant-leadership is a long-term, transformational approach to life and work – a way of being – that has great potential for creating positive, non-violent change throughout our society and the world." This seminal approach was a metaphorical 'Copernican revolution', that is, a fundamental turning point in thoughts, on leadership applicable to different spheres of life such as business, religion, education or governance. The relevance of servant-leadership in these different contexts is commensurate to the submissions of this chapter.

In light of the above, it is important to note that servant leadership has a long tradition in practice among different communities. Notwithstanding the contributions of Greenleaf and his followers to the discipline of leadership, it is interesting to note that Greenleaf came up with an idea of leadership that is similar to that of Jesus Christ and the African philosophy of *Ubuntu*. The African philosophy of *Ubuntu* teaches that a person is a person through other people. In the context of leadership, the Shona adage that "*Ishe vanhu*" (A king is a king through the people) comes to the fore. This statement suggests that a leader is a leader if s/he expresses the collective will of the people. S/he does not represent him/herself, but exits for the sake of the people (Ngara 2014: 66). This is servant-leadership par excellence. Along the same lines, Jesus' teaching on leadership captures the moral virtue of *Ubuntu* as it illustrates the relationship between leaders and those they lead. It is prudent to refer to the biblical example of Jesus where it is said:

When the ten heard about this, they became indignant with James and John. Jesus called them together and said, 'You know those who are regarded as rulers of the Gentiles lord it over them, and high officials exercise authority over them. Not so with you. Instead, whoever wants to become great among you must be your servant, and whoever wants to be first must be slave of all. For even the son of Man did not come to be served but to serve, and to give his life as a ransom for many (Mark 10: 41-45, NIV).

The relevance of religion to matters of leadership becomes apparent. The *Ubuntu*-based leadership and that of Jesus Christ are closely related to that of Greenleaf (1977) who stresses that the servant-leader willingly chooses to be a servant first instead of being a leader first. At the base of this kind of leadership, there is emotional intelligence, responsibility and accountability, which can facilitate African development and transformation.

Understanding Development and Underdevelopment

This section explores how development and underdevelopment is understood in the academy. Such an interrogation begins with the concept of development. There is no universally accepted definition of development (Ngara 2014). Thus, the notion of 'development' is notoriously difficult to define. Development specialists and other researchers disagree on "how to define development, how to measure it and how to achieve it" (Ranger 1987: 29). These are complex issues that are necessary to interrogate when trying to understand the multi-dimensional phenomenon of development that is seen from diverse perspectives. In fact, there is an inadequate understanding of development with many perceiving it solely in a materialistic manner. This anchors on numerical or economic indicators such as growth in production per capita and the ability to attract investment capital measured by Foreign Direct Investment (Ngara 2014). At another level, Walter Rodney (1989) says development is understood at individual and societal levels. In his words, he writes thus:

> Development in human society is a many-sided process. At the level of the individual, it implies increased skill and capacity, greater freedom, creativity, self-discipline, responsibility and material well-being. Some of these are virtually moral categories and are difficult to evaluate – depending as they do on the age in which one lives, one's class origins, and one's personal code of what is right and wrong. .... At the level of social groups... development implies an increasing capacity to regulate both internal and external relationships (Rodney, 1989: 9).

Along the same lines, Churches in Manicaland (2006: 102,103) rightly observe:

> True development is holistic. It touches the body, mind and soul. Holistic development includes the struggle to remove all that diminishes us at a personal and societal level. It means unbinding all that binds: crippling poverty because of economic mismanagement, closure of public space because power and control are kept in the hands of a few, inefficiency in public service, apathy and indifference.... True development is a fruit of respect for human rights... protection of the marginal and the poor. Development is the new name for peace.

The above quotations delve into the definition and the measurement of development as something that is a process and not an event, which encompass the transformation of the individual and society. This has implications on the kind of leadership in place geared towards the service of the human person in terms of material needs and the intellectual, moral, spiritual and religious aspirations. Authentic development is a transition from less human conditions to those that are more human.

The basis for development reminds one about Ranger's (1987) third element noted above on the puzzle of how to achieve development. For development to take place, a number of factors are vital to consider. For instance, all citizens must have a deep respect for laws that safeguard basic democratic principles; the government must provide authentic service to improve the lives of the people; the local entrepreneurs must have the confidence that hard work and initiative are rewarded and not threatened by political chaos; foreign investors need an assurance that government officials stick to their promises; creditors expect loans to be repaid by responsible governments; donors look for credibility to support a deserved assistance (Churches in Manicaland 2006: 104). Therefore, some of these factors are useful in assessing the kind of leadership in place and the levels of development or under-development in society.

As in the case with development, an attempt to define the concept of 'underdevelopment' is equally elusive. Rodney (1989) gives a warning that underdevelopment does not imply absence of development. Following Ngara (2014) underdevelopment is characterised by a low production per capita in a country; low Foreign Direct Investment, a significant proportion of the population lives in abject poverty on less than US$1,25 per day (Ngara 2014: 459), among other factors. As such, underdevelopment from the economic perspective places most of the developing countries of the South in the category of 'underdeveloped' as compared to the countries in the global North. This has implications on the kind of leadership that are currently found in most African countries at the backdrop of the long history of underdevelopment caused by western colonialism and exploitation. The Sustainable Development Goals (SDGs) can also be used as an indicator to gauge levels of underdevelopment through economic empowerment, social inclusion and environmental sustainability in the world. It has to be asked: Is there hope for African development? Rodney (1989) expressed hope for African development basing on a radical break with the international capitalist system, which has been the main agency for the underdevelopment of Africa. In addition to this insight, the chapter demonstrates that African development is possible through, *inter alia*, the service of leaders inspired by the African philosophy of *Ubuntu*, which is servant leadership characterised by responsibility, accountability, relevance and ethical consciousness. Such an approach is being explored with reference to Zimbabwe as a microcosm of the macrocosm, to which the call to reinvent the past for sustainable development in 21st century Africa can be established. At this juncture, the chapter turns to the case of servant leadership in Zimbabwe.

Servant Leadership for Sustainable Development: The Case of Zimbabwe

In this section, servant leadership is being applied in the context of religion and matters of governance in order to illustrate the paradoxes of leadership that exist in Zimbabwe. Both religion and politics are fundamentally 'systems of survival' seeking to empower individuals, families, communities and the nation at large. Therefore, the presentation refers to religious and political functionaries as specific religious or political leaders, ecumenical perspectives, selected church or political party as well as pronouncements of specific religious bodies. This has a bearing on leadership and development or underdevelopment evaluation in Zimbabwe.

Narratives on the Church Bodies: ZCBC, EFZ and ZCC
In the context of religion, one can draw examples of leadership from the religious bodies, which are the main platforms through which Christianity manifests itself in Zimbabwe, namely, the Evangelical Fellowship of Zimbabwe (EFZ), the Zimbabwe Catholic Bishop Conference (ZCBC), and the Zimbabwe Council of Churches (ZCC). Notwithstanding that during the colonial era

missionary Christianity was regarded as the 'handmaid of colonialism', there are countless instances where they also sided with the oppressed black majority. This saw many nationalists getting schooled at Christian mission institutions. Since colonial times, the Roman Catholic Church and churches under the ZCC offered humanitarian services. The Roman Catholic Church established the Catholic Development Commission (CADEC) as the developmental arm of the Church whilst the Zimbabwe Council of Churches created Christian Care as its arm for emergency relief services and development. They undertake rural communal development projects for the alleviation of poverty, disease and hunger. Assistance has been rendered to address emergency situations like floods, war and internal displacements through government clean up campaigns such as Operation Murambatsvina (Sibanda Maposa and Makahamadze, 2008). The Zimbabwe National Pastors Conference of the Catholic Church issued a press statement on 30 May 2005 in line with government action. It condemned Operation Murambatsvina and called upon the government to "engage in a war against poverty and not a war against the poor" (The Zimbabwe National Pastors Conference, cited in Mashingaidze, 2006: 14). In addition, Christian Care and CADEC in rural districts of Masvingo Province provided food, clothes, blankets, school fees and back up psychosocial counselling to the HIV and AIDS affected orphaned and vulnerable children (Mashingaidze 2006: 31). This epitomizes servant leadership by the church bodies.

As intimated above, the Christian Care Brochure (2006) states that Christian Care is tasked "to witness the presence of God among the poor and disadvantaged who are burdened by oppression, poverty, ill health, lack of freedom or knowledge to make sustainable life supporting choices." Thus, the majority of the intended beneficiaries are the poor – the poorest of the poor who live on the "underside of history" (Gutierrez 1973: 189). Yet, the gamut of all the rural development projects by CADEC and Christian Care was to enhance self-reliance through engaging them in conservation agriculture, livestock breeding and fish farming. In other words, CADEC and Christian Care are giving skills to empower communities in order to avoid "donor-syndrome" and the piece-

254

meal solutions of providing people with "fish" instead of "fishing lines". By helping the needy to help themselves perpetually, these church organs are providing servant leadership for sustainable development in Zimbabwe.

In an ecumenical document, "The Zimbabwe We Want", the ZCBC, EFZ and ZCC (2006) pronounced their dismay with the deterioration of the socio-economic and political situation in Zimbabwe in the first decade of the New Millennium. They were self-critical about the lackadaisical attitude of the Church, as the conscience of the nation, for failing to defend the values of love, peace, justice, forgiveness and truthfulness trampled to the detriment of the majority (ZCBC, EFZ and ZCC, 2006: 10). These religious bodies, as a prophetic voice of the church, taught "the value of human solidarity, the value that says that human beings must never loose [sic] sight of the humanity of others" (Churches in Manicaland 2006: xii). This is a candid reflection on the role of the Church in society. The prophetic mandate of the church has also been expressed by the ZCBC in various Pastoral Letters that they have produced to address different situations. One such Pastoral Letter entitled, "God Hears the Cry of the Oppressed" (ZCBC 2007), said Zimbabwe was facing a moral crisis on the leadership front. In this way, informed by the Gospel and guided by the Holy Spirit, the church is providing servant leadership to address the social ills and lives of the needy in society. The church is therefore a watchdog of human rights, justice and peace as part of its humanitarian work. This creates a platform for sustainable development in Zimbabwe. In the religious front, Zimbabwe has witnessed the leadership of different spiritual leaders in various traditions including African Indigenous Religion (AIR) and Christianity.

Individual Spiritual Leaders: African Indigenous Religion

The popular sayings which pronounce that 'one wo/man's meat is another wo/man's poison' or 'one wo/man's hero is another wo/man's villain' are applicable to both religious and political leadership. In the context of African Indigenous Religion, reference is often made to the spiritual leaders such as Mbuya Nehanda, Sekuru Kaguvi and Mukwati who waged a war of resistance against colonial rule in the First Chimurenga (1896-7). On one hand, these are heroes and heroines for the indigenes of Africa who sacrificed their lives for the restoration of land and the liberation of the people. On the other hand, the colonialist and Christian missionaries labelled them as 'witches' and 'wizards', the very status under which Nehanda and Kaguvi were hanged in 1898 and why the colonial government later promulgated the Witchcraft Suppression Act (1899). Essentially, the First Chimurenga was a war between two religions, Christianity and AIR. In the history of Zimbabwe, T.O. Ranger is among the scholars who argue that traditional religious leaders played a significant role in the First Chimurenga war contrary to Beach and Cobbing who minimise their role (Sibanda and Maposa, 2014: 56). This chapter subscribes to Ranger's position as it shows how the war was fought under traditional religious leadership, the root of all subsequent Chimurenga wars in Zimbabwe. In the words of Beach (1986: 120) "there was a strong element of continuity between the 1896 Chimurenga and the nationalism of the 1960s [and 1970s]". The prophecy attributed to Mbuya Nehanda which says "*Mapfupa angu achamuka*" (My bones shall rise again), supports the view that she was an inspirational spirit behind the Second Chimurenga war (1965-1980) and beyond.

Chief Rekayi Tangwena of Kaerezi in Nyanga was among the traditional leaders of great repute in leading the resistance of the removal of his people from their homeland in the 1960s and 1970s by the Rhodesian Front regime. He also assisted young men and women to cross into Mozambique to join the liberation struggle (Sibanda and Maposa 2014). Among those assisted to cross into Mozambique by Chief Tangwena were Robert Mugabe and Edgar Tekere. In recognition of his servant leadership, the postcolonial government elected him to be a Senator and was eventually accorded a national hero status when he died. Today, cultural songs and spirit mediums like Nehanda and Kaguvi are invoked for "guidance, protection, inspiration and courage" (Bhebe 1999: 97) as part of the history and memory about the servant leadership they presented.

Individual Spiritual Leaders: Christianity

The diversity of Christianity makes it a mammoth task to do justice to the exploration of spiritual leadership. It would suffice to focus on a few selected spiritual leaders in the Pentecostal fold of churches. There are old and new players in Pentecostal Christianity in Zimbabwe. Among the 'old-timers' is Archbishop Ezekiel H. Guti of ZAOGA who has supplied a charismatic leadership to the church with his wife, Eunor Guti. Propelled by the Holy Spirit and having embraced transformation through information and communication technologies, Guti has created a transnational church that ZAOGA has become, anchored on the teachings of *kupa* (giving) and *matarenda* (talents) to engender self-reliance (Biri, 2013). The construction of large state-of-the-art infrastructure in the form of cathedrals, churches, hospitals, schools, colleges, a University in Zimbabwe named after the founder as Zimbabwe Ezekiel Guti University (ZEGU) constitute other milestones of ZAOGA's impact to society and evidence of Guti's visionary leadership. This makes ZAOGA FIF a 'super power without a sword' (Sibanda, Moyo and Muyambo, *forthcoming*) and an epitome of Guti's servant leadership.

Nevertheless, arguably, the case of ZAOGA presents the 'carrot and stick' sides of Pentecostal Christianity in Zimbabwe, in general and the leadership of Ezekiel Guti, in particular. The leadership of Guti provides a paradox. Kudzai Biri (2013: 115) puts up a comparative critique of the leadership styles of Ezekiel Guti and Robert Mugabe where she describes the two as charismatic leaders who 'bulldoze' their way to achieve their goals. Along the same lines, David Maxwell (2006) cited in Biri (2013: 114) describes ZAOGA as "a cult sustained by a heavily edited sacred history to discredit co-founders" such that "[o]nly Guti's literature must be used in the church, alongside the [B]ible." Therefore, the servant leadership of Ezekiel Guti can be put to question. In addition, it can be asked: How far 'innocent' is ZAOGA FIF ministry and mission at the backdrop of rampant accusations of abuses and errors in some Pentecostal churches as modes 'gospreneurship' in Zimbabwe?

With the emergence of new mega-churches at the turn of the new millennium, Zimbabweans witnessed the birth of new prophetic indigenous churches under leaders who are "young, male and polished" (Chitando, Manyonganise and Mlambo 2013: 153). The leaders were associated with healing episodes and the gospel of prosperity which made people to wonder whether the so-called prophets were 'men of God' or 'men of Gold' on the basis of what has been termed 'gospreneurship' or 'gospelneurship'. This was a new art of spinning money in the church (Guvamombe 2012). The spiritual leaders of interest here are Prophet Emmanuel Makandiwa of the United Family International Church (UFIC) and Prophet Walter Magaya of the Prophetic Healing and Deliverance (PHD) Ministries. Like Makandiwa's UFIC, Magaya's church is a crowd puller that has attracted people from far and wide. Through the charismatic leadership of Makandiwa and Magaya, congregants have been promised deliverance and economic emancipation through miracles (The Zimbabwean Situation 2014). Although Makandiwa is a major spiritual competitor to Magaya, Makandiwa's miracles have also attracted a lot of debate, which left people wondering whether these were "miracles or magic" (Sibanda, Marevesa and Muzambi 2013: 256). However, Magaya's moral leadership has also been questioned. His 'permissive ethics' has seen him being accused of rape charges. Whether it is for being gullible or expressing their faith, many followers are still lured by a possibility of attaining health and prosperity through such prophets who have brought the office of the prophet into disrepute. The paradox brought by the gospel of prosperity to development is that some people might resort to laziness with the hope of getting rich miraculously. For instance, Finance Minister, Patrick Chinamasa said only hard work and commitment would transform the economy and not to bank on miracles as those performed by Emmanuel Makandiwa (Mandizha 2014). This would echo one of Gandhi's social sins: wealth without work. In a country that has become a 'miracle society', the integrity of the spiritual leadership of some religious functionaries falls short of being responsible, accountable, relevant and ethical. Apparently, some prophets have manipulated the people and sought to enrich themselves instead of empathising with the poor and suffering by sharing their pain through accompaniment that addresses day to day realities (Biri and Togarasei, 2013: 91). The same puzzle characterises political leadership in Zimbabwe today.

The ambivalent analogy attached to religious leaders as being a hero/heroine and a villain is also found among the political and civil leaders in the context of governance in Zimbabwe. This produces a paradox to the political leadership plane. An interesting example of this paradox is that of President Robert Mugabe. In 1980, Mugabe was portrayed as a Messiah, Deliverer or Liberator. Mugabe was a distinguished revolutionary who ushered in a new dispensation that replaced the unjust racist regime of the Rhodesians by extending a hand of reconciliation to the former colonisers. He was referred to as 'Baba Mugabe' (Father Mugabe) as a sign of respect and to acknowledge his role in co-founding the nation. This suggests that Robert Mugabe was the provider and protector of his people. He was a 'shepherd' (Chitando, 2013: 86). Many followers compared Mugabe as a Moses for the nation of Zimbabwe because through his leadership, political independence was attained that was followed by socio-economic developments in education, health and industry up to the end of the 20th century, notwithstanding the alleged Gukurahundi atrocities. Gukurahundi was a militarised government action in the first decade after independence in 1980 that was as a counter move to deal with the problem of dissidents mainly among the Ndebele people in Matabeleland and Midlands provinces. So ruthless was the 'scotched-earth-like' strategy by the North Korean-trained Fifth Brigade in the Gukurahundi genocide that over 20 000 people lost their lives and many others were displaced and maimed (CCJPZ and LRF, 1997). Arguably, Gukurahundi was 'moment of madness' on the part of the political leadership (Ndebele, 2008). Nevertheless, the visionary leadership of Mugabe was recovered after the Unity Accord between ZANU-PF and PF-ZAPU in 1987, which brought relative peace and development that transformed Zimbabwe at that time into the 'Bread Basket' of the SADC region. In the face of neo-colonialism, Mugabe encouraged African agency and self-reliance under the guise of Pan Africanism. Therefore, outside the Gukurahundi disturbances, in general, peace, unity and development prevailed to a certain extent in this period.

The pendulum for President Mugabe to be regarded as a 'good shepherd' shifted due to the Zimbabwe crisis, one of whose landmarks was the Third Chimurenga-instigated Fast Track Land Reform Programme from February 2000. Whereas the quest for land acquisition was a common cause for concern among the landless black majority in Zimbabwe, it was through the mechanics of land allocation that the leadership was blamed. Land became an important tool by the leadership to benefit the ruling ZANU-PF supporters resulting in multiple farm ownership (Sibanda and Maposa 2014). There was under-utilisation of land by some of the cronies who concentrated on looting what they found on the farms in place of enhancing productivity of the land. Eventually, there was very low production on the farms, where instead of finding, say, soya beans, one finds 'sora (grass) beans'. In this way, land reform was no longer giving Zimbabweans their daily bread. This was blameworthy on the leadership because no serious land auditing has been done up to now.

In addition, to show that Zimbabwe is facing a moral crisis on the leadership front, one can make reference to weak governance, policies and institutions. In Zimbabwe, corruption has become endemic in state-owned enterprises and large amounts of funds have been siphoned out for personal gain, thereby reducing Zimbabwe to poor economic back water. Some of the state entities involved in corruption include Zimbabwe Electricity Supply Authority, Net One, Air Zimbabwe, Zimbabwe Revenue Authority, Central Mechanical and Equipment Department and Zimbabwe Broadcasting Corporation. Zimbabwe has about seventy-eight state enterprises which were contributing 40% of the Gross Domestic Product such as National Railways of Zimbabwe, Cold Storage Commission, Zimbabwe United Passenger Company, Agricultural and Rural Development Authority, Grain Marketing Board and Zimbabwe Iron and Steel Company, but due to mismanagement, corruption and debts, they have been reduced to wrecks (Muleya 2016). What is surprising is the inaction to corruption by the Executive and the government. Why is there no action? Why the executive is not doing anything to bring the perpetrators to book is because the government ministers and other cronies are also corrupt. There is a looting spree by government mandarins, crooks and charlatans, robbing the state and people under the disguise of entrepreneurship (Muleya, 2016; Hungwe, 2016; Mambo, 2016). This shows that corruption is eroding the already damaged economy due to reluctance of the leadership to take action. The Zimbabwe Anti-Corruption Commission (ZAAC) set up in 2005 is a toothless bulldog in fighting corruption because it is underfunded and understaffed. The problem of graft has extended to NGOs, political parties, the private sector and the judiciary. This shows that there is no political will to fight corruption as the Executive's concern is only a lip-service (Mambo 2016). Because of the moral crisis and atrocities committed by the regime's officers, Mugabe's traditional status of 'good shepherd' has been eroded as it has become 'toxic'. The *laissez faire* approach by the leadership towards delivering the core functions of the state to the majority of the population brought fission instead of fusion with the people. This places the servant leadership of Mugabe to be a paradox at a time when the Zimbabwean economy remains at the crossroads.

Tapping the African Philosophy of *Ubuntu* for Moral Leadership: Critical Reflections

Leadership is an intricate and fluid process. The diversity of leadership styles and contexts demands that Africans must tap from their African culture and world view for answers. This suggests that the African philosophy of *Ubuntu* becomes the template for a pro-people leadership. It can be argued that Africans are co-authors of their fortunes and misfortunes in Africa. The prevalent scenario is that former liberators from colonial rule have sometimes been caught up in 'bad governance and corruption' in order to cling to the privileges of power and wealth (Chitando, 2013). Along these lines, Musa Dube (2015) uses the analogy of 'the Ghost of Pharaoh' to argue that the ghosts of oppressors stay and travel with the oppressed. Citing Masiiwa Gunda, Dube (2015: 890) fervently argues that, "Many Moseses of African countries have become Pharaohs of today". For some analysts, this is what some of the Zimbabwean leaders have become – liabilities and toxic leaders. It is in this context that the African philosophy of *Ubuntu* to leadership becomes relevant. Such type of leadership ushers in servant leadership, which has people at heart. As Nussbaum cited in Muzvidziwa and Muzvidziwa (2012) asseverates, "*Ubuntu* is a capacity in African

261

culture to express compassion, reciprocity, dignity, harmony and humanity in the interests of building and maintaining a community with justice and mutual caring." *Ubuntu* is action-oriented and people-centred just as servant-leadership. There is in it a realisation that greater privilege means greater responsibility. A servant leader anchored in *Ubuntu* realises that s/he is a leader because of people.

Whether in religious or political circles, an *Ubuntu*-inspired leader accompanies people and shares their pain through thick and thin without expressing preferential treatment on the basis of colour, creed, gender, class or political affiliation. Such a leader fulfils the truth in the African proverb which says, 'a leopard licks its black and white spots', suggesting an egalitarian and empathetic approach to leadership. Servant leadership evinces an aura of critical thought whose attributes include fairness, objectivity, courage and tolerance. A continual dependence on this philosophy in leadership is a typical reinvention of the past to forge sustainable development in contemporary times. Servant leadership that is responsible, accountable, relevant and ethical provides a fertile ground for sustainable development in Africa. Nevertheless, Adjibolosoo (2003: 3) rightly observe that "the absence of truth, integrity, responsibility, accountability, trust, and commitment leads to serious social, economic, and political problems." This shows that *Ubuntu* and human factor are critical to servant leadership and development.

Conclusion

The chapter concludes that Africans in general and Zimbabweans in particular, are their own oppressors or liberators from the jaws of underdevelopment on the basis of quality of leadership in place. Overall, servant leadership, anchored in the African philosophy of *Ubuntu*, could be a remedy that would keep organisations and the government at large, focused on their mandate to deliver on promises to their clients and stakeholders. To realize development, the best leadership models, philosophies and strategies have to be put on board. Arguably, the philosophy of *Ubuntu* is a sustainable leadership model that is human-centred. Yet, until there is servant leadership that is responsible, accountable, relevant and ethical for sustainable development in Africa, among the religious and political functionaries, it is important to keep saying with Musa Dube (2015) '*Aluta continua*', for the development and transformation of the 21st century Zimbabwe.

References

Adjibolosoo, S. 2003. Pillars of Economic Growth and Sustained Human-centred Development, In: Muzvidziwa, V.N. and Gundani, P. (Eds.), *Management and the Human Factor: Lessons for Africa*, Harare: University of Zimbabwe.

Andersen, J.A. 2014. Ladies and Gentlemen: Leadership has Left the Building, *Leadership and the Humanities*, 2(2): 94-107.

Asante, M.K. 1998. *The Afrocentric Idea*, Philadelphia: Temple University Press.

Beach, D.N. 1986. *War and Politics in Zimbabwe*, Gweru: Mambo Press.

Bhebe, N. 1999. *The ZAPU and ZANU Guerrilla Warfare and the Evangelical Lutheran Church in Zimbabwe*, Gweru: Mambo Press.

Biri, K. 2013. African Pentecostalism and Politics in Post-colonial Zimbabwe: A Comparative Critique of the Leadership Styles of Ezekiel Guti and Robert Mugabe, In: Chitando, E. (Ed), *Prayers and Players: Religion and Politics in Zimbabwe*, Harare: SAPES Books.

Biri, K and Togarasei, L. 2013. '...but the One who prophecies, Builds the Church': Nation Building and Transformation Discourse as True Prophecy: The Case of Zimbabwean Pentecostal Women, In: Chitando, E. Gunda, M.R. and Kugler, J. (Eds.), *Prophets, Profits and the Bible in Zimbabwe*, Bamberg: University of Bamberg Press: 79-94.

CCJPZ and LRF. 1997. *Breaking the Silence Building True Peace: A Report on the Disturbances in Matabeleland and the Midlands 1980-1988*, Harare: CCJPZ and LRF.

Chitando, E., Manyonganise, M., and Mlambo, O. 2013. 'Young, Male and Polished: Masculinities, Generational Shifts and Pentecostal Prophets in Zimbabwe', In: Chitando, E. Gunda, M.R. and Kugler, J. (Eds.), *Prophets, Profits and the Bible in Zimbabwe*, Bamberg: University of Bamberg Press, pp. 153-170.

263

Chitando, E. 2013. God Hears the Cry of the Oppressed: Analysing a Provocative Pastoral Letter by the Zimbabwe Catholic Bishops Conference (2007), In: Chitando, E. (Ed), *Prayers and Players: Religion and Politics in Zimbabwe*, Harare: SAPES Books.

Churches in Manicaland, *The Truth Will Make You Free: A Compendium of Christian Social Teaching*, Mutare: Churches in Manicaland.

Dube, M. 2015. Aluta Continua: Toward Trickster Intellectuals and Communities, *Journal of Biblical Literature*, 134(4): 890-902.

Greenleaf, R.K. 1977. *Servant Leadership: A Journey into the Nature of Legitimate Power and Greatness*, Mahwah, NJ: Paulist Press.

Gutierrez, G. 1973. *A Theology of Liberation*, New York: Orbis Books.

Guvamombe, I. 2013. Gospreneurship – Are they looking for God or Gold? *The Herald*, 13 September.

Hallencreutz, C.F. 1987. Preface, In: Petersen, K.H. (Ed), *Religion, Development and African Identity*, Uppsala: Nordiska Afrikainstitutet: 7-9.

Jackson, H. 2002. *AIDS Africa: Continent in Crisis*, Harare: SAfAIDS.

Kaulemu, D. 2006. The Role of the Church in Society, In: Churches in Manicaland, *The Truth Will Make You Free: A Compendium of Christian Social Teaching*, Mutare: Churches in Manicaland.

Kondlo, K. 2014. Introduction: Africa's 'Unended Quest' for Emancipation – North Africa and Beyond, In: Kondlo, K. (Ed), *Perspectives on Thought Leadership for Africa's Renewal*, Pretoria: Africa Institute of South Africa: 1-19.

Ladkin, D. 2010. *Rethinking Leadership: A New Look at Old Leadership Question*, Cheltenham, UK: Edward Elgar.

Mambo, E. 2016. Graft: Ex-Convicts, Drug Dealers Live it Up while Economy Bleeds. *Zimbabwe Independent* May 20-16.

Mandizha, T. 2014. 'Don't Follow Makandiwa': Chinamasa, *News Day*, 16 January, Available at: https://www.newsday.co.zw/2014/01/16/dont-follow-makandiwa-chinamasa/ Accessed: 12 December 2016.

Mashingaidze, T. 2006. An Investigation into the Role played by the Roman Catholic Church in Combating Socio-economic Problems in Masvingo District, Unpublished Research Project Submitted to the Department of Humanities, Masvingo State University, Masvingo.

Mawere, M. 2016. 'Beyond the Politics of Power and Violence,' In: Mawere, M. & Marongwe, N. (Eds), *Violence, Politics and Conflict Management in Africa: Envisioning Transformation, Peace and Unity in the Twenty-First Century*, Langaa Research & Publishing CIG: Bamenda, pp. 1-12.

McVay, M. H. 2014. Discursive Resistance as a Tool for Servant-Leaders: The Tactics of Eugene V. Debs, *Leadership and Humanities*, 2(2): 108-119.

Mudimbe, V. Y. 1998. *The Invention of Africa: Gnosis, Philosophy, and the Order of Knowledge*, Bloomington: Indiana University Press.

Muleya, D. 2016. Zim Govt Fantastically Corrupt, *Zimbabwe Independent*, May 20-26.

Muzvidziwa, I. And Muzvidziwa, V.N. 2012. Hunhu (*Ubuntu*) and School Discipline in Africa, *Journal of Dharma: Dharmaram Journal of Religions and Philosophies*, 37(1): 27-42.

Ndebele, Z. 2008. Gukurahundi a Moment of Madness, Available at: http//www.gukurahundicorner.blogspot.com/2008/09/gukura hundi-moment-of-madness.html, Accessed: 23 February 2017.

Ngambi, H. 2014. RARE Leadership: An Alternative Leadership Approach for Africa, In: Kondlo, K. (Ed), *Perspectives on Thought Leadership for Africa's Renewal*, Pretoria: Africa Institute of South Africa: 110-129.

Ngara, S. 2014. Pan Africanism and the African Renaissance: Extracting Paradigms of Underdevelopment, In: Kondlo, K. (Ed), *Perspectives on Thought Leadership for Africa's Renewal*, Pretoria: Africa Institute of South Africa: 458-478.

Ranger, T. 1987. Religion, Development and African Christian Identity, In: Petersen, K.H. (Ed), *Religion, Development and African Identity*, Uppsala: Nordiska Afrikainstitutet: 29-57.

Rayment, J. And Smith, J. 2010. *Misleadership: Prevalence, Causes and Consequences*, Farnham, UK: Gower.

Rodney, W. 1989. *How Europe underdeveloped Africa*, Zimbabwe Publishing House: Harare.

Sibanda, F., Marevesa, T. & Muzambi, P. 2013. Miracles or Magic?: Theological Reflections on the Healing Ministry in Pentecostal Churches in Zimbabwe, *JLARM*, 1(8): 248-261.

Sibanda, F. and Maposa, R.S. 2014. Beyond the Third Chimurenga?: Theological Reflections on the Land Reform Programme in Zimbabwe, 2000-2010, The *Journal of Pan African Studies*, 6(8): 54-74.

Sibanda, F., Moyo, J. and Muyambo, T. Super power without a Sword?: Power of Communication and Prosperity Gospel in Pentecostalism, In: Machingura, F. (Ed), *Pentecostalism and Human Rights in Zimbabwe*, Cambridge Scholars Publishing, Ltd. (forthcoming).

ZCBC, EFZ and ZCC. 2006. *The Zimbabwe We Want: Towards a National Vision for Zimbabwe: A Discussion Document*, Harare: ZCBC.

ZCBC. 2007. *God Hears the Cry of the Oppressed: Pastoral Letter on the Current Crisis in Zimbabwe*. Holy Thursday, 5 April 2007. Harare: ZCBC.

ZCC. 2006. *Christian Care Brochure*, Harare: ZCC.

Chapter Eleven

Dilemmas and Controversies Surrounding the Land Debacle in Zimbabwe: Appropriating Some Ideas from the Shona *Unhu (Ubuntu)* Justice

Erasmus Masitera

Introduction

The land question[2] in Zimbabwe is associated with controversies and vexing positions which are not easy to resolve. Implicitly this means that the land issue is one that has not really been amicably resolved and is likely to explode in the near future, that is to say the land question has serious implications upon social justice. Four particular problems are dominant in the Zimbabwean land question. Problem number one rests on ownership since the colonial period (over 150 years ago) protracted disagreement over land ownership, on one hand colonial settlers claiming ownership of land through titles granted them by the colonial government and the indigenes claiming that land belongs to them by virtue of being first occupancy. Further, by virtue of the Fast Track Land Reform (F.T.L.R) the indigenes claim that ownership and title over land was granted them through repossession (through historical connections) and government assurance that land now belongs to the 'occupiers'. Problem number two, in all the land redistributions that have occurred, that is the colonial redistributions and the post-colonial distributions especially the F.T.L.R, unjust methods of land exchanges and other forms of injustices transpired[3]. Problem number three, the problem of rectification, taking into consideration the injustices that have

---

[2] Land in question here, is arable agricultural land. Urban and rural land ownership is not a bond of contention, the land ownership in urban areas is less disputed.

[3] However, that is not to say all land redistributions are unjust, there are instances where individuals legally and procedurally acquired lands.

occurred, this is closely related to the forth problem. Problem number four, how to attain justice? In considering all these problems and associated controversies, the chapter will be guided by the Shona *Unhu* thinking. The argument advanced in this chapter is that resolving the problems or controversies will require utilizing the local *Dare/Indaba* (court) system of settling differences and social difficulties that establishes respect of pluralism at the same time. This will also include adapting the Shona thinking and understanding of injustice and inequality, and the way of redressing such social ills. The supposition of the chapter is that the Shona *Unhu* can be adopted as one way in addressing historical injustices and thus plausible for use in social justice.

Zimbabwean Land Redistribution: An Overview

A brief overview of the Zimbabwean land distribution is important at this juncture. In Zimbabwe, land alienation span from the colonial period that began around 1884 up to the year 2000. Effective colonisation of Zimbabwe began with the signing of the Rudd Concession of 1888 (Sachikonye: 2012, 227 - 228), following from then, land alienation among other colonial expedience followed. Notable on this point is that the alienation of land from the native occupants of the Zimbabwean land marked the beginning of 'land redistribution' in the colonial Zimbabwe. However, the colonial 'land redistribution' was skewed towards the colonial masters. Moreover, the general colonial practice reflected an exclusive system that favoured the colonialists at the expense of the natives; thus establishment of social injustice and inequality in the colonial state. The social injustices and inequalities were particularly shown in the legal, economic, political and social dimensions of the colonial system. The colonial practices were reinforced by legal instruments such as the Master and Servant Ordinances (1901), and the Native Regulation Ordinances (1910). The major aims of the legal instruments were to fully exploit and manipulate the blacks' or indigenes" labour force. Under the laws blacks were not free to move around but were to be confined to particular places allocated them by the colonial government and above all were to be under the

268

control of the immediate white or settler farm or mine owner. Inevitably, the indigenes were open to manipulation and exploitation. Apart from the legal instruments that confined blacks to particular areas there were also legislations that prohibited and restricted the kinds of areas and land size that natives could buy and own. Laws such as The Land Tenure Apportionment Act (1930), The Native Husbandry Act (1951), and The Land Tenure Act (1969) were promulgated aiming at allocating large arable areas to the settlers and restricting the indigenes to dry and arid lands that were referred to as Tribal Trust Lands (TTLs). The 1930 Land Tenure Apportionment Act states clearly, "… that each race has its own area … neither race may own or occupy land in area of other race except by permit …." The real intention was to separate and segregate races with the net effect that the settlers or white race get to occupy the best land in areas that also had good rainfall patterns while other races occupy poor areas. It also meant easy facilitation of preferential treatment for the colonial settlers. For this to happen, the locals were force marched into dry inhabitable areas so as to make way for the settlers. This was an unjust practice in land distribution due to the fact that the blacks were forced off their lands and thus their rights to the lands were abrogated willingly and knowingly by the colonial government. The colonial government in turn justified the violent land takeovers by issuing title deeds to the settlers. In order to disempower the indigenous people, the colonial government promulgated laws that limited the indigenes' herds of livestock (5 beasts at most) per family.

As a matter of fact and as an attempt to do away with partiality in land distribution (became one major, among other, grievances), the indigenous Zimbabweans waged a war of liberation from 1966 - 1979. After the war the post-colonial Zimbabwean government's key focus (among others) was land redistribution and reform[4]. The land redistribution programs were designed to correct the skewed racial land distributions. The major aims of the government were to reduce

---

[4] Through colonial land redistribution, the T.T.Ls were congested with natives such that, by 1980, the T.T.L's were located on 16.4 million hectors shared among 4.3 million natives, while the occupiers who amounted to 6000 owned 15.5 million hectors of Zimbabwean land.

imbalances in colonial land distribution it inherited from the colonial system and at the same time promote and maintain political stability and economic viability of the independent Zimbabwean state. Reducing racial land imbalances through land reforms proved to be a cumbersome process as there were legal, political and economic constraints. This dragged on from 1980 to 1999. After the year 2000 a new form of land redistribution began and it was generally referred to as accelerated land reform or the Fast Track Land Redistribution (F.T.L.R). The F.T.L.R became a new way of seeking social justice; however, the methods implemented in the land redistribution included violence, force, legal, and political protection from the Zimbabwean government. F.T.L.R targeted mostly white owned farms. The methods that had been used by the settler regime in appropriating land from the blacks were almost replicated against them during the F.T.L.R, except that the white farmers were not force marched into reserved areas and were not legally excluded from the social, political, or economic livelihoods but the practice confirmed the exclusion. This was done through abrogating the rights of the settler farmers through unjust and unequal treatment in the legal, political and social dimensions of the Zimbabweans livelihoods. The F.T.L.R saw the repudiation of land titles and the introduction of lease agreements that were guaranteed by the independent Zimbabwean government. This was and is considered a way of countering the colonial system.

A point to note is that the Zimbabwean land redistribution from the colonial period to date symbolises partial distributions along racial lines that are punctuated by unjust and unequal distributions. It is un-doubtable that the continuation of such distributions created perpetual antagonism among the inhabitancy of and users of Zimbabwean agricultural land. It is no surprise, therefore, that controversies around the method and philosophy used in Zimbabwean land redistributions stirred questions linked to justice and equality. In particular how is justice and equality to be attained through land reform? To adequately reflect on this question, the chapter proposes that land redistribution should be enriched by the Zimbabwean Shona thinking of and on achieving justice and equality. The chapter first reflect on the controversies that emanate from the

Zimbabwean land reforms then turn attention to the Shona conception of justice.

Controversies from Land Redistributions

i. Who owns the land?

The major question here is on determining ownership of land. As already mentioned controversy exists as to which form of ownership should be honoured. On one hand there is the colonial title deeds ownership (that has its dark side that is land forcibly appropriated from the indigenes) and there is the ownership ushered in through the F.T.L.R that is the lease agreements. The lease agreements only apply to lands that were seized after the year 2000, apart from that title deeds stand for other agricultural lands. The title deeds of former farmers in some way still stand; in that regard there are chances of the former owners claiming that they still own the lands that are now leased by government to resettled local farmers. In fact there exist two kinds of ownership confirmation, of the two questions linger, which one is to be honoured. Both are legitimate as they are legally binding and underwritten by the government. Interestingly politicking surrounds the land ownership. With this in mind, the chances are high that conflicts and possible wrangles will arise over ownership. To show the extent to which there are disagreements with regards to land ownership, there are some farmers who still contest the legitimacy of the government takeover of their farms. There are pending cases within the Zimbabwean High Court and even with the Southern Africa tribunal (2007, Mike Campbell *et al* versus Republic of Zimbabwe; Sachikonye: 2012, 227).

Closely related to the above is the question of who actually owns Zimbabwean land?[5] This question invites theories that vary from first occupancy theory (Pufendorf) to the labour theory of property ownership (John Locke). Pufendorf (1991, 84) proposed the First Occupancy Theory which accords ownership or entitlement to the first person to use in whatever way a natural resource such as a piece of land. The theory further states that displacement of others and any

---

[5] Determining the actual owners of the land, helps define the form of entitlement and ownership as well.

form of unfair and unjust property possession is unacceptable. In that case, it goes without saying that the Zimbabwe locals were the first occupancy and therefore the rightful owners of the land. Historically as well, the indigenes were displaced by the colonialists, this further gives testimony as to who first occupied the Zimbabwean land and further attests to the fact that the indigenes were the actual owners and is entitled to the land. The colonialists thus rely on the goodwill of the locals to occupy, use and own Zimbabwe land. Through colonization and colonial land expropriations, the colonizers displaced the locals, thus violating property owning rights of the locals or first occupiers, according to Pufendorf. Though it can be established through Pufendorf, First Occupancy Theory, who is the actual owners of Zimbabwe lands? A further question lingers on the natives as to who first occupied the lands among the local inhabitancy. Shaw (2003, 82) conjures that historically, Zimbabwe has been a country characterized by dislodging which probably began with the Khoisan being displaced by the Shona, Ndebele displaced the Shonas is some areas, before the Ndebeles were dislodged by the colonisers.

On the other hand John Locke, an 18th century philosopher contradicts Pufendorf's First Occupancy Theory. Locke (2013: Chapter II, Section 27), unlike Pufendorf, thinks that acquiring property especially natural resources should be through the use of labour and not merely being the first to be in a place. In cases of land acquisition, Locke advocates that cultivation[6] or some other productive way of utilizing the resources reflects claim to particular area (for this reason, he doubted the indigenous hunters or nomadic peoples' claim as owners of the land over which they roamed, hunted and gathered fruits). Locke' perspective is a misconception of or limited understanding of labour. Locke further says that common ownership, which characterised the non-western way of land ownership is a primitive way of claiming property instead, individual and, or, private property ownership was necessary. By failing to claim lands, Locke thinks that it is also the failure of communities to put

---

[6] Questions can be raised on what is meant by 'cultivation' since for Locke this meant a broad understanding which included working on the land, to claiming or pegging area, and even to mere improvements done on a piece of land.

value to land (Chapter IV, Section 38 and Section 40). It seems therefore that it was the Lockean acquisition procedure which the colonisers adapted when viewing the Zimbabwean indigenous way of ownership and entitlement; this was despite the shortcomings of disregarding others' property rights to owning and using natural property in a different way. Thus according to Locke, the colonisers can rightly be considered as the rightful owners and thus entitled to the Zimbabwean land and thus can decide the form in which entitlement and ownership can take.

From the foregoing arguments, it is clear that there is a challenge as to determining which form of ownership and entitlement is to be followed. From the historical and the first occupancy theory, it is the locals' conception of ownership and entitlement which should be followed. From the labour theory it is the settlers,' since according to Locke owning a person in the form of slave equals to owning the labour that the enslaved individual produces. The challenge that exists is that there is no one particular theory that can be used to control the form of land ownership and entitlement in Zimbabwe. In fact, the stated understanding of land ownership deviates from the locals understanding of ownership which is based on communal ownership and hugely depend on communal allocation. There is therefore a conflict on land ownership and entitlement. In that case there is need to resolve the conflict while at the same time promoting a system that is multifaceted.

ii. Unjust and unequal land redistributions

The colonial land redistribution was skewed towards one race. The colonizers implemented legal frameworks that supported their takeover of the locals' lands. The bias by which they did this was meant to ensure their superiority position which had begun being theorized by some respected scholars, among them philosophers of the 16th and 17th Century. The colonizers as already mentioned in the previous section relied on the propositions of John Locke among others to ensure their appropriation of the indigenes lands and abrogate the rights of the natives. Thus the indigenous were considered as inferiors to the colonizers. The inequalities were reflected in standing before the law, access to medical facilities and attention among others. Beyond this, the locals did not have legislative represented or if there were any, these were individuals who were subservient to the colonial masters. Even in land redistribution during the colonial period, the locals were displaced and confined to TTLs that were characterized by poor rainfall and poor soils (Sachikonye: 2012, 227). Again only a few natives were allowed to own lands near areas that settlers were located. To ensure the success of such a project the colonizers made it a point that the cost of the lands were beyond the reach of the indigenes. This was done by underpaying and at times not paying the indigenes as well. Furthermore, there were no mortgages for the locals as was with the case with the settlers who wanted to acquire land in good areas (Scoones *et al*: 2010, 66).

From the year 2000 to date the locals reciprocated the land redistribution activities of the colonial period. For the locals, the arguments forwarded for the 'new' redistribution were largely related to the need to redress skewed colonial land imbalances and the following arguments were used to justify the Zimbabwe government and the landless indigenes' actions and policies for embarking on F.T.L.R. The first argument is the economic argument that argues that the major outcome of colonial land redistribution was poverty for locals. Locals suffer from economic and social exclusion as a result of colonial land exclusion. The second argument, the historical argument, postulates that as a matter of fact illegitimate transfer and acquisition of arable land in Zimbabwe exists; the arable lands were stolen from the locals who were the initial owners of the lands (Shaw: 2003). To this end it was necessary for the locals to reclaim their lands; thus the arguments have compounded in the rebuttal and were a search for a reversal of European and colonial land establishments through expelling those considered as colonialists from productive farms. To that end, violent and forced removals were employed to remove settler and mostly white farmers (Mukodzongi: 2013, 346). Over and above all, the Zimbabwean government legalized the F.T.L.R by issuing lease agreements instead of land titles. In doing so, the rights of the white farmers were equally abrogated just as those of the locals during the colonial period. Thus the white farmers who are closely connected and conceptualized as settlers or colonialists suffered at the hands of the indigenous. Exclusion, marginalization and victimization of the considered settlers thus ensued. Exclusion from political lives of the Zimbabwean people became apparent through political slogans that demonized and threaten any collaboration with the colonizers. Land now is considered as solely reserved for the natives and thus excluding any other people considered as 'Zimbabweans.' In light of the unjust land appropriations and redistributions, three major challenges thus emerge. First challenge relates to the achieving justice especially in light of unequal land redistributions that are skewed towards particular races. Second challenge relates to the kind of land ownership or entitlement is to be considered legitimate considering that the injustices in Zimbabwe have become a vicious circle of unjust appropriations. Third challenge, is connected to the already noted, who is the legitimate owner of the land in light of the protracted disagreements. All these challenges point to the third difficulty controversy that is rectification. Importantly, a matter of concern is that there is confusion over land ownership conception, in that there is ownership coming from colonial land tittles and land ownership emanating from lease agreements, over and above there is also land ownership acquired through traditional conception that is communal land ownership. The confusion is on which one to respect and consider as entitling one to a particular piece of land.

iii. The Problem of Rectification

It has been established that injustices exists in the Zimbabwean land redistributions, as such the redistributions require rectification so as to correct the injustices and to some extend propose a just future. Rectification according to Nozick (2013 [1974], 152 - 153) is correcting injustices that have occurred in the past. Scholars such as Shaw, Perez, Alexander, and Hill and Woermann among others share Nozick's sentiments by arguing that rectification refers to the correcting or altering of unjust conditions so as to make the conditions right or acceptable in accordance to parties involved. Thus rectification addresses injustices with the aim of attaining justice and eventually establishing a perpetual just society. To this end, scholar such as Shaw (2003b, 219), Mawondo (2008, 15) Perez (2011, 151 -

275

152), Alexander (2014, 2), and Hall and Woermann (2015) aver that restitution, compensation, repossession, reparation, restoration and affirmative action are some of the ways through which societies (or groups of people) acknowledge that wrong was done, at least in the past, and ways of forging and fostering a dignified sense of identity and coexistence (just society) in the present and the future as well.

But in the Zimbabwean land question scenario the questions that become pertinent are: Who is wrong, and who should (re)pay or compensate who and compensating for what, who should repossess the land? It has already been established that injustice and inequalities have been the hallmark of the Zimbabwean land redistribution and hence the controversy emanates in answering these questions. In fact land dislodging has been on-going and will thus continue if no acceptable solution is found soon (Openshaw and Terry: 2015, 40). An important fact then is that it is important to establish who the perpetrator is and who the victim of injustice and inequality is. However, considering that this is not an easy task because of difficulties noted through the historical theory, labour theory and first occupancy theory, it becomes clear then that injustice and inequality are acknowledged as facts that have occurred in the Zimbabwean land redistributions. The bottom line is that the injustices and inequalities deserve to be corrected. This brings us to the other focus of this work, how is justice to be achieved? To that end the chapter proposes utilizing the Shona *Unhu* justice process. To reveal the Shona justice system and philosophy, the chapter identifies the Shona people first and goes on to expose their justice system.

Achieving Justice and Equality through the Shona Understanding

i. The Shona People

The Shona people are found in Zimbabwe, they are one of the largest ethnic groups of people in Zimbabwe (Chemhuru and Masaka: 2010, 121). The word Shona refers to "a conglomeration of a number of linguistic groups … namely the Korekore, Karanga, Zezuru, Ndau, Kalanga and the Manyika" (Chemhuru and Masaka:

2010, 121). This group of people is widely spread in the country though some have migrated to neighbouring states. As a cultural group, the Shona abide by the principles of *Unhu* which in other traditions is known as *Ubuntu*. In fact the Shona people though made up of different dialects or of different linguistic grouping have similarities in their cultural beliefs and behaviours. The different groupings firmly share the thinking that justice is a shared process that is reached through a communal process of discussing issues that pertains to human living. For the Shona people justice is achieving consensus or agreement on issues that relates to communal living, this ranges from relations among individuals, and the use of resources among others. Consensus and agreement is always an expectation for realizing acceptable relations that is reached through discussions.

ii. Shona Conception of Injustice and Inequality and Addressing the Anomaly

For the Shona any form of injustice is considered as a social ill that affects and harms a particular community (Gwaravanda: 2011, 148). There is no particular word for justice in the Shona language however, there exists characteristics of it. In characterizing justice, the Shona expect good social relations. In other words justice is concerned with establishing good and accepted social relations among people and the environment, and for an individual this implies abiding and upholding the ethos *Unhu* sometimes referred to as *Ubuntu*. For the Shona people *Unhu/Ubuntu* is a cherished epistemic and moral Shona social heritage that is concerned with values, and conducts aimed at attaining social harmony and cohesion. *Unhu* put emphasis on the community as the basis for social living (Ramose: 2014, 12; Mangena 2015, 6). Communal effort and ethos is important in building the individual to such an extent that the community is an expression of the individual or the individual interests and worries find fulfilment in the community. In this sense the community ethos is a sum total of individual interests. Moreover, *Unhu* is a lived and living experience of the Shona people on how to live together and foster future social cohesion. It is from this understanding then that for the Shona, justice is described and characterized as *jekerere* that is doing or acting in such a way that makes everyone happy and satisfied. Following from the just said, injustice is thus a departure from the good, injustice is upsetting the societal expectation of social harmony. Injustice is considered as departing from the norm hence understanding injustice as *kureswa* and or *kukanganisa*. *Kureswa* or *kukanganisa* is making a mistake. Since injustice is a departure, it follows that it is a social ill that harms the whole society and the individual or group that commits the offence as well. Wrongdoing is further understood by the Shona as part and parcel of life and a problem that deserves attention or that has to be solved peacefully (Gwaravanda: 2011, 149). Most importantly is the fact that wrongdoing in the Shona set-up is a departure from the expected and as such it is important to reconcile the offender with the rest of the society or community. In reconciling the offending member the Shona employ critical reflections on human life that are based on logical conclusions (drawn from consultations and connections from what the offender and offended present) and epistemological and ethical principles or tools for fostering social harmony. The Shona people are convinced that good social relations are the bedrock of common good. Thus for the Shona people, correcting wrong demands that the whole community be involved as this helps in amending relations that would have been severed by the wrong. The basis of this thinking is that (injustice and inequality) affects the community, hence the need of involving all members of society in correcting the wrong.

The correction of wrong is done through communal discussions, which are normally referred to as *matare* [single known as *Dare/Indaba*] (local courts that vary from local, village to chiefdom courts). The Shona justice largely has to do with eliminating disharmony among people in community or communities this is achieved through discussions and mutual agreements; Metz (2007, 321) has observed that this is characteristic of African justice system in general as well. Mangena (2015, 6) adds to this by saying that *dare/indaba* necessitates a new beginning especially after serious violations of people's rights. The principle behind the *dare/indaba* was that discussions and mutual agreements were necessary for solving communal mishaps such as violation of rights, and thus rebuilding society's cohesion and inspiring collective aspirations and hopes

(Mandova and Chingombe: 2013, 105). By employing discussions as a way of solving social mishaps or wrongs or injustices, the Shona had realised that true justice is people generated and people driven. In addition, the *dares/indabas* are necessary as arenas for learning, recognising and enlightening each other. Coming together despite tensions and disputes is always considered as one of the best ways to avoid further straining relationships in society, and even for relations degenerating into anarchy. Also coming together to discuss is a characteristic of human relations, that is, it affirms the sociality of humans as Aristotle observed. In that sense then, discussions help build respect, understanding and tolerance among members of the society, and common good is also encouraged. Justice for the Shona was a process reached through and a result of people's input and not something imposed upon the people. During the *dare/indaba* meetings, members of society were given chances to contribute their views without any form of discrimination; and in the final stages of making up a decision, all the inputs would be put into perspective (thus employing simple logical tools to come to a conclusion and settle disagreements). The views of the people were in this sense taken seriously by so doing the whole society (under the leadership of the chief and his advisors) was responsible for producing, upholding justice according to people's perspectives. This was necessary for changing society for the better. There is a sense in which diversity of ideas is promoted through the *Dare/Indaba* system.

Through society's participation in correcting wrong, the principles or ideals of equality were achieved through equal participation, recognition and consideration. This was besides the aim of attaining and promoting social harmony which could only be achieved through discussion rather than fighting or continuing disagreeing. By promoting equal communal participation the Shona people reveal their commitment to communal effort of solving problems without violating anyone's rights. The idea of engaging in dialogue and reaching mutual agreement was and is meant to encourage social cooperation and cohesion that is achieved through repaired relation (and rehabilitating individuals in social ethos). In this sense justice was promoted.

It is important to note that for the Shona people, correcting any wrong doing aimed at reconciling members of society rather than alienate them or further create animosity among feuding parties. This is why some scholars such as Moyo (2015, 73), and Mangena (2015, 6) refer to African justice system, including the Shona justice system as therapeutic and corrective mechanisms in nature because its major intention is to achieve harmony and social cohesion through having good relations in society. The therapeutic aspect emanate from the fact that the Shona justice always aimed at bringing people together and especially reconciling contending parties, that is the reconciling the victim and the perpetrator or violator of rights. Through discussions the community (as the facilitator) encouraged the two sides to come to an agreement and understanding each other, thus eliminating any form of bias that may accrue in partial discussions. This would also influence the kind of reparations to be paid. Noteworthy, was the fact that the society would continue to guide the feuding parties on the acceptable form of reparation(s), this was done so as to promote and facilitate continued living together in peace and in harmony. Plurality is also thus respected.

Important and beautiful as the ideas reflected above are, there has been little or no effort at all to encourage the political dispensation to adhere to the *Unhu/Ubuntu* ideals. Besides, there is also no willingness among the political leadership to encourage the adherence to these concepts. Perhaps this shows that there is rejection, neglect and marginalization of the traditional way of living among contemporary Zimbabweans.

iii. Appropriating Shona Justice and Equality into Zimbabwean Land Redistribution

The Zimbabwean land question is not easy to deal with and as reflected in the preceding paragraphs and sections. However, that does not deter one from making efforts towards forwarding suggestion(s) on addressing the vexing position and contentions. In that regard, the proposal of this chapter is that addressing the land question in Zimbabwe ought to appropriate the local Shona system of dealing with injustices. The argument being forwarded here is that land redistributions that have taken place in Zimbabwe over the past hundred or so years have generally resulted in injustices and inequalities. This position has already been reflected upon earlier. The Shona understanding of justice, inequality or any other form of violating people's rights or crime is understood as an anomaly or mishap that deserve correcting. The correcting of the wrong requires a communal approach that aims at establishing social harmony and cooperation while at the same time removing any form of discontentment. In other words, this means revoking all forms of ownership and starting afresh a new ownership structure that is agreeable to all in society. The idea proposed here is that first people through their representatives discuss on how land is to be (re)distributed and the ownership structure to be followed. The idea is that all should benefit, not for land be of advantage to one (and or groups) over others. This structure presumably will not be selective in its application and it will at the same time take the different social and economic dispositions of people into consideration. Thus, in the spirit of repairing relationships, land ownership and redistribution patterns will have to be based upon agreements of people in society. This means bringing together people (groups) interested in land use (and redistribution) together, these people vary from political leaders, agricultural expects, environmental groups, traditional leaders, farmers' representative groups. These are just some of the stakeholders that can be considered for the discussions on how land is to be (re)distributed. Land distribution will thus be guided by views of the people. At the same time such *dares/indabas* will eliminate biases and possibly usher a new beginning in land redistribution in Zimbabwe.

It is anticipated that the discussions that will ensue will undoubtedly focus on settling ownership and compensation contentions through discussions. People will discuss on issues of compensation for those who deserve; beyond that they will inevitably settle the ownership debacle, in fact the land tenure systems can be discussed here and be rearranged at the same time. In other words, the discussions will be a platform to enlighten each other on past mistakes and also platform for settling differences of the past. In fact negotiations, accepting mistakes, and working towards reconciliation thus become the main thrust of the *dare/indaba* meetings

(Gwaravanda: 2011, 149). In saying this, the therapeutic and corrective aspect of *Unhu* philosophy becomes apparent, that is reconciling competing parties and making them agree on how they are to live together[7]. Yet the important aspect of *Unhu* philosophy which exalts being there for others and thinking for others will be the guiding principle for the discussions. By saying this, the *Unhu* philosophy is steeped in people's experience and not a mere hypothetical proposition. This idea also takes into consideration the experiences and the histories that people have gone through, thus *Unhu* philosophy respects people's views, experiences and their conception of the good, while at the same time aiming at unifying and forging a situation that promotes the common good that respect diversity of ideas and plurality of cultures. This means that the negotiations that people engage in leads to compromises on their conceptions of living. Compromises thus offer people a new beginning (a transition from injustice and unequal system to a just society) which is necessary especially in societies that have a lot of differences (Castiglione: 2015, 162). In the same manner the discussions on land redistribution will take the same course.

Of great importance is that the discussions offer society a chance to realize different forms of equality. Equality of participation and equality of standing in discussions among others are the forms of equality that are realized. All people will be accorded a fair chance to contribute in the discussions and will all receive a fair consideration of their contributions. In such a situation there will be no domination of one group or person over others; thus the discussion platforms will offer people equal standing and consideration. Over and beyond, by engaging in such discussions there are chances of mending relationships through discussing and to some extend working together in the effort of correcting past mistakes (Gwaravanda: 2011, 148; Castiglione: 2015, 164). The participation that ensues in the discussions assures people that their rights are respected and that they carry out their responsibility in society. The duties and

---

[7] Reflections can be made here that pertains to laws. Laws are generally believed to be made by people to regulate their conducts. In the same vein people arrange and rearrange how they are to live and even how they are to view ownership and entitlement to land.

responsibilities of people in society is to ensure social stability and social prosperity and thus contributing to political and economic development as well. Essentially by respecting equalities, it is anticipated that inequalities in standings are reduced during discussions and the same practice will be exported into social practices that deal with land redistribution as well.

However, the *Unhu* philosophy just like Ubuntu philosophy has been described by certain philosophers and scholars as less effective in addressing social disturbances. Minow (2007, 621) asserts that court systems and reconciliation process only serve to reopen old wounds and thus dividing the society. Shaw *et al* (2010) augment the argument by saying that the court system does not conform to international standards and ways of seeking justice and redress. In response to the concerns raised here, Anders and Zenker (2014, 402), and Mangena (2015, 6) argue that court systems reflect the cultural practices and cultural beliefs in dealing with social problems. Besides that local court systems are necessary as they offer people chances to reconcile (through perpetrators taking responsibility and victim forgiving and all showing commitment to ending feud) and bring about a new beginning after violations of different forms. Thus court systems are necessary in building good relations among people rather than perpetuate hatred and divisions that are sometimes brought about by 'international justice systems'. The idea of repairing relationships and restoring harmony in society has been the driving force in the South African Truth and Reconciliation Commission, the Rwanda's and Uganda's Gacaca Courts. The repairing of relationships and restoring harmony will include forgiving each other and reconciling with each other so as to forge a new beginning together. It is in the same sense that this chapter proposes for *Indabas* or *Matare* to address the Zimbabwean land debacle, through emphasizing on establishing social harmony and eventually contributing to economic development and respecting cultural diversity. In fact reasonable stability has been experienced and witnessed in states that have attempted utilizing the court system. However, the chapter recognize the fact that in some instances the traditional court systems maybe manipulated by some individuals so as to work to their advantage. This has to be guarded against through appealing to honest, truthfulness, openness, and honest among engaging members.

Conclusion

The Zimbabwean land redistribution poses difficult and vexing positions which beg for urgent attention. Through this work, a suggestion that advocates for a humane approach to solving vexing and contentious issues has been forwarded. In that regard, the Shona *Unhu* Philosophy provides a framework to work within. It provides for opportunities for people to start afresh, to remodel their way(s) of life through discussions. The discussions are meant to provide people with the opportunity to iron out differences and thus usher in a new beginning. Furthermore, common good is built when people engage each other and this contributes to respect, recognition, tolerance, and forgive and reconcile with each other; over and above this will contribute significantly to reaching compromises on how people are to live together. More importantly, it will respect diversity of the Zimbabwean culture and even ideas as well. The Zimbabwean Land redistribution requires such an approach so as to avert any future squabbles over land ownership and entitlement.

References

Alexander, S. G. 2014. 'The Complexities of Land Reparations', *Law and Social Inquiry: The Journal of the American Bar Foundation*, 3 (4): 1 – 28.

Anders, G, & Zenker. O. 2014. 'Transition and Justice: An Introduction,' *Development and Change*. 45 (3): 395 – 414.

Castiglione, D. 2015. 'Introduction: The Logic of Social Cooperation for Mutual Advantage – The Democratic Contract,' *Political Studies Review*, Volume 13, pages 161 – 175.

Chemhuru, C, & Masaka, D. 2010. 'Taboos as Source of Shona People's Environmental Ethics,' *Journal of Sustainable Development in Africa*, 12 (7): 121 - 133.

Gwaravanda, E. T. 2011. 'Philosophical Principles in Shona Traditional Court System,' *International Journal of Peace and Development Studies,* 2 (4): 148 – 155.

Hall, S, & Woermann, M. 2014. 'From Inequality to Equality: Evaluating normative Justifications for Affirmative Action as Racial Redress,' *African Journal of Business Ethics*, 8 (2): 59 – 73.

Locke, J. 2013. *Two Treatises of Government.* www.efm.bris.ac.uk/het/locke/government.pdf

Mandova, E, & Chingombe, A. 2013. 'The Shona Proverb as an Expression of Unhu/Ubuntu,' *International Journal of Academic Research in Progressive Education and Development* Volume 2 #1.

Mangena, F. 2015. 'Restorative Justice's Deep Roots in Africa,' *South African Journal of Philosophy* 34 (1): 1 - 12.

Mawondo, S. 2008. 'In Search of Social Justice: Reconciliation and the Land Question in Zimbabwe,' *The Struggle After Struggle: Zimbabwean Philosophical Studies 1.* Edited by Kaulemu D. Washington D. C: The Council for Research in Values and Philosophy.

Mertz, T. 2007. 'Toward an African Moral Theory,' The Journal of Political Philosophy, pages 321 – 341.

Minow, M. 2007. 'Historical Justice.' *A Companion to Contemporary Political Philosophy* Volume 2. Edited by Goodin R. E, Pettit P, and Pogge T. Malden: Blackwell Publishing

Moyo, K. 2015. 'Mimicry, Transitional Justice and the Land Question in Racially Divided

Former Settler Colonies,' *International Journal of Transitional Justice,* Number 9, pages 70 – 89.

Mukodzongi, G. 2013. 'New People, New Land, New Livelihoods: A Micro-Study of

Zimbabwe's Fast-track Land Reform,' *Agrarian South Journal of Political Economy*, 3 (2): 345 – 366.

Nozick, R. 1974. *Anarchy, State and Utopia*, Oxford: Blackwell.

Openshaw, K.S. & Terry, P. C. R. 2015. 'Zimbabwe's Odious Inheritance: Debt and Unequal

Land Distribution,' *McGill International Journal of Sustainable Development*, 11(1): 39 – 86.

Pafendorf, S. 1991. *On the Duty of Man and Citizen According to Natural Law*. Edited by J Tully. Cambridge: Cambridge University Press.

Perez, N. 2011. 'On Compensation and Return: 'Can The Continuing Injustice Argument' for Compensating for Historical Injustices Justify Compensation for such Injustices of the Return of Property,' *Journal of Applied Philosophy*. Volume 28, Number 2. Pages 151 – 168.

Ramose M. B. 2014. 'Ubuntu: Affirming a Right and Seeking Remedies in South Africa,' *Ubuntu: Curating the Archive*, Edited by Praeg L and Magadla S. Pietermaritzburg: University of KwaZulu-Natal Press, pages 121 – 136.

Sachikonye, L. M. 2012. 'From 'Growth to Equity' to 'Fast Track' Reform: Zimbabwe's Land Question.' *Review of African Political Economy*, Number 30 (96): 227 - 240

Scoones, I, & Marongwe, N, & Mavedzenge, B, & Mahenehene, J, & Murimbarimba, F, & Sukume, C. 2010. *Zimbabwe's Land Reform: Myths and Realities*, Harare: Weaver Press.

Shaw, R. & Waldorf, L. & Hazan, P. 2010. *Localizing Transitional Justice: Interventions and Priorities after Mass Violence*, Stanford, C. A: Stanford University Press.

Shaw, W. H. 2003. 'They Stole Our Land': Debating the Expropriation of White Farms in Zimbabwe,' *The Journal of Modern African Studies*, Volume 41 #1. March, pgs. 75 – 89.

Chapter Twelve

The Trans-Atlantic Slave Trade from the 15th -19th Centuries: A Major Setback to the Development of the Indigenous Economy of the Niger Delta Region of Nigeria

Odeigah, Theresa Nfam

Introduction

The Trans-Atlantic slave trade began in the 15th century during the period of the Portuguese exploration of the coast of West Africa This illicit trade became lucrative such that it spread to the other parts of Africa including Nigeria. The Slave trade was a popular business among the Portuguese, because it was the Portuguese who were first granted the opportunity to have a licence by their king to purchase other human beings - slaves. The other major slave trading countries, ordered by trade volume, were Britain, France, Spain and the Dutch. In the 16th century, the demand for labour increased as a result of the establishment of more plantations, and also the discovery of America by the Spanish explorers like Christopher Columbus and Leif Eriksson, during their four voyages to the region between 1492 and 1502. This paved the way for massive influx of the Western Europeans in to the region (Enochs, 2016). That was how it was discovered that the "new" land was fertile and could be profitable for European agricultural pursuits (The Niger Delta, 2016).

The Dutch and the English found their way to the Caribbean and the West Indies and started the development of huge plantations, which required a lot of extra labour to cultivate and make profits for themselves. The local Red Indians were perceived inadequate for the labour required in their plantations, because they were few. Besides, they could not muster the physical straight and stamina required for the job. Because of these factors, the Europeans intensified their efforts in the slave trade business, mainly from Africa. For Britain and France, the settlements in North America by migrants from Europe made them demand for more slaves to assist in the cultivation and maintenance of the sugar plantations among several other plantations (Wrigley, 1971). Most of the slaves that were forcibly taken from Nigeria were from the Niger Delta Region (Paul and Toyin, 2003).

The Trans-Atlantic slave trade has been described as the greatest human deportation in the history of the Niger Delta Region of Nigeria and indeed in Africa as a whole. From time immemorial, the Niger Delta Region with its abundant natural resources and great economic potentials had sustained the indigenous peoples even before the arrival of the Europeans (Naana and Paul, 2008). With the advent of slave trade, the region was seen as a cheap source of slaves to the Europeans, firstly, because of the region's early contact with the Portuguese, and secondly, because of the enormous economic potentials of the region. In 1481 emissaries from the king of Portugal visited the court of the Oba of Benin in exchanging correspondences and after which in 1504 and 1550 the Portuguese established a diplomatic and trade relations with Oba Esigie of Benin. From thence, the Portuguese maintained a cordial relationship with the Oba of Benin. It became imperative for a cordial relationship because of their economic motive. It was from the Niger Delta Region that the Portuguese seamen found a sea-route to India. This was an easy route for the European Merchants to convey slaves from the Niger Delta Region to Europe (Paul and Toyin 2003).

The negative effects of the Trans-Atlantic slave trade in Nigeria included among others, the collapse of the thriving Niger Delta indigenous economy. As already highlighted, the Niger Delta Region was known for its enormous agricultural productivity that attracted traders from far and near (Boahen, 1992). Historical and ethnographic evidence abound that show that there was intensive and massive production of several agricultural products in the Niger Delta Region even before the coming contact of Africa with European (Onwubiko, 1967). The indigenous economy flourished at that time and the people were involved in palm oil production, fishing, trading, and hunting. Some indigenous technologies like gold smiting and salt production also flourished. The Trans-Atlantic slave trade was considered by the indigenous people as a major setback to the economy and development of the area, as it caused enormous depopulation of the region as well as massive economic loss that affected negatively, the livelihood of the indigenous people. It is this factor among others that truncated the indigenous Niger Delta economy (Akpofure, 1962).

The indigenous economy was not a mono-economy as we are generally made to believe, but colonial exploitation and several other inhuman activities shattered the blooming that would have enabled the full realisation of the great economic potentials of the Niger Delta Region.

That said, this chapter examines the extent of the damage to the indigenous economy of the Niger Delta Region of Nigeria by the Trans-Atlantic slave trade. The chapter adopts a historic-structural and multi-disciplinary approaches to this problem (Tidy and Leeming, 1981).

Sources of Slaves in the Niger Delta Region

Before the advent of the Portuguese, the Niger Delta Chiefs were into what was called indigenous slavery. Indigenous slavery is a situation whereby the chiefs or the rich people in the communities "purchased" individuals who worked for them and also ran errands for them. It should be noted that a personality like King Jaja of Opobo, who later became a merchant prince and the founder of Opobo city in the present Rivers state of Nigeria was also a slave that was sold in Bonny at the age of twelve (Cookey, 1974). This entails that slave trade was not a new business to the people of the Niger Delta Region. It became a new business, however, when the slaves were taken outside the African continent. The Europeans that infiltrated the Niger Delta Region for the purpose of buying slaves were received by the Oba of Benin and other. Initially the Europeans were also friendly with the influential Chiefs in the region as the trading relationship developed within the region (Obong, 2016). The Portuguese soldiers helped the people of the Benin kingdom to fight wars with their neighbours using guns, guns power and other sophisticated weapons against their neighbours. The Oba of Benin was impressed with such assistance and this was the main reason for offering Portuguese, slaves and ivory among other things as gifts. The discovery of the West Indies and America by Spaniards in 1942 increased the demand for more slaves to assist in working at the various sugar plantations that were established during the time. The increased demand for labour as a result of the new sugar plantations was met by the increase in the number of slaves acquired by the European slave merchants (Hakeemm, 2001).

The methods that the Niger Delta chiefs used in acquiring slaves even before the advent of the Europeans were the same methods and logistics the Portuguese used to acquire slaves that were eventually taken to Europe, but the Portuguese slave merchants were more aggressive and business-like in getting the slaves. It was recorded that an Englishman by the name John Lock kidnapped five West Africans in 1554 (Stride and Ifeka, 1971). The slave trade business was lucrative in the Niger Delta Region of Nigeria, which was the reason the Gwatto depot became a major and also an important depot in the area. This depot was a centre where slaves were kept for their final departure to Europe. The exportation of slaves and other important items like cowries and shells which were used as currencies were all taken away through this depot from the Niger Delta Region. In the process of the Portuguese trading with the Niger delta people, their economic monopoly was broken in the sixteen century by other European countries coming into the slave business (Olikeze, 2016). Other European countries saw the Niger Delta and indeed Africa as major suppliers of slaves and cheap labour, which was the main reason France, the Dutch and many others countries came into the business. The European slave merchants set up trading posts along the coast of West Africa for easy evacuation of slaves. Some of these slaves were however, captured and taken through the Sahara Desert to the Mediterranean (Anene and Brown, 1966).

Kidnapping

In the Niger Delta Region, one of the sources and methods of acquiring slaves included kidnapping. In places like Calabar, the European merchants were fond of kidnapping people and taking them into slavery. Kidnapping occurred through the lonely bush paths to the farms and even on the lonely paths to the streams. People who could not walk in groups were most times fall prey in the hands of the European slave merchants or even the indigenous slave's traders (Akin, 1975). It should be noted that the Europeans did not force the slave trade business on the indigenous people, but the local Chiefs gave the Europeans the opportunity and support to trade with them, because of the various valued gifts they received from the Europeans (Cosmas, 2016). Another method of acquiring slaves in the Niger Delta Region was directly through the chiefs, who were already into domestic slave trade business before the coming of the Europeans. Initially, the chiefs were the only people with the power to buy slaves. The slaves that were sold to the chiefs were labelled as criminals or murderers or those who had committed various atrocities in the land (Domingo, 2016). Warri Town was another big centre that responded to the stimulus of slave trade with a sea port. This sea port was believed to have been founded and financed by Ginuwa, the son of the King (*Oba*) of Benin. Because of the sea port in Warri, Warri became a powerful kingdom because of slave trade. Ginuwa was recorded to have exported slaves in exchange of a wide range of goods to Europe (Lolomari, 2016).

Inter-Tribal Wars

Inter-tribal wars were another major source of acquiring slaves. In the Niger Delta Region, during the pre-colonial and colonial periods, there were always communal conflicts and wars with neighbouring towns and villages. Those conflicts and wars were seen as part of the struggle for the survival of the people and their territories. The wars that were fought and the various conflicts during the era of the slave trade aided the destruction of property and lives in the Niger Delta Region. The wars and conflicts were aided and orchestrated by the Europeans who then used their guns and higher fire power to capture slaves (Umukoro, 2016). This group of slaves were of individuals who were captured during the conflicts and wars. Some other people who were captured as slaves were those who were missing because they could no longer locate their towns and communities in the confusion following the conflicts. The local chiefs used this opportunity too in capturing innocent people as slaves because slave trade was a lucrative business among the chiefs. The Europeans provided guns and other dangerous weapons, which gave the people more impetus and capacity to fight with their neighbours and this process therefore offered the slave merchants the opportunity to kidnap and capture more of the people. This was a dangerous vicious cycle of events orchestrated by the Europeans that yielded their desired result of having a lot more slaves from the Niger Delta Region (Ekpen, 2016).

The European merchants were only interested in people who were strong able-bodied, marketable and not the weak or sick ones. Slaves were gotten from the interior parts of the Niger Delta Region to the coastal areas where the European merchants took them across Europe. No compensation was given to families of the victims of the kidnapped slaves, that is why till today the issue of lack of reparations to Africa remains vexatious to Africans. Places like Calabar, Okrika, Bonny and Benin where all major markets for slaves. The Europeans only compensated the chiefs with alcoholic drinks, guns, gun powers, textiles and calico among others. These were all finished goods brought from Europe (Ekaette, 2016). The relationship between the Niger Delta Region with the Portuguese merchants was purely economic and exploitation.

The Impact of Slave Trade on the Economy of the Niger Delta Region

The Trans-Atlantic slave trade had far reaching consequences on the economy of the Niger Delta Region. The slaves that were sold had profound economic prospect in the region and the Europeans merchants undermine the region development. The region lost lots of its young and able-bodies population. Walter Rodney in his book How Europe Underdeveloped Africa emphasised the subjugation, oppression and oppression of the Europe over Africans. The trans-Atlantic slave trade increased, encouraged and developed the capacity for inter-tribal wars and conflicts (Akpofure, 1962). Lives were lost during the conflicts and people were displaced and some were also taken away as slaves. These inter-tribal wars were frequent because most of the times the communities were assisted in very subtle ways by the slave merchants who kidnapped people from neighbouring communities during the resulting confusion (Effiong, 2016). This brought a setback to the economic activities of the indigenous people. Most of the local chiefs got slaves through inter-tribal wars and this encouraged more raids against their neighbours. Some of the slaves that were taken across to Europe were already into advanced canoe building, rare crafts and dearth of these skills and services negatively affected the indigenous economy. Some of those slaves left their crops and businesses unceremoniously, terminating all these economic plans and their potentials (Hakeem, 2001).

Other spheres of life that were seriously affected by slave trade were the political, social and cultural as of the life of the Niger Delta people. The Ijaws in the Niger Delta Region were friendly and open to the Europeans. They gave the Europeans land to establish trading posts and these trading posts eventually became centre points for European penetration into the interior. The Trans-Atlantic slave trade destroyed the communal life and co-operation that had hitherto existed among the communities. Suspicion, distrust and acrimony became the characteristic of the politics and social life of the people of the Niger Delta Region (Obong, 2016). The devastation of the villages through kidnapping of people affected farms, livestock and other economic activities in the Niger Delta Region. It can be reasonably argued that the criminality and banditry that are very rampant in the Niger Delta Region of Nigeria today have their roots in the negative experiences of the people during the slave trade era in the region (Etuk, 2016).

Economic diversification

The Niger Delta Region has always been recognised as a region endowed with immense economic and natural resources even before the coming of the Europeans. The diversification of the indigenous economy had long existed and the economy flourished in spite of the pre-colonial slave trade carried out by a few greedy local Chiefs from the Niger Delta. Domestic slave trade was a lucrative business among the people of the Niger Delta Region. Even at that, it did not affect the economy negatively or cause displacement of the people of the Niger Delta Region, because it was a recognised institution at that time. It was only the chiefs and the wealthy men at that time who could afford to acquire slaves (Isichie, 2016). The slaves, also known as *Osu* in the local indigenous language, were over worked and poorly fed but this cannot be compared to the maltreatment t the European merchants meted out to the slaves that were taken across the Atlantic. The advent of the Europeans definitely disrupted the commercial transactions between communities since most men and women that were enterprising in nature were taken as slaves to Europe. It also resulted in a diversified local economy for the reason that, the farm and agricultural produce were different as long as it was mainly the women who were into agriculture after the men were taken into slavery. The indigenous people were into farming, fishing, smiting, canoe, building, palm oil production and trading among others (Mafiana, 2016).

Depopulation

No one can dispute the danger and harm that was brought to bear on the people of the Niger Delta Region by the Europeans during the Tran-Atlantic slave trade period. It will not be easy to estimate the total number of people taken away from the Niger Delta Region as slaves to the "new world" This demographic evacuation of the population of the people was significant and it greatly endangered the society (Olikeze, 2016). Some scholars have claimed that almost over 20,000 people were taken from Bonny alone. Others like Dike and Fage had conservatively estimated figures that are said not to be correct. This is because many slaves died in transit and, many others were abandoned that could have also died (Anene, 1966). It is therefore difficult to really estimate the number of slave taken to Europe from the Niger Delta Region, the net result of all this could not but be catastrophic Njoku, 2001). The Niger Delta region as a coastal area suffered greatly the impact of the Trans-Atlantic slave trade more than any other region of Nigeria because of it closeness to the coast and it was the first area to come in contact with the

Europeans. The choice of slaves was only naturally restricted to the strong able-bodied women and men, the physically defected people were rejected by the slave merchants. Places like Nembe, Calabar, Kalabari and Brass suffered greatly in the hands of the slave merchants as a result of the adoption of the "House Rule" in the slave trading communities. The "House rule" was a place where slaves from different parts of the Niger Delta were brought and kept with other slaves before being evacuated (Abu, 1964).

Dehumanisation

Another negative impact of the Trans-Atlantic slave trade on the indigenous people was the dehumanising effects of slavery on the slave families. Slaves were taken forcefully by the slave "masters" against their will and slaves were separated from their families. Most of the men were bread winners of their families. According to Bisong slaves were also seen as inferior to the Europeans and were treated as domestic slaves. Slaves were also humiliated, maltreated and over-worked in the European plantations (Bisong, 20016). Slaves were thrown overboard on the high seas from the ships in the process of ferrying them across the Trans-Atlantic and a lot of them drowned in the process (Basil, 1965). The women who were also captured in slavery were most times sexually molested by the male officers specially the captains and the male crew of the ships and some of the female slaves were raped by their male captors. Slaves that were weak and sick were dumped and abandoned in unknown destinations. The slaves were kept under very harsh conditions and their complaints were not addressed by the slave masters (Stride and Ifeka, 1971). This made life very difficult for the slaves both physically and psychologically. Slaves were mismanaged, shackled with chains and some were short by the slave masters. It is also pertinent to note that the dehumanisation of slaves went as far as in the West Indies where these slaves were sold to the European farmers who disfigured them and gave them terrible marks of identification on the body (Clepperton, 1966).

Insecurity

Insecurity in the Niger Delta Region of Nigeria during the Trans-Atlantic Slave Trade was the order of the day. Armed robbery, kidnapping and other forms of attacks created fear in the hearts of the indigenous people and it also truncated the economy of the Niger Delta people. The people could no longer go to farm or engage in fishing and other businesses because of fear of being kidnapped. People were afraid to move on their own to transact business with their neighbours and this hindered the process of development in the region. Insecurity was not restricted to certain areas alone, virtually every part of the region that was involved in slave trade. All these factors affected very negatively the economy of the region and caused a serious setback to the development of the region (Abu, 1964).

The Abolition of the Trans-Atlantic Slave Trade

In 1807 the British abolished the trans-Atlantic slave trade, this was not really based on humanitarian grounds, but it was mainly because of the economic necessity at that time in Europe. The parliament in London passed a legislation prohibiting the British and its loyalists from trading in slaves. The Trans-Atlantic slave trade would not have lasted the duration it did, without the co-operation and connivance of the coastal chiefs and some of the indigenous Niger Delta slave traders who were making large sums of profit from the trade. It was also the quest of the indigenous people for the European goods in exchange for slaves that kept long the trade. The Europeans did not offer any form of development in the region rather, they took away slaves and brought in dangerous weapons and intoxicating drinks into the Niger Delta Region. Despite the evils in the Trans-Atlantic trade, in the 18th century, a combination of factors necessitated the sudden change of attitude in Europe calling for the abolition of the slave trade. The abolition of slave trade was facilitated by the British government and Great Britain was one of the most powerful countries at that time even though other countries like Portugal and France resisted the abolition vehemently, the British

296

influence and diplomatic pressure sow the abolition through (Basil, 1965).

It should, however, be noted that it was not easy for the British government, because between 1776 and 1805 almost eight attempts were made for the parliament to pass the legislation against trading in slaves. All these attempts failed because of the vast interest and profit in the trade. The abolitionists however, put all the modalities in place before the abolition was successful. In 1807, Great Britain won the battle when the British Parliament eventually passed the law making the Trans-Atlantic slave trade illegal for Britain and all British loyalists. In 1807 other countries like Denmark, America in 1808, Spain and Portugal in 1816, France in 1815 and many other countries actively joined the fight against human trafficking and slavery. The British also enforced the law banning slavery by it warships patrolling the Atlantic to ensure that no county conveyed slaves from Africa to Europe. The British government showed good example by paying the sum of $20,000 USD as compensation to slave owners and this example was followed by some other European countries (Adiele, 2006).

As earlier mentioned, combinations of factors were responsible for the abolition of the slave trade. The Industrial revolution in Europe was one of the major reasons for the abolition of the slave trade. Some of the other factors were the revolt of the American colonies against Britain and the activities of the missionaries among others. The religious Organisations like the Catholics, Anglicans and Presbyterians were always preaching and condemning slave trade among the Europeans and the local chiefs. Prominent people like Pope Benedict XIV protested against slave trade and also prohibited it (Encyclopaedia).

The abolition of the slave trade ushered in a new trend in the relationship between Europe and Nigeria. One of the most important developments was the formation of colonies in Africa following the Industrial revolution in Europe. Because of the vast economic potentials in the Niger Delta Region and Nigeria as a whole, the European countries picked a lot of interest in the region. After the scramble in 1885, Nigeria became the territory of the British government. The British traders then began to explore the interior of the Niger Delta Region with the view of creating and developing markets for their manufactured goods and also avenues of getting raw materials back to Europe. Britain, for example, needed palm oil, Cocoa, timber, rubber and tobacco for lubrication of their factory machines and for the production of other goods such as soap, candles and others. The above views therefore, helped in bringing to an end the Trans-Atlantic slave trade in the region and Nigeria as large (Odeigah, 2015).

Conclusion

The Trans-Atlantic slave trade was a major setback to the growth and development of the Indigenous Economy of the Niger Delta Region of Nigeria between the 15th and the19[th] Centuries. This is mainly because the Trans-Atlantic slave trade took away able-bodied man and women who were the productive force of the indigenous economy in the Niger Delta Region. The indigenous people also abandoned their farming activities and trading in slaves became the dominant economic activity with no attention being paid to other sectors of the economy. Local cloth weaving, pottery, smiting, local crafts and hunting were all paid very little attention. Insecurity caused by the trading slave merchants arising from regular kidnapping and frequent devastation of villages, affected the farmers, livestock and other economic activities in the region. Indigenous people could no longer work in their farms freely for fear of being kidnapped unceremoniously by the European slave merchants. The industrial revolution in Europe and British powerful diplomacy eventually led to the abolition of Trans-Atlantic slave trade.

The introduction of legitimate trade did not stop European exploitation in the region and other parts of Africa because Nigeria and other African countries became colonies where cheap raw materials were sourced for their factories in Europe and finished expensive luxury goods were then shipped back to the colonies which served as markets for their finished products. The political, social and cultural life and internal security of the Niger Delta Region was also shattered by the activities of the slave merchants. It has been argued that some of the present day insurgency and criminality in the Niger

Delta Region of Nigeria have their roots in the insecurity characterised by the regular kidnappings, raids and violence perpetrated during the period of slavery. The lack of payment of reparations to Africa remains a very vexatious issue because this would have helped to address some of the economic challenges resulting from Trans-Atlantic slave trade in Africa.

References

Abu, B. 1964. *Topic in West African History*, Longman: Ghana.

Adiele, A. 2006. The Abolition of the Slave Trade-in South-eastern Nigeria, 1885-1950, https:// boydellandbrewer.com, 2006, Accessed 15th Oct, 2016.

Akinyemi, A. 1975. *Essential of West African History, (AD. 1000-1800),* Ibadan, Nigeria.

Akpofure, R. and Crowder, M. 1962. *Nigeria A Modern History for Schools*, Faber and Faber, London.

Anene, J. C. and Brown, G. 1966. *Africa in the Nineteenth and Twentieth Centuries,* University of Ibadan, Ibadan.

Anene, T. C. 1966. *Essays in African History 19th-20th centuries,* University of Ibadan Press, London.

Basil, D. 1965. *A History of West Africa 1000-1800*, Longman, London.

Bisong Banku, age 98[+] years, status women Leader, occupation Farmer, place of Interview Ikom, 6/11/2016.

Boahen, A. 1992. Britain, *The Sahara,* pp.119-125, Elizabeth Savage(ed), The *Human Commodity: Perspective on the Trans-Sahara Slave Trade, London:* Jan Hogendorn, "The Economics of Trade in Eunuchs," Seminar Paper on African Slavery, York University, 1996.

Chief Cosmas Etta, age 95[+] years, status clan head, occupation Chief, place of Interview Oron, 6/11/2016.

Clapperton, H., 1966. *Journal of a Second Expedition into the Interior of Africa*, Frank Cass, London.

Cookey, S. J. S. 1974. King Jaja of the Niger Delta, NOK, London.

mingo Edward, age 102[+] years, status Elder, occupation farmer, place of Interview Effurun, 1/11/2016.

Effiong Duke age 103⁺ years, status Elder, occupation farmer, place of Interview Oron 6/11/2016.

Ekaette George age 91⁺ years, status Women Community leader, occupation messenger during the colonial period, place of Interview Uyo, 8/11/2016.

Ekpen Onoroide age 102⁺ years, status Women leader/singer, occupation retired trader, place of Interview Aladja, 3/10/2016.

Encyclopaedia History, Slave Trade in Nigeria, logbaby.com.

Enochs Kevin, 2016. The Real Story: Who Discovered America, http: www.voanews.com.

Etuk Enebong age 101⁺ years, status Elder, occupation retired civil servant/colonial Clark during the colonial period, place of Interview Calabar, 10/11/2016.

Hakeem .B. Harunah, 2001. *The Political and Socio-cultural Factors in the West Africa Slave Trade 1450-1897, Lagos: Centre for Black and African Arts and Civilization*, Lagos: Nigeria.

Isichie Jumbo age 79⁺ years, status retried director of Education, occupation teaching, place of Interview Port Harcourt, 14/11/2016.

Lolomari Dede age 100⁺ years, status Elder, occupation Farmer, place of Interview Ugep, 23/2/2017.

Lolomari Dede age 89⁺ years, status Elder, occupation Trader, place of Interview Warri, 2/11/2016.

Mafiana Udeh age 81⁺ years, status Elder/retired school principal, occupation teaching, place of Interview Asaba, 15/11/2016.

Naana Opoku-Agyemany, Paul. E. Lovejoy and David Trotman, 2008. (Ed.), *Africa and Trans-Atlantic Memories: Literary and Aesthetic Manifestation of Diaspora and History*, Longman: London.

Njoku, O. N. 2001. *Economic History of Nigeria, 19th and 20th Centuries*, Magnet Business Enterprises: Enugu.

Obong Okokon Ittah age 100⁺ years, status Elder, occupation farmer, place of Interview Calabar, 10/11/2016.

Obong Okokon Ittah age 100⁺ years, status Elder, occupation farmer, place of Interview Calabar, 10/11/2016.

Odeigah, T. N. 2015. *The Eastern Niger Delta Economy under Colonial Rule 1885-1960,* Unpublished Master's dissertation, Kogi State University, Nigeria.

Olikeze Okocha age 83⁺ years, status Elder, occupation farmer, place of Interview Agbor, 15/11/2016.

Olikeze Okocha, age 83⁺ years, status Elder, occupation farmer, place of interview Uyo, 12th October, 2016.

Onwubiko, K. B. C. 1967. History of West Africa, A.D. 1000-1800, Anambra: Africana Educational publishers, in association with FEP, International Private Limited, Nigeria.

Paul. E. Lovejoy and Toyin Falola, (Eds.), *Pawnship, 2003. Slavery and Colonialism in Africa*, Heinemann: London.

Stride. G. T. & Ifeka Caroline, 1971. *People and Empires of West Africa, West Africa in History 1000-1800,* Thomas Nelson and Sons: Hong Kong.

The Niger Delta in the 19th Century-Culture, 2016. http://www.nairaland.com/1027145/niger-delta-19th-century, 2016, Accessed 15th Oct, 2016.

Tidy Michael and Leeming Donald, 1981. A History of Africa 1840-1914, Volume two, Holder and Stoughton, London.

Umukoro Jefia age 79⁺ years, status Elder, occupation fisherman, place of Interview Warri, 2/11/16.

Wrigley, C. C. 1971. Historicism in African Slavery and State Formation, *African Affairs*, 70, pp115-22.

Chapter Thirteen

'Eating a Pig in a Pie?' – A Philosophical Paradox of Women Rights in Human Rights Discourse in Zimbabwe

Jowere Mukusha

Introduction

The paradoxical nature of women rights in Human Rights discourse poses a serious challenge in all sectors of development in any biosphere that is primarily centred on humanity. In the contemporary global world there is a contentious talk and fierce struggle for the respect for human rights between men and women. This is in spite of the fact that the people at the centre of the human rights enigma – men and women – are both human beings. The struggle for the need to respect human rights ushers in the paradox of women rights in the realm of human rights in Africa and Zimbabwe in particular. It is on this note that this chapter seeks to explore almost all of the gnawing issues with regards to women rights covering the following areas: land, culture, political democracy and education. The nature and scope of the women rights paradox is typically similar to the saying that: 'Eating a pig in a pie' as women are susceptible to a barrage of human rights abuse despite their existential presence in the realm of humanity, including the whole discourse of human rights. It is like eating 'a pig in a pie' in many different forms. Firstly, women are just human beings like their male counter-parts but the talk of women rights in the Human Rights discourse presents a challenging situation faced by women. Secondly, women seem to be fully covered whenever the issue of Human Rights is addressed by virtue of their being human but the situation on the ground seems to suggest otherwise.

In this chapter, the term men refer to males whilst women denote all females. In addition, the term 'pig' has a metaphorical analogical meaning in this chapter. The situation on the ground with regard to the treatment of women is just a mixed bag thereby handing the women rights discourse its paradoxical nature. In other words, women are pictured in a situation whereby the patriarchal dominated society is making significant effort to accord them rights in all sectors of life; however, some of those efforts are coincidental thereby making it a paradox. Taking the instance of Zimbabwe, a great majority of women are still under-privileged in many ways but are sort of covered up by the few privy to certain positions of influence, hence, another 'eating a pig in a pie' paradoxical scenario obtains. As Boss (2008: 444) observes "men are socialised to be both protectors and sexual predators; women are socialised to be weak and to be sexual prey." This implies that the Western and African patriarchal interpretation of men/males upholds the superiority of men/males over women. However, in certain African matrimonial societies women are dominant over men in the traditional domain. It should however be noted that in the current public domain, women in Africa are threatened by male dominance in the observations of their rights. In this light, the chapter's main port of call is: the Universality of Human Rights, the controversial nature of Human Rights for women as enshrined in the Convention of the Elimination of All Forms of Discrimination against Women (CEDAW), land rights, education and women political democracy in Zimbabwe. In Zimbabwe's Millennium Development Goals Status Report (2010: 16), goal number 3 target 1, categorically states the need to, "Eliminate gender disparity in primary and secondary education, preferably by 2005, and to all levels of education no later than 2015." This goal in Zimbabwe has been addressed in the education sector where females are more than males. For example, at Great Zimbabwe University in the year 2016, 59% were females whilst 41% were males. There are positive steps being taken in the implementation of the gender policy in Zimbabwe. Laws have been put in place by parliamentarians after consulting the public to address the issue of gender parity in the Zimbabwean society although still women rights are sometimes received with suspicion due to men's fear of being dominated by females. A succinct conclusion as well as a sound reference section marks the closure of this chapter but open for criticism and affirmation by any interested researchers.

The universality of Human Rights

The universality of the issue of Human Rights can only be understood by first looking at the concept of Human Rights in line with the United Nations Universal Declaration of Human Rights Act, 1948. As Crawshaw (1999: 37) notes, "Human Rights can best be understood as those rights which are fundamental to the human condition, and as fundamental principles of justice." This implies that Human Rights are an indispensable entity accorded to every human being for equity and justice to prevail in society. Although Crawshaw looks at rights, a better approach would have been to avoid the tautologous use of the term rights by replacing it with the term entitlements. It is not always the case in Zimbabwe that the issue of women rights are properly addressed and this is evidenced by several campaigns advocating for women human rights consideration in the civic society and parliament.

Acknowledging the same position, Understanding Gender and Gender Based Violence: Resource Manual for Training Trainers Sida and UNICEF (2010: x) notes, "Zimbabwe introduced a National Gender Policy to act as a guideline for examining and redressing gender issues at national level." It is the duty of the gender policy to inform policy implementation in an attempt to correct gender disparities in all spheres of life in Zimbabwe and beyond. In other words, in Zimbabwe, without respect for the fundamentals of Human Rights for both males and females, development endeavours are highly likely to be threatened to stagnation. Jayasuriya and Jayasuriya (1999: 30) allude to Principle I that, "… all human beings are born free and equal in dignity and rights, including all the rights and freedoms of the Universal Declaration of Human Rights, and have the right to life, liberty, and security of persons." This suggests that no one should enjoy his/her rights in another; thus, women in Zimbabwe and elsewhere should experience their full human dignity independent of men and vice versa is true for they are not a 'pig in a pie'. Crawshaw's (1999: 37) clarification is apt when he argues that "Human rights are also "inherent", 'equal' and "inalienable" – which means that: every human being has them by virtue of his or her humanity, without distinction; and they cannot be taken or given away." Principle 1 summarises the conception of Human Rights under the United Nations' Universal Declaration of Human Rights Act of 1948. Neither men nor women should be regarded as 'window' dressers who are not accorded their human worth in the Human Rights discourse in the world.

Skewed Implementation of Human Rights

Crawshaw (1999: 67) sums, "Human Rights are those inalienable rights inherent in every human being, and enshrined in the Universal Declaration of Human Rights and other international instruments promulgated for the protection of human rights." In view of this, the paradoxical nature of the skewed implementation of the Human Rights policies between men and women is deliberately manipulated by politicians in Zimbabwe as well as in other countries ending up developing a false consciousness of women freedom and general emancipation from the traditional cultural practises faced by women. Thus, their participation in the human rights discourse renders them a second fiddle, a real 'pig in a pie' situation. In this light, Zimbabwe Millennium Development Goals Status Report (2010: 16) stresses the need to "increase the participation of women in decision-making in all sectors and at all levels (to 40% for women in senior civil service positions and to 30% for parliament) by 2005 and to a 50: 50 balance by 2015." This is a clear indication that women rights in Zimbabwe are given attention but the implementation has not yet satisfied what is suggested by policy. Women are still in a paradoxical situation thereby taking up the status of 'pigs in pies' when it comes to the universal treatment under the banner of the human rights discourse. Women enjoy their rights in highly assumed and swallowed state of affairs where men seem to dominate and benefit more than them.

The high degree of controversy of women rights in Human Rights gives an asymmetrical relationship between men and women thereby subjecting women to a number of disadvantages in Zimbabwe. Men generally assume a masculine dominance over women's so-called feminine passivity. However, this situation is currently under serious challenge by a plethora of women movements anchored on the banner of feminist philosophy buttressed by the United Nations Convention on the Elimination of All Forms of Discrimination against Women (CEDAW) Act of 1979. Waldorf (2007: 5-6) observes: "The human rights obligation to eliminate sex-based discrimination against women in order to achieve gender equality has been at the centre of international human rights from the beginning." Thus, for any meaningful development across all spectrums of life, women should not be discriminated against but be active equal partners in any society, Zimbabwe included. Meer (1997: 1) posits, "Women are generally disadvantaged, compared with men of the same race and class, in access to land, employment, labour and training…" This depicts a situation in need of urgent redress in order to enable women to participate and compete with men on an equal footing as a way of boosting economic development in Zimbabwe. In light of this, women should not be seen as just 'pigs' in 'pies' but respected participant in their right in different spheres of life in a bid to meet the millennium goals in Zimbabwe and abroad. Waldorf (2007: 6) confirms that "in 1993, the Vienna World Conference on Human Rights took the centrality of women's rights to the international human rights regime as one of its primary concerns." It is, therefore, the sole function of CEDAW and indeed an obligation for all people to ascertain women emancipation in the world and Zimbabwe in particular.

Legislation attempting to address Women Rights

Jayasuriya and Jayasuriya (1999: 17) note, "Women rights need to be demystified and information about them must be made available in the public domain." In an attempt to achieve the millennium goals in Zimbabwe, a number of legislative efforts were implemented and reviewed to guard against the general abuse of women. Most of the legal Acts covering a period from 1980 to 2010 as cited in Zimbabwe Millennium Development Goals Status Report (2010) are: Equal Pay Regulations of 1980, all women to given equal pay to men doing the same job; Legal Age of Majority Act (LAMA) of 1982, this allows women to be fully independent citizens who should enjoy the full benefits in all spheres of life by virtue of attaining the age of eighteen years; these Acts are gender inclusive thereby not disadvantaging either sex. The Labour Relations Act of 1984 Chapter 28: 01, this suggests the need to practise indiscriminate labour practices that is, regardless of sex. Marriage Act of 1987 Section 21 Chapter 5: 11, which deals with empowering women through a marriage contract that is acting as a form of security in terms of property inheritance and the stability of the family. Equally important are the Matrimonial Causes Act of 1987, attempts to address the maternal rights; and the Maintenance Amendment Act of 1989, which one of the most crucial legal instrument put in place in Zimbabwe in order to protect children in case of a divorce or strained relations between the spouses. Usually, women used to carry the burden of looking after their children while the errant husband or impregnator enjoys himself elsewhere. The other important Acts with regard to women rights in Zimbabwe are the Electoral Act of 1990, which allows women to participate in general and by- elections for the Presidency or in Parliament and local elections as voters or candidates without discrimination; and the Domestic Violence Act of 2007 and the launch of an Anti-Domestic Violence Council in 2009. These two were/are attempts to curb violence between men and women in Zimbabwe thereby according them Human Rights in the proper sense. All this legislation endeavours to achieve gender equality and equity as the sole means to do away with gender parity in different spheres of life. In the colonial era, that is, before Zimbabwe's independence in 1980, women were treated more like objects who do not qualify to be accorded human rights in a number of areas. However, currently, Zimbabwe is putting a lot of effort and resources in an attempt to make women enjoy their right to good health, right of choice, political participation, and freedom of expression among other rights. These rights among others were deprived of women both during the pre-colonial, colonial and part of the post-colonial era. For example, women in Zimbabwe did not have voting rights in the colonial era and most were denied of owning a national identity card. In other words, women were treated as second class citizens in the society.

Demystification of Human Rights in the eyes of women

The successful demystification of women rights information will enable the full emancipation of women in Zimbabwe and beyond for the benefit of developmental programmes without which it will derail sustainable development. Waldorf (2007: 6) states, "As stated in the Vienna Declaration and Programme of Action, and affirmed many times since, including in the Beijing Platform: The human rights of women and of the girl-child are an inalienable, integral, indivisible part of universal human rights." In view of CEDAW, Waldorf (2007) stresses that CEDAW is an anti-discrimination treaty, meaning that gender inequalities are understood to have been produced due to sex-based discrimination. It is, therefore, the responsibility of the state to eliminate the many different forms of gender-based discrimination that women face. CEDAW embodies both a theory of women subordination and a strategy to overcome this subordination. In other words, women fight gender discrimination under CEDAW so that they can take part in various forums locally and internationally.

From a Zimbabwean perspective, women are lobbying for their rights through a number of civic organisations such as Musasa Project, Women's Forum, Women Lawyers Association, and many others. Zimbabwe has realised a considerable formulation and reformulation of policies in a bid to serve women interests. This has managed to enable women participate actively and productively for the good of the country that is currently reeling of the illegal sanctions imposed by the West. The first paragraph in the Preamble to the Universal Declaration in Crawshaw (1999: 39) states, "Recognition of the inherent dignity and of the equal and inalienable rights of all members of the human family is the foundation of freedom, justice, and peace in the world." Therefore, for realistic development to take place in the world and Zimbabwe in particular there is need to sustain peace and justice through the respect for women rights in Human Rights. Women in Zimbabwe have the potential to contribute to the development of the country if they are supported in the banking sector, agricultural sector, engineering sector and in the small and medium enterprises. For instance, the current campaign by women in Zimbabwe to be afforded a chance to develop a women's bank is a noble example. The beneficiation of women projects in the small and medium industries has a strong impact on women realising their rights through constructive production. Women rights are also realised to a greater extent in the cross border trade which is dominated by women where they have the potential to contribute positively to the gross domestic product (GDP) of Zimbabwe. However, the impact of corruption in the cross border trade activities derails the economic gains for women and Zimbabwe as a country.

Although positive steps are being taken in Zimbabwe to empower women through the national policy, there is still need to broaden and deepen the recognition of women rights in the Human Rights discourse in all walks of life. This would enable some form of compensatory development among women, as they will put lots of energy in the country's developmental programmes thereby complementing men's efforts. In this way, women in Zimbabwe will not be like pigs eaten in pies but productive beings in themselves outside the male dominated social pie. Brock-Utne (1985: 73) also notes that "only through respect for the equal rights of others and through work for the cessation of all forms of oppression on a major and minor scale will the concept of peace become a reality." Women and men should not be viewed as separate entities under the Human Rights discourse but both are important partners. Although Brock-Utne (1985: 149) states, "As women we have to believe in ourselves and other women to have the strength, endurance, compassion, and passion to continue our struggle for a better, more humane, and truly peaceful future." This feminist stance can only succeed if men realise the need for women emancipation through constructive dialogue at both national and international levels. Women and development projects are an essential entity in the study and analysis of gender and development proponents in Africa and beyond. Julia Dolly Joiner in Heyns and Killander (2006: vi) observes, "Human rights, human security and human development are interdependent, inter-related and indivisible and, thus, constitute inseparable ingredients for Africa's quest for prosperity." Clear as it, Human Rights respect for both women and men are crucial for the development of Africa and Zimbabwe in particular. Boss (2008: 444) notes that, "According to radical feminists such as Catherine Mackinnon… one cannot be a woman without being objectified as objects for sexual violence. To use a well-known slogan… the most important difference between men and women is that "men fuck and women get fucked." Thus, no one should be treated like a by-product of Adam's rib whereby women are rendered a second class product in the creation of humanity with regards to the Human Rights discourse in Zimbabwe and elsewhere. The chapter now turns on to the address of women rights in Human Rights in a number of areas in the Zimbabwean context.

Women Rights to Land

Access to land: A contestation between women and men in Zimbabwe

The land question is a contested issue in Zimbabwe (Mukusha 2010). Women and men are brought in a heterogeneous contest in as far as the access to land is concerned in Zimbabwe where men enjoy a larger stake in land ownership. In any country, Zimbabwe included, Meer (1997: 26) observes, "Men fear that if women gain land rights, they will use this leverage to overthrow the male-oriented system of power relations. This system centres on the control of land, but ultimately involves control of the social order as well." It is clear that generally women are disadvantaged in as far as the ownership of land is concerned. This lack of many women who own land has both direct and indirect impacts on the economy and the potential of women to gain power in the so-called men dominated spheres of power. Hence, for sustainable development to take place in Zimbabwe, access to land especially for women should be supported and accelerated. In the current Zimbabwean context, most women who own land are those who are politically influential such as women war veterans, war veterans' wives and relatives as well as vibrant women political activists. It is high time those other women who do not have a strong political base be included in land ownership schemes in order to attain indiscriminate economic development in Zimbabwe like what happened immediately after independence in the country. The coming in of more women in the land ownership train should liberate both, for men will see that women are not enemies but indispensable partners in development. Meer (1997: 5) states, "In both the South African and Zimbabwean contexts it would seem that specific policies are directed at women, while other policies are regarded as gender neutral. However, ostensibly gender-neutral policies have gender impacts. Thus, policy that does not take into account differences in the needs of men and women most often ends up being gender-biased in favour of men." Land ownership is generally gender-neutral in Zimbabwe but when it comes to the actual implementation many women are dislodged by their male counterpart. This is because of the patriarchal tendencies where men dominate in the ownership of land and other essential resources. Men dominate meetings to do with the redistribution of critical resources such as land in Zimbabwe. This scenario discriminates against women thereby hampering effective development in Zimbabwe.

Gender equality: A Women Human Rights solution

It is also important to note that in farming activities women provide the bulk of the labour force required in the rural and commercial farms in Zimbabwe. Given the fact that women are a treasure in them due to their child bearing potential, a factor that increases labour force in agricultural activities in Zimbabwe and elsewhere, they seem to be better candidates than men to own a larger percentage of land though it is not the case. The rate of productivity is most likely to improve significantly if more women in Zimbabwe are legally allowed to own more land than men. Hence, Waldorf (2007: 12) emphasises: "Not everyone who works to advance gender equality approaches it as a human right. For example, it can be treated exclusively as a development concern. From that view, gender equality has importance because of its instrumental value in furthering development – because a country's development objectives cannot be reached unless the situation of both men and women are significantly improved, attention must be paid to the challenges women face. It is self-explanatory that for meaningful development to take place in a sustainable manner there is need to treat both women and men equally. Thus, Waldorf (2007: 13) notes, "One of the central principles human rights law has established is that all human beings, women included, are equal and should not be subjected to discrimination." Discrimination of either sex automatically discriminates against development in a country and Zimbabwe is not an exception. Meer (1997: 2) quotes Bernstein (1992) pointing out that, "better strategies for land reform will emerge when the diversity among and within communities and households is noted. Such diversity should include differentiation along the lines of gender and class." Therefore, the consideration of women as one element of that diversity is cardinal for sustainable development in the country's economic sector through land ownership and maximum utilisation of the land in Zimbabwe. Without the potential to use the land wisely productively in Zimbabwe by either sex, productivity will nose-dive thereby worsening the already sanction ridden economic situation. This suggests the need for support mechanisms to empower both women and men in the administrative and technical areas in the utilisation of land in order to achieve development in the positive way. Sue Middleton in Meer (1997: 74) states, "The case study suggests that some women may have more rights to land in a situation of land invasion, and at a time when rules of allocation are in a state of flux." This situation has been realised in Zimbabwe since the year 2000 when the landless Zimbabweans, women included embarked on what is commonly dubbed the 'Land invasion' exercise. The so-called land invasion had negative and positive impacts at its initial stages, it destabilises commercial farming activities thereby affecting the rate of productivity. It also enables the landless and land hungry Blacks to get a golden chance, not to be missed, to access and own a piece of land that is currently in use for agricultural purposes in Zimbabwe. Before this so-called land invasion in Zimbabwe, very few women owned pieces of land as it was seen as primarily a male's domain. It was the bedrock of the so-called "land invasion" that catapulted the Zimbabwe Government to enact the Fast Track Land Acquisition Act in the year 2000 in order to try and bring peace in the commercial farming areas. This has seen a large number of both men and women enjoying the right to own land for agricultural purposes that has a decongesting effect on the densely populated rural populace in Zimbabwe. The land issue is even captured in the Global Political

Agreement of 15 September (2008: 1) thus, "Recognising and accepting that the Land Question has been at the core of the contestation in Zimbabwe and acknowledging the centrality of issues relating to the rule of law, respect for human rights, democracy and governance." This implies that the land contestation is poly-focal that is, between Whites and Blacks and among Black males and females. Positive development in Zimbabwe could be realised if women are equally treated in land ownership. The land issue in Zimbabwe and elsewhere always cascades women's political rights where land is used as a means of production as well as a source of power.

Women Rights to Politics

Power struggles between women and men

By virtue of being part of the human species, women should also take up major roles and positions in the political arena in Zimbabwe. According to the Mena Development Report (2004: 14) "The public sphere is the sphere of power, influence, and patronage and, as such, has been traditionally reserved for men. A call for gender equality is effectively a 'transgression' of women into this space and a claim to share power and control." Women should be seen penetrating the once regarded as the male domain under the policy of gender equity in Zimbabwe. In Zimbabwe, though not yet adequate, women are currently gradually increasingly taking posts in the political realm occupying the Vice Presidency, Vice Prime Minister, and a number of ministerial and senatorial posts. The benefits of CEDAW with regards to the social and political rights are firmly becoming a reality in Zimbabwe. Thus, women in Zimbabwe as a political community are grappling with national politics in a meaningful manner coupled with the support they get from the Presidium or the Executive. However, according to the Zimbabwe Millennium Development Goals Status Report (2010: 17), "Although approximately 52% of the population in Zimbabwe is female, women are disproportionately represented in politics and in other decision-making positions." In simple terms, women are still very much like 'pigs in pies' (swallowed by men) suffering from ill representation coupled with a false conscious of their consciousness of their rights to take up important posts in Zimbabwe. Colonialism perpetuated women suffering due to severe discrimination practices that were targeted at women. Freire (1972) would view such a situation as the perpetuation of the culture of silence and a dehumanising state of affairs where there is need to humanise women by according their rightful human rights in the sphere of freedom that is liberating. Hatchard and Ogowewo (2003: 6) posit, "The most prized right of any political community is the right to govern itself." The women community though still disadvantaged as compared to men in Zimbabwe is gaining some political milestones. In this regard, Mena Development Report (2004: 14) points, "Gender equality will remain an abstraction unless a substantial number of women believe that they must do something to exercise their rights and governance, and unless they realise that they must play an active role in promoting gender equality." Therefore, it is still a mountain's climb to the bottom for women in Zimbabwe and in the African continent to enjoy a lion's share in the much chauvinistic political arena. In relation to development, positive development can only take place when women are not subjugated by men in different forums in life including in the political cosmology/structure.

Women Liberty under Threat: A Feminist Perspective

Harrison-Barbet (2001: 253) notes, "… for Mill, liberty meant protection against the tyranny of the political rulers." This implies that even in Zimbabwe women need to be protected against the political rulers in the name of men for them to enjoy freedom and contribute in national development. In Zimbabwe and Africa in general, law must be put in place in order to safeguard women's Human Rights in the political arena. Shaw (1997: 1) says, "Law is the element which binds the members of the community together in their adherence to recognised values and standards." From what Shaw tells us, there is a link in this instance between law and ethics especially when law addresses community related issues which are morally binding although law is generally perceived to be amoral. This kind of law will inevitably abate the controversial nature in gender equality currently experienced among men and women of Zimbabwe.

Without such laws, women's discrimination in various spectrums of life will culminate in the lack of development in Zimbabwe. Thus, Rawls (1971: 259) emphasises, "A doctrine of political economy must include an interpretation of the public good which is based on a conception of justice." The women's Human Rights should be legally treated as a public good in Zimbabwe and beyond for sustainable development to take place. In other words, women should be liberated legally in the political terrain. Women must experience what Chung (2007: 66) calls, "Uhuru… the Swahili word for freedom and liberation." Total women rights consideration and implementation in the political arena would see women enjoying freedom and liberation which are important ingredients for social, economic and political development.

Taking the bull by the horns is the pressure exerted by feminism as an attempt to attain total emancipation of women in Zimbabwe. Shulamith Firestone, a radical feminist activist and founder of the New York Radical Women in Gould (1989: 463) reiterates, "A person is free if she is neither constrained nor coerced… she contends that women are badly constrained and/or coerced in lone situations." Thus, for this radical feminist love is at the centre of women rights abuse, oppression and exploitation in any country. In Zimbabwe, women also face the wrath due to their femininity coupled with the chauvinistic demands of the African Traditional Culture which has strong tallies with the dogmatic Christian Bible in making women objects of men's satisfaction at the expense of them expressing their liberal rights as entities belonging to the realm of humanity. However, the problem with this radical feminist approach is that society cannot develop in the absence of sexual love and its products in any country. Firestone in Gould (1989) fires that women's sexuality is so important to men that it becomes equated to her individuality. She refers to this equation as sex privatisation where men's emphasis on beauty as an ideal also serves a political function establishing a pecking order when some women are left out. The denial of love for Firestone will empower women in the political domain. It seems better to take up the Liberal feminist stance that there is need to redress the situation in an attempt to have men and women share certain responsibilities such as child rearing, kitchen chores and outdoor labour intensive responsibilities in all spheres of life. By so doing women will not be like 'a pig in a pie' in the human rights discourse in Zimbabwe and the world at large. Women's Human Rights are also catered for in the United Nations as observed in Waldorf (2007: 70) that:

> The human rights guaranteed by the International Covenant on Civil and Political Rights include the right to life, freedom from torture... right to liberty and security of the person... rights relating to citizenship and political participation, minority groups' rights to their culture, religion and language.

Thus, in the political realm women and democracy are sometimes at polar relations in Zimbabwe due to male dominance over females thereby stifling social, economic and political development.

The Culture of Women Suppression

In any country, education should embody the culture of its society. A patriarchal biased education curriculum inevitably suppresses and exploits women's Human Rights. This is likely to have negative impacts on production and the level of peace in a society. Meer (1997: 93) avers:

> Women identified a number of obstacles to their participation in decision-making structures within the community. These were linked most crucially to their own lack of information and the lack of confidence due to men's alienating tendencies that hand the inferiority complex tag to women thereby preventing women from participating at meetings, and to the time-consuming domestic work that prevents women from attending meetings.

There is a form of submissive culture engendered in women that obstructs them from taking courageous steps into challenging areas such as politics. In Zimbabwe, there are a number of women who have opted out of marriage and are now into politics that is sometimes observed as 'the 'I don't care' type of women. Unmarried women politicians in Zimbabwe are a clear example of those females allegedly categorised as radical for example, Margaret Dongo and others. There is still controversy with regards to women's Human Rights in the ever-intimidating presence of men in Zimbabwe almost creating Freire's (1972) culture of silence among many women in Zimbabwe. This should not be the case because following an African feminist dose women were alright with the responsibilities bestowed on them. This twist is a clear manifestation of the impact of colonialism coupled with patriarchalism in the way women rights have been distorted in Zimbabwe and Africa as a continent. Echoing the same sentiments, Shulamith Firestone, a radical feminist in Gould (1989: 463) stresses, "... one reason is that culture has been built on women's love; that men have used the emotional strength of women to build culture." This kind of thinking is too radical in any normal human society because it is based on hate and emotional reasoning against men. It therefore implies that women rights in Human Rights in the face of the male counterpart are a contested issue with the potential to derail possible development programmes in the Zimbabwean community. Because of this, Jayasuriya and Jayasuriya (1999: 17) states, "... 1995-2004 – the General Assembly proclaimed the UN Decade for Human Rights Education, underlying the importance of creating awareness." This in Zimbabwe enabled the demystification of women rights and the respect for gender equality in the economic and political environments. This is evidenced by the fact that currently Zimbabwe's level of literacy is at first position, 92% in Africa followed by Tunisia according to the UN report. It is primarily because Zimbabwe has managed to go against some cultural barriers inhibiting the education of the girl child which were caused by Western education that sacrificed the girl-child for the boy-child in an attempt to create a strong semi-literate labour force. In a nutshell, despite an avalanche of sanctions imposed on Zimbabwe, it has managed to democratise its education from the grassroots up to the highest echelons thereby fighting the segregatory tendencies of the colonial type of education. Rapid development, however, is on the wait in Zimbabwe if the political polarisation coupled with illegal sanctions imposed by the West that are currently stifling the efficient achievement of the millennium goals due to the lack of international funding and the existence of some trade embargoes which are severely affecting the marginalised groups that include children and women, are removed – a call for the international passion.

Conclusion

'Eating a pig in a pie' may qualify to describe the respect and disrespect for women's Human Rights in Zimbabwe. The main paradox necessitates the need for universal consideration of Human Rights to all human beings against the skewed implementation of Human Rights to women. This has resulted in the invention of Women Rights as though women are not human enough like their male counterpart. It has been noted that the use of the term "Women Rights" is an indication of a situation that is not level where women rights are sort of assumed in the male dominated Human Rights discourse. This brings the paradox of eating a pig in a pie. The chapter is philosophical in its tone of analysis as it attempts to reveal the nature and level of Women Rights in Human Rights discourse. It has been stressed in this chapter that there are sheer levels of women rights' Human Rights controversy in the universality of Human Rights' right to land, right to politics and right to education and culture. This Human Rights controversy hampers sustainable development throughout Zimbabwe's social, economic and political domains due to the fact that women are somehow treated as second-class citizens. CEDAW is handy in as far as the improvement of women rights is concerned in Zimbabwe and beyond its borders. Although women rights issues in Zimbabwe are being constantly revisited, there is still a great deal of work to be done in order to do justice to the contestations between women and men in terms of power, resources, education, representation and discrimination in different spheres of life. The use of legislative powers seen to be one possible way of levelling the Women rights in Human Rights issues. Women rights remain inherently a socio-political philosophical paradox for sustainable development efforts in Zimbabwe and the world at large.

References

Boss, J. 2008. *Analysing Moral Issues*, New York: McGraw-Hill Companies, Inc.

Brock-Utne, B. 1985. *Educating for Peace: A Feminist Perspective*, New York: Pergamon Press.

Chung, F. 2007. *Re-Living the Second Chimurenga: Memories from Zimbabwe's Liberation Struggle*, Harare: Weaver Press.

Crawshaw, R. 1999. *Police and Human Rights: A Manual for Teachers, Resources Persons and Participants in Human Rights programmes*, The Hague: Kluwer Law International.

Friere, P. 1972. *Pedagogy of the Oppressed*, New York: Penguin Books Ltd.

Global Political Agreement 15 September. 2008. Harare: The Ministry of Constitutional & Parliamentary Affairs.

Gould, J. A. 1989. *Classic Philosophical Questions*, Ohio: Merrill Publishing Company.

Harrisson-Barbet, A. 2001. *Mastering Philosophy*, New York: Palgrave.

Hatchard, J. & Ogowewo, T. I. 2003. *Tackling the Unconstitutional Overthrow of Democracies: Emerging Trends in the Commonwealth*, London: Commonwealth Secretariat.

Jayasuriya, S. & Jayasuriya, D. C. 1999. *Women and Development, The Road from Beijing*, New Delhi: Har-Anand Publications Pvt. Ltd.

Joiner, J. D. "Foreword", in: Heyns, C. & Killander, M. 2006. *Compendium of Key Human Rights Documents of The African Union*, Pretoria: Pretoria University Law Press.

Meer, S. (Ed.). 1997. *Women, Land and Authority: Perspectives from South Africa*, Cape Town: David Philip.

Mena Development Report. 2004. *Gender and Development in the Middle East and North Africa: Women in the Public Sphere*, Washington D.C., World Bank.

Millennium Development Goals Status Report Zimbabwe. 2010. Harare: Ministry of Labour and Social Services, United Nations Development Programme.

Mukusha, J. 2010. Land?: *The Socio-Political Engine-room for Controversy and Development in Zimbabwe*, Unpublished.

Rawls, J. 1971. *A Theory of Justice*, Cambridge: The Belknap Press of Harvard University Press.

Shaw, M.N. 1997. *International Law*, Cambridge: Cambridge University Press.

Understanding Gender and Gender Based Violence: Resource Manual for Training Trainers (2010), SIDA & UNICEF: Harare.

Waldorf, L. 2007. *CEDAW and the Human Rights Based Approach to Programming*, New York: UNIFEM May 2007.

Chapter Fourteen

Female Initiation as a Preventative Measure to Teenage Pregnancy: A Reflection on Zimbabwe's Vhavenda Cultural Practices

Silibaziso Mulea & Kelibone Choeni

Introduction

Teenage pregnancy is a matter of concern across all cultures in Zimbabwe. Since the advent of colonialism, various Western methods and programmes were utilised on the reduction of teenage pregnancy, but to no end. Despite the various methods used to prevent teenage pregnancies, the teenage percentage pregnancy rate continues to soar even higher. It is, therefore, on this pretext that the present chapter explores the Vhavenda's female initiation process as a means of teenage pregnancy reduction. The chapter focuses on the initiations which the Vhavenda women undergo to prepare them for womanhood and mature sexual practices. The initiation schools discussed in this chapter are: *vhusha,* which is a ceremony attended by a girl as soon as possible after her first menstruation, during which she is taught about good behaviour and custom, *Musevhetho* which is a circumcision "school" which may be attended by girls of all ages. It is an operation of cutting the clitoris and also *tshikanda* which refers to a culturally induced phenomenon that physical anthropologists have, in other contexts, called the *Hottentot apron*, and it is interesting that the Venda also think of it as an 'apron'.

The chapter argues that among the Vhavenda people, initiation is perceived as a safe place where women learn about their cultural belief system, admire and understand their respective roles, and learn to develop a sense of self. Initiation is the preparation of girls for marriage and the control of young mothers. Within this authority system, a woman's status depends chiefly on her seniority, which is established by her attendance at the initiation school. As ascertained by Haralambos and Heald (1980), most importantly, the initiation enhances a person's emotional intelligence. Despite the limited research that exists on the Vhavenḓa female initiation process which is enshrined in secrecy, this chapter explores the process through the lived experiences of Vhavenḓa initiated girls in the rural areas of Rukange and Dumba east of Beitbridge in Zimbabwe. It draws on qualitative research principles based on sociological approach; interviews were carried out with girls of adolescence stage and elderly women who are in charge of the initiation process as the mentors.

The chapter reveals that in Zimbabwe, indigenous methods of preventing teenage pregnancy have since been abandoned due to the Western influence yet the modern methods seem to do more harm than good. Most of the so-called modern programmes and methods seem to boost their sexual appetite than controlling the sexual desires resulting in the teenagers being reckless on their sexual activities. On this note, the chapter brings to the fore the argument that the revitalisation of these African traditional methods on teenage pregnancy may also be embraced as means to promote women's social and reproductive health. These methods have proved to be worthwhile in the Vhavenḓa lived experiences and define their true national character and values. Basing on our findings during research, the chapter recommends that focus should be cast to bring together the peculiar qualities of the past and the present, without, of course, returning to the old but to transform it in a manner that is productive and progressive. This is how the study of the survival becomes meaningful from the historical and socio-cultural perspectives.

Initiation ceremonies as a form of indigenous knowledge system

In view of the efficacy of indigenous knowledge system in most African countries, initiation ceremonies are rooted deep in the cultural history of most traditional groups. For indigenous African women, ceremonies are seen as important because the event is perceived as an entry into the realm of adulthood. For example, in most African countries female initiation ceremonies are practised. Initiations for girls are marked as an important sign in most societies of Africa. However, women initiation varies from one society to another. It is also stated by other anthropologists such as Van Gennep (1960) that there are differences in the sanctions that apply to these practices: some threaten terrible consequences and some are promised great benefit (see also Brown, 1963). In African countries, such as Kenya, Ghana and Tanzania, female initiation rituals are widely practised (Van de Walle; Franklin, 1996). These ceremonies are regarded as major rites of passage for girls entering womanhood. These are a symbol for a girl's readiness for marriage. The rite of passage from childhood to adulthood also figures highly among various ethnic groups worldwide. For example, the Americans celebrate the sweet sixteen parties, 21st birthday party and graduation from college even entering into marriage (Van Gennep, 1960). Hence, these initiation practices are part of the Zimbabwean culture. The Vhavenḓa as an ethnic group also believe in initiation schools as a way to develop the girl child holistically, that is, socially, economically and politically.

Teenage pregnancy is a social issue which has an impact on the lives of the adolescent in Zimbabwe. In 2015, statistics pointed out that child pregnancy for the past five years has harshly increased in Zimbabwe (Newsday 29/07/2015). Even though teenage pregnancy is a social issue occurring in different social contexts it tends to be high in developing countries. Its impact depends on individuals' attitudes towards certain behavioural patterns as well as their background. As part of an intervention, a number of pregnancy prevention strategies have been implemented. These include educational programmes, access to family planning such as contraceptives and condoms, as well as termination of pregnancy. Even though these strategies have been put into practice, the incidence of teenage pregnancy is still very high. South Africa has been identified as a country with high levels of teenage child-bearing (Rutenberg, Kaufman, Macintyre, Brown and Karim, 2003: 123). Since it has been acknowledged that an individual's background has an important influence on sexual behaviour, an intervention based on the different conditions and perspectives is necessary.

Pregnancy prevention strategies based on universal or Western perspectives often tend to overlook the importance of indigenous knowledge. In other words, there is a gap in literature and service delivery incorporating indigenous knowledge and traditional practices. Failure to incorporate individual's cultural norms, values and beliefs may provoke disinterest and lack of co-operation. Sillitoe, Dixon and Barr (2005: 13) argue that research based on indigenous belief is needed to adopt a more modest stance and allow others to teach about their understanding of their natural resources and thus create solutions to jointly perceived problems, rather than an attempt to impose inappropriate ideas. No matter how graceful a solution, scientific or otherwise, if people reject it on cultural grounds, it will meet with local disinterest or opposition. In other words, individuals' participation in needs identification and the subsequent implementation of intervention strategies is significant as it promotes a sense of belonging and motivation. In so doing, the implementation of relevant strategies will bring changes in individuals' lives. For instance, applying indigenous knowledge, especially in urban areas, when dealing with the issue of teenage pregnancy may be the answer, as individuals may be motivated to practise what they believe is part of their own values and beliefs. In this case, reference to indigenous knowledge means local traditions, customs, norms, beliefs and values of a particular society which are significant, respected and valued by the members of the society and which is more concerned with human behaviour. The purpose of this chapter is to ascertain indigenous perspectives in relation to teenage pregnancy prevention. The aim is to explore the Vhavenḓa female initiation schools towards teenage pregnancy and to gain different perspectives based on the knowledge of indigenous ways used to prevent teenage pregnancy.

In an effort to appreciate female initiation perspectives towards indigenous methods traditionally used to prevent teenage pregnancy the Socio-Cultural Theory has been used. According to Swartz *et al.* (2006: 69), "Lev Vygotsky's socio-cultural theory focuses on how culture – the beliefs, values, traditions, and skills of a social group – is transmitted from generation to generation". Each and every group of persons is characterised by its own culture which determines suitable manners within that particular group. Through social interaction and socialisation, social group culture can be transmitted from one individual to another in such a way that influences their judgement, views and attitudes towards certain behavioural patterns.

Classification of normal and abnormal behaviour depends on an individual's social and cultural perspectives. The Socio-Cultural Theory is significant to this study as the indigenous practices that were previously used to prevent teenage pregnancy will be explored. The indigenous practices if revitalised could be useful to the modern society. Since adolescents are viewed as being more vulnerable to risk taking, it is important that they are socialised in such a way that enhances their flexibility and strengths to deal with risk exposures.

The main focus of this chapter is to gain knowledge of the Vhavenḓa cultural practices that can be transmitted to the current generation as a means of dealing with teenage pregnancy. For example, cultural practices such as initiation schools may be viewed by particular individuals as a meaningful way to promote self-efficacy and resilience to young girls. In this case, culture is viewed as a self-regulatory process providing power to deal with temptations to risky sexual behaviour. However, individuals who are viewed as sources of information, in this case the Vhavenḓa elderly women who possess indigenous knowledge concerning teenage girls, rarely play a major role. Vygotsky viewed "cognitive growth as a socially mediated activity, one in which children gradually acquire new ways of thinking and behave through co-operative dialogues with more knowledgeable members of society" (Swartz, *et al.*, 2006: 69). Making the effort to take indigenous knowledge into consideration from the viewpoint of traditional practice experts may have a great impact on teenagers' sexual choices. As a result, young people could be able to identify sexual risk behaviour that may expose them to unintended pregnancy and sexually transmitted infections. As mentioned earlier, most teenage pregnancy studies are based on a western perspective and are at least implicitly critical of cultural practices without exploring the essential meaning of these practices. However, socio-cultural theory emphasises the importance of transmission of a social group's culture through generations, since there is no universal culture.

Western teenage pregnancy intervention programmes such as family planning and termination of pregnancy, may not hold the same value for indigenous individuals. In summary, socio-cultural theory emphasises the significance of recognising that individuals have their own cultural beliefs, values, norms and traditions which shape their *habitus* and modus operandi as part of a unique social group. Whatever happens to the individual happens to the whole group and whatever happens to the whole group happens to the individual. This is applicable to any ritual regardless of the type we are dealing with. Mbiti (1969) rites of passage are rituals and they strengthen one's behaviour.

The research was conducted in two villages east of Beitbridge District in the Matabeleland province that is, Rukange and Dumba. The study relies primarily on qualitative data, which was obtained through in-depth interviews with adolescents attending initiation school and elderly women who manage the initiation process as mentors. The qualitative method was found to be appropriate for this study as it provided detailed insights into the personal and private experiences of adolescents attending traditional initiation schools. Furthermore, qualitative methods are useful for providing an understanding of the meaning and context of behaviours and the processes that take place within social relationships and provide an opportunity for explaining in more detail complex and sensitive issues (Brannan, 1992).

What is teenage pregnancy?

Teenage pregnancy is when a girl in adolescence becomes pregnant before adulthood. An adolescent girl is a girl within the ages of thirteen to nineteen. Nodin (2001) states that Erickson and Freud's theory defines adolescences as the period of life between puberty and maturity, which is generally, accepted as the ages 12 through 17, inclusive, however, there are some extreme cases were some get pregnant at the age of 10 or 11 . For example, it is the period of physical, psychological, social and moral/ethical growth following childhood and preceding maturity; a period characterised by intensified pre-occupation with issues of identity and independence; often associated with intensified pre-personal and inter-group competition. Nodin (2001) defines an adolescent as an individual living through the period of major change at various levels: physical, family, social, emotional and personal. It is during this phase that, in a way, the adolescent becomes a person who tries to become self-sufficient and determine her position in the world, something necessary to give some significance to her own existence (Heaven, 2001). According to the Zimbabwean constitution, an adult is someone who is eighteen years however this legal age for adulthood varies across the world. In teenage pregnancy the pregnancy may be in a marriage or out of marriage. In most cases the pregnancy is unwanted due to many factors. As a result, this brings a lot of challenges in the girl child. The challenges mostly are based on the fact that the pregnancy is not planned and the teenager is not mature or ready for adulthood.

Causes and challenges of teenage pregnancy

The causes of teenage pregnancy are numerous. The following are some of the causes of teenage pregnancy, some cultural and religious norms, such as child marriage, contribute to teenage pregnancy. In most cases the girl child has no right to choose not to enter into that kind of marriage. Conformity to peer norms and certain values also expose teenagers to high risk behaviour. Teenagers may engage in sexual relationships to gain material support from their partners who are today addressed as "blessers" as a means to gain certain status within their groups. Some teenagers engage in sexual relationships with older partners to gain material support for themselves and their families as well. In Burkina Faso, a study based on interview with schoolgirls was conducted in a small town. Girls are surrounded by a modern reverence for material wealth, which is attained most easily by entering into a sexual relationship with an older, wealthy man and finally, girls are usually involved with an older and experienced partner, which makes it difficult to demand the use of contraceptives. They have too little self-esteem to oppose the partner who does not support the idea of contraception (Görgen *et al.*, 1993). Due to poverty some parents view education as a major obstacle and they force their daughters into marriage as a way to support the family financially. The relationships between young girls and older partners are usually characterised by a power imbalance and lack of communication. As a result, young girls are unable to negotiate condom use. Poor access to resources, such as condoms, contraceptives and sexual health education also exposes teenagers to risky sexual behaviour. In fact these teenagers are exposed to health risk factors, such as HIV and AIDS, Sexually Transmitted Diseases, sex force, unwanted pregnancy and rejection. The above patterns of sexual relations make young girls extremely susceptible to STDs, in particular infections with HIV in regions with a high prevalence of the virus. In particular, the fact that older and experienced men seek sexual relations with young girls without using barrier contraceptives leads to the dissemination of these diseases. In countries with a high prevalence of HIV some men even purposely have sex with young girls in an attempt to avoid becoming infected with HIV. In South Africa, one in five pregnant adolescents is infected with the virus (Jewkes *et al.*, 2001).

Unprotected sexual intercourse is the risk behaviour common to both unintended pregnancy and HIV infection (Whaley, 1999). Above all lack of knowledge on African indigenous practices such as initiation schools contribute too. In the urban areas teenagers have adopted the Western way of life and have no idea of their cultural practices. Teenagers need to be equipped with life skills which include their cultural practices. These may be done through the formal school curriculum. The inclusion of these forms of teachings for example the initiation schools may help in curbing teenage pregnancy since this harmer on good morals and sex education. Anthropologists and health educaters are now re-examining traditional circumcision and seclusion rites, particularly the teaching that was considered a key part of the process. (Feldman, 2008) The rites together with the modern teachings may reduce teenage pregnancy and HIV and AIDS infections.

Teenage pregnancy also come with its own challenges such as, having children out of wedlock, this in an African perspective depicts being immoral to the girl child. Mostly the community will see the teenager as someone who lacks *vhuthu/ubuntu/uhnu*, the high cost of raising the child alone as a single parent becomes a problem to both the mother of the child and the child. Raising the child alone may also result in poor performance at school and school dropouts since the teenage mother cannot support self. There are high chances of the girl not getting married. The lack of adequate, accurate information on puberty leaves young people dependent on uninformed sources.

Western preventative methods of teenage pregnancy and their challenges

Most of the programmes that have been implemented to affect teenage childbearing have been small, and poorly designed short-term projects lacking a useful evaluation strategy. Condom use is a very common method that is used to prevent teenage pregnancy however; its effectiveness is questionable since condoms are not 100% effective. Moreover, teenagers in relationships with elderly people do not have the power to negotiate condom use. The "fear of losing her partner or incurring his anger appear to be important factors inhibiting young females from exercising choice in the timing of sexual activity or negotiating the use of condoms or other contraceptives" (Jejeebhoy *et al.*, 1999). The ways in which condoms are dispatched seem to encourage sex desires than controlling sexual behaviour. In fact, condoms seem to communicate that one can engage in sexual activities any time. The same applies to many other modern family planning methods. These methods do have side effects to the teenagers. Abortion, for instance, has been used as one of the methods for preventing teenage pregnancy. In addition, planning services also have been found to reduce unwanted births, primarily because contraceptive services help sexually active persons prevent pregnancy, but perhaps also due to increased access to abortion. Services that reduce shame to obtaining reproductive care among adolescents are more likely to affect contraceptive use than traditional service delivery approaches. Although the modern methods do help in a way they are not very much effective as teenage pregnancy still goes high.

This chapter aims to prove that indigenous methods for example the Vhavenḓa initiation schools may be used as preventative measures together with these other methods. The Vhavenḓa most set goals on the initiation schools, are a set of family strengths including nurturance and love, monitoring and discipline, clear values and respected communication which they instil in children and adolescents the will and ability to delay parenthood until they can form strong and stable families. In addition many girls attend such initiation ceremonies to conform to their culture and gain respect from their society (Van de Walle and Franklin 1996).

Vhusha, Musevhetho and Tshikanda as ways to curb teenage pregnancy

An initiation ceremony is something a young girl eagerly looks forward to, prepares for, and takes part in. The ceremony is usually viewed as a cultural practice that upholds African culture. Furthermore, it functions as a form of entertainment, a place of fun and freedom that teaches respect and "*ubuntu*" to young girls (Milubi, 2000). Richards (1956) defines initiation as a rite of passage, usually performed during puberty. It is a cultural tradition that is practised in most communities in Africa. Lincoln (1981) concurs and goes further to define initiation as a process that a woman goes through, resulting in a change of status and becoming "fertile, productive, experienced and whole. Women initiation is performed differently in other countries. Turner (1987) and Mönnig (1967) concur that, in Nigeria four lines are cut in the girl's abdomen, to make her a woman and the mother would teach a girl to "love magic." The initiated women could teach her of the female powers and the physical changes marking womanhood. This culture is exclusive, but some families still hold on to this tradition. Initiation rites develop an individual into building good social relationships; understanding, and moral decision making. Moral decision making is key especially on this topic since teenage pregnancy relay mainly on the teenager's decision on sexual issues. It is viewed as a major developmental task for a girl who is learning how to fit in and be accepted socially by her peers. When initiation rites are done appropriately, they meet teenagers' needs such as a sense of belonging, understanding the history and culture of their nation. It serves the purpose of building relationships and if not done properly can cause psychological harm to a girl's ego or self-concept.

In addition initiation rites create solidarity among women and are used for passing knowledge from one generation to another (Rasing, 1995). Women initiation ceremonies, much like their male counterparts, provide instructions to females on what society will expect of them as responsible adults (Mlama, 1990). Through imitation and positive reinforcement by their mothers and elderly women, most girls are fully aware of what is expected of them as women in the Venda, Pedi and Tsonga cultures. Within the Vhavenḓa community, an initiation ceremony is something a young girl eagerly looks forward to. Van Gennep (1960) proposed that the initiation ceremony conveys three sub-meanings, namely; a) separation from society, b) transition in the case of adolescence, from child to adult, and c) incorporation- a welcoming back into society with acknowledgement of the adolescent's changed status. All of this may be summarized as social transition; these moratoriums are connected with personal transitions between different stages that occur during developmental stages. These changes are life crises from birth until death. However, rites of passage in many cultures are used to mark the socially recognized transition to sexual maturity (Van de Walle *et al.*, 1996). The graduates (initiates) of initiation schools perceive initiation to be a high degree of solidarity, brotherhood and sisterhood. The importance of socialising with one another brings unity towards each other. During the process of initiation, the initiates accept and treat each other with respect. Respect is understood as a spirit of unity and humanity towards each other in respect of their particular schools. That is, the graduates from *'musevhetho, 'vhusha', 'domba' and 'vhutamba vhutuka' and 'murundu'* are related humanely towards each other after they have realised that they have gone through a similar experience together. The initiates believe that initiation teaches them tolerance, discipline and responsibility (Stayt, 1969). The Vhavenda in the Beitbridge district villages view initiation as a culture and an initiation school as a place of socialisation.

The whole process of initiation schools according to Vhavenḓa is some form of education. Farrant (1992) defines education as the process of learning or acquiring new skills. People can learn in a formal or an informal education set-up. Whatever particular social structural features may account for the presence of adolescent initiation rites in different societies, all such rituals seem to also have one purpose in common, and that is the function of educating the young person. Initiates are given detailed instructions about their roles, responsibilities, and privileges as adults in the culture in which they live. They are also instructed in the culture's mythology and system of ethics, the manner in which they should conduct themselves and others, (i.e. to respect the boundaries when sharing initiation information with uninitiated women and adulthood life) (Young, 1965).

The following initiation schools are discussed as ways of reducing teenage pregnancy: *Vhusha, musevhetho* and *tshikanda*. These initiations have been practised for decades by people in the Beitbridge district to pass on knowledge and culture to the young women before marriage. The initiation school is perceived as a cultural norm that enables the new and old generations to cope with life, childbirth, marriage and taking good care of the family. It is believed by the Vhavenḓa that initiation schools help in reducing divorce, teenage pregnancy, youthful misbehaviour, drug abuse and HIV and AIDS.

Musevhetho is a circumcision rite for a girl, which initiates girls from a baby to the stage of puberty. Stayt (1969) claims that *Musevhetho* is an initiation adopted from the Northern Sotho people. It is the cutting of the clitoris as a way to maintain cleanliness and preserving virginity. The cutting of the clitoris is done by the elderly women. This practice helps in reducing teenage pregnancy. The girls are taught to respect themselves and others. They are taught discipline and to respect their rituals and customs. They are taught to abstain from sex until they get married. Abstinence also acts as a preventative measure of reducing teenage pregnancy. 'Ukwevha' is part of the activity that takes place during *musevhetho*. Ukwevha is when girls are taught how to stretch their labia minora. The reason given was that it prepares girls to harness men into fulfilling relationships during the time of marriage. Most of the girls who attend '*musevhetho*' are virgins. At *musevhethoni*, the young girls are taught to respect their bodies and are discouraged from engaging in sexual intercourse with boys in order to prevent unplanned pregnancies. After the initiation, girls are labelled, that is there are left with a mark on the thigh, as proof that they attended the initiation. The scar would be the identification to go through to the next stage of initiation. The main function of *musevhetho* is to teach girls songs and rules. *Musevhetho* is believed to play an important role in reducing early sexual engagement amongst young girls and boys. To support the above Mulaudzi *et al* (2015) confirm that virginity testing was introduced during labia elongation sessions to check out which girls were sexually active. For example, girls who are not virgins are not accepted at '*musevhetho*' initiation school. The practice is believed to encourage girls to abstain from sex and discourage girls not to lose their virginity before marriage hence this will reduce teenage pregnancy.

Vhusha is a ceremony attended by a girl as soon as she experiences her first menstruation. She is taught about good behaviour and manners. According to Stayt (1969) Vhusha marks the passage from childhood to adolescence. Girls pass through this ceremony after experiencing their first menses. Before this stage a girl is called *musidzana (a* little girl*)* afterward she is called *khomba* meaning (dangerous) implying that sexual intercourse may result in pregnancy. At *vhushani* girls were taught *milayo*. The *milayo* are laws taught to the initiates at *vhushani*. Warmelo translated *milayo* as precept, a formulation of what is traditionally right, customary in support of traditional standards of behaviour. *Milayo* are regarded as rules of behaviour, commandment and law. The *milayo* are only taught at the vhusha ceremony. When a woman wants to visit other ceremonies the *milayo* are then recited. Blacking (1969) concurs that the *milayo* are thus regarded as the passwords, proving that a woman has been initiated into the ceremony. The purpose of this is to separate the initiated from the non- initiated based on the secrecy of this initiation. *Vhusha* is thus characterised by secrecy and a newly-initiated woman is understood to be vested with a status she did not possess beforehand through acquiring knowledge of these secrets. The secrets constructed differences in status between women and acted as boundary mechanisms between the different social categories (Murphy 1980: 193). *Milayo* is also a teaching technique for good behaviour. Good behaviour was expected for the initiates' marriage and onwards. According to Jeannerat (2007) the *milayo* of etiquette and behaviour is concerned with the differential status system of the community within which the initiate would henceforth be placed and within which she would take a subordinate position. The main purpose of *vhusha* is an initiation which prepares a girl child for adulthood. At this ceremony girls are also tested if there are still virgins.

After the virginity testing girls who were found to be virgins were decorated and embraced by the community and their families. The function of *vhusha* was to instil, discipline, respect and responsibilities and that girls should maintain their virginity, to prevent HIV and AIDS and other sexually transmitted diseases. These rites were used as a transition to prepare girls from childhood to adulthood life. Louw and Edwards (1997) concur with the above statement that initiation schools are rituals associated with adult life. It is a passage to adulthood. Some villages no longer checked the virginity status, but the girls were taught good manners, except those that are taught at family level. Initiates were taught about matters relating to sex, sexual behaviour and marriage, with emphasis on avoiding pregnancy outside marriage. They further reported that initiates were taught to sing, dance and learn rules norms and values that would entitle the initiates to participate in traditional meetings and important ceremonies. Participants believed practice can be regarded as a good way to ensure delayed sexual involvement among the youth and a way of preventing teenage pregnancy (Mulaudzi *et al.,* 2015).

Tshikanda is an initiation that reflects the sociological significance of the Vhavenda. It is a ceremony that takes place shortly before marriage. *Tshikanda* may be taken in the same light as the puberty school vhusha however the Vhavenda prefer to call it vhusha ha halwa *vhusha* of beer. Stayt (1931) and Warmelo (1932) describe *Tshikanda* as part of pre-marital initiation school for both boys and girls. Blacking (1969) claims that *Tshikanda* emphasis unity and alliance among the initiates, cross-cutting their family backgrounds. The initiates at this school are socialised with their cultural knowledge. At this school the rites and cultural interests of commoner women are respected. The cultural knowledge that the girls gain from this initiation also has a function of instilling in them good morals that will help them behave well and abstain from sex. This practice may also reduce teenage pregnancy.

Critical reflection and its viability

The Vhavenḓa female initiation school major role and concern is to educate the adolescence on how to have good moral values. If good moral values are instilled in a teenage girl, good behaviour will also be the end result. The interviewed teenage girls from the Rukange and Domba villages revealed that they feel honoured that they were initiated. The girls claimed that they are now aware of what their society expects from them, for example, that they should not engage in sex before marriage. Abstinence from sex was very much possible since at the initiation school there was virginity testing. For this reason virginity testing contributes in the curbing of teenage pregnancy. Besides that the Western methods are not 100% effective, it is clear from the modest to zero success of most programmes to date, that these approaches alone are insufficient to produce substantial impacts on teenage childbearing, particularly for adolescents who are at greatest risk. There is need to develop broader programmes that focus on poverty, school failure, and behaviour problems. The programmes are to help teenagers in practicing good moral behaviour patterns as means to curb unwanted pregnancy.

Female initiation is a process of undergoing an expansion of consciousness, as part of the normal process of evolutionary development, viewed on a large scale, and not from a standpoint of an individual. Primarily, it involves the capacity to see, hear and comprehend, and to synthesise and correlate knowledge and recognise the purpose of pervading circumstances (Maluleke & Troskie, 2003). *Vhusha* and *musevheth and tshikanda* initiation schools should be considered in teaching the young generation *"vhuthu, ubuntu, unhu"*, discipline, respect, morals and standards in making informed decisions. The initiation ceremony is usually viewed as a cultural practice that holds African culture. Furthermore, it functions as a form of entertainment, a place of fun and freedom that teaches respect and ubuntu to young girls (Milubi 2000). However, initiation ceremonies like, *vhusha, musevhetho and tshikanda* are thought to help build respect in teenagers and prepare them for womanhood. Therefore, if these indigenous practices together with Western methods would be implemented teenage pregnancy may be reduced.

This may be possible if such programmes on indigenous practices like initiation schools would be included in the school curriculum so that every girl child is equipped with the same knowledge nationwide. In many developed countries sex education is part of the curriculum of primary and secondary schools (Wight *et al*, 2002). The teenagers in the urban areas will also be reached out as there have moved from their cultural behaviour and adopted the Western way of life. Initiation knowledge is found mainly with the older generation because adolescent initiation rituals tend to be found in rural communities. Adolescents need good information about their sexual development and ways of avoiding pregnancy. Moreover, they need information on Sexual Transmitted Diseases including HIV and AIDS. In the past it was the parents' task to educate the adolescent but studies have shown that parents do not talk to their children about matters anymore. Parents are ill-informed and embarrassed about the topics (Hughes and McCauley 1998) yet the chapter advocates for the teaching of indigenous methods to curb teenage pregnancy. Embracing the African cultural practices to the modern way of life by the teenagers will help as preventative methods of reducing teenage pregnancy.

Conclusion

Different methods on teenage pregnancy have been implemented in Zimbabwe and abroad however teenage pregnancy still increases. The research revealed that indigenous methods of preventing teenage pregnancy have since been deserted due to the Western influence hence the modern methods seem to do more harm than good. Most of the so-called modern programmes and methods seem to boost their sexual appetite than controlling the sexual desires resulting in the teenagers being reckless on their sexual activities. Through this rite of passages of initiation, the girl child is groomed into adulthood. This research brings to a close that the revitalisation of these African traditional methods on teenage pregnancy may also be embraced as means to curb teenage pregnancy. These methods have proved to be worthwhile in the Vhavenda lived experiences and define their true national character and values. The chapter recommends that focus should caste to bring together the peculiar qualities of the past and the present, without, of course, returning to the old but to transform it. This is how the study of the survival becomes meaningful from the historical and socio-cultural perspectives. The major role for these initiation schools is to instil good behaviour hence thereby helping the girl child in self-control on matters concerning sexual behaviour. The Vhavenḓa initiation schools have proved to be of help in curbing teenage pregnancy.

References

Blacking, J. A. R. 1969. "Songs, Dances, *Mimes and Symbolism of Venda Girls' Initiation Schools,* Part Two: (*Milayo*). "*African Studies.* 28 (2).

Brannan, M. 1992. Nursing process in Telephone Advice, *Nursing Management* 23(5): 62-66.

Brown, J.K. 1963. *A Cross Cultural Study of female Initiation rites,* American Anthropologist: New Series, 65 (4): 837-853.

Farrant, J.S. 1992. *An Introduction to Language and Linguistics,* Heinemann, London.

Feldman, D.A. 2008 *AIDS, Culture and Africa*: Gainesville, University Press of Florida.

Görgen R, Maier B, Diesfeld, H. J. 1993 *Problems related to schoolgirl pregnancies in Burkina Faso,* Studies in Family Planning, Burkina Faso.

Harralambos, M. & Heald, R. M. 1980. *Sociology: Themes and perspectives,* Great Britain: University Tutorial Press.

Heaven, P. C. L. 2001. *Contemporary Adolescence: A Social Psychological Approach,* New York: Palgrave.

Hughes, J. and McCauley, A. P. 1998. Improving the fit: adolescents' needs and future programmes for sexual and reproductive health in developing countries, *Studies in family planning,* 29: 233-245.

Jeannerat, C. 1997. Invoking the female vusha ceremony and the struggle for identity and security in Tshiendeulu, Venda, *J. Contemporary African studies* 15 (1): 87-106.

Jewkes, R., Vundule, C., Maforah, F., & Jordaan, E. 2001. Relationship dynamics and teenage pregnancy in South Africa, *Soc Sci Med*, 2 (3): 12-21.

Jejeebhoy, S .J, Shah, I. H., &Young, M. 1999. *Sexual and reproductive health of Adolescents, WHO Department of Reproductive health and research, Annual Technical Report.*

Lincoln, B. 1981. *Emerging from the chrysalis, studies in rituals of women's Initiation,* Cambridge: Harvard University Press.

Louw, D. A., & Edwards, D. 1997. *Psychology: An introduction for Students in South Africa,* Johannesburg: Lexicon Publishers.

Maluleke T. X & Troskie, R. 2003. The views of women in the Limpopo Province of South Africa concerning girls' puberty rites, *Health SA*, 58: 47-60.

Mbiti, J. S. 1969 *African Religion and Philosophy,* London: Heinemann.

Milubi, N.A. 2000. *Sexual images: Essence of presence. South African Journal for Folklore Studies,* 20 (2): 56-61.

Mlama, P. 1990. *Tanzanian traditional theatre as a pedagogical institution: The Kaguru as a case study,* Doctoral dissertation, University of Dar es Salaam: Tanzania. Mulaudzi, F.M., Chinouya, M. & Ngunyulu, R.N 2015 *Perceptions of the Vhavenda Regarding the Significance of IKS Rituals and Customs in Women's Health: "The Other Side of The Coin"* Asian Journal of Social Science 44 (1): 21-27.

Newsday, 29-07-2015. The challenges of teen pregnancy, *Newsday,* Harare: Zimbabwe.

Nodin, N. 2001. *Adolescents, sex and other: sexual education in the school environment,* Sexual and Family Planning, 31, 10-17.

Rasing, T. 1995. *Passing on the Rites of Passage: Girls' Initiation Rites in the Context of Urban Roman Catholic Community on The Zambian Copperbelt,* African Studies Centres: Amsterdam.

Richards, A. L. 1956. *Chisungu: A Girl's Initiation Ceremony among the Bemba of North Rhodesia,* Grove Press: London.

Rutenburg, N., Kaufman, C. E., Macintyre, K., Brown, L. & Karim, A. 2003. Pregnant or Positive: Adolescent Childbearing and HIV in KwaZulu Natal, South Africa, *Reproductive Health Matters,* 11(22): 122-133.

Sillitoe, P., Dixon, P. & Barr, J. 2005. *Indigenous Knowledge Inquiries: A Methodologies Manual for Development,* Bangladesh: The University Press Limited.

Swartz, L., de la Rey, & Duncan, N. 2006. *Psychology: An Introduction,* South Africa: Oxford University Press.

Stayt, H. A. 1968. *The Bavenda,* Oxford University Press: London.

Turner, D. 1987. In Mahdi L. C, Foster S., & Little, M. (Eds). 1987. *Betwixt & Between: Patterns of Masculine & Feminine initiation,* Illinois, Open Court Publishing Company.

Van de Walle, E. & Franklin, N. 1996. *Sexual of Initiation and the Transmission: Reproductive Knowledge,* University Pennsylvania.

Van Gennep, A. 1960. *The Rites of Passage,* University of Chicago Press: Chicago.

Whaley, A. L. 1999. *Preventing the high-risk sexual behaviour of adolescents: focus on HIV/AIDS transmission, unintended pregnancy, or both? J Adolesc Health;* 24: 376-382.

Wight, D., Raab, G. M., Henderson, M., Abraham, C., Buston, K., Hart, G., & Scott, S. 2002. *Limits of teacher delivered sex education: interim behavioural outcomes from randomised trial. Br Med J;* 324: 1430.

Young, F.W. 1965. *Initiation Ceremonies: A Cross-Cultural Study of status dramatisation,* New York: Bobbs-Mernil Company.

Chapter Fifteen

Pentecostalism as a Drive for Religious Tourism Development in New Millennium Zimbabwe

Tendai Chibaya

Introduction

Religious tourism represents one of the oldest forms of tourism and dates back over centuries ago. Religious tourism augments and is augmented in turn by other segments of tourism such as leisure, business tourism, cultural tourism, heritage tourism, educational tourism, rural tourism, eco-tourism and garden tourism, among others. On the whole, and globally, the tourism industry is significant and it contributed up to US$ 7.6 trillion annually, which is about 10 per cent of the global Gross Domestic Product (GDP) in the year 2014 (World Travel and Tourism Council, 2015). Based on estimates, the UNWTO (2014) reveals that an estimated six hundred million national and international religious travellers were recorded across the world in 2014, with approximately forty percent of these recorded in Europe. In line with this, and making reference to the statistics obtained from the World Religious Travel Association, every year it is estimated that over three hundred million religious arrivals are yielding revenues of up to US$ 18 billion across the globe (Wright, 2008). Considering the significant lucrative benefits brought to various economies across the globe, this form of travelling is found to be a crucial niche of the worldwide travel market and has grown into an industry of its own (Wright, 2008). Due to the tremendous benefits that accrue from this segment, many countries across the globe have begun to seriously compete for religious tourists because of the lucrative benefits that are derivable from this segment.

Like most of African countries, Zimbabwe is not an exception in witnessing an increased growth of people visiting different church denominations. In Zimbabwe, the Pentecostal group is one of the fastest growing segments exemplified by the new age mega churches that have outgrown and outnumbered old traditional churches (Greatzimtraveller, 2016). In this chapter, the new age mega church represents new millennium Pentecostal Churches, namely United Family International Church (UFIC) and Prophetic Healing and Deliverances (PHD) Ministries which were born in 2010 and 2012 respectively. These new Pentecostal churches are led by young and predominantly male charismatic leaders (Chitando, Manyonganise and Mlambo, 2013). The churches also represent African indigenous churches. Using the cases of Zimbabwe's charismatic Pentecostal prophets namely Walter Magaya (PhD Ministries) and Emmanuel Makandiwa (UFI Church), the chapter discusses the link between the Pentecostal-led Christian revivalism and the resuscitation of Zimbabwe's tourism sector.

The central questions raised in this chapter are: 'What is the contribution of new millennium Pentecostal churches to the development of religious tourism in Zimbabwe? Going forward, with what effect do these new Pentecostal churches have to the Zimbabwean tourism sector and the larger economy when hosting mega church events? What have been the negative externalities incurred from these huge religious gatherings in Zimbabwe?'

Broadly, the chapter argues that the presence of these two Pentecostal ministries, together with others, has ratcheted up peoples' desires, *inter alia*, to be healed, listen to their sermons, acquire prosperity for themselves and miracle searching. Other people wanted to be born again in Christianity and find 'truth' about their lives as they visit Pentecostal Founders and Prophets of Zimbabwe.

Historical overview of religious tourism

Religious tourism, as one of the segments of cultural tourism, is mainly related to faith-based travel. According to Cardenas (2012: 10), religious tourism "is the result of a faith which leads a segment of the population to travel from one place to another in order to enter a place that is considered sacred, and whose main peculiar characteristic is that it allows visitors to have a closeness with the divine that cannot be achieved anywhere else or appreciated as profanely." In India, the Strategic Initiatives and Government

Advisory (SIGA) Team (2012: 8) views, religious tourism as travel with the core motive of experiencing religious forms, or the products they induce, like culture, arts, architecture and traditions. In this chapter, religious tourism is summarised as the travelling of groups or individuals who are motivated by spiritual, religious or associated with religious heritage sites (Multifaiths, n.d). The definitions show that faith and motivation are the key selling points of religious travel to a particular destination. Religious tourism as a segment, has been found to be best at attracting all segments of the market. Thus, in the process it fundamentally promotes the travel of all age groups of all nationalities (Tourismandmore, 2014), with an appropriate disposable income which allows them to travel. The segment is not easily influenced by the politics of the country and promotes the fair treatment of people from different races and cultures across the globe.

The concept of religious tourism started almost with the genesis of humankind. Since the dawn of history, religious travelling and gatherings were observed during festivals of the religious character to commemorate three harvest seasons in the Holy Land of Israel. The Biblical era provides much history of key religious practices, holy sites and how the concept of spiritual travelling came into existence. In the Old Testament, for instance, the Israelites gathered three times a year to celebrate seven harvest festivals, namely the Passover, Pentecost, the Feast of unleavened Bread, the Feast of Trumpets, Feast of Tabernacles, Day of Atonement and the Eighth day (Exodus 23 verses 14-17, Deuteronomy 16 verse 16 and 2 Chronicles 8 verse 13). The first three festivals were celebrated within 8 days of the same month of the spring season while the last four festivals were celebrated in the late summer and autumn of the harvest time. These occasions were done as part of thanksgiving to God as well as celebrating their harvest with a religious character. This act of pilgrimage progresses very well to the New Testament when faith based travellers were witnessed in Matthew 2 verse 1, when three men called the Magi came from Iran to Bethlehem in Judea to see the newly baby Jesus (Ashiegbu and Achunike, 2014). During the Passover festival, Jesus' parents travelled to Jerusalem on a yearly basis (Luke 2 verses 41-42) and Jesus was also accompanying his parents on a pilgrimage as part of their custom. Also, when Jesus was in his ministry, various multitudes of people travelled to Galilee for healing from all sickness and to listen to his articulation of the gospel of the Kingdom of God (cf. Matthew 4 verse 23).

In countries like Turkey, religious tourism is a key component of the country's tourism geography as the destination is endowed with many Christian and Islamic sites. Faith based travellers are visiting places such as House of Virgin Mary which is believed by Catholics as the last resting place for Mary (Sayin, 2014). The Saint Nicholas Church, the Cave churches, Saint Peters Church (one of the oldest churches in the world), Saint John's Basilica, the Hagia Sophia and Ephesus are Christian popular sites which are drawing people to visit Turkey (Sayin, 2014).

In China, religious groups have historically been visiting religious monuments of Buddhist and the Taoist faiths (UNWTO, 2011). Elsewhere in the Russian Federation, tourists travel to the mountain sites for their retreats for peace and relaxation from the tension of urban lifestyles. Islamic faith travellers travel to Indonesia's spiritual sites to pray for specific blessings or guidance. Also, Moslems are encouraged to visit the Holy city of Mecca, at least once in their lifetime, during the annual *hajj* to Mecca (Mecca Pilgrimage, 2015). This sacrament of pilgrimage to the holy city of Mecca is said to go back thousands of years to the era of Abraham and his son Ishmael who are believed to have erected the shrine of worship (Mecca Pilgrimage, 2015). The *hajj* pilgrimage travel to celebrate Muhammed the prophet and Abraham, for example, attracted fourteen million pilgrims to Mecca in 2015 (Whitman, 2015). Thus, this holy travel to Mecca is important for Muslims and their travelling is a way of fulfilling the commandment of their religion. As well, many in the Japanese society also visit the place of Shintoism (Shinto Shrines) and Buddhism and they engage in their local religious practices such as Syugendo, which is believed to be a unique combination of animistic mountain worship with Tantric Buddhism, Taoism and Confucianism (UNWTO, 2011).

Another popular destination in France is the Sanctuary of Our Lady of Lourdes which is a popular holy site for the Roman Catholics. People travel to Lourdes as an act of devotion and to be close to the site of a miraculous event (Sacred-destinations, n.d). Besides France, other pilgrimages travel to the land of Jordan which is richly endowed with five Christian holy sites which include Baptism site, Mount Nebo, Mukawir, Our Lady of the Mountain in Anjara and Mar Elijah. In addition to that, Jordan has eight Islamic holy sites viz Abu Ubaydah Amir ibn al-Jarrah Shrine, Dirar bin al-Azwar shrine, Shurhabil bin Husnah shrine, Amir bin Abi Waqqas shrine, Mu'ath bin Jabal Shrine, Ja'far bin Abi Taleb shrine, Zaid bin Harithah shrine, Abdallah bin Rawahah shrine (Sacred-destinations. N.d).

The African continent is not an exception as it is also richly endowed with religiously sacred places. Large numbers of tourists and faith based travellers are motivated to travel to Egypt to see the pyramids for their religious, social or cultural significance. Egypt is also rich in religious heritage, as some faith based travellers visit Mount Sinai, where Moses received the Ten Commandments from God. Mount Sinai also has small chapels and spectacular sunrise views. Luxor temple dates from the period around 1300 BC and has full of monumental statues, ancient carvings and tall walls. Ibn Tulun Mosque was built in 879, is the 3rd largest mosque in the world (Sacred-destinations. n.d). Karnak Temple was initially dedicated to Pharaoh Amun and begun around 1600Bc. St Paul's Monastery, Citadel, Temple of Hatshepsut and Philae Island (one of the last sanctuaries to be converted to Christianity) are among the drawing cards to Africa. Egypt is also a place where Jeremiah one of the Christian Prophets was stoned to death (Sacred-texts, n.d: 69). Outside of Egypt, Ethiopia also contains sacred sites which include Axum Stelae Field, Chapel of the Ark of the Covenant, Axum, Debre Birhan Selassie Church, Gondar, Bahar Dar, New Church of St. Mary of Zion, Axum and Rock-Cut Churches of Lalibela (Sacred-destinations. n.d). Ivory Coast has one key sacred site by the name Basilica of Our lady of Peace, Yamoussoukro (Sacred-destinations. n.d). Morocco also attracts large numbers of travellers who wish to visit such sites as Almoravid Koubba Marrakesh, Ben Youssef Medersa Marrakesh, Tomb of Moulay Idriss, Tomb of Sidi and Saadian Tombs, Marrakesh. Tunisia has Great Mosque of Kairouan, Three doors Mosque, Kairouan (Sacred-destinations. n.d).

Moreover, it is observed that Christian Evangelism in Africa has gained currency in Europe and America (Kenya and beyond Safaris, n.d). Africa is a place where Bishops, for instance, the Catholic popes from the West (Europe and the USA) hold their Evangelism Conventions on a yearly basis (Panoratoursafrica, n.d). The popularity of Temitope Balogun (TB) Joshua of the Synagogue Church of All Nations (SCOAN) in Nigeria has resulted in Nigeria receiving numerous tourists yearly. Of late, as well, Zimbabwe has gained international prominence due to the advent of Pentecostal Christian faiths rooted in charismatic leadership. For example, through the miracles performed by Archbishop Ezekiel Guti and wife prophetess Eunor of ZAOGA FIF, Mathias and Mildred of the Mathias and Mildred Church and Andrew Wutawunashe and wife prophetess Ruth of Family Of God (Vengeyi, 2013). It is also worth noting that other governments in Africa go on a step further to promote pilgrimage travel, for instance the Nigerian Government in the year 2015 sponsored an approximate of 76 000 Muslims for pilgrimage to Mecca and 30 000 Christians to Jerusalem (Nigerian Anarchist, 2015). In a way, Africa is seen as a burgeoning epicentre for the spiritual expansion.

From the above, the travelling of Christians, Hindus, Buddhists and Muslims from and to different parts of the world is mainly based on the spirituality that may be based on the physical, intellectual and emotional needs of the pilgrims (Wright, 2008: 111). It can also be realised that faith is a magnetic element which draws out the attention of faith based travellers together with tourists to visit various destinations across the world. The commercialisation of religious products is encouraging many economies of the world to compete and get the best out of their religious heritage in order to induce greater and accelerated investment in their vicinities. The well-known pilgrimage destinations like Jerusalem, Fatima, Rome, Mecca and Lourdes have been remodelled up as tourist attraction centres. Due to the commercialisation aspect of religious tourism, a study by Yalghouzaghaj and Shorbolagh (2013) reveals that in India, most of the bazaars, economic departments, schools and caravansaries were built besides tombs, mosques, shrines and other religious sites. The idea of building the facilities near the religious sites is to tap the various opportunities brought by tourists as well as faith based travellers like income generation as well as job creation. To illustrate this, Yalghouzaghaj and Shorbolagh (2013) cite the example of Abbassi Hotel in Isfahan and the King's mother school, which benefited more or less income from the Tabriz Bazaar which was built beside Sahib Alarm mosque in Iran.

Contextualising religious tourism in Zimbabwe

In Zimbabwe, religious tourism has a long genealogy with pre-colonial Shona people visiting the Great Zimbabwe Monuments and the Njelele shrine and later Ndebele people, visiting the Njelele shrine in the Matopos Hills to ask for, among others rain and for relief from calamities. Zimbabwean nationalist leaders also visited the Njelele shrine during the 1960s and 1970s to seek spiritual guidance that helped strengthen their fight against colonialism.

With the advent of African independent churches, such as Johane Masowe and Zion Christian Church, some of the adherents of these sects have been making annual pilgrimages to selected shrines such as Rusape and Defe in Gokwe, respectively. In the 1980s and early 1990s, there were also streams of tourists who visited Boniface Muponda's shrine in Norton seeking, *inter alia*, baby making and or baby conceiving powers. Furthermore, the Zion Christian Church members travel to Mbungo in Masvingo and Defe-Dopota in Gokwe for their church conventions. The Roman Catholic Church adherents travel to Muchemwa Mountain in Mutoko and the Anglican Church travel to Bernard Mizeki Shrine in Marondera for their spiritual rebirths (Ncube, 2015, Rusare, 2014). More so, the Zimbabwe Assemblies of God Church Forward in Faith (ZAOGA FIF) members visit a prayer mountain in Bindura which was founded in 1963 by Archbishop Ezekiel Guti for their prayers. Every September of each year, the Apostles of Johane Masowe travel to Gandanzara Shrine in Rusape (Rusare, 2014). The Spirit Embassy has a prayer mountain called Eagle Mountain off Beatrice road along the Masvingo-Harare highway.

More so, religious tourism in Zimbabwe got much of its support from old and new Pentecostal churches like the Zimbabwe

Assemblies of God Africa Church Forward in Faith Ministries (ZAOGA-FIF), Family of God (FOG), Apostolic Faith Mission in Zimbabwe (AFM), Harvest House International church, Faith Ministries, United Family International Church (UFIC) and Prophetic, Healing and Deliverance Ministries (PHD Ministries), among others. Every year, most of the Pentecostal churches usually host their mega Easter Conventions in various cities for instance the UFIC-Harare, PHD ministries in Waterfalls- Harare, AFM congregates meet at Rufaro Chatsworth-Gutu, and ZAOGA FIF congregates meet at the Conference Centre in Harare. Other annual events hosted by these Pentecostal churches include prayer convention, youth conventions, deeper life leadership Conventions as well as Pastors' conferences or leadership conventions. In addition to shrines, the country also held the United Methodist Church Ebenezer Convention from 15-17 August 2014, and the Jehovah's Witnesses Convention from the 22nd to 24th August 2014 in Harare, which drew an approximate of 55 000 and 89 000 congregates respectively (Zimbabwe Tourism Authority (ZTA) report, 2014). What is interesting is that the pilgrims have been drawn from both the local and international markets.

The new millennium religious events in Zimbabwe were also modelled by the events of the new Pentecostal churches through the hosting of crusades and/or mega conferences when large numbers of believers visit the United Family International Church (UFIC) led by Prophet Makandiwa and Prophetic, Healing and Deliverance (PHD) Ministries led by Prophet Magaya for these events. For instance, in 2012, the Judgement Night 1 hosted by UFIC attracted an approximate of 100 000 congregates at the National Sports Stadium (Dube, 2012) while the Judgement Night 2 held in 2014, attracted approximately 150 000 congregates at the same venue (*Nehandaradio*, 2014). Judgement Night 3 of 2015 attracted more than two hundred thousand congregates in the country (Matenga, 2015). In addition, the PHD Ministries' Night of turnaround 3 which was held in 2014, was attended by more than 350 000 people at its Waterfalls headquarters in Harare (Kamhungira and Chaya, 2014), while the 2015 Night of turn round 4 recorded more than 500 000 people at the same venue (*Newsday*, November 2015). The gospel of prosperity, miracle searching as well as healing, among others is some of the key reasons for attending Prophet Makandiwa and Magaya's crusades.

Pentecostal-based religious tourism in Zimbabwe

Zimbabwe is one of the Southern Africa countries with a vibrant Christian tradition alongside other nations such as Botswana, South Africa, Lesotho, Zambia and Namibia. Based on the statistics from the Religion in Zimbabwe (2012), Christianity has the highest share of adherents measuring up to 84 % against African traditional religion (3%), Islam and other religions (1%) and non-religions (12%) of the demographic survey of 2010-2011. Within the eighty-four percent Christianity composition, the Apostolic has a stake of 33%, Protestant 16 %, Pentecostal 17%, Roman Catholic 10% and other Christians 8% (Religion in Zimbabwe, 2012 in Marongwe and Maposa, 2015). This composition reveals that Zimbabwe is a multi-religious nation with denominations which co-exist legally.

Of the 17 %, which represents Pentecostal segment, the churches are evangelical in character (Religion in Zimbabwe, 2012) and belonged to the Evangelical Fellowship of Zimbabwe, which was founded in 1962. Most of the Pentecostal churches fall under the banner 'African Initiated church' (AIC) referring to churches which started in Africa by Africans, not by missionaries from other continents (Ibid). The Pentecostal churches emphasise the 'African gifts of the Spirit' which include healing (Ibid). These African indigenous churches include Apostolic Faith Mission in Zimbabwe, Faith Ministries, Gospel Assembly Church, Harvest House International church, United Family International Church, Spirit Embassy, Heartfelt International Ministries, Revival Centre World Ministries, Zimbabwe Assemblies of God, Prophetic Healing and Deliverance Ministry, among others. These Pentecostal churches attract people from various corners of the globe to come and witness the power of God.

In the context of tourism, Zimbabwe through the Ministry of Tourism and Hospitality Industry in its tourism policy of 2013 included religious tourism as a strategy to expand other segments of

351

tourism destinations like leisure, business and cultural tourism. The country's religious policy sought to promote equity and access to religious products (*The Financial Gazette, 13 October, 2013*). The policy was born out of the realisation that Zimbabwe was one of the Southern African countries that is richly endowed with religious sites which attract various segments to its various shrines or sacred places as well as popular Prophets of the Pentecostal churches.

More prominently, the buzzword in religious tourism in Zimbabwe in new millennium Zimbabwe is anchored on the crusade-like mega-events hosted by the various millennium Pentecostal churches. Among others, have been the Judgement Night 1, 2 and 3 revival crusades hosted by the UFIC that attracted thousands of faith based travellers to Zimbabwe to witness and experience the power of God through the Founder Prophet Emmanuel Makandiwa (Ruzvidzo, 2015). On its part the PHD Ministries has held Nights of Turnaround, which have been mega-events drawing people from far and wide corners of the world. As an illustration of this power of attraction, the Night of Turnaround 4 held on the 6th of November 2015 attracted an approximate of five hundred thousand of congregates to the PHD Ministries headquarters along Masvingo highway near Waterfalls in Harare (Ncube, 2015). The essence of the discussion is to demonstrate that religious gatherings which attract both domestic and regional people into the country continue to grow. This is notwithstanding the fact that mega religious tourism is in its infancy stage of development.

The history of United Family International Church

United Family International Ministries' founder is Emmanuel Makandiwa. The church began as an interdenominational church in 2008 under the name United Family Interdenominational Ministry. The interdenominations met for a lunch hour fellowship at the Anglican Cathedral in Harare (UFIC, n.d). After a week as the fellowship numbers rose sharply, the Anglican Cathedral failed to accommodate all the worshippers, and they moved to the State Lotteries hall (UFIC, n.d).

Emmanuel Makandiwa was a former pastor of the Apostolic Faith Mission in Zimbabwe (AFM) before he became a Prophet. It is said that there was a conflict between AFM (parent church) and Makandiwa for reasons that were not clear (Manyonganise, 2013). As a way of resolving the conflict, the Nyoni (2012) avers that the AFM executive asked Pastor Makandiwa to choose between UFIC and the AFM, and he chose UFIC. In 2010, United Family International Church was born and renamed from United Family Interdenominational Ministry (Manyonganise, 2013; Nyoni, 2012; UFIC, n.d). In the same year, it was estimated that 17 000 people joined UFIC in a period of three months (Religion in Zimbabwe, n.d).

Emmanuel Makandiwa changed from being a Pastor to a Prophet because of his prophetic activities, and currently people call him Prophet Makandiwa (Manyonganise, 2013). Church assemblies were planted in Harare, Masvingo, Bulawayo, Zvishavane, Chinhoyi, Mutare, Muzarabani, Gweru, Kwekwe. The UFIC Ministries host Judgement Night on a yearly basis, which draws huge congregants in the country. From this background, it shows that UFIC is a relatively new church that is fast growing in Zimbabwe. The church also plays a significant role in attracting many congregants to Zimbabwe, thereby promoting religious tourism of the country.

The history of Prophetic Healing and Deliverance (PHD) Ministries

The founder of PHD Ministries is Walter Magaya. The Ministry started in 2012, after his visit to TB Joshua of Nigeria, who anointed him to become a 'great prophet' (Kamhungira, 2014; Zuze, 2014). Before his new ministry, he was a member of the Blood of the Lamb Christian Community (Kupe, 2015). After the visit to Synagogue Church of Nations (SCOAN), Prophet Magaya has been performing miracles which are believed to have drawn the attention of many Zimbabweans and foreigners. PHD Ministries headquarters is in Waterfalls, Harare, with other branches across Zimbabwe. The main goal of the church is to bring spiritual, physical and economic deliverances to people who are oppressed by the devil

(Prophetwmagaya, n.d). The PhD ministries introduced Night of turnaround (all night prayer session) in 2012 when the Ministry was still in its infancy with less than 100 church members. The Night of turnaround 2, 3, 4 and 5 drew large numbers of locals as well as foreigners. Because of the significant numbers of congregants recorded, the Night of turnaround was endorsed by the Government of Zimbabwe as a religious tourism attraction (*The Sunday mail*, 30 October 2016). From the discussion, it points out that the Ministry is also a relatively new church and it is of interest to note how it is contributing to Zimbabwe's religious tourism and the country at large.

Religious tourism as an economic development tool in Zimbabwe

It is increasingly being realised that religious tourism is fast becoming a vital tool for the economic development of many regions of the world, Zimbabwe included. For the Zimbabwean situation, the revival of religious tourism in Zimbabwe in the new millennium is fledgling and an ongoing phenomenon. Thus, literally we are chasing a moving shadow and it is not easy to get all the details partially relating to earnings and expenditure patterns. Secondly, the lack of detailed information has been worsened by the desire of the state authorities to tax these incomes (Manyukwe, 2015). As a result, inferences that speak to potential earnings based on reasoned probabilities will be used where actual figures are not available.

As a way of contributing to the economic advantages of the country, faith based travellers spend as much as those of the non-religious travellers. Gone are the days when faith based travellers used to pitch their tents around or use classrooms for their overnight stays when attending their crusades, retreats or conventions. The modern faith-based travellers are now using the hotels, lodges and guest houses for their accommodation services and other ancillary services. As the faith-based travellers usually travel in groups or as families they need accommodation so they make use of nearby hotels, motels, chalets, guest houses as well as lodges for their overnight stays rather than pitching up their tents. They require 1st class hotels for comfort, security and health reasons (Wright, 2008). Service providers would offer tailor made family facilities as religious tourism is closely related to family tourism.

To elaborate this further, when faith-based travellers visit Prophet Makandiwa of UFIC and Prophet Magaya of PHD Ministries in Zimbabwe, among others, they make use of the national accommodation sector. In the Zimbabwean context, Ruzvidzo (2015) pointed out that the faith-based travellers usually book hotels and spend an approximate of US$ 500 per person per visit as they came to witness and experience the power of the Almighty God through Prophet Makandiwa of UFIC or Prophet Magaya of PHD Ministries. Regional and international religious travellers have also been recorded coming from Australia, New Zealand, Botswana, South Africa, Kenya, among others for their healing and weekly sessions at least once a month (Ruzvidzo, 2015). The congregants who came from other countries and far away from the hosting towns usually travelled a day before the prayer session and put up for the night in the nearby accommodation waiting for the event. After the event, they also need to rest before returning to their places of residence. To complement this, in the Zimbabwean context, the PHD Ministries has seven guest houses and a hotel dotted around Harare, which charge US$300 as the minimum rate up-to US$900 for executive lodging for three day stay while the UFIC Life Haven facility in Mt Hampden accommodates 27 people with a minimum charge of US$ 300 to US$ 900 (Chitemba and Ncube, 2016). The executives Life Haven in Glen Lorne offer services for a minimum rate of US$1 200 and US$1 500 as the maximum rate (Chitemba and Ncube, 2016). This helps to boost the church's coffers and also to improve the tourism services in the country.

According to the ZTA report (2014), the Jehovah's Witnesses International Convention held from 22 to 24 August 2014 and the Ebenezer United Methodist Convention from 15 to 17 August 2014 posed economic contribution to the country as shown in table 1 below:

Table 1: Economic benefits from conventions

	Jehovah's Witness Convention		Ebenezer Convention	
	Foreign	Local	Foreign	Local
Accommodation per person	US$ 1 073	US$148	-	US$31
Food per person	US$425	US$66	-	US$9
Transport per person	US$ 1 329	US$64	-	US$21
Shopping per person	US$ 316	US$108	-	-
Tourist activities per person	US$405	-	-	-

Source (ZTA survey, 2014)

The Jehovah's Witnesses International Convention resulted in a hundred per cent occupancy for Harare hotels which included the Rainbow Towers, Meikles, Cresta Oasis, Cresta Lodge, Crowne Plaza, Holiday Inn, Selous hotel, Jameson hotel, Courtney and Bronte hotel from 20 to 26 August (ZTA, 2014). However, the low intake of accommodation was recorded when the Ebenezer Convention was held because most of the participants were staying with friends and relatives while others used the hall venue (ZTA, 2014).

In addition to accommodation, faith based travellers make use of restaurants, fast food outlets and nearby supermarkets for their food and beverages, thus creating brisk business in the hosting area. Vendors also took advantage to erect their temporary stalls outside the venues to sell airtime, fruits, food and soft drinks. For instance, an approximate of 40 vendor stands and 131 vendor stalls were erected during the Jehovah's Witnesses Convention and Ebenezer Convention respectively (ZTA report, 2014). The business of selling airtime brought innumerable vendors at the convention venues. Companies such as Delta Beverages sell various brands of soft drinks. Dairiboard Zimbabwe sold ice creams, yoghurts, mineral water and juices. The Lyons Maid sold juices and ice creams to congregates while Alpha Omega dairy company sold ice creams and yoghurts. Additionally, other groups of Christians hire caterers to offer catering services when they are gathering for their religious ceremonies thus supporting other sectors of the economy indirectly. Travel agencies and tour operators are also benefitting from these travellers as they book their religious holidays via these travel intermediaries.

The transport sector is not an exception as it has also tremendously benefitted from these religious events. To this extent, congregants and entrepreneurs at these conventions are ferried from one area to another, thus making business for all modes of the transport system around the globe. Some of the people made use of public transport, thus giving business to buses, commuter omnibuses and taxis, while others used their own private vehicles to get to the venue. To exemplify the transport business, the Jehovah's Witnesses Convention hired 118 buses and 28 minibuses from different transport operators. The highest number of 25 coaches was hired from Pioneer Bus Company (ZTA report, 2014). This gave business to fuel service stations across Zimbabwe. All these stakeholders were assumed to make profits, although there were no recorded revenues from these events. The airline industry was used by those travelling across regions, continents as well as from country to country. The airlines are also supported by road as well as rail transport system for landlocked countries. This implies that employment is generated for the casual employees as well as maintaining full time employment of their employees in all supporting services. Because of substantial benefits derived from religious tourism, it is no longer a niche, but an industry in its own right (Wright, 2008). Thus, it can be observed that various sectors of the economy are benefiting from religious tourism directly and indirectly.

Most of the Pentecostal churches in Zimbabwe do not own church buildings like the main line churches so they use venues at various stadiums, colleges or local government facilities for their mega conferences, all night prayer sessions or Sunday or Tuesday church services. This helps in the generating of income to the venue suppliers. For instance the Heartfelt International Ministries use the Belvedere Technical Teachers' college for their conferences in Zimbabwe. The municipality of Harare is also benefiting a lot of revenue from other churches like the Kingdom Church, which usually books Harare Gardens for their gospel festivals. The UFIC Church also pays rentals for the use of the Harare City Sports Centre for their Sunday and Tuesday church gatherings (Matenga, 2012). According to the UFIC's spokesperson, the church paid an approximate of US$2 million rentals to the Harare City Council since 2009 up to mid-2016 for the venue (Mabehla, 2016).

Business is also created to companies which specialize in décor and companies that sell décor material because most of the Pentecostal churches' pulpits are usually professionally, if not expensively, decorated in a way that is attractive depending on the level of the occasion to be held. The churches make use of technological advancement in Public Address System (PA). Most of the Pentecostal churches tape their sermons, gospel music and make DVDs which are sold to their church congregates at a price of one to two United States dollars each, thus generating a lot of income, not only for the church but for those that supply these services and materials. Other denominations sell scripture stickers, T-shirts, wristband and bandanas to both their members or to the outsiders at a profit. For instance, the UFI Church sold church regalia and paraphernalia towards Judgement Night 3 to people, which include T-shirts which were priced at US$ 10, hats at $10, berets at $10, helmets at $10 and wristbands at $5 each (Matenga, 2015). In addition to that, before the Judgement Night 3 of 2015, the UFIC was rendering car décor services at a price of US$ 15. This was part of fundraising activities which contributed positively to the coffers of the church. The financial benefits were used for the benefit of the church as well as the community at large. In another way, it also creates employment to the local people who manufacture church regalia and other church stuffs thus improving the residents' standards of living.

Religious travellers through Pentecostal churches usually bring in foreign currency to the hosting destination as well as contributing to government revenue. Its contribution to the revenue of the economy contributes to the view of religious tourism as one of the multi-billion market. Pentecostal churches usually host crusades in different countries and they need travelling documents such as passports to cross international boundaries. At the country's borders when they are using their own vehicles or buses they pay road access fees as well as gate passes and other toll fees along the ways. For instance, when the PHD Ministries host crusades in neighbouring countries such as South Africa and Botswana, significant revenue is generated for the revenue collection departments. As an example, a PHD Ministries crusade which was held between 2 to 4 July 2015 in Botswana, used more than 15 buses to ferry congregates from Zimbabwe to Gaborone (Mike, 2015). Furthermore, in October 2015, the same ministry used eighteen buses from Zimbabwe to Johannesburg, which is estimated to contribute a significant amount to Zimbabwe Revenue Authority (ZIMRA) totalling US$540-00 approximately (18 buses x (US$ 20 gate pass fee to and from + US$ 10 road access fee) per trip.

In the Zimbabwean context, the taxation of churches is also expected to contribute to government's revenue. The Zimbabwe Revenue Authority highlighted in 2014 that churches acting as employers and pay their pastors, caretakers, secretaries, gardeners, priests, among others, some allowances or salaries or wages were to remit employees' tax to the government. These church employees are entitled to contribute pay as you earn (P.A.Y.E) tax (Zimbabwe Revenue Authority, 2014). In the end, the taxing of churches and church-based activities will help boost the country's coffers. For example, the other churches like the PHD Ministries operates lodges or guest houses would be entitled to pay value added tax to the government.

When international faith based travellers as other categories of tourists visit various countries, they create business opportunities for local people in the art and craft industry. Besides purchasing church-based souvenirs and anointing waters, these faith based travellers purchase souvenirs and other kinds of local foods or products for their family members or friends left behind in their home countries. These business transactions act as a source of income for the local communities. This shows that religious tourism supports other small scale markets as well as the churches they are visiting. The revenue generated improves the living conditions of the local church residents and the economy at large thus eliminating poverty. Additionally, it improves the balance of payments of many economies especially developing economies. What has emerged over the years is that Zimbabwe produces many curios that many tourists favour to take back to their home countries. These include sculptures made from wood and stone, traditional music instruments, cloth, beads and basketry, among others. What also emerges is that some of the artists who produce and market these souvenirs belong to the Pentecostal churches. This dovetails with the articulation of the gospel of prosperity in the doctrines of the Pentecostal churches. This gospel implores the adherents to seek earthly riches as they also seek spiritual salvation. Possibly as a way to set examples, the prophets have taken the lead in the investment of economic ventures or income generating projects like the operating of lodges in the country. Fundamentally, these forms of entrepreneurship that are sponsored by the Pentecostal churches have trickle down effects to the national economy.

Religious tourism is an all year round activity which provides a steady flow of income during economic hard times (Tarlow, 2014). Faith based visitors tend to travel regardless of the state of the economy. However, some groups of faith based travellers want to experience and enjoy the landscape of the visited place after church business. Religious travellers can have an opportunity to engage in other leisure activities for instance the 2014 Jehovah's Witness travelled to Victoria Falls-Zimbabwe and other tourist attraction places in Harare and nearby areas after the conference (Rusare, 2014). This promotes both religious and leisure tourism of Zimbabwe.

Socio-cultural benefits

Religious tourism based on the Pentecostalism in Zimbabwe attracts various groups of different nationalities across the globe to visit Zimbabwe in the name of Christianity. There is intermingling of attendees through the spirit of the one Creator, thus creating and rebuilding a friendship among them. These people can visit one another at a later date for various reasons beyond religious reasons. Religious tourism promotes peace. Pentecostal churches are said to provide places of spiritual security and personal communities for people unsettled by rapid social change. Some of people are visiting religious sites or religious conferences to find the hidden facts about their life because of the challenges faced in their day to day living. Wilson *et al.* (2013) further add that other people want to get some answers to some of the specific questions relating to their life's meaning from God through the prophets. For instance, people are travelling to Zimbabwe for Prophet Makandiwa and Magaya to get clarification on their lives. The seeking of solutions helps to bring global understanding which may open avenues for future cooperation.

The social desire to be physically and spiritually healed prompts people to travel frequently to countries with religious sites and Prophets. People with poor health or suffering from various diseases such as cancer, Acquired Immune Deficiency Syndrome (AIDS), arthritis, stroke, asthma, heart disease, respiratory disorders, among others, as well as the disabled travel to Zimbabwe for their healing from the Prophets such as Prophet Makandiwa and Magaya. Other people who are facing problems of infertility are visiting the Prophets in Zimbabwe for miracles to happen in their lives. For those who are rejected by their family members, with no jobs, experience misfortune in their day to day living are travelling to get solutions through the visitation of holy places or Pastors. Others are visiting the prophets to find ways of reuniting their families or rebuilding their marriages. Some travel to these religious gatherings to perform a deed of gaining remission of their sins. This is one way of trying to bring peace within their minds.

Some faith based travellers to the PHD Ministries as well as the Judgement Night of UFIC to pray to God as a way of trying to reverse every negative situation, covenants and curses made by their relatives without their knowledge in their life. In the Christian sense, this is supported by a verse in the Old Testament, Isiah 54 verse 7 which says 'no weapon formed against you shall prosper'. Other Christians travel to religious conventions to find significance in one's life, fulfil the promise, follow the footsteps of others who have travelled the journey over the past years, meet other pilgrims, find a favourable environment in which to believe and reflect, experience the heritage along the way, give a significance of belonging to life or to prayer, in chronicled remembrance and because of testimonies told by other pilgrims, believe in one of the Church founders who they believe are very close to their gods and apply and make offerings for the varied needs (Dominguez, 2010). It is also a way of showing loyalty to their faiths, to express gratitude for the blessings sent from the Creator, participate in church processions as well as in religious celebrations. Such religious gatherings gave participants time to commune with others and confess their wrong doings to each other. It is also through collective prayers that divine guidance may be released, got divine protection as well as averting disaster. Other congregates would like to witness the answers of their prayers together. Other people after attending such religious gatherings felt encouraged, refreshed and empowered.

Religious tourism promotes the growth of education among both faith based travellers and other tourists. According to Stephanie (2012), some people travel to religious sites to observe and learn about the intended religion, people in their group of travellers, culture, food, customs and lifestyle buildings or the environment. Some faith based travellers visit their religious sites as a way of fulfilling their religion's commandment thus enhancing their statuses among their peers after the journey (Mansfeld et al., 2006: 3 in Bader, 2012). This is part of self-actualisation to these faith based travellers. As an example, the congregates returning from such church conferences usually display stickers on their cars, wristbands and or t-shirts describing the event they recently attended. On the whole, although these items are inexpensive, they are significant as status enhancers.

Within the economy of Zimbabwe, religious tourism is assisting in the revival of the nation's international reputation as a safe and desirable tourist destination (Agere, 2014). This cements to what the UNWTO (2014) asserts that religious tourism is beneficial in the building of cultural dialogue as well as peace. To the Zimbabwean scenario, religious tourism is working as one of the marketing tools to reverse the bad publicity that was spread with some sections of the media about the country as an unsafe destination. Religious tourism is one of the segments within the economy which does not cause any harm related to alcoholism, crime (Terzidou et al., 2008) as well as prostitution. This tourism segment promotes peace and harmony amongst the people.

Negative impacts of religious travel

Religious travel is also accompanied with adverse effects to the hosting destination. Huge congregates tend to cause congestion or traffic jams in cities where these events are hosted. This can lead to long queues in the supermarkets as well as shortages of parking space. Some of the local people can have challenges of access to these areas because of the religious events being hosted. According to (Rinschede, 1992, in Gedecho, 2014), huge numbers of people at sacred or holy sites can lead to the violation of the area's rules and regulations. In some cases there will be overcrowding at these places, thus influencing the character of the site as large crowds of congregates can affect the way people experience a religious place. On another lens, a sudden increase in the number of congregates or tourists can lead to overuse of resources for instance, water and wood thus leading to the depletion of resources. Large crowds of people can stampede on the surrounding natural environment, thus jeopardizing the natural resources around the holy site.

An illustration of the potential effects of congestion in Zimbabwe came from the PHD Ministries stampede that was witnessed at Mbizo Stadium in Kwekwe-Zimbabwe in 2014, when the overcrowding congregates led to the death of eleven people while some fifty-four more were injured (Musiiwa, 2014) when exiting the stadium after the Church service. Idler (2014) adds that the spread of diseases such as flue through the air, by handshakes or via the sharing of drink and food as religious people gather, thus affecting the public health. Other congregates can engage in illicit sexual activities, thus resulting in the spread of AIDS, Human Immunodeficiency Virus (HIV) infection and other sexually transmitted diseases. These mass gatherings can result in high noise levels, causing increased stress, blood pressure and other mental health problems (Paulus *et al.*, 1978; Ising & Kruppa, 2004).

Opportunities from Pentecostal-based gatherings to the Zimbabwean community

For the Zimbabwe's tourism industry, it is also an opportunity to showcase the tourism products to some of the religious congregates after or before their main events. The church participants have the opportunity to visit nearby tourist places surrounding Harare, which include the Lion and Cheetah Park, Snake Park, Kuimba Shiri, Lake

Chivero and other tourist destinations at low rates. This boosts domestic tourism of Zimbabwe. Zimbabwe as a nation can use its own prophets rather than travelling to other countries seeking healing and other benefits, thus promoting the religious tourism of the country. This helped to reduce the leakages of the country's revenues. The local unemployed people can also take an opportunity to sell various products to the congregates when attending their church gatherings, thus improving their living standards.

Conclusions

From the foregoing discussions, it can be deciphered that religious tourism or faith based travel is one of the tourism segments for which many of those economies which are richly endowed with religious sites/holy places or religious products are opting for as it brings numerous benefits to both the travellers as well as the hosting destination. Within the Zimbabwean context, religious tourism is in its infancy and gained momentum through the charismatic prophets Makandiwa and Magaya of UFIC and PHD Ministries, respectively, in the new millennium. Thousands of people came to Zimbabwe to witness various events such as the Judgement Night 1, 2, 3 and Night of Turnaround 3 and 4. This is creating business to various sectors of the Zimbabwean industry such as accommodation, transport, travel intermediaries, retail shops, banks, florists, fuel service stations, small and medium enterprises as well as customs and immigration department. Its growth is a welcome relief for the Zimbabwean economy, which has been heavily affected by negative publicity and near collapse since the year 2000. As such, religious tourism is becoming a cornerstone of the positive marketing of the country's tourism potential that had been damaged by negative publicity and negative effects of the new millennium crisis.

References

Agere, H. 2014. Religious Tourism: In search of the holy cash cow Retrieved from http://www.sundaymail.co.zw/religion-in-search-of-the-holy-cash-cow/. Accessed 09 November 2015.

Bader, M. 2012. Religious tourism in Jordan: Current situation, future developments and prospects. A case study on Islamic and Christian holy site. A dissertation submitted to the Katholischen Universitat Eichstatt-lngolstadt.

Cardenas, R.M. 2011. Regional development through Religious tourism. Retrieved from https://etudescaribeennes.revues.org/5352. Accessed 19 October 2015.

Chitando, E., Manyonganise, M. and Mlambo, O.B. 2013. Young, male and polished masculinities: Generational shifts and Pentecostal prophets in Zimbabwe. In *Prophets, profits and the Bible in Zimbabwe, (eds)* E. Chitando, M.R. Gunda and J. Kügler. University of Bamberg Press. Bamberg.

Chitemba, B and Ncube, D. 2016. Makandiwa and Magaya charge US$1 500 per person for 'solutions'. Retrieved from http://nehandaradio.com/2016/05/22/makandiwa-magaya-charge-us1500-per-person/. Accessed 07 September 2016.

Dube, J. 2012. 100 000 at Makandiwa's Judgement Night, New Zimbabwe, 8 April http://www.newzimbabwe.com/news-7672-100,000%20at%20Makandiwa%20Judgement%20Night/news.aspx

Egresi, I, Bayram, B and Kara, F. 2012. Economic Impact of Religious Tourism in Mardin, Turkey. *Journal of Economics and Business Research*, 2, 7-22.

Gedecho, C.K. 2014. Challenges of religious tourism development: The case of Gishen Mariam, Ethiopia. *American Journal of Tourism Research*, 3 (2), 42-57.

Greatzimtraveller. 2016. Religious tourism and Spirituality. Available at https://www.greatzimtraveller.com/2016/04/religious-tourism-and-spirituality/. Date of access 14 March 2017.

Ising, H. & Kruppa, B. 2004. Health effects caused by noise: Evidence in the literature from the past 25years. *Noise Health* 6: 5-13.

Kamhungira, T and Chaya, V. 2014. Magaya draws 350 000 to church. Retrieved from http://nehandaradio.com/2014/11/10/magaya-draws-350-000-church/. Accessed 18 January 2016.

Kamhungira, T. 2014. Magaya opens up. Daily news 6 November, https://www.dailynews.co.zw/articles/2014/11/06/magaya-opens-up. Ate of access 15 March 2017.

Kenya and Beyond Safaris. n.d. Religious and Pilgrim Tourism. Retrieved from http://www.kenyandbeyond.com/safaris/kenya/pilgrim. Accessed 09 December, 2015.

Kupe, L .2015. 7 Things true about Prophet Walter Magaya. Available at http://www.ocradio.co.za/7-things-true-about-prophet-walter-magaya/. Date of access 14 March 2017.

Mabehla, A. 2016. Plot to push out Makandiwa. Retrieved from https://www.dailynews.co.zw/articles/2016/05/02/plot-to-push-out-makandiwa. Accessed 30 August 2016.

Magazine for tourists. n.d. Pilgrimage Tourism. Retrieved from http://psna.ru/index.php?p=turist&st=3-1. Accessed 03 November 2015.

Manyonganise, M. 2013. Pentecostals responding to Gender-based violence: The case of the United Family International Church in Harare, *in Justice not silence: Churches facing sexual and Gender-based violence (eds)* E. Chitando and S. Chirongoma, Stellenbosch, South Africa

Manyukwe, C. 2015. Taxing of churches to start January. Retrieved from http://www.chronicle.co.zw/taxing-of-churches-to-start-january/. Accessed 20 January 2016

Marongwe, N and Maposa, R, S. 2015. PHDs, Gospreneurship, Globalisation and the Pentecostal 'New wave' in Zimbabwe. Afro Asian Journal of Social Sciences, 1 (1) 1-22.

Matenga, M. 2012. Council wants more money from Makandiwa. Retrieved from http://nehandaradio.com/2012/06/30/council-wants-more-money-from-makandiwa. Accessed 15 January 2016.

Matenga, M. 2015. UFIC cashes in on Judgement Night 3. Retrieved from https: //www.newsday.co.zw/2015/08/29/ufic-cashes-in-on-judgment-night-3/. Accessed 14 December 2015.

Mecca Pilgrimage. 2015. About the Pilgrimage to Mecca-Hajj. Retrieved from http: //www.meccapilgrimage.com. Accessed 04 November 2015.

Mike. 2015. Prophet Walter Magaya's followers flood Botswana. Retrieved from http: //www.zimbabwelatestnews.net/prophet-walter-magayas-followers-flood-botswana/#sthash.B00vV2Of.dpbs. Accessed 16 December 2015.

Miltifaiths. n.d. Religious tourism cultural diversity. Available at http://www.multifaiths.com/faith-communities/religious-tourism. Date of access 15 March 2017.

Musiiwa, M. 2014. 11 die at Magaya crusade… cops teargas congregants, spark stampede. Retrieved from http://nehandaradio.com/2014/11/22/11-die-magaya-crusadecops-teargas-congregants-spark-stampede. Accessed 11 December, 2015.

Ncube, D. 2015. A Religious boost to the economy. Retrieved from http://www.sundaymail.co.zw/a-religious-boost-to-the-economy/ Accessed 09 November 2015.

Nehanda radio. 2014. Makandiwa Judgement Night 2 in pictures. Retrieved from http://nehandaradio.com/2014/04/20/makandiwa-judgement-night-2-pictures/. Accessed 15 January, 2016.

Newsday, 9 November 2015. Pictures Magaya's Night of turn around 4. Retrieved from https://www.newsday.co.zw/…/pictures-magayas-night-of-turn-around-4/. Accessed 18 January, 2016.

Nigerian anarchist. 2015. Nigeria sends 76 000 Pilgrims to Mecca http://nigeriananarchist.blogspot.com/2015/09/nigeria-sends-76000-pilgrims-to-mecca.html. Date of access 15 March 2017.

Nyoni, P. 2012. Who is Prophet Emmanuel Makandiwa? http://www.zimdiaspora.com/index.php?option=com_content

&id=7392:who-is-prophet-emmanuel-makandiwa-&Itemid=299. Date of access 14 March 2017.

Panoratoursafaris, n.d. Religious safaris. http://www.panoratoursafaris.com/index.php/religious-safaris. Date of access 14 March 2017.

Paulus, P, McCain, G & Cox, V. 1978. Death rates, psychiatric commitments, blood pressure and perceived crowding as a function of institutional crowding. *Environ Psychol Non-Verbal Behaviour* 3: 107-116.

Prophet Walter Magaya. n.d. About PHD ministries. http://www.prophetwmagaya.com/phd-ministries/. Date of access 14 March 2017.

Religion in Zimbabwe. N.d. Pentecostal and African Initiated Churches. Available at https://relzim.org/major-religions-zimbabwe/pentecostal-aic/. Date of access 15 March 2017.

Religious Travel. N.d. Religions. Retrieved from http: //www.leahlarkin.com/Religions.pdf

Rusare, P. 2014. Religious Tourism Pays Off. Retrieved from http://www.thepatriot.co.zw/old_posts/religious-tourism-pays-off/ Accessed 09 November, 2015.

Ruzvidzo, V. 2015. Zimbabwe: Judgement night 3...Religious tourism assumes new level. Retrieved from http://allafrica.com/stories/201508270028.html Accessed 06 November 2015.

Sacred destinations. n.d. Sacred sites and Religious Travel, Retrieved from http://www.sacred-destinations.com. Date of access 27 November 2015.

Sacred sites in Jordan, Retrieved from http://www.sacred-destinations.com/jordan/sacred-sites. Date of access 27 November 2015.

Sacred-texts. n.d. chapter XXXII of the death of the prophets, how they died, and where each one of them as buried. Available at http://www.sacred-texts.com/chr/bb/bb32.htm. Date of access 15 March 2017.

Sayin, N. 2014. A Christian Tour: Religious Tourism in Turkey. Retrieved from http://www.turkeytravelcentre.com/blog/christian-tour-religious-tourism-turkey. Accessed 03 November, 2015.

Stephanie, B. 2012. Potential benefits of religious tourism. Retrieved from https: //cplondon.wordpress.com/2012/06/25/potential-benefits-of-religious-tourism-44-2/. Accessed 27 November 2015.

Strategic Initiatives and Government Advisory (SIGA) Team. 2012. Diverse Beliefs: Tourism of Faith Religious Tourism gains ground.

Tarlow, P. 2014. The importance of the religious tourism market. Retrieved from.
http://www.eturbonews.com/50998/importance-religious-tourism-market. Accessed 27 November 2015.

The Financial Gazette. 2013. Zimbabwe embarks on religious tourism. Retrieved from.
http://www.financialgazette.co.zw/zimbabwe-embarks-on-religious-tourism/ Accessed 12 November 2015.

The Sunday mail. 30 October 2016. Magaya ready for Night of turnaround. http://www.sundaymail.co.zw/magaya-ready-for-night-of-turnaround/. Date of access 14 March 2017.

Tourismandmore. 2014. The importance of the Religious Tourism market. Retrieved from
http://www.tourismandmore.com/tidbits/the-importance-of-the-religious-tourism-market. Accessed 25 October 2015.

UFIC. n.d. Our brief history. Available at
www.ufiministriesinfo.co.Date of access 14 March 2017.

United Nations World Tourism Organisation. 2011. Religious Tourism in Asia and the Pacific, Madrid, Spain. Retrieved from http://dtxtq4w60xqpw.cloudfront.net/sites/all/files/pdf/1103 25_religious_tourism_excerpt.pdf. Accessed 04 November, 2015.

UNWTO. 2014. Tourism can protect and promote religious heritage. Retrieved from http://media.unwto.org/press-release/2014-12-10/tourism-can-protect-and-promote-religious-heritage. Accessed 26 November, 2015.

Vengeyi, O. 2013. Zimbabwean Pentecostal Prophets; Rekindling the "True and false Prophecy" debate, In: *Prophets, Profits and the bible in Zimbabwe (eds)* E. Chitando, M. R Gunda and J. Kugler, University of Bamberg Press: Bamberg.

Whitman, E. 2015. Ramadan 2015: Mecca Visit Top 14 million, Breaking record for the first 16 days of Muslim Holy Month. Retrieved from http://www.ibtimes.com/ramadan-2015-mecca-visits-top-14-million-breaking-record-first-16-days-muslim-holy-1997555. Accessed 04 November, 2015.

Wilson, G. B., McIntosh, A.J., and Zahra, A.L. 2013. Tourism and spirituality: A phenomenological analysis, *Annals of Tourism Research*, 42, 150-168.

Wong, C.U.I., Ryan, C., and McIntosh, A. 2013. The Monasteries of Putuoshan, China: Sites of Secular or Religious Tourism? *Journal of Travel & Tourism Marketing*, 30 (6), 577-594.

Wright, K. 2008. Religious tourism: A new era, a dynamic industry, *Tourism review*.com, 33-35.

Zamani-Farahani, H., and Musa, G. 2012. The relationship between Islamic religiosity and residents' perceptions of socio-cultural impacts of tourism in Iran: Case Studies of Sare' in and Masoole, *Tourism Management*, 33 (4), 802-814.

Zimbabwe Revenue Authority. 2014. Tax obligations for church or religious organisations. Retrieved from http://www.zimra.co.zw/index.php?option=com_content&view=article&id=2105: tax-obligations-for-church-or-religious-organisations&catid=21: did-you-know&Itemid=91

Zimbabwe Tourism Authority Report. 2014. The Ebenezer Convention, 15-17 August 2014 (Unpublished report), Harare, Zimbabwe.

Zimbabwe Tourism Authority Report. 2014. The Harare International Convention of the Jehovah's Witnesses, 22-24 August 2014 (Unpublished report), Harare, Zimbabwe.

Zuze, L. 2014. Prophet Magaya's breath-taking miracles, Daily news 9 January 2014.